Mirrors of Our Playing

THEATER: Theory/Text/Performance

Enoch Brater, Series Editor

Recent Titles:

Staging Place: The Geography of Modern Drama by Una Chaudhuri

The Aesthetics of Disturbance: Anti-Art in Avant-Garde Drama by David Graver

Toward a Theater of the Oppressed: The Dramaturgy of John Arden by Javed Malick

Theater in Israel edited by Linda Ben-Zvi

Crucibles of Crisis: Performing Social Change edited by Janelle Reinelt

Fornes: Theater in the Present Tense by Diane Lynn Moroff

Taking It to the Streets: The Social Protest Theater of Luis Valdez and Amiri Baraka by Harry J. Elam Jr.

Hearing Voices: Modern Drama and the Problem of Subjectivity by John H. Lutterbie

Mimesis, Masochism, & Mime: The Politics of Theatricality in Contemporary French Thought edited by Timothy Murray

Approaching the Millennium: Essays on Angels in America edited by Deborah R. Geis and Steven F. Kruger

Rooms with a View: The Stages of Community in the Modern Theater by Richard L. Barr

Staging Resistance: Essays on Political Theater edited by Jeanne Colleran and Jenny S. Spencer

Sightlines: Race, Gender, and Nation in Contemporary Australian Theatre by Helen Gilbert

Edges of Loss: From Modern Drama to Postmodern Theory by Mark Pizzato

Postmodern/Drama: Reading the Contemporary Stage by Stephen Watt

Trevor Griffiths: Politics, Drama, History by Stanton B. Garner Jr.

Memory-Theater and Postmodern Drama by Jeanette R. Malkin

Performing America: Cultural Nationalism in American Theater edited by Jeffrey D. Mason and J. Ellen Gainor

Space in Performance: Making Meaning in the Theatre by Gay McAuley

Mirrors of Our Playing: Paradigms and Presences in Modern Drama by Thomas R. Whitaker

Mirrors of Our Playing

Paradigms and Presences in Modern Drama

Thomas R. Whitaker

Ann Arbor

THE UNIVERSITY OF MICHIGAN PRESS

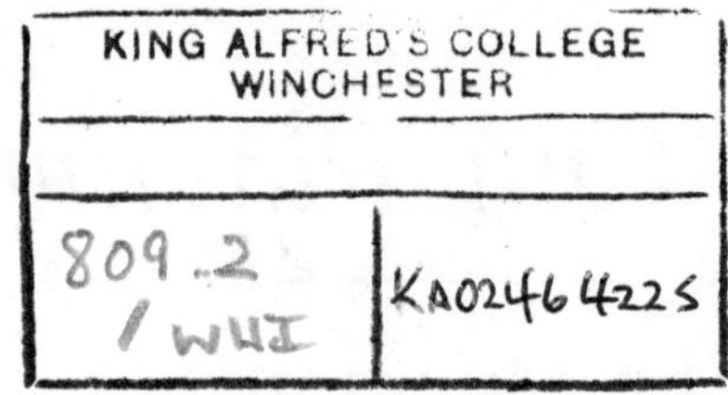

Published in the United States of America by
The University of Michigan Press
Manufactured in the United States of America
⊗ Printed on acid-free paper

2002 2001 2000 1999 4 3 2 1

A CIP catalog record for this book is available from the British Library.

Library of Congress Cataloging-in-Publication Data

Whitaker, Thomas R.
Mirrors of our playing : paradigms and presences in modern drama / Thomas R. Whitaker.
p. cm. (Theater : Theory/Text/Performance)
Includes bibliographical references (p.) and index.
ISBN 0-472-11025-X (acid-free paper)
1. English drama—20th century—History and criticism. 2. Influence (Literary, artistic, etc.) I. Title.
PR736 .W53 1999
822'.91509—dc21 98-58110
CIP

remembering
Dorothy Vera Barnes Whitaker
1927–1995
who taught me that
the horizon of playing is love

The generation of the spirit is not as the generation of the flesh
for its virtue is diffused like light, generously, unpriced.
Doing and suffering and the work of thought must take its toll of us.
And all that life corrupts, death can destroy. Then we may cease to know.
But, freed from self's claim upon it, scattered, dissolved, transformed,
that inmost thing we were so impotently may but begin, new-breathed,
the better to be.

—Harley Granville Barker, *The Secret Life*

Souls were rising, from the earth far below, souls of the dead, of people who had perished, from famine, from war, from the plague, and they floated up, like skydivers in reverse, limbs all akimbo, wheeling and spinning. And the souls of these departed joined hands, clasped ankles and formed a web, a great net of souls. . . .

—Tony Kushner, *Angels in America*

Acknowledgments

While this project was forming itself, I presented installments and tentative readings to many people, who responded with suggestions and encouragement. I am especially grateful to Maynard Mack, Declan Kiberd, Joseph Ronsley, Frederick P. W. McDowell, Stanley Weintraub, George K. Hunter, Paul H. Fry, Enoch Brater, Henry Louis Gates Jr., Bruce King, John Hollander, and Arien Mack, who invited such early versions; to the students in my Yale seminar on Peter Brook, especially Julian Davies and Jon Dean, who taught me much about playing; and to two anonymous readers for the University of Michigan Press, who helped me to clarify and strengthen my argument. I wish also to thank my father, J. Russell Whitaker, who urged this project upon me, and my son, Tom O'Hara Whitaker, whose work in the theater continues to delight and inform me. My deepest debt, acknowledged in the dedication, is to the playful spirit who shared with me so many of the thoughts and occasions reflected in these pages. Even as I write these sentences I can hear her singing the haunting cadences of "Isla" that she composed, two years before her death, for my seminar presentation of Eduardo Machado's *Broken Eggs:* "En una isla/Lejos de aquí . . ."

A portion of the introduction was published in "Holding Up the Mirror: Deception as Revelation in the Theater," in *Social Research* 63, no. 3 (Fall 1996): 701–30. Part of chapter 1 is reprinted with the permission of Simon and Schuster from *Twentieth Century Interpretations of "The Playboy of the Western World,"* ed. Thomas R. Whitaker (Englewood Cliffs, NJ: Prentice-Hall, 1969), 1–20. An earlier version of chapter 2, first offered at a W. B. Yeats seminar in Sligo, was published in *Omnium Gatherum: Essays for Richard Ellmann,* ed. Susan Dick, Declan Kiberd, Dougald McMillan, and Joseph Ronsley (Gerrards Cross, Buckinghamshire: Colin Smythe, 1989), 407–23. A small portion of chapter 3, first offered at an MLA session on George Bernard Shaw, was published in *Shaw: The Annual of Bernard Shaw Studies* 10 (1990): 85–94. Copyright © 1990 by the Pennsylvania State University, reproduced by permission of the Pennsylvania State University

Press. An earlier version of chapter 4 was published in the *Yearbook of English Studies* 9 (1979): 167–87, reproduced by permission of *The Yearbook of English Studies*. Much of chapter 5 was first offered at a Byron conference at Yale University. An earlier version of chapter 6 was published in *Beckett at 80 / Beckett in Context,* ed. Enoch Brater (London and New York: Oxford University Press, 1986), 208–29. Copyright © 1986 by Oxford University Press, Inc. Used by permission of Oxford University Press, Inc. And an earlier version of chapter 7 was published in *Post-Colonial English Drama,* ed. Bruce King (New York: St. Martin's Press, 1992), 200–216. Copyright © Bruce King, editor, reprinted with permission of St. Martin's Press. I thank the respective presses for their permissions.

Contents

Children of Paradise: Shooting a Dream

I

Although forced by economic and technological change to the margins of our society, the theater still offers an interpersonal vitality not present in any other artistic medium. A backward glance at the end of this century may suggest what we are in danger of losing. How does that vitality relate to the theater's diversity of styles and forms? And how does it mirror our life in community? In *Fields of Play in Modern Drama* I approached such questions through Continental European plays from Ibsen to Genet, with some reference to Shaw, Eliot, Beckett, and Stoppard. I argued there that the dramatic medium is participatory and perspectival, that plays are constituted by relations between a "performed action," outlined by a script and represented onstage, and an "action of performance" in which actors and audience participate. Here I want to extend that argument by looking mainly at modern English-speaking drama—from its Anglo-Irish beginnings in Wilde, Shaw, Yeats, and Synge to the cross-fertilizations and international dispersals represented by such figures as Tennessee Williams, Athol Fugard, Wole Soyinka, Howard Brenton, Eduardo Machado, Brian Friel, Anna Deveare Smith, Peter Brook, and Tony Kushner.

I start with the premise that a play in performance is a manifold mirror of the playing that constitutes our lives, shaped through the interaction of received paradigms and living presences. These paradigms are more comprehensive than genres or styles as usually understood, for they include both the "performed action" and the "action of performance." They interact with playwrights, directors, actors, and audiences as well as "presences" from the past. The most comprehensive paradigm in our theater, rivaling the Shakespearean romance, is that developed by Bertolt Brecht and his collaborators, followers, and revisers. Not just "epic" but "dialectical" and "dialogical," it foregrounds through episodic structure, shifting styles, theatrical montage, songs, and ironic commentary the very consciousness of playing. By subsuming other paradigms, it encourages in actors and audience a variety of relations to both the performed action and the action of performance. It also encourages an explicit recognition that all scripts, theatrical events, and lives are collaborative at heart. It makes both actors and audience aware of the fact that theater is a participatory event. Tony Kushner, no doubt the foremost practitioner in America of a dialectical and dialogical aesthetic that is at once Brechtian, counter-Brechtian, and meta-Brechtian, has put the matter succinctly in his afterword to the revised version of *Perestroika:* "Marx was right: The smallest indivisible human unit is two people, not one; one is a fiction. From such nets of souls societies, the social world, human life springs. And also plays" (155).

How this collaborative paradigm of paradigms can structure our playing I suggested in an interpretation of Brecht's *Caucasian Chalk Circle* that is included in *Fields of Play in Modern Drama* (130–43). Here I will recognize its importance for Howard Brenton, Peter Brook, and Tony Kushner—and I might as easily have adduced the work of Caryl Churchill and the Joint Stock Company. Because this paradigm provides an accessible imaginative frame for the various mirrors of our playing, I want to open this book with one recent instance, *Children of Paradise: Shooting a Dream* (1992–93), and close it with another, *Angels in America* (1990–95).

Children of Paradise: Shooting a Dream was developed by Théâtre de la Jeune Lune, a French-American ensemble company based in Minneapolis. Written by four members of the company—Steven Epp, Felicity Jones, Dominique Serrand, and Paul Walsh—it draws on the Brechtian tradition, using a kind of stylistic collage as it engages in historical reflection and self-reflection. On the literal level it is a somewhat fictive account of the writing (by Jacques Prévert) and filming (by Marcel Carné) of *Les Enfants du Paradis* (1943–45), which starred Arletty (as Garance), Jean Louis Barrault (as Baptiste Debureau), and Pierre Brasseur (as Frederick Lemaître). That film was itself a fictive account of some historical events in Paris in the 1830s, in and around the Théâtre des Funambules, that were shaped by romantic dreams, criminality, social power, and artistic disclosure. For both the film and the play the nuclear event is the theft of a watch by the histrionic assassin Pierre-François Lacenaire, in the presence of an actress, Garance, whom the police erroneously accuse of the theft. Baptiste discloses the thief, miming the theft as he has observed it—but, even as he does so, he is falling in love with Garance, who is well aware of Lacenaire's behavior. Baptiste, who is already married, soon becomes Garance's lover, but he must compete for her attention with the romantic actor Frederick Lemaître—and he finally loses her when she accepts the protection of a wealthy aristocrat, Alexandre Trauner. A film produced with great difficulty by Carné in occupied Paris, *Les Enfants du Paradis* amplifies both the romantic desire and the ethical questions implicit in those events as it follows Garance's involvements with Lacenaire, Baptiste, Lemaître, and Trauner. It was attacked after the Liberation as escapist art, and the director and some of the cast were charged with collaborating with the Nazis. But the film was interpreted by others as an allegory of just such temptations. *Children of Paradise: Shooting a Dream* probes this ambiguity by doubling the action of the 1830s with the action of the filming in the 1940s, and doubling that again with aspects of the present performance. We watch an episodic and theatricalist unfolding of what is simultaneously the original story, its filming, and our own participation in the meanings of both.

In ways that Brecht and others have made familiar, the play reaches out to incorporate the audience in its interrogation. The prologue, rather like the opening of Ariane Mnouchkine's *1789,* places the entire audience onstage (behind a proscenium scrim) as the crowd on the nineteenth-century Boulevard of Crime that observes the episode of the watch theft and Baptiste's disclosure, with actors here in the historical roles that they will later enact before the camera. We start as actors and witnesses on the historical stage. Then, assuming our seats in the theater, we watch scene after scene of the filming of *Les Enfants du Paradis* with an intensifying estrangement from the nineteenth-century events, as those events are approached and inhabited—sometimes through repeated "takes"—by a film director and actors of the 1940s who increasingly seem analogous to the characters they direct and play. Carné, a fitfully brooding directorial consciousness, is painfully caught between artistic integrity and the appearance of political compromise. Arletty, the French Garbo, plays a Garance who, in transcending class boundaries to enter a histrionic world, embodies both a romantic ideal and a persistent temptation. Indeed, Arletty herself is being compromised by a liaison with a member of the German-sympathizing French Militia. (In 1944 she was in fact imprisoned for collaboration.) Robert Le Vigan, playing Jericho, the fence and spy who embodies our collective shadow, is a Nazi sympathizer finally tried for his crime. And Barrault, playing the Pierrot figure who seems a romantic self-idealization of each witnessing consciousness, becomes in the documentary and elegiac epilogue a clear instance of the life of theater as a humane project despite all the temptations and pressures of the structures of power. The complex action that we share by analogy with both actors and characters is "to discover the meanings of our artistic collaboration."

Carné's film suffused the nineteenth-century action with the poignancy and irony of a romantic theater dream confected of erotic desire, criminality, social power, and aesthetic delight. Tracing that action and its later filming from a cooler distance, the play finds a more sardonic set of meanings. Felicity Jones plays Arletty/Garance with a throaty voice that is almost parodic. Steven Epp brings to Brasseur/Lemaître a brash narcissism unredeemed by charm. Robert Rosen offers a Barrault/Baptiste whose vulnerability and gaucheness are more evident than his gestural finesse. A jagged pacing prevents our emotional indulgence, and the motifs of romanticism are edged with uneasiness, anger, and guilt. But the play does not simply suggest the ambiguity of artistic collaboration in Nazi-dominated France. It focuses on what resides in the hearts of such actors and witnesses as we may be, and its analogies between the present action of performance and the historically doubled action offer a wry commentary on our potential collaboration in a time that is still greedy, unjust, and escapist. It is appropriate that, as we leave the theater, the members of the company are lined up in the lobby to shake our hands.

That is one kind of self-conscious playing, developed by a company aware of its traditions and of our current situation. Through its dialectical structure and ironic capaciousness it aims to diagnose a social illness that results from the ego's self-aggrandizement, inattentiveness, and duplicity. By inviting us to adopt various perspectives upon the action, to inhabit and criticize its characters, and to recognize the problematic implications of our own playing, it demonstrates that the multiplicity of consciousness that invites such illness can also lead toward self-knowledge and community rapport. The dialectical and dialogical paradigm that is exemplified by *Children of Paradise: Shooting a Dream* suggests an appropriate imaginative frame for the examination of paradigms and presences to which this book is devoted.

II

In part 1 I focus on four paradigms, with attention to the persons who have actualized, developed, and modified them. Although the paradigms cover a range of modern playing, I do not arrange them in a neat system. I want to avoid the abstraction that characterizes Northrop Frye's phases of comedy in *Anatomy of Criticism* (163–86), in which the temporality of performance has almost disappeared from a "spatial" vision of dramatic form. Paradigms illuminate one another not only through similarities and differences but also through overlappings, collaborations, transformations, and cross-fertilizations. I do not intend, however, a sociological analysis of the various sectors of "audience" at different historical moments. That is an important inquiry, but not mine. Like Francis Fergusson, Kenneth Burke, and much "reader-response" theory, I emphasize our obligation to the text and to the performance. The crucial aspect of "audience" for me, therefore, is not the social or historical conditioning we bring to the theater but what, given our implicit potential, we may become or see ourselves as becoming when we participate with full attention in the event.

Each chapter in part 1 attempts a different approach to a paradigm as it has persisted within the untidy openness of our shared history. Chapter 1 considers Synge's *The Playboy of the Western World* in the context of its traditions, antecedents, and composition, its major productions and reception, and its analogues in the modern theater. This play of eclectic design, which blends farce, romance, tragicomedy, satire, and allegory, might be called in its own non-Brechtian way a paradigm of paradigms. Continually refocusing the relations between the grotesque onstage community and the community of performance, it understands role-playing as the basis for ironic self-recognition, personal growth, and the discovery of mutuality. Chapter 2 then takes up Wilde's *The Importance of Being Earnest,* Shaw's *You Never Can Tell,* Orton's *What the Butler Saw,* and Stoppard's *Travesties,* which offer versions of a single paradigm of playing. They show how farce can subsume a range of serious concerns—satirical, sentimental, savagely grotesque, and didactic—and sweep them into a shared music of performance. Chapter 3 turns to a more complex and flexible paradigm in which the ironic and pathetic failure of a represented community stands in contrast to the resources of the community implicit in our playing. Here the historical trajectory runs from Chekhov's major plays, Shaw's *Heartbreak House,* and Granville Barker's *The Secret Life* on to plays by Sean O'Casey, Clifford Odets, Lillian Hellman, David Storey, Eduardo Machado, Lanford Wilson, and Brian Friel and the performance art of Anna Deveare Smith. Despite great differences in style, these works use analogous strategies for setting a panorama of isolation, blockage, and waste against a faith in the potentialities that inform our action of performance. Chapter 4 then focuses on the paradigm that became in mid-century the main theatrical vehicle of the so-called pessimism and nihilism of our time. The infernal stage worlds of Sartre's *No Exit,* Beckett's *Play,* Genet's *The Screens,* and Pinter's *No Man's*

Land seem very far from Synge's collaborative playfulness, the farcical music of Wilde and his successors, and the emotional ambivalence of the Chekhovian answers to heartbreak. But, in ways that have often been overlooked, these instances of "playing hell" incorporate actions of performance that radically qualify, and indeed overturn, their explicit bleakness and entrapment.

Part 1 will have suggested how paradigms can be transformed by encounters with various styles, genres, and thematic concerns. But it will also have made evident that such interactions require the participation, the dialogical response, of personal presences. Part 2, shifting the focus, emphasizes those presences. I select to illustrate the twentieth-century process a nineteenth-century English antecedent of the modern European sensibility, a self-exiled Anglo-Irish playwright who has had international influence, a Nigerian essayist and playwright who has related European theater to his African heritage, and an English director who has taken world theater as his province. The spirit of that histrionic poet-playwright, Lord Byron, has directly or indirectly shaped much of the work surveyed in part 1. In midcentury Samuel Beckett most subtly defined the Byronic sensibility in its state of crisis. The African-European eclecticism of Wole Soyinka has pursued a difficult course through several ancient and modern paradigms of playing. And, as a director, Peter Brook has sought most boldly to move through and beyond the modern European sensibility in search of the meaning of playing itself. Each of these presences has brought into focus certain histrionic potentialities, mediated by an array of theatrical forms. And each has evoked dialogues with others that can suggest some of the many ways in which we inhabit and transform theatrical paradigms.

Chapter 5 examines the continuing presence of Byron by now placing Wilde, Shaw, Beckett, and Stoppard in a wider context that includes Yeats, Eliot, Auden, O'Neill, Williams, Linney, and Brenton. Through paradigms that reinvent Byron's "mental theater," they bring his hypnotic blend of romantic passion, self-conscious damnation, and satirical verve into relation with more beneficent powers of playing. Chapter 6 turns to the continuing vitality of Beckett, who might seem to have carried the Byronic mental theater to a point of no return. Plays by Fugard, Soyinka, Shepard, Mamet, and Friel acknowledge but overcome the self-conscious finality of Beckett's minimalism, as they sustain the community life implicit in his actions of performance and move toward more expansive images of social concern. Chapter 7, considering more closely Soyinka's understanding of theater as a participatory event, takes up four plays in which, through quite different versions of an African-European eclecticism, he charts approaches to an ecstasy of transformation. Chapter 8 then reflects upon a presence for whom the directorial art itself has constituted a paradigm of self-transformation. Peter Brook's assimilation of many genres, styles, and paradigms of acting and witnessing led to major productions of *King Lear* and *Marat/Sade.* His later work, with scripts and companies both English and international, may seem to have offered a strange mix of theatricalism, pessimism, mythology, and clinical observation. But Brook has been unfolding the possibilities of playing itself as a continuing search in which we all may participate. It is no accident that he has translated into very different international terms the commitment to individual transformation and community realization that informs *The Playboy of the Western World.*

Given world enough and time, I would have added a chapter on what Marc Robinson has called "the other American drama"—from, say, the Gertrude Stein / Virgil Thomson *Four Saints in Three Acts,* as recently staged by Robert Wilson, to Suzan-Lori Parks's *African Venus,* as directed by Richard Foreman. In that paradigm an often enigmatic performed action speaks to us through a beautifully lucid and self-conscious action of performance, informed by the principles of visual and musical art. But these chapters are at least notes toward a "thick description" of the mirrors of playing in our time. The afterword will invoke Tony Kushner's *Angels in America* as the most powerful recent exploration in English of the mental theater (or what Kushner calls the "Theater of the Fabulous") as a field in which we may engage, dialectically and dialogically, a multitude of paradigms and presences through the mirrors of our playing. But some readers may want at this point a fuller account of what I mean by "playing," "paradigms," and "presences."

III

The "purpose of playing," said Hamlet to the First Player, "was and is, to hold as 'twere the mirror up to nature" (3.2.17–19). Today that formula may strike us as rather naive, for we know that the "mirror" of drama always distorts and believe that our "nature" has become irreversibly problematic. Even the theater's most "realistic" images are shared illusions. Hollis Huston, in *The Actor's Instrument,* has insisted that the "circuit of signals" onstage is objectively different from what it causes us to imagine. The theater "must create public signs of what cannot happen in public space." And, "when spectators accept those signs as signifiers of what they encode, actors live the peculiar illusion that their preposterous behavior is appropriate" (114). How can nature be mirrored by such illusions—or, indeed, by anything? According to Richard Rorty in *Philosophy and the Mirror of Nature,* the mind itself is no such mirror. Perception, thought, and language all subdue experience to their own structures, and nature remains unknowable except as so transformed. If so, can we still speak of the "purpose" of playing? Or even of playing as a determinate mode of action?

Many believe that we cannot. "It seems hardly possible today," says Michael Vanden Heuvel, "for books to be written with titles like *The Elements of Drama,* much less *The Idea of a Theater*" (10). But I think we can still speak of the purpose of playing if we accept the premise, justified by theatrical practice of all kinds, that playing holds the mirror up to our "playing." We need not accept some fashionable notion of the world as irreducibly plural or indeterminate. At the very least we can look through the variety of theatrical forms toward the spontaneous and self-reflexive activity that generates them. Drama always assumes that we behold in its mirrors a human nature as histrionic as the mirrors themselves. In fact, most of what Hamlet means by *nature* is the histrionic. His words to the First Player are part of his own theatrical project, which includes an antic disposition and the insertion of lines in the Player's performance that will smoke out the murderous performance of Claudius. Hamlet is obsessively alert to the theatrical projects of others—from Gertrude, Ophelia, and Polonius to Rosencrantz, Guildenstern, and Laertes. Shakespeare's play discloses a whole theater of playing. As much recent commentary has shown—we may think here of Ann Righter, James L. Calderwood, Thomas F. Van Laan, Michael Goldman, and others—the playing of Shakespeare's actors mimes the playing of his characters. And so it is in other kinds of plays, in which the characters may be less self-conscious. A Stanislavskian probing of subtext can reveal that every character in a "realistic" play by Ibsen, Chekhov, or Miller is at least spontaneously and unwittingly histrionic. Moment by moment, they engage in self-presentations for others and for themselves. "Acting," as Michael Goldman has said in *The Actor's Freedom,* "is not a matter of assuming a fixed role but of showing how the character *acts*—that is, how he moves in and out of his repertory of roles." That is one reason why the "powers of the actor determine the playwright's art, as the possibilities of language determine the poet's" (92, 100). What, then, of plays in which characters have little or no depth or continuity? Bertolt Brecht sometimes thought the human being an atom that perpetually breaks up and forms anew. Samuel Beckett put all presumed continuities or identities yet more radically in question. But every *gestus* in *Man Is Man,* every disjunctive speech in *Endgame,* is just such an action of conscious or unconscious self-presentation. Even "flat" or "abstract" characters like Goods in *Everyman,* the Fool in *King Lear,* the Mummy in Strindberg's *The Ghost Sonata,* or the partial, fleeting, or composite beings that inhabit plays by Heiner Müller, Richard Foreman, or Suzan-Lori Parks are engaged at every moment, directly or symbolically, in a project of role-playing.

When playing holds the mirror up to playing, it reflects not only the histrionic behavior in its stage world, its performed action, but also its own modes of histrionic behavior. We always behold not merely the represented "characters," "actions," and "world" but also ourselves—as actors and witnesses in the action of performance. As a participatory and self-reflexive art, drama mirrors its own act of "holding up the mirror." The full meaning of a play therefore includes the implications of the performance event. Hollis Huston has mistakenly said: "You can't think of representation and of that which it represents at the same moment—you must choose" (114). But in fact dramatic art, like all art, requires its creators and appreciators to oscillate rapidly between those seemingly incompatible thoughts, or to "think" them simultaneously and nonverbally at different levels of awareness. How else could one extemporize an artful and elaborate sentence or gesture? Or appreciate a brilliant performance in a gripping play? Throughout most of its history the theater has privileged "playful" styles that emphasize just that doubleness of attention, heightening our impressions of offstage nature and bringing us into a shared game of disclosure. In this century, after some decades of commitment to realistic or naturalistic acting, we have been rediscovering the complex resources of those styles. J. L. Styan has shown in *Drama, Stage, and Audience* (141–79) how "role-playing" and not realistic characterization has been central to dramatic tradition. Huston's own phrase, "public signs of what cannot happen in public space," should remind us that naturalism itself is a kind of theatricalism in which the game is to disguise the game. In the plays of Ibsen, Chekhov, and their many successors, that disguise is fairly transparent, and the fiction of objective observation may itself become a major theme. Whatever the style, we are peripherally aware of the distance between the actor's persona and the role being played—a distance that Brecht exploited as a means of ironic reflection to be shared with the audience. Unlike the Stanislavskian actor in a realistic play, who seeks to give the illusion of merely inhabiting the character, the Brechtian actor establishes a variable distance from the character, moving back and forth along a spectrum that runs from empathy to ironic commentary. In doing so, the Brechtian actor foregrounds *the actor's role as actor in this play*—and we are encouraged to share that variable perspective.

A play, then, does not merely "imitate an action" or "make a statement" about a human condition from which it has somehow withdrawn. It is a form of attentive playing, which is partly about our own participation—for every actor is also an implicit witness, every witness an implicit actor. From such reciprocity each moment is shaped. Indeed, we already bring to the theater a histrionic self-awareness and an interior multiplicity. We are compulsively mimetic beings. We constitute our "selves" and imagine the selves of others through a conscious and unconscious role-playing that includes Freud's "introjection" and "projection," Jung's dialogues with the "shadow" and the "anima," and of course our more deliberate taking on of roles. As both Freud and Pirandello have taught us, a "consciously chosen" role may result from a role-playing that is unconscious and obsessive. Our "personality," or "persona," is a complex role that has become entrenched in a system of mental and emotional habits. We may withdraw certain projections, revise the identities of "self" and "other," and detach ourselves to some degree from our possessed experience—but those are tasks of some difficulty. As Ernest R. Hilgard and others have shown, our role-playing is further complicated by the fact that the unity of personality is for the most part illusory. Milton Erickson and Ernest Lawrence Rossi have hypothesized that all experience is "state-dependent," acquired and recalled within specific states of awareness. "The apparent continuity of consciousness that exists in everyday normal awareness," Rossi has said, "is in fact a precarious illusion that is only made possible by . . . associative connections" (41). Each of us is a community of "subpersonalities" who voice their feelings and knowledge when provoked by our present situation. Charles T. Tart calls them "identity states" within a consensus trance that we think of as "normal" consciousness (*States of Consciousness* 163–70; *Waking Up* 85–106, 115–25). At different moments and at different levels of consciousness we assume a variety of roles—and the drama of this "interior community" shapes our perceptions of a community "outside" ourselves.

How to render this situation onstage? Actors in a realistic play like Ibsen's *Ghosts* must often enact feelings and intentions of which the character is not fully aware and provide the illusion of a behavior more transparent to us than to other characters. In other kinds of plays interior communities may receive external embodiment. In Aeschylus' *The Oresteia,* Orestes first sees the Furies, who then become apparent to all. In Pinter's *The Birthday Party* Stanley undergoes an interrogation by Goldberg and McCann that turns his hidden story into manifest nightmare. Caryl Churchill, David Lan, and the Joint Stock Company have taken from Euripides' *The Bacchae* the issues of possession, psychic transformation, and projection, explored them through improvisation, and produced the remarkable play *A Mouthful of Birds.* More generally, of course, the hypnotic power of mimesis rests in large part upon its eliciting of just such projections of our interior roles.

And so does its therapeutic power. Here, as elsewhere, the pathological, because it exaggerates the normal, makes the normal easier to see. Colin A. Ross and other clinicians have offered accounts of multiple personality disorder, in which consciousness is dissociated into centers at least partly separated by trauma-induced repression and amnesia. Therapy must begin by bringing those personalities into communication with one another. For the less seriously disturbed, Erickson's therapeutic hypnosis, Jung's active imagination, and Frederick Perls's Gestalt therapy are among the quasi-dramatic arts that encourage an integrative dialogue among state-dependent centers of awareness. The playfulness of the theater operates in much the same way. Actors find that playing a role taps not only specific feelings but entire personalities they did not know they contained. Some with rather fragile "ego identities" may know "who" they are only when playing a role. Others, like Anthony Hopkins, have testified that acting has given them a way of getting in touch with "deeper" or "darker" or "more capable" aspects of their own being.

Playwrights, acting instructors, directors, and psychologically oriented critics have often recognized these facts. Synge's *The Playboy of the Western World* explores with rich ironies some of the personal and social implications of therapeutic role-playing. Keith Johnstone has described in *Impro* his work at the Royal Court Theatre with masks from several non-European traditions, which induced trance states that allowed "spirits" to take possession of the actor's body (143ff.). Ned Manderino's *The Transpersonal Actor* modifies Stanislavski's "system" to include exercises that arouse energies and "action choices" in the self and its surrounding field. Margaret Brenman-Gibson, drawing upon Erik Erikson's revisionary dream analysis, has hypothesized that *"in every play the cast of characters represents a projection of the playwright's identity elements and fragments, a distribution of the self and its conflicts."* The playwright finds in the dramatic structure "a psychohistorical bridge to an audience who collectively then share his conflicts, his liberation, and his renewal of inner cohesion" ("Creation of Plays" 227). Clifford Odets, in a note quoted by Brenman-Gibson, sums up this process: "Theatre, in a certain sense, is the outward play of inner play" (189). What she infers from

Odets's realistic scripts we can see more directly in Strindberg's *A Dream Play,* in which, as the playwright said in his introduction, characters split, double, redouble, evaporate, condense, fragment, and cohere. Pirandello shaped *Six Characters in Search of an Author, Henry IV,* and *Tonight We Improvise* by confronting the impossibility of attaining an objective distance from the dream of multiplicity that we both project and inhabit. As he said in the preface to *Six Characters,* "the multiple personality of everyone" corresponds to "the possibilities of being found in each of us" (367). Nina daVinci Nichols, in "Pirandello and the Poetics of Desire," has traced the spirals of self-creation and self-consciousness generated by his repeated attempt to realize in dramatic form a unified vision of our relation to the impulses welling up from the unconscious. The post-Pirandellian and post-Brechtian works of Heiner Müller rethink such multiple role-playing in the context of an apocalyptic fragmentation of culture. "I was Hamlet," says the actor who opens *Hamletmachine* (53), as he embarks upon a densely textured histrionic collage that often recalls the themes and strategies of T. S. Eliot's *The Waste Land.*

Whatever its style, a play solicits and mirrors our plural and multidimensional consciousness through its total form and not just through the character with whom we may most easily "identify." "Expressionist" plays—from Strindberg's *A Dream Play* and *The Road to Damascus* to O'Neill's *The Emperor Jones,* Williams's *Camino Real,* and Mamet's *Edmond*—make the entire scene respond to the psyche of a central character. But "actors as characters" in any play are intensified and distorted by our projections of our internal communities. For me the magnetism of Morris Carnovsky as Shylock, Lear, and Chekhov's old servant Firs had much to do with the "father" that my ego both resists and tries to incorporate. On one occasion that projection was intensified by the fact that Carnovsky was also directing me in *The Merchant of Venice.* But my response to his Lear at the American Shakespeare Theatre in 1965 did not preclude my finding Ruby Dee's Cordelia a similarly magnetic image, compounded no doubt of ego and anima projections. And I might as easily adduce here Ian Holm's brilliant and poignant rendering of Lear at the National Theatre in 1997. Indeed, the entire gamut of role-playing, from Edmund's "Nature, be thou my goddess" to Edgar's "Tom's a-cold," can disclose and name some of the creatures that inhabit me. We all move through such fields of projections and affinities. As we find ourselves everywhere in the acting of a play, we take a step toward a psychological and social integration that may, of course, finally elude us, as it did Pirandello.

Theater gains its power from what is most problematic in our lives: the instability of our "I," the ease with which we are immersed in a waking dreamwork. These vulnerabilities open us to an art form that, bodying forth our shared condition, can become a locus of playful exercises that help us to access our feelings, change our perceptions, revise our understanding of the world, and, perhaps most important, discover the ways in which we are already immersed in several communities. By inviting us to explore the roles that inhabit and largely control us and by introducing us to yet other roles, playing illuminates the process through which our lives are shaped and leads us toward a fuller awareness of the intersubjective field in which we participate.

Bruce Wilshire, in *Role Playing and Identity: The Limits of Theatre as Metaphor,* has cogently described theater as a "perceptually induced mimetic phenomenon of participation—an imagined experience of total activity," which illuminates "through its fictive variations the actuality of mimetic relationships between persons" (26, 16). He argues that, because "behavior and identity were laid down bodily, mimetically, and together, their recovery and recognition may very well be achieved only bodily, mimetically, and together" (16). During a performance we in the audience "stand in" for actors who themselves are "standing in" for characters who "find themselves through each other's presence" (10). In this way theater gives "release to our primal mimetic absorptions in types of doing and being," which "are constitutive . . . of our identity as persons, and are usually quite unspeakable by us even when they are released" (23). Wilshire warns against any a priori separation between self and other. The self, he says, is "involved essentially in a body which is involved pre-reflectively and non-thematically in others and in other things" (156). Theatrical encounter is "a communal experimentation in which models and metaphors for life are tried out" (89), as we work through the struggles and discoveries that make possible the emergence of a "vital and authentic individuality" (296).

Wilshire is pessimistic, however, about our finding such "individuality" in the modern theater. He speaks of the "tragic limitations" of theater as a metaphor for life and as a social institution. In "our time of need" it is "not clear whether vital and authentic individuality is still possible for us" (296). And he hopes for a "rite of authorization and authentication" that the theater "suggests but does not provide" (295). It seems to me that our situation is both more complex and more hopeful than Wilshire suggests. His emphasis on individuality deflects attention from the fact that we always participate in the entire play as performed by the actors. It may be hard to find any "vital and authentic individuality" in plays by Ibsen, Strindberg, Chekhov, Pirandello, O'Neill, Beckett, or Genet, in which characters are so often confused, isolated, and imprisoned by self-deceptive role-playing. But the larger meanings of such plays reside in the dialectic between their stage worlds and the actions of performance in which we participate. When acting and witnessing Beckett's *Waiting for Godot,* we are not lost with Vladimir and Estragon in the wasteland of the perverse or problematic. In discovering and assessing their situation, we also discover our reciprocity in the theater and the rich coherence of the playwright's subtle, intellectually complex, often humorous, and often lyric discourse. Such relations between the represented action and the action of performance constitute an implicit critique of what we might otherwise take to be Beckett's despairing vision.

This effect is no accident. Plays must employ and therefore endorse a good many human possibilities that their stage worlds may sometimes ignore, question, or even deny. But very often—as in Beckett's work—their dramatic forms call our attention to just such contradictions. Why should that be? Like every work of art, a play tends to focus its meanings through a coherent structure of analogies. As Francis Fergusson pointed out in *The Idea of a Theater,* the action represented by a play tends to become one that the characters share by analogy—a Stanislavskian insight into dramatic form that we may also find in Odets's preface to *Awake and Sing!* or Harold Clurman's notebooks in *On Directing.* But, because a play in performance is both participatory and self-reflexive, its "action shared by analogy" is likely to expand to include the participants as well as the characters, if only with some sharp contrasts. A realistic play like *Rosmersholm* can therefore become a participatory drama that interprets its own paradoxical invitation for us to pretend that we are not there. And a self-conscious parable of absurd blockage, disintegration, and isolation like *Endgame* can point through its style toward the powers of rationality, heuristic action, and community that are implicit in its performance. Some modern plays incorporate a conscious reflection upon the complexity of our present role-playing. In Brecht's *The Caucasian Chalk Circle* the relations between the performed action and the action of performance greatly expand the meaning of a play that is already "about" the possibility of constructive familial and political action. Modern plays are therefore more complex and more optimistic in their mirroring of our life than most accounts have recognized. Whatever their style, they lead us not so much toward a "vital and authentic individuality" as toward a more lucid, comprehensive, and balanced awareness of the "inner" and "outer" communities of playing in which we already participate.

That, in fact, is precisely what we find in the dialectical paradigm explored by Théâtre de la Jeune Lune's *Children of Paradise: Shooting a Dream*. Because the self is no stable "substance," the unity of our consciousness as it mediates an internal multiplicity must reside in a constantly reaffirmed "act." And, because we are community beings, our aim must always be an attentive act that transcends the ego's understanding of individuality. Even when seemingly pessimistic in its representations, the theater can orient us toward that end through its mirrors of playing. That is why the director Peter Brook, whose understanding of this matter has been deepened by the work of G. I. Gurdjieff, has sought through playing itself to waken actors and audiences from our consensus trance, our shared sleepwalking, to an awareness of what he calls the "invisible."

IV

Our role-playing off and on the stage emerges from a complex interaction of paradigms and presences. Each of us, as a presence more responsive and plural than we often believe, has come to consciousness through an exploration of paradigms of action or gesture that help to organize and interpret our experience. Responding subliminally and reflectively to those patterns of behavior, we incorporate them into selves reinforced by habit. Language, in its slowly changing versions, may be the most complex of those paradigms, but many others help to sustain the fabric of our lives. But every paradigm, whatever its biological or metaphysical foundations, comes to us as a possibility already informed by other presences. As Wilshire has said of a dramatic text, a paradigm is "the evolving precipitate of encounters of persons with each other in time, the precipitate of a tradition" (89). Every encounter of a presence with a paradigm is a doubly evolutionary dialogue. We revise the paradigm, even as it enables or provokes our self-revision. That dialectic is fundamental to our historical life—and to the life of all our institutions. Of course, we may deny our reliance upon preexisting paradigms. Jean-Paul Sartre could sometimes claim for the *pour-soi,* or reflexive subjectivity, an unfettered existential freedom. We may also deny that the source of our experience is an inherently nonobjectifiable presence. Jacques Derrida has often described that presence as a verbal illusion, an absence masked by the infinite slippage of language. But in practice, I think, each of us recognizes that we are constituted by a dialectic between what Louis Lavelle has called the appearances "given" to us and the subjective "act" that we are. One form of that dialectic is the interaction of paradigms and presences. By shaping that dialectic into art, theater invites us to participate in formally controlled instances of what happens everywhere.

Neither paradigms nor presences, of course, can ever be regarded from an entirely objective distance. We cannot objectify a paradigm because we always inhabit some model of understanding and must therefore always interpret one in terms of another. Those that guide our play, moreover, are especially protean. The paradigms that Thomas Kuhn traced in the sciences succeed one another in linear fashion, with victories so absolute that textbooks "disguise not only the role but the very existence of the revolutions that produced them" (137). The theatrical analogue of Kuhn's "normal science" would be an ossified conventionality, like that evoked by Peter Brook's account in *The Empty Space* of a rehearsal at the Comédie-Française in which "a very young actor stood in front of a very old one and spoke and mimed the role with him like a reflection in a glass" (12). But playing, especially in our own time, is even more fluid than Kuhn's "revolutionary science." A "paradigm shift" is here no great matter: we slide or jump from one to another, readjusting our attention and expectations as we go. Paradigms of playing can coexist, compete, overlap, merge, develop, and undergo sudden mutation—as Tony Kushner's *Angels in America* seems designed to demonstrate. Nevertheless, each has a certain coherence and a tendency to replicate itself as a way of organizing and interpreting theatrical experience. It offers its own relationships, patterns of development, and routes of exploration. It can therefore be a heuristic model for the playwright, and for actors and witnesses, leading us toward fresh discoveries.

In this respect the theater of our time has become more and more like contemporary philosophy. Pragmatic treatments of knowledge and meaning, Rorty says, "seem to license everyone to construct . . . his own little paradigm, his own little practice" (*Philosophy and the Mirror of Nature* 317). In the "central" areas of analytic philosophy "there are now as many paradigms as there are major philosophy departments" (*Consequences of Pragmatism* 216). The modern theater is a similar "conversation" among paradigms, through which we may gain new skills in using partly incommensurable models as ways of discovery (*Philosophy and the Mirror of Nature* 264, 319). But, unlike the paradigms that may guide the philosopher, psychologist, or anthropologist, a paradigm of playing invites a shared activity that is polyphonic, fully embodied, and artistically ordered. The knowledge arising from our participation in that activity must largely remain what William James called "knowledge-by-acquaintance" (*Pragmatism* and *The Meaning of*

Truth 184–86, 196–97), though its outlines and major themes can be rearticulated through the rather different paradigms of critical interpretation.

We can most easily discover a paradigm's power of organizing and interpreting experience by looking at a group of related plays. Genres and styles, as critics usually describe them, mainly pertain to the imitated or represented action. I will therefore be showing how a number of paradigms include both the imitated action and the action of performance. They can bring various genres and styles into their magnetic fields—simultaneously as in Synge's *The Playboy of the Western World,* through serial transformation as in Wilde's *The Importance of Being Earnest,* Shaw's *You Never Can Tell,* Orton's *What the Butler Saw,* and Stoppard's *Travesties,* or through a pervasive shaping of different period styles as in Sartre's *No Exit,* Beckett's *Play,* Genet's *The Screens,* and Pinter's *No Man's Land.* When such paradigms interact with one another and with specific presences, their transformations can point toward the inherent possibilities of our fields of play.

Nor can we fully objectify a presence, though historians, biographers, and autobiographers have often tried—even when recognizing the multiplicity of their individual subjects and understanding that the "unity" of the self must reside in an "act" or "project" and not a substance. On that scale of description a presence is the goal-directed action that inhabits the life course of an individual. But I shall also use *presence,* as we do in ordinary parlance, to refer to the appearance or manifestation of an individual from the past. In that sense a presence is a field of "influence"—though *influence* mistakenly suggests a one-way causation. We engage in dialogue with a presence from the past—putting questions, receiving answers, offering interpretations, and putting further questions, even if we can never finally separate such dialogues from those with our interior presences. Under the pressure of such recognitions the idea of a unitary biographical presence is likely to merge with some larger field. Again, for our time, Kushner's *Angels in America* seems the exemplary text.

No doubt all such notions of presence are convenient oversimplifications. Even a pluralistic or skeptical mind, convinced of the irreducible reality of its own conscious life, may suspect that behind what Louis Lavelle called the "given" and the "act" there may be an immanent and transcendent presence. Speaking as a psychologist, William James insisted upon the concrete particularity of the personal consciousness. "Absolute insulation, irreducible pluralism, is the law" (*Principles of Psychology* 1:221). And yet, in the very same textbook, when considering how a "passing thought" might be "more" than a "passing brain-state," James could say: "when we are once trying metaphysical explanations we are foolish not to go as far as we can. For my own part I confess that the moment I become metaphysical and try to define the more, I find the notion of some sort of *anima mundi* thinking in all of us to be a more promising hypothesis, in spite of all its difficulties, than that of a lot of absolutely individual souls" (1:328). Merleau-Ponty insisted that phenomenology must be all or nothing (94–95), but Jung, who believed that analytical psychology must remain phenomenological, could also hold that our role-playing is grounded in a psyche more extensive than our ego consciousness, a field of dramatic activity open to the transpersonal and the cosmic. Such an immanent and transcendent field of consciousness, accessible through the configurations of energy that we call "body" and "psyche," seems a plausible inference from our psychosomatic and histrionic experience. That would correspond with what Peter Brook calls the invisible. But the following chapters bracket all questions of personal faith or doctrinal adherence. They offer empirical approaches based on the interpretation of scripts, productions, and historical contexts, though they are oriented toward possibilities that we may glimpse through the mirrors of our playing.

Part 1

Paradigms

Chapter 1

Playing with *The Playboy*: Synge and Tradition

I

For nearly a century we have been responding to Synge's invitation to join him in an exuberant, astringent, and self-illuminating playfulness. In its own way *The Playboy of the Western World* is like *Oedipus Rex, Hamlet,* and *Waiting for Godot,* a complex paradigm of the theatrical. Its eclectic style, naturalistic-romantic-tragicomic-farcical-satirical-and-allegorical, is an exemplary instance of early modernism. And its continual refocusing of the relations between the onstage community and the community of performance shows richly and economically how playing can elicit from actors and witnesses their diverse potentialities, complicate their self-understanding, and invite their transformation. The playboy himself, that mock-Christ and mock-Oedipus, is an archetypal instance of transformation through role-playing. But it is the play's elaborate structure of analogous actions that becomes in performance our interlocutor and histrionic mirror. If we look at *The Playboy* in the context of its traditions and antecedents, its productions, the responses of audiences and critics, and its relations to other works in the modern theater, we can begin to grasp its paradigmatic qualities.

In the early years, of course, Synge's invitation was sometimes rudely turned down, most notably in Dublin during the turbulent week of January 1907, when *The Playboy* was first produced, and again in New York and Philadelphia during the winter of 1911–12, when the Irish Players had to cope with riotous audiences and the arrest of the entire cast. The Philadelphia liquor dealer who brought charges had stayed in the theater, according to Lady Augusta Gregory, "only till Shawneen's 'coat of a Christian man' was left in Michael James's hands. He made a disturbance then and was turned out, but was able to find as much indecency even in that conversation as would demoralise a monastery. His brother, a priest, had stayed all through, and found we had committed every sin mentioned in the Act"

(227). Those early rejections were also political, for Arthur Griffith's *United Irishman,* the New York *Gaelic American,* and the Clan-na-Gael whipped up an indignation that depended in part on the touchy sensibilities of an aggrieved nationalism. As Bernard Shaw put it to an interviewer from the New York *Evening Sun,* the Clan-na-Gael had hit upon "the brilliant idea that to satirise the follies of humanity is to insult the Irish nation, because the Irish nation is, in fact, the human race and has no follies and stands there pure and beautiful and saintly to be eternally oppressed by England and collected for by the Clan" (qtd. in Gregory 300). Shaw was unfair, as usual, but he had a point. We all traffic in such brilliant ideas, though sometimes we think our purity destined not to be oppressed but to impose its own will upon the Western world. And *The Playboy*'s yoking of naturalism to the extravagantly satirical seems aggressively designed, as Edward Hirsch has argued, to provoke outrage from the least playful sector of its audience.

The play tempts all of us, however, toward self-disclosure and self-recognition. Recognizing that our potential resistance to its playfulness is rooted in fear, projected guilt, and a consequent desire to control, to hurt, and to escape, it leads us through its naturalism into a Mayo funhouse, where we may recognize ourselves in such mirrors as an anxious suitor, an insensitive father, a scapegoating community, and a lonely young woman who helps to create the hero whom she then indignantly and fearfully rejects. The first scene already invites our laughing complicity in Mayo scapegoating, as the clergy-haunted Shawn Keogh barely escapes from the pub to the amusement of a father more interested in an alcoholic wake than in the safety of his adventurous daughter. And the closing moments of act 3, after Christy has survived a more violent scapegoating and has left the stage with his wry blessing upon the Mayo community, sound a complex chord of resistance to the play's own unsettling burden. "By the will of God," says Michael James, "we'll have peace now for our drinks," whereupon Shawn tries to reassert his and Father Reilly's rights over Pegeen Mike, and the stage erupts with her swift blow and wild lament: "I've lost the only Playboy of the Western World" (4:173). We share her painful recognition that she has trapped herself by collaborating with the anti-playful impulses toward a repressive safety and order.

Those early attacks on the play and its mirroring of our motives can lead us toward a fuller understanding of its import. Central, of course, is the humor that Synge later called "the test of morals" and a sign of "that instinct of sanity that we call so many names" (2:349). As William Butler Yeats said at the time, "The outcry against *The Playboy* was an outcry against its style, against its way of seeing" (*Explorations* 253). That way of seeing encompasses its own opposition. If we refuse to see ourselves in the comic protagonist, who is both victim and victor, or in the society that longs for such a protagonist, half-creates him, projects on him its deepest desires and delights, celebrates him, and then casts him out, then we make a scapegoat of the play itself. And the play knows why. Not for nothing is Christopher Mahon a potato-digging poet, ostensible father-murderer, seeming savior, and lord of misrule. But Synge's dramatic style, in which Yeats found a "delight in setting the hard virtues by the soft, the bitter by the sweet" (*Essays and Introductions* 308), and a combination of "lyric beauty" and "violent laughter" that holds "so much of the mind of Ireland" (*Essays and Introductions* 337), can also lead us toward that comprehensive knowledge and delight.

Although we are not likely at this end of the century to reject *The Playboy* out of moral, religious, or political indignation, we may still be tempted to regard it somewhat condescendingly as a masterpiece of the Irish dramatic movement. It has been said that Synge "looked backward, not forward" (R. Peacock 115), and that his imaginative strengths and formal complexities are circumscribed by "very definite limits" (N. Grene 186). But *The Playboy* is not a splendid dead end or an instance of transcendent provinciality. It foreshadows a great deal of Irish drama—from Sean O'Casey, Denis Johnston, and Brendan Behan on to Samuel Beckett, Brian Friel, and Martin McDonagh—that is devoted to a counterpointing of laughter and violence, lyricism and irony, trenchant talk and collapsing action. Friel's recent *Dancing at Lughnasa,* for example, makes clear the centrality of such counterpoint to modern theater. It takes certain themes and strategies from *The Playboy*—lonely women, insensitive or incompetent men, an emotionally desolate Ireland counterpointed against what is now specified as the festival of the pagan god Lugh, with its games, horse races, and marriages—and expands them with the help of Anton Chekhov's more panoramic focus on analogous emotional predicaments in *Three Sisters* and Tennessee Williams's distancing of such a predicament through the "memory play" in *The Glass Menagerie.* Quite appropriately, when the Abbey Theatre brought *Dancing at Lughnasa* to New York, the dementedly histrionic Uncle Jack was played by Donal Donnelly, who had played Christy Mahon in Dublin three decades earlier.

Nearly ninety years after *The Playboy* opened, McDonagh's *The Beauty Queen of Leenane* has shown how a humorous, violent, and poignant play can still rely upon elements inherited from Synge: an economically marginal

Connemara cottage, village jokes about deliberate cruelty to animals, an isolated woman longing for a partner, a tyrannical parent murdered by a long-suffering child, and a wild mixture of exuberant laughter and painful violence, a hesitant or bold erotic lyricism and the darkest irony. Even Maureen Folan's brutal burning of her mother Mag on a hot stove seems drawn from Pegeen Mike's burning of Christy Mahon with a coal from the fire. In *The Beauty Queen,* as in *The Playboy,* stock farcical characters repeatedly complicate the melodrama. When Ray Dooley (who is somewhat reminiscent of Shawn Keogh) gives the love letter from his brother Pato not to Maureen Folan but to her mother, Mag, the farcical-melodramatic suspense is milked for all it is worth. Ray's comic fascination with the poker that could kill a man then prepares us for an astonishing climax. And his fury on discovering the string ball Maureen had once taken from him, which rises to farcical but ominous violence even as she threatens him with that poker, seems to avert a second such climax. In *The Beauty Queen,* however, McDonagh has heightened the irony, horror, and pathos by transposing genders, grounding the tragic in the pathological, and surprising us with an actual murder. It is not the lonely girl Pegeen Mike but the hesitant suitor Pato Dooley who discloses his mind in writing a letter, not the shyly attractive Christopher Mahon but the unbalanced middle-aged virgin Maureen Folan who rebels against a parent after years of tyranny, and not the farcical-pathetic Old Mahon but the farcical-ugly Mag Folan who abuses the adult child. And yet Maureen's murder of Mag, when under the illusion that she still has a chance to wed Pato, leaves her in an exacerbated version of Pegeen's ironically self-produced predicament. "I've lost the only Playboy of the Western World!" cries Pegeen at the end of all. In a similar situation, but with greater restraint and so with a sudden poignancy, the desperate and disappointed Maureen asks Ray to tell Pato that "the beauty queen of Leenane says *good-bye.*"

There are many other affinities between *The Playboy* and modern theater. Cyril Cusack said that in Paris at the First International Theatre Festival, to which he had taken his own production in 1954, *The Playboy* "found its true home and audience" (305). Of course, the play had long since reached Paris in translation: in 1914 Lugné-Poë directed *Le Baladin du Monde Occidental* at the Théâtre de l'Oeuvre. (Barrett Clark thought it farther from the original than the Künstlertheater production of *Der Held des Westerlands* that he had seen in Munich [25].) But Cusack rightly suggested that Synge's play is genuinely *of* our larger Western world. "The striking feature of modern art," Thomas Mann once said, "is that it has ceased to recognize the categories of tragic and comic, or the dramatic classifications, tragedy and comedy. It sees life as tragi-comedy, with the result that the grotesque is its most genuine style" (240–41). And Synge's masterpiece in that style is a remarkably full engagement with what is also the central subject of modern drama: life as a question of role-playing.

Synge may not have known Arthur Schnitzler's "grotesquery in one act," *The Green Cockatoo,* in which a Paris cafe is an improvisatory "theater" rather like his Mayo pub: "There are people here who play the criminal—and others who are criminals without knowing it" (189–90). There an actor, Henri, gives a histrionic account of killing a duke whom he pretends to believe is his wife's lover. Then, in a *coup de théâtre* that foreshadows the complexities of Pirandello's *Henry IV,* Henri discovers that the duke really is his wife's lover, the duke enters, and Henri kills him. As the poet Rollin has already said: "Truth dissolves into pretense, pretense into truth" (214). Synge did not live to read the words given by Hugo von Hofmannsthal to a player in his "Prologue to Brecht's *Baal*": "The actor is the amoeba among all living things and therefore he is the symbolic man" (119). But, because *The Playboy* develops similar insights, Synge's understanding of the histrionic must be viewed in the context of dramatists from Ibsen, Chekhov, Pirandello, and Genet onward who have been haunted by such implications of their medium.

II

Stripped of its many ironies, *The Playboy* sets forth a remarkable parabolic action. The shy and lonely farmboy threatened by an oedipal fate (a forced marriage with the widow who "did suckle me for six weeks when I came into the world" [4:103]) has erupted in panicky violence against the father whom he fears. Now, finding himself among those who shelter him and draw his story from him, he gradually lends himself (with a childlike creative faith) to the role of glorious parricide—whereupon, through the ups and downs of exploratory prevarication, he discovers his poetic power, his ability to love and be loved, his strength and courage. After surviving the appropriate ordeals (exposure as a liar, confrontation with the repeatedly resurrected Old Mahon, rejection as a murderer), Christy leaves the stage a new man, independent and reconciled with the father—indeed, having gaily swapped places with him. Although "master of all fights from now" (4:173), he no longer seems tempted to maintain an insecure ego by violence and deceit. In fact, he invokes blessings on those (including his once-beloved Pegeen) who had seemed fools or worse a moment before. The playboy as hoaxer has become the playboy as genuine champion, beyond their understanding—though not beyond Pegeen's longing. Role-playing has led to the authentic; lies have led to truth.

Or so it seems—for such an interpretation contains difficulties. Una Ellis-Fermor said that, whether this finale is Christy's "self-realization, as he thinks," or "the expansion of a superb fantasy, as we half-suppose, matters little" (179). But Howard Pearce has argued that it matters very much, and that the play drastically qualifies Christy's vision. Cyril Cusack, perhaps still weighting the play's naturalism more heavily than its theatricalism, as he did in his early renderings of Christy, has said the finale is weak because a "void," the artist's "flight from reality," has become the resolution (304). And Patricia Spacks, who sees the "man" and the "pose" as finally identical in Christy, suggests that language comes to control him as much as he comes to control language. Surely we must then ask: Has Christy's kind of playing really led him to the actual? Or has Synge's kind of playing led *us* from the actual into the realm of myth? Or has the play enabled us to participate in both possibilities? And, if so, how are those possibilities related to each other?

The Playboy locates itself quite firmly in a difficult territory: the educational function of role-playing in life and in art. Its ambiguities are clues to its meaning. The play's grotesque style elicits from us an unusually sustained combination of spontaneous sympathy and detached irony. We share in Christy's passionate improvisation and in the formal patterns of Synge's precise comic control. Located both "inside" and "outside" Christy, we follow the reciprocal process of his self-construction and self-discovery. And, in assessing that process, we share Synge's marvelously balanced awareness of the wry fictiveness of the seeming actual and the potent actuality of our most profound fictions. But these effects point toward the central mysteries of drama itself. For drama is that art of collaborative role-playing that submits passionate improvisation and its spontaneously doubled response in the spectator to formal control, locates us both "inside" and "outside" the action, and so brings to awareness much that remains hidden in the more compulsively histrionic texture of our lives. *The Playboy,* then, is "about" both the drama of life and the life of drama. There is ample reason to agree with Mary King that it is a double-edged "apotheosis of the metadramatic" (133, 148). By inviting us to focus the self-blinding and self-illuminating possibilities of our shared histrionic sensibility, it transcends the ambiguities of its central parable. Its role-playing does lead us to the authentic.

That paradox has deep roots in Synge's own persona and his writing. Here, as elsewhere, "paradigms" attain their fresh artistic form through the mediation of "presences." At first glance there is a striking distance between the sometimes violent and frequently prevaricating Christy and Synge himself. Although W. B. Yeats saw in his friend "that egotism of a man of genius which Nietzsche compares to the egotism of a woman with child" (*Autobiography* 311) and Stephen MacKenna cut out great patches of violent speech from his friend's letters to protect his memory (Saddlemyer, "Vision and Design" 311), Synge's persona was one of attentive and truthful simplicity. John Butler Yeats said that "Synge was morally one of the most fastidious men I ever met," a "man of peace" whose conversation "had the charm of entire sincerity, a quality rare among men and artists" (60–61). MacKenna said that he never knew "a man with so passionate, so pedantic a value for truth as Synge. He didn't so much judge the lie intellectually or morally as simply hate it—as one hates a bad smell or a filthy taste" (39). And John Masefield, on observing Synge at the first London performance of *The Playboy* in June of 1907, reflected "that he was the only person there sufficiently simple to be really interested in living people, and that it was this simplicity which gave him his charm" (qtd. in Greene 269).

That testimony indicates how fully Synge had let go of our usual hypocrisy and evasive sophistication. Indeed, his frequent praise of what is most simple in life recalls the firm belief of another master of the tragicomic, Chekhov. Such distance between the playwright's persona and his theatrical personae derives in part from the fact that alertness to the histrionic impulses of our lives may help us to avoid their most seriously self-hypnotic effects. Chekhov's rendering of histrionic lives in *The Sea Gull* and *The Cherry Orchard* invites us to inhabit and transcend our usual narcissistic role-playing. A similar paradox enters Ibsen's drama. Peer Gynt, an ancestor of Christy Mahon, works through the theatrical onion skins of his life to confront his nothingness and the possibility of a new authenticity. *The Wild Duck,* unlike its sardonic and self-justifying Dr. Relling, does not prescribe "the life-lie" but invites us to engage in an alert and sympathetic playing of roles that are themselves constituted by a more defensive role-playing. Quite similar is the strategy of Synge's *The Well of the Saints*—that bleak precursor of Beckett's theater and, indeed, of Brian Friel's *Molly Sweeney*—which does not celebrate Martin Doul's choice of blindness and self-delusion but leads us, through qualified sympathy with that choice, beyond the habitual blindness of those who think they see.

No doubt Synge's own persona was to some extent a paradoxically antitheatrical mask, a self-effacing social role that enabled him to observe others and did not exhaust his protean self. It is clear that his romanticism and exoticism provided a field for self-projection that compensated for the lack of active richness in his social role. W. B. Yeats remarked upon that quality: "He was a drifting silent man full of hidden passion, and loved wild islands, because there, set out in the light of day, he saw what lay hidden in himself" (*Essays and Introductions* 330). Two early "imaginary portraits"—"Vita Vecchia" and "Étude Morbide"—indicate Synge's own understanding of romantic projection in art and life, as mediated through the styles of J. K. Huysmans, Walter Pater, and Oscar Wilde. *The Aran Islands* and the later travel sketches are informed by a quieter and more profound awareness of how the natural scene and its inhabitants may focus and articulate the impulses of the observer's own depths—as can occur in the theater itself. In *The Aran Islands* Synge explicitly remarks on the "affinity between the moods of these people and the moods of varying rapture and dismay that are frequent in artists, and in certain forms of alienation" (2:74) and relates a dream in which his consciousness seemed merged with the "psychic memory" attached to a locality (2:99–100). And in "The Vagrants of Wicklow" this young man who a few years later would die of cancer declares that "in moments when one is most aware" of the "ceaseless fading" of nature's beauty "some incident of tramp life gives a local human intensity to the shadow of one's mood"—and then simply describes his meeting with a tramp "suffering from some terrible disease" (2:204).

In the plays Synge carried such self-projections and intuitions further toward what we often misleadingly call dramatic "objectivity"; that is, he increased their solidity, purged them of the defensive and self-gratifying, and opened them to our collaborative participation. *Riders to the Sea* focuses with a difficult simplicity the passions aroused by the overwhelming sense of death's immanence in life, and it enables us to follow them, with Maurya, to the point of acceptance beyond tragedy, all passion spent. *Deirdre of the Sorrows,* written after Synge's engagement to Molly Allgood and left uncompleted at his death, invites us to explore the gestures of another kind of heroic acceptance. And the four other plays allow Synge to engage his audiences with an aggressive but therapeutic playfulness that the silently observant writer chose not to employ in his own person.

As Synge shaped those solid and translucent projections, he developed his distinctive speech. That speech was based, in ways that Declan Kiberd has analyzed, on the English of the West of Ireland, with its elements of Gaelic syntax and archaic English vocabulary. It was enriched by contact with the English Bible, Elizabethan plays, and Lady Gregory's *Cuchulain of Muirthemne:* "Your *Cuchulain,*" Synge wrote her, "is a part of my daily bread" (Gregory 124). But it is, above all, a stage speech, condensed and refined through many drafts in accord with the dynamic relations of the theater. Its temptations are obvious: the mechanical lilt, the predictable lyric inflation, the too neatly sardonic counterpoint. But in Synge's best work its fluctuations of tone enact the dance of an alert consciousness responding to the total dramatic situation. The difficulties that this speech made for the Abbey players, about which W. G. Fay has commented (137–38), indicate not merely its distance from their everyday language and from the "stage Irish" to which they were accustomed but also its unusual demand for sustained alertness. In *The Playboy* the characters themselves become contrapuntal vehicles of the style's extravagant but subtle playfulness, leading us through an ironic and often startling sequence of impressions.

In such ways Synge moved as artist through a complex role-playing toward the authenticity of continually renewed openness. Christy Mahon, his seeming antithesis, was also his twin. W. B. Yeats clearly learned from that relation between Synge and his art. "If we cannot imagine ourselves as different from what we are and assume that second self," he said in 1909, "we cannot impose a discipline upon ourselves, though we may accept one from others. Active virtue as distinguished from passive acceptance of a current code is therefore theatrical, consciously dramatic, the wearing of a mask" (*Autobiography* 285). That same year, in "The Death of Synge," he said: "I think that all happiness depends on the energy to assume the mask of some other self; that all joyous or creative life is a re-birth as something not oneself, something which has no memory and is created in a moment and perpetually renewed" (306). And in 1907, the year of *The Playboy,* Yeats began to write *The Player Queen,* that tragedy that became a farce, about the fulfillment that comes with finding one's antithetical self. Yeats's Decima finds that self as she assumes the role of the Queen in expectation of imminent death. She is a cousin of Christy's—one of a number. Our minds may be carried forward, past Pirandello's more sardonic study of related paradoxes in *Henry IV,* to Ugo Betti's *The Queen and the Rebels,* in which the prostitute Argia discovers her true queenliness by a similarly bold role-playing, and on to Genet's *The Balcony,* in which Madame Irma with a darker irony assumes the role of Queen as she initiates us into the meaning of a skillful speeding toward absence.

The modern theater offers many playboys. Sometimes, as in Shaw's *Heartbreak House,* the role-playing seems to work in reverse: "In this house," says Hector Hushabye, "we know all the poses: our game is to find out the man under the pose" (133). In Edward Albee's *Who's Afraid of Virginia Woolf?* the updated name of that game is "Get the Guests." Sometimes, as in Pirandello, Genet, or Beckett, this self-conscious role-playing may seem—but, as I shall later argue in some detail, only seem—to define for us a brothel of mirrors, the self's closed room, or a circle of hell. "Me—(*he yawns*)—to play," begins the Hamm of *Endgame* (2), who knows more than Shaw's Hector about such matters. Indeed, when James Knowlson asked Beckett who he felt had influenced his own theater most of all, "he suggested only the name of Synge," being drawn to his "resilient tragicomic vision" (*Damned to Fame* 71). But sometimes, as in Betti or Brecht in their different ways, a play more explicitly recognizes that the histrionic sensibility can be both a trap and a means of self-understanding. Another cousin of Christy's is Azdak in Brecht's *The Caucasian Chalk Circle,* whose swift rise from cowardly intellectual to lord of misrule, scapegoat, and ironic judge depends partly on his own learning through bold improvisation and partly on the play's comic control of his relations to the triply layered audience that is learning with him through such role-playing (Whitaker, *Fields of Play* 130–43). Not surprisingly, the next step for *The Playboy* after finding "its true home and audience" in Paris in 1954 was its entry into the repertory of the Berliner Ensemble in 1956, directed by Peter Palitzsch and Manfred Wekwerth.

In Synge's own time Oscar Wilde had most boldly summed up romantic aesthetics with the skeptically histrionic accent that points toward such twentieth-century developments. As often and as outrageously as possible, he declared the necessity of a self-consciously histrionic point of view: "The first duty in life is to assume a pose; what the second duty is no one yet has found out" (qtd. in Ellmann 311). Behind such statements was the sober philosophical position that appearance is all and reality is unknowable. And yet Wilde also had a striking sense of the value of masks: their ability to release us from habitual fixations, to focus the impulses of the subliminal self, and to provide the forms through which we apprehend experience. Wilde's own social persona had little in common with the personal simplicity of John Synge. But when Synge was in France he had persuaded a Breton friend, Albert Cugnier, to write a French translation of Wilde's *Intentions* and had helped him with that project (Bourgeois 47). In that book, among several remarks that foreshadow *The Playboy,* we may find this: "Many a young man starts in life with a natural gift for exaggeration which, if nurtured in congenial and sympathetic surroundings, or by the imitation of the best models, might grow into something really great and wonderful" (*Artist as Critic,* 294).

III

"All art is a collaboration," wrote Synge in the preface to *The Playboy* (4:53) Although he was there referring to the process of composition, he could as easily have been describing the condition of art in itself. He once argued, for example, that poetry has or should have a dual existence, "in the voice of the poet and in the voice of the reader, who is, or should be, a kind of performer" (qtd. in Greene 84). His musical training in harmony and counterpoint, as Ann Saddlemyer has observed, prepared him to undertake "the rhythmical balance and formal intricate structure of his plays." And his comments on the "extraordinary excitement" of participation in an orchestral performance make clear that music, for him, was above all a formal and emotional shaping of a community activity that can give individual access to the transpersonal. "To realize that all emotions depend upon and answer the abstract of ideal form," he said, "and that humanity is God, is but the first step towards a full comprehension of this art" (qtd. in Saddlemyer, "'A Share'" 211, 210). Synge found it appropriate to transpose the major attributes of that many-voiced and participatory art into theatrical terms. Indeed, the full meaning of *The Playboy* begins to appear only when we read the text as a "score" for a participatory event. Its shaping of our collaborative role-playing attains the wholeness or many-sidedness that Synge equated with "sanity." And it does so through a grotesque style that compresses into a single form all that he meant when he said: "it is only the catastrophes of life that give substance and power to the tragedy and humour which are the true poles of art" (2:350).

The larger structures of that style depend first of all upon a synthesis of comic convention and naturalism. The dramatis personae descend from traditional types that had been used by Greek and Roman comedy, the commedia dell'arte, the Elizabethans, Molière, and more recent playwrights. We see the hero of New Comedy (modified in the direction of farcical fool and braggart), the heroine (with a touch of Boucicault), the rival youth (a simpler and more effeminate fool), the two "heavy" fathers (each with his distinctive humor), the older woman who trades on her fading sexual attractiveness (worldly wise, a matchmaker, rival of the heroine), the two parasites (humorous and suspicious), and the peripheral group that represents society. The situations, too, are highly traditional: the hero's violence against the oppressive father, the complex love rivalry (with suggestions of incest), the victory of the lord of misrule and his rejection as a scapegoat, the torture of the tricky slave, the resurrection of the old man (as adversary and as rescuing agent), the reconciliation of son and father, and the final transcendence of the closed society. Patricia Spacks has pointed to the folktale for analogies to the strange action of this play, but one might also point to comic tradition. Indeed, one could almost fit the play into Northrop Frye's *Anatomy of Criticism* as a complex instance of the second, or "quixotic," phase of comedy, in which a society is formed by or around the hero but cannot sustain itself. The hero, Frye remarks, "is usually himself at least partly a comic humor or mental runaway, and we have either a hero's illusion thwarted by a superior reality or a clash of two illusions." But *The Playboy* ends with something of Frye's third phase, too, as the *senex iratus* "gives way to the young man's desires" (180). Although we cannot see everything from the abstractive "middle distance," Frye's typology makes a useful dictionary for this level of *The Playboy*'s style.

Within such traditional comic plotting the complex and vacillating relations of actor to role and play to audience have always been prominent. William E. Gruber has commented shrewdly on how the "extreme formalism" of Plautus's comic theater "manifests tensions that the playwright and his audience were unable to express directly" and serves as medium within which problems of acting, identity, and theatricality can be explored with remarkable subtlety (46). *Epidicus,* for example, does not merely depict a temporary inversion of society's rules and customs but provides a "somatic representation of intense inner conflict as a mechanism of self-invention." The slave Epidicus "appears before the audience as a Figur who has literally created an identity that he can manipulate at will" (52, 53). Through the actor's "conspiratorial intrusions" a "correspondence" is developed between "an onstage Figur, which shows the way in which to live out the role of the tricky slave, and spectators, who partly set aside their normal selves in order to frame the events as play" (55–56). Such self-conscious role-playing, with its focus on identity formation, is part of the traditional matrix from which Christy Mahon has developed. And by the time of Molière's *Le Malade Imaginaire,* as Gruber has also demonstrated, the role-playing of New Comedy has begun to suggest yet more strongly that we "must surrender any claim to an original self-hood. The *acting* constitutes the identity" (121).

Synge grounded or rediscovered the plotting and the self-conscious role-playing of New Comedy in an intensely local naturalism. His earlier plays had already blended the conventional and the naturalistic, in the symbolic economy of *Riders to the Sea* and the anecdotal spareness of the comedies. Lady Gregory's Kiltartan versions of Molière also provided partial examples, as did her farces of Irish gossip, *Spreading the News* (which she first thought would be a tragedy) and *Hyacinth Halvey*. Synge's own complex interest in what he called "the psychic state of the locality" did the rest (qtd. in Greene 265). As a performance of *The Playboy* begins, with Pegeen's slow composition of the letter to Mister Sheamus Mulroy, Wine and Spirit Dealer, Castlebar, the naturalism of setting, situation, and vocabulary seems to dominate—and we never quite lose the sense of that inclusive frame. But our expectations are swiftly expanded by an alert speech that can flicker into farce, lyricism, satire, or pathos, by a rich and self-conscious fantasy that all characters share in varying degrees, by the constantly shifting perspectives that involve us (as J. L. Styan has shown) in the total action, and by the larger orchestration of moods, or "currents," to which Synge devoted much attention in his preliminary notes. The play has fused the particular and the archetypal, naturalistic intimacy and comic distance. Hence its strange use of violence, which requires us to experience the painful meaning of our accepted conventions of farce; hence the poignancy of its comic reversals, abandonments, and reconciliations; and hence its interior exploration of a naively perceptive *miles gloriosus*. The growth and self-transcendence of Christy, which needs a stage time much more rapid than naturalistic clock time, is one function of the play's expansion of mode. The resulting tonal ambivalences, as Synge knew, may recall those of *The Merchant of Venice* and *The Misanthrope* (4:364), but they are reached through stylistic means unlike anything in Shakespeare or Molière. The play demands that a production find a comparably balanced style of playing—one that remains in touch with the naturalistic ground as it moves toward the choreography of farce.

"The aim of literature," Synge once said, "is to make the impossible seem inevitable or to make the inevitable seem impossible" (2:349). Because *The Playboy*'s grotesque style contains a good bit of both, we are continually tempted to simplify it in one direction or another. Padraic Colum felt that the somewhat "sardonic" Christy of W. G. Fay (whom Synge had in mind for the part and who then received the benefit of Synge's advice) detracted from "the extravagance of the comedy" and that the "horribly-bloodied bandage" on Old Mahon's head "took the whole thing out of the atmosphere of high comedy." He preferred the Abbey production of 1909, when Old Mahon "was made a less bloody object" and Fred O'Donovan's

Christy had more innocent "charm and gaiety" (368–69). Colum's feeling was shared by such different judges as Joseph Holloway (129) and George Moore. O'Donovan, said Moore, "was no doubt occasionally against the words, but that was unavoidable; the part cannot be played any other way." Moore even presumed to ask Maire O'Neill (Molly Allgood, who had played Pegeen from the beginning) to mitigate in 1909 the reversals of act 3: "I wonder if you could speak your words so that the audience would understand that your anger against Christy was simulated?" She said "she didn't think she could" (2:317). But later Abbey performances, if one may judge from P. P. Howe's comments in 1912, further reduced the play's complexity through cuts and the overplaying of comic business.

In 1939, on the other hand, the critic for the *New Statesman and Nation* found Ashley Duke's London production too "naturalistic," insufficiently "flamboyant." He was not asking for a less painful tone. Cyril Cusack's Christy, he said, "was wilful, but excellent . . . at once rueful and swaggering," though with "less violence than volatility." But he regretted that Pegeen, who "should have a touch of the fury in her," was played by Pamela Gibson "as a limpid young girl." In contrast the Widow Quin (a role now assumed by Maire O'Neill, after many years as Pegeen) had "a gloomy richness that overtowered Miss Gibson temperamentally." Cusack himself in 1954, now directing as well as playing Christy, sought to bring the play "out of the too naturalistic style" he had "helped to foster," into "a wider acting orbit nearer to extravaganza" (305). In that production, and again at the Dublin Theatre Festival of 1960 with Donal Donnelly as Christy, Siobhan McKenna returned to Pegeen's role a necessary vibrant depth and wildness.

The many-sidedness of the grotesque style, in fact, had provided a strange challenge to Synge himself in 1905 and 1906. How should a play of such protean sympathies end? Synge's notes read like the combinations and permutations in Frye's *Anatomy:* "Pegeen hesitates between Christy and Shawn. Marries Shawn, marries Old Man, or goes out with Christy" (4:298). Or again: "Pegeen scoffs Christy and the Widow Quin takes him into her care" (4:299). Then he tried expanding the plot to include a proposal by Widow Quin to Michael James, with the Widow seemingly to become Christy's mother-in-law, and a final reversal in which "old Michael James renounces Widow Quin so she takes Christy instead" (4:301). Only by late spring of 1906 did he pose these possibilities: Christy is "dragged away to . . . justice" or "set free by Widow Quin[,] Old Mahon being really dead," or "Old Mahon revives on stage and there is grotesque scene of the two of them on their knees"—whereupon "they shake hands on a prodigiously fantastic treaty of amity and curtain on that" (4:303–4).

Synge's final shaping of Christy's end—"Ten thousand blessings upon all that's here, for you've turned me a likely gaffer in the end of all, the way I'll go romancing through a romping lifetime from this hour to the dawning of the judgment day"—is not simply the resolution of a naturalistic story. Both Christy and the play have expanded beyond that perspective, though it remains to suggest the irony and pathos beneath the exuberance. Nor does that end simply endorse a myth of the self-constructed man or the hero at dialectical odds with society: the play itself does not so easily abandon the grotesque world of the stage. And yet the final Christy is no baseless fantasy—or, as Cusack himself was tempted to think, "a void which is made the play's resolution": within the terms provided by that world his growth has a strange cogency. His movement through role-playing to the ambiguous authenticity of romance becomes an image of our own participation in the richer movement of the entire dramatic event.

The Playboy's "action," its quasi-Stanislavskian "spine" or "superobjective," might be called the desire "to play the comedy to the end of all." That self-consciously histrionic action is shared by each character in various ways. Each wants to discover in himself or herself a comic or romantic role, to witness his or her own "play"—of which the self-delighting and expansive speech is a pervasive sign. (Christy with his glass is one visual image of that desire.) But each character is also a fascinated witness of the "play" of others, encouraging or provoking it by various means. And, as Pegeen says with more inclusive truth than she intends, "It's queer joys they have, and who knows the thing they'd do" (4:109). The gamut of comic play runs from killing to wedding—from the romantic murder and sadistic farce in which an anxiously repressive and frustrated society finds release, through subtler kinds of "playing upon" others (to tease, entrap, explore, or woo), to the more genuine "playing with" that arises from the mutual discovery of loneliness and reciprocal identity: "We're alike, so" (4:81).

Each note in that scale reverberates in our own responses to the play as actors and witnesses—including what Synge once called "the thin relish of delightful sympathy with the wildness of evil which all feel but few acknowledge even to themselves" (2:6). If much of our comic play comes from our being allowed to transcend the limited perspective of each character, *The Playboy* also treats *us* as it treats its characters—turning the tables on us, undercutting our delight, showing us our vain and grotesque face in its glass. And behind all that playful counterpoint moves the desire for finality, which flowers in the hyperbolic metaphors, in such phrases as "the end of all," "the end of time," and "the dawning of the judgment day," and in the heightened style of the stage action itself. Through the dissonance of the grotesque we strive toward the ultimate harmony of romance.

Contrapuntal to Christy's version of that shared action is Pegeen's. His growth through the discovery of role-playing is balanced by her vigorously sustained but ambivalent play as she half-creates, holds, and then both rejects and loses her man. Her opening speech toys imaginatively with the end of her self-defined romance, but we soon see that she lacks a real partner. Her second kind of play—the scornful teasing of Shawn, echoed in her acquiescent witnessing of his farcical entrapment—arises from her own frustration. Those two kinds of play, interacting and expanding, lead toward a third. She pries the secret from the Shawn-like Christy, identifies his shy violence with her dream of desire's release, engineers his employment, and ejects Shawn. Then she grows toward the fresh play of mutuality (4:81–85) in the first of those increasingly lyric climaxes, duologues between Pegeen and Christy, which are also major stages in Christy's growth. Soon, however, she turns swiftly and cagily to defend her new property against Widow Quin. In act 2, yet more on the defensive, she ejects her rivals and uses her skill in role-playing to intimidate and recapture her pot-boy hero, moves then through the second lyric climax, another stage in their reciprocal growth (4:109–13), only to be diverted by the stratagem of Shawn and Widow Quin.

The final sardonic and poignant amplification of such mixed play occurs in act 3. After the races, in the third lyric climax, Pegeen fully discovers the heart's wonder in her own histrionic glass (4:147–51). That moment is her fullest equivalent of Christy's more complex growth through role-playing. The reciprocity of these "gallant lovers" already points, I think, toward the remarkably earthy elevation that Synge would explore in his Anglo-Irish versions of Petrarch (1:86–102)—as Reed Way Dasenbrock has shown (85–98)—and would then employ in the lyrically and tragically distilled speeches of *Deirdre of the Sorrows*. But Pegeen soon turns on Christy—in embarrassment and disappointment over his lie, in harder condemnation and self-justification over his second "murder," and in fear of the mockery and judgment of others. Rejecting the "dirty deed" that he thought would redeem himself in her eyes, she vents upon him all the violence of frustration that his "gallous story" had vicariously expressed for her—and more (4:169). When she forces herself to burn his leg (quite as if he were the tricky slave in a Menander fragment to which Northrop Frye alludes [179]), that action—more violent in the theater than any offstage "murder," real or pretended—is crucial for them and for us. Our lust for farce and romantic cruelty—which has been verbally mirrored in such things as Marcus Quin's "maiming ewes" (4:59), Jimmy Farrell's hanging his dog (4:73), Sara Tansey's driving ten miles to see "the man bit the yellow lady's nostril" (4:97), and Pegeen's vicariously anticipatory description of Christy's hanging (4:109)—now shows its full face.

Partly through that burning, and through reconciliation with Old Mahon, Christy becomes fully the "playboy" and vanishes from the onstage society—not into the "desert" of Molière's Alceste in *The Misanthrope* or the "night" of Shaw's Marchbanks in *Candida* but into the realm of companionable romance. Pegeen, however, playing out her comedy of frustrated romanticism to its appropriate end, condemns herself to isolation within that society, and her startling blow and her wild lament are the play's final gestures. *The Playboy* in its sanity has not merely followed the playboy. It has invited us to discover in ourselves, with increasing sympathy, irony, and painful gaiety, these two mutually dependent roles. That discovery is part of our own grotesque reconciliation—"We're alike, so"—as we play our comedy to the end of all.

But our reconciliation includes more. Widow Quin is for Pegeen a "sneaky kind" of murderer and manstealer (4:89), and at first she may seem to us little more than a Mayo version of that stagey type. But in this play the static types are surprisingly dynamic: every seeming opposite is a secret double and may prove to be an ally. Although Widow Quin's mode of playing is a tougher version of Pegeen's, it is really not more grasping or less open to new insights. Before Pegeen turns against Christy, the older temptress has begun to seem his double and his maternal savior. By the end of act 2 she has sent away Old Mahon as well as Pegeen, and she has bargained with Christy as well as with Shawn. Her closing soliloquy—which counterpoints Christy's at the end of act 1 ("it's great luck and company I've won me in the end of time" 4:93])—shares with us her readiness to play out a new comedy: "Well, if the worst comes in the end of all, it'll be great game to see there's none to pity him but a widow woman, the like of me, has buried her children and destroyed her man" (4:131). It is not merely ironic that Christy can say to this lonely woman, as he has said to Pegeen: "You're like me, so" (4:127).

Thanks to Widow Quin's perspective, act 2 also prepares us for the parallel reversal of that other negative type, Old Mahon. As she playfully draws him out (and we recall how Pegeen drew Christy out) the dialogue interweaves the differences and similarities between father and son. Her description of that son hiding behind the door—"A hideous, fearful villain, and the spit of you" (4:123)—summarizes with affectionate humor for her and us their childlike self-inflation, naive folly, and real violence. In act 3 Widow Quin takes Old Mahon a step further when she persuades him that he is a "sniggering maniac" (4:143). His cheerfully proud acceptance of that fate ("there'll be a welcome before me, I tell you") foreshadows his final acceptance of the role of "heathen slave" to Christy's "gallant captain," in the reversal that expresses their newfound mutuality. "Is it me?" he will then ask (4:173), as he asked when Widow Quin marveled over his wickedness (4:121), and as his son had asked when Pegeen praised his "noble brow" (4:79), and he will continue: "Glory be to God! (*With a broad smile.*) I am crazy again!" For him, as for us, to role-play one's craziness is to journey toward sanity.

Amid such parallels and reversals, in which every new discovery of identity is the discovery of a new reciprocity and a new role, we cannot separate ourselves even from the lesser and more truly static characters. They often express our own momentary point of view; and their comic vanity, self-pity, or cruelty is never theirs alone. Perhaps the least sympathetic is Shawn, who thinks he wants a wedding that will end "trouble" (a version of Michael James's more affable desire for the peace of intoxication) but who really enjoys playing the role of anxious child, inviting the attention of parental surrogates and contemptuous baiters. But even Shawn has a whining lyricism—"and I'm after feeling a kind of fellow above in the furzy ditch, groaning wicked like a maddening dog" (4:61)—and that fellow, the Christy who exits like a Mahon, entered much like Shawneen. Having lived through his own self-pity, his longing for attention, his baiting and being baited, Christy can include Shawn in his final blessings. We can do no less, though we also share Pegeen's desire to give him a hard box on the ear.

As we respond to these role-playing characters, whose gestures are clarified and pointed up by a language always alert to its own excesses, we discover ourselves in each fragment of Synge's histrionic glass. The "imitated" or "represented" action of *The Playboy* depicts a society that the playboy himself must transcend, the father reconciled but the bride unredeemed. But in the performance of *The Playboy* a more inclusive society finds in itself the full gamut of the grotesque as it moves toward that openness that is the psychological equivalent of Christy's final state. When the curtain falls or the lights darken, we have seen that nothing human can be alien to us.

Synge has given another turn to the process that C. L. Barber elucidated in *Shakespeare's Festive Comedy*. As the playboy is to that Mayo community, so the play is to us—but the abortive saturnalia of that "imitated" action is completed by the action of performance. Our lord of misrule and potential scapegoat, *The Playboy* leads us through controlled and reflected release toward self-understanding. Has Synge, with a modern self-consciousness, brought the conventions of saturnalian comedy back toward their presumed origins in the "psychic state" of the folk milieu? The notion does not seem beyond a writer who attentively followed d'Arbois de Jubainville's lectures on mythology at the Sorbonne, who had taken notes on Sir James Frazer's *The Golden Bough* in 1900, and who could speculate on Dionysos while visiting the Puck Fair. Presiding over the fair, as the essay "In West Kerry" tells us, was "Puck himself, a magnificent he-goat (Irish *puc*), raised on a platform twenty feet high." And at the foot of this platform, "where the crowd was thickest, a young ballad-singer was howling a ballad in honour of Puck, making one think of the early Greek festivals, since the time of which, it is possible, the goat has been exalted yearly in Killorglin." Synge transcribed in full that ballad, which tells how "the lads and lassies coming gaily to Killorglin can be seen, / To view the Puck upon the stage, as our hero dressed in green" (2:265–66).

In any case our puckish Christy transcends that stage as he romps on toward the "dawning of the judgment day" (4:173). And that image focuses the emergent end of Synge's orchestrated play. For *The Playboy* the final harmony of romance and judgment is now, at the end of time within time, whenever we recognize our participation in the dissonances of the grotesque. On the play's own terms such openness leads us past the manipulative forms of role-playing toward growth and mutuality. Yeats thought Synge to be "one of those unmoved souls in whom there is a perpetual 'Last Day,' a perpetual trumpeting, and coming up to judgment" (*Autobiography* 311). The play invites us to share its grotesque version of that state.

Such, I think, is the implicit *telos* of this kind of playing, its journey and its journey's end. Playing with *The Playboy,* we discover intentions that we did not know we had. "Well, the heart's a wonder," says Pegeen (4:151). And at the height of his romance with her Christopher Mahon understandably feels "a kind of pity for the Lord God is all ages sitting lonesome in his golden chair" (4:147). But Christy's theology has dropped from view the divine consort, that creative Wisdom of *Proverbs* who said: "I was by his side, a master craftsman, delighting him day after day, ever at play in his presence." It is possible that this remarkably capacious paradigm, written by a skeptic who hoped to translate an essay on role-playing called *De Imitatione Christi,* participates more than Christy knows in that immanent Wisdom "at play everywhere in his world, delighting to be with the sons of men" (8:30–31).

Chapter 2

The Music of Serious Farce: Wilde, Shaw, Orton, and Stoppard

I

Mingling naturalism, farce, romance, and satire, Synge offers us an exploratory role-playing that leads through the grotesque toward self-recognition and mutuality. Another paradigm of playing, less rich in its tonalities but perhaps more in accord with the taste of this century, asks a fuller commitment to the farcical without abandoning its claim to the serious. "For me," says Gwendolen Fairfax to her nervous suitor, "you have always had an irresistible fascination." And why? "We live, as I hope you know, Mr. Worthing, in an age of ideals. The fact is constantly mentioned in the more expensive monthly magazines, and has reached the provincial pulpits, I am told; and my ideal has always been to love someone of the name of Ernest" (*Plays* 263). That, of course, is from Wilde's masterpiece of 1895. Almost eighty years later Tom Stoppard's *Travesties* has Old Carr recall or imagine another Gwendolen, who gave the same assurance to Tristan Tzara in Zurich about 1917, but with a different explanation. "As you know," she says, "I have been helping Mr. Joyce with his new book, which I am convinced is a work of genius, and I am determined to secure for him the universal recognition he deserves." On learning that Tzara edited "a magazine of all that is newest and best in literature," she knew she was "destined" to love him (55).

Victorian high seriousness is out; devotion to the avant-garde is in. But ideals propagated by journalism can still serve a pragmatic young lady as masks for erotic impulse, personal vanity, and social power. In both plays the mask-wearing invites satirical judgment, but the absurdities disarm us. Our critical animus yields to delight. Even if we wanted to assess the degrees of disingenuousness, self-deception, and folly in the Gwendolens Fairfax and Carr, we would find it hard to do so. They are not real persons, not even rounded characters whose motives we might plumb.

These mask wearers are themselves playfully earnest masks that we must wear, directly as actors or indirectly as members of an audience, as we share in the performance.

Although we always respond in the theater to the actors' invitation to enter into their role-playing, that invitation may range in style from the sympathetic inhabiting of a character to the ironic wearing of a brittle or grotesque mask. The actors may relate to us through a shared solitude (as in Chekhov), a sardonic commentary (as in Brecht), a farcical mugging (as sometimes in Shakespeare or Molière), or yet more complex mixtures of representation and presentation. In "serious farce" the detachment that arises from our wearing of outrageous masks is balanced by a spritely intellectual engagement, and both are incorporated into a characteristic "music" that sweeps our playful community toward a transpersonal end. Katharine Worth has noted some of the ways in which *The Importance of Being Earnest* prepared for the twentieth-century "use of farce to make fundamentally serious (not earnest!) explorations into the realm of the irrational" (*Oscar Wilde* 179), and she has mentioned Stoppard's *Travesties* and Joe Orton's *What the Butler Saw* in that connection. We can gain a fuller view of this paradigm, which aggressively cannibalizes other paradigms, if we think of these three plays in relation to a fourth—Shaw's *You Never Can Tell*—and place them all in a somewhat wider context.

Soon after he reviewed *The Importance of Being Earnest* in 1895, Shaw started work on *You Never Can Tell,* partly in reaction against what he took to be the intellectual frothiness and lack of feeling in Wilde's play. He clearly wanted to free the truth in Wilde's title from self-irony without lapsing into the solemn or sentimental. Orton read *The Importance of Being Earnest* when in secondary school—aloud, and with relish, to his sister Leonie. Much later, after echoing Wilde repeatedly in *The Good and Faithful Servant* and *Loot,* he began *What the Butler Saw* at least partly in revisionary homage to a precursor whom he had come to think insufficiently tough-minded. That was 1966, the year in which Stoppard published both *Rosencrantz & Guildenstern Are Dead,* which approaches Wilde through Pirandello and Beckett, and a novel *Lord Malquist and Mr. Moon,* which approaches him through Joyce. When Orton's play was posthumously produced in 1969, it helped Stoppard to shape *Jumpers.* And Stoppard's Wildean permutations came to a climax in 1974 with *Travesties,* which also reached out to incorporate some Shavian political and emotional dialectics.

These plays belong to a modern tangle of traditions that has raised farce to a master genre, able to subsume not only burlesque, satire, comedy of manners, and romantic comedy but also the didactic, the pathetic, and even—as in Dürrenmatt's *The Visit*—the tragic. Although earlier playwrights could mix up the genres, there may never have been such a various flood of mingled levity and gravity as that which includes Jarry's *King Ubu,* Chekhov's *The Cherry Orchard,* Pirandello's *Six Characters in Search of an Author,* Brecht's *The Threepenny Opera,* Beckett's *Waiting for Godot,* Ionesco's *The Chairs,* Pinter's *The Birthday Party,* and the satirical commedia dell'arte of Dario Fo. Similar outpourings in film (from Chaplin to Truffaut and Allen) and fiction (from Faulkner and West to Heller, Nabokov, Pynchon, and Grass) have contributed to the flood. Perhaps some future Gwendolen, in a meta-farce called *The Importance of Being Absurd,* might explain her fascination in words like these. "We live," she might say,

> in an age that refuses to take things simply in earnest or simply in fun. Ten years before Wilde wrote his "trivial play for serious people," Nietzsche said we must learn to laugh if we are hell-bent on remaining pessimists. Ten years after Wilde's play, Freud showed that every joke is serious. Farce, as we know, enacts our secret desires and guilts. Saturnalia and carnival are the safety-valves of all repressive societies. And the historians of modern drama have fully explained our need for Dark Comedy, the Grotesque, and the Absurd. My ideal must therefore be to love someone like *you,* whether you are Alec or Buster or Charlie or Didi or Hulot or Humbert or Krapp or Quilty or Woody or Yossarian or Zero.

Such an eclectic Gwendolen, however, could not begin to describe the music of serious farce or the communities that dance to its measure. Nor can the many academic definitions that imply that a "community" of farce would be a contradiction in terms. Jessica Davis has said that the spirit of farce "delights in taboo-violation" but "avoids implied moral comment or criticism" and "tends to debar empathy for the victim" (86). Maurice Charney has said that farce is "a destroyer and detractor," a "negating force" (*Classic Comedies* viii). For Albert Bermel farce "tends to exclude such worthwhile human emotions as tenderness, sensitivity, sympathy, and compassion" (14). For Eric Bentley its principal motor is the "impulse to attack": "in farce hostility enjoys itself" (Corrigan 210). And Barbara Freedman has declared that farce "enacts something like a primitive superego punishment for the characters' libidinal release in the form of a maniacal plot which both arranges libidinal gratification and punishes them for it" (Charney, *Classic Comedies* 590). Those definitions point to elements in many farces, including those of Feydeau and Orton, but they have little bearing on the work of Wilde, Shaw, or Stoppard. And they cannot explain why so many modern plays with farcical tone or structure do incorporate moral comment, social criticism, and even tenderness and compassion. Indeed, if we define farce simply in terms of a staged world of madness, a blocking of humane feelings, and an acting out of secret cravings and hostilities, we ignore the fact that, like every kind of play, a farce is an artwork created and interpreted by a community.

More helpful, therefore, are some statements by writers who never lost sight of the theater's central artistic and social impulses. "In a sense," said Stark Young, "all drama moves toward the condition of farce. That is because the theatre's very essence consists in the heightening of its material. Heightening that is free, fluent, almost abstract, unless it has the restrictions of character and rational measure, floats off into farce; which is closer to poetic drama and serious tragedy than to plain everyday prose realism" (177). W. B. Yeats would have agreed. "What attracts me to drama," he said, "is that it is, in the most obvious way, what all the arts are upon a last analysis. A farce and a tragedy are alike in this, that they are a moment of intense life." They focus "an energy, an eddy of life purified from everything but itself" (*Explorations* 153–54). Indeed, Yeats could take abortive tragedies and translate them into farce, producing *The Player Queen* and *The Herne's Egg*. Near the end of his life he said: "The arts are all the bridal chambers of joy." He heard "dance music" in Hamlet's last speech, and in the last moments of Cleopatra, Lear, and Oedipus he read signs of the "energy" that Blake had called "eternal delight" (448–49).

Yeats understood that the actors and spectators must participate in that delight. In the poem "Lapis Lazuli" he imagines Hamlet and Lear as actors on the stage of history, the choric spectators as figures in a Chinese work of art, and all as sharing in the artist's "gaiety." Their script is a tragedy, but their real play is a transcendent comedy. His distinction between the tragic heroes on the historical stage and the musical Chinamen within the quasi-eternity of art and nature echoes that made by the young Nietzsche, in *The Birth of Tragedy Out of the Spirit of Music,* between the Apollonian heroes and the Dionysian satyr chorus that projects them. The "metaphysical joy in the tragic," said Nietzsche, translates the "instinctive unconscious Dionysian wisdom" of the chorus into the language of images. The hero as manifestation of the will is annihilated, but "the eternal life of the will is not affected by his annihilation" (104). Tragedy enables us to share an "eternal life" of which "music is the immediate idea." Indeed, Nietzsche proposed a "*mystery doctrine of tragedy:* the fundamental knowledge of the oneness of everything existent, the conception of individuation as the primal cause of evil, and of art as the joyous hope that the spell of individuation may be broken in augury of a restored oneness" (74).

What, then, of farce? Although insisting that the Greek chorus derived from the satyr play, the young Nietzsche believed farce to be a sign of decadence. Wagner's music-drama was for him "the gradual awakening of the Dionysian spirit" in the Alexandrian modern world (*Birth of Tragedy* 119). Later, after turning against Wagner, he began to praise Bizet and Offenbach. "What is good is light," he could then say; "whatever is divine moves on tender feet" (157). And his Zarathustra declared: "Come, let us kill the spirit of gravity" (*Portable Nietzsche* 153). Morton Gurewitch has argued that we should therefore understand farce in Nietzschean spirit, though against the letter of *The Birth of Tragedy,* as "our only source of Dionysian comedy" (127–28). And he has provided a suggestive anatomy of the "imagination of farce," which includes the sexual, psychic, social, and metaphysical. I would go yet further. In the persistent effort of farce to encompass that gamut of the serious, I think, we can often discern the Dionysian spirit struggling to awaken from the nightmare of our modern Alexandrianism. There it enacts what we might call—conflating Nietzsche's earlier metaphysics and his later celebration of levity—a "mystery doctrine of farce." In a time of psychological and social alienation, objectifying knowledge, and chronic doubt, such farce can enable us to participate in a music that sustains the joyous hope that the spell of individuation may be broken and oneness may be restored.

To understand that power of farce we must recognize that its negativity can be balanced, contained, and transmuted by its artistic and social form. In the Plautine tradition, from *The Menaechmi* through Shakespeare's *The Comedy of Errors* to the sexual farces of Feydeau and Orton's *What the Butler Saw,* the imitation of madness, confusion, and frenzy occurs within quite rational dramatic designs. *The Comedy of Errors,* as it revises Plautus, develops with rigor the permutations and combinations of error made possible by its premise of not one but two sets of twins. So too within the British, Irish, and French tradition of the short farce, from John Maddison Morton's *Box and Cox* to Ionesco and Beckett. *Waiting for Godot* explores its bog of uncertainty within a symmetrical pattern of paradoxical doublets, reversals, and repetitions. In farce, moreover, every reduction in sympathy for the characters as victims is balanced by our heightened identification with the actors who play them or sometimes with the clownish characters themselves as players of their own life roles. Farce tends to replace the world's gravity with the levity of our shared playing, not blocking our social feelings but redirecting them into the action of performance. Having invited us to identify with a player, or a character-as-player, it can then lead us toward a new kind of pathos, as in Chaplin's films, or toss us back and forth between levity and gravity, as in the plays of Beckett, Ionesco, or Dürrenmatt. And, because the unfolding designs of farce are abstract and musical, they enable us to participate in a nonverbal unity. That is why the version of *The Comedy of Errors* produced by Greg Mosher in 1983 at the Goodman Theatre in Chicago, and then at Lincoln Center, with the Flying Karamazov Brothers and the Vaudeville Nouveau, was so strikingly appropriate. As Ron Jenkins has noted, "Some critics were concerned at the loss of the play's moral center, but the vaudevillian approach gives the production a muscularity that American actors rarely achieve in Shakespearean comedy" (68). But much more important to the success of this interpretation, I think, were the continually surprising ways in which the troupe's juggling, doubling of roles, disguises, and acrobatics exuberantly translated Shakespeare's own design of oppositions, mirrorings, reversals, and symmetries.

These formal strategies lead to a single end. As Stuart Baker has argued with reference to Feydeau, farce "makes a game of reality," and its devotion to laughter is not "an invitation to anarchy" but "the key to a unifying principle" (22–23). The hostile and confusing aspects of the world become aspects of a brisk and even frenzied game of music and masking in which we are invited to participate. The game's design, moreover, suggests that our ideas, our social roles, and even our cherished personalities may be no more than changeable masks for the rigorously playful mind that moves through us. A farce therefore willingly abandons rounded characters, individualized speech, and realistic action, preferring to use the heightened rhythmic and rhetorical forms that we can adopt as the exhilarating gait of our shared mind. Committing itself to what J. L. Styan has called "the echo/mirror tradition in Western comedy" that descends from Plautus and the commedia dell'arte (*Drama, Stage, and Audience* 89–93), it is likely to concoct its plot from bits and pieces of those old stories about masters and servants who change places, lovers who are disguised, families who are dispersed and reunited, antagonists who are blood brothers or even twins, and opposites of all kinds that finally disclose their unity. Farce delights in burlesquing those premises of melodrama and romance partly because they express its own deep desire to break the spell of individuation and alienation that holds us in thrall.

This is clear, for example, in Morton's short farce of 1847, *Box and Cox,* which became in 1867 the musical farce *Cox and Box,* by F. C. Burnand and Arthur Sullivan, W. S. Gilbert's future collaborator, and which seems to have bequeathed some of its motifs and devices to Wilde, Beckett, Ionesco, and Stoppard. Here Box the printer, who works by night, and Cox the hatter, who works by day, accidentally discover that they have been renting the same room and sleeping in the same bed. (Michael Booth has speculated, in his essay on "Early Victorian Farce," on the French connections between this play and Ionesco's *The Bald Soprano,* in which Mr. and Mrs. Martin make a similar discovery [Richards 109n].) Quarreling about their rights to the room, Box and Cox soon discover that they have both been engaged to the formidable widow Penelope Ann, a proprietress of bathing machines, whom they now both wish to escape. Box has already faked suicide and therefore enjoys a condition of life-in-death that Cox envies. They quarrel over whose proposal to Penelope Ann is now valid (somewhat as Wilde's Gwendolen and Cecily will quarrel over their proposals to Ernest), but each man here wishes to pass the lady on to the other. Deciding to dice for her hand, they throw only sixes. Tossing coins, they throw a steady run of "heads," rather like Stoppard's Rosencrantz and Guildenstern. On receiving news that Penelope Ann has drowned and left her property to her intended, they suddenly take up all their arguments in reverse. The apparent arrival of Penelope Ann at the rooming house leads to yet another reversal as they join forces to stave off her entry. But another letter suddenly announces her "immediate union" with a Mr. Knox—whose name, as often in Beckett's work, suggests the possibility of an endless series of rhyming characters neither dead nor alive. And the dénouement—which echoes the device whereby Figaro, in act 3 of the Mozart-da Ponte *The Marriage of Figaro,* learns his true mother and father—weds Box and Cox as firmly and enigmatically as Beckett's Didi and Gogo or Hamm and Clov will be wed. As they are about to embrace, Box stops, seizes Cox's hand, and looks eagerly in his face. "You'll excuse the apparent insanity of the remark," he says, "but the more I gaze on your features, the more I'm convinced that you're my long-lost brother." "The very observation I was going to make to you!" replies Cox. "Ah—tell me—in mercy tell me—," says Box, "have you such a thing as a strawberry mark on your left arm?" "No!" exclaims Cox. "Then it is he!" exclaims Box—and, with this demonstration that true brothers require neither birthmarks nor other evidence of consanguinity, they rush into each other's arms (232).

The stylization of this farce—its repetitive pattern of speech and counter-speech, violent reversals, and puppetlike gesticulations—ensures, according to Jessica Davis, that the interest of the audience is "strategic, rather than empathetic" (56). But, if we do not respond seriously to the loves and fears of this Tweedledum and Tweedledee, surely we do participate with empathic delight in the playing out of their absurd duet to its harmonious close. We can see why Burnand and Sullivan thought of transposing the action into the literally musical. And the play finally reverberates, amid our laughter, with feelings of unity that we can take quite seriously—just as we can warmly assent to Dromio of Ephesus (and the actor who plays him) when at the end of *The Comedy of Errors* he says to Dromio of Syracuse, "Methinks you are my glass, and not my brother," and brings our game of mirrors to a close with a couplet that dismisses the world's concern for hierarchy:

> We came into the world like brother and brother:
> And now let's go hand in hand, not one before another.

Antagonisms, differences in rank, characters, actors, spectators—what are they all but different masks of one playful mind?

The greatest of the late-nineteenth-century British farceurs, W. S. Gilbert, who helped to pass on the tradition to Wilde and Shaw by way of *Engaged* and the Savoy operas, knew very well that in farce the musically scored dissonances must lead to a final consonance. Recall, for example, that opera of 1878, *H.M.S. Pinafore,* in which Little Buttercup finally reveals that when she was young and charming she had practiced baby farming and had nursed two tender babes, one of low condition, the other of a patrician—but she mixed those children up. "Then I am to understand," exclaims Sir Joseph, "that Captain Corcoran and Ralph were exchanged in the childhood's happy hour—that Ralph is really the Captain, and the Captain is Ralph?" (135). Precisely so: hierarchy is now reversed, individuality is negated, and three loving pairs can be happily united. With that the tradition of farce was well on its way to Miss Prism's mixing up of a baby and the manuscript of a sentimental novel, John Worthing's discovery that he is Algernon Moncrieff's brother Ernest, and the union of three more loving pairs. And Wilde's play led in turn to the discovery by Shaw's Clandon children that their father is Mr. Crampton and the discovery by Orton's Geraldine Barclay and Nicholas Bennett that they are the twin children of the Prentices and the mixing up by Stoppard's Gwendolen and Cecily of Joyce's manuscript for an episode of *Ulysses* (that in which a baby and modern prose come to simultaneous birth) and Lenin's manuscript for a revolutionary tract.

II

Each of these four plays is a rhythmic or musical game of doublings, oppositions, analogies, and reunifications that revises the tradition and reinterprets some aspect of the modern world. *The Importance of Being Earnest* finds our social and intellectual life to be a construct of masks. *You Never Can Tell* puts those masks in a more serious historical context and discloses behind them a common heart. *What the Butler Saw* puts them in a psychological context, updates their manners and the intellectual chatter, and discloses behind them a polymorphous sexuality. And *Travesties* asks us to discern in the earnest, arch, or Dionysian masks that we project into politics, art, and history the protean mind of a single but multiform player. In effect, these plays invite us to discover four versions or aspects of the mystery doctrine of farce.

The first production of *The Importance of Being Earnest,* as Joseph W. Donohue Jr. has noted (Richards 125–43), was both "modern" and realistic in its costumes, social setting, and topical references. (The 1923 Haymarket production was the last to use modern dress, updating the fashions of thirty years earlier. Only since then has it become customary to do the play in "period costume.") For that first audience, however, the play's revisionary artifice would have been amply evident. The witty rakes, so similar and yet so different, the imperious aunt who controls the issue of marriage, the adroit young ladies, and the document produced at the end that establishes legitimate power—all these recall Congreve's *The Way of the World* and other Restoration plays. Closer at hand was the melodrama of social concern, which used the mechanics of the well-made play and often involved both a long-hidden secret and a woman with a past—items that lead directly to Miss Prism. But the "farcical comedy" that took London by storm in the 1870s had already burlesqued those mechanics. As Lynton Hudson has noted (101–5), the absurd amatory and gustatory obsessions in *Earnest,* the blend of romantic idealism and crass self-interest, and such details as Algy's Bunburying and Jack's wearing of mourning for someone who has not died are reminiscent of Gilbert's play of 1875, *Engaged,* which also required of its actors "the most perfect earnestness and gravity" (Booth 3:330).

Wilde himself had written such comedy-melodramas as *Lady Windermere's Fan* and *An Ideal Husband,* in which sentiment was complicated by dandies who voice a sardonic and paradoxical wisdom. *Earnest* echoes Wilde's plays so often that it seems in part a loving self-parody. Lady Windermere, refusing to think of her unknown mother as a "fallen woman," makes the pronouncement that Gwendolen will travesty: "We all have ideals in life. At least we all should have. Mine is my mother" (*Plays* 66). A witty thrust and counterthrust between Lord Illington and Mrs. Allonton in *A Woman of No Importance* become a single speech for Algernon: "All women become like their mothers. That is their tragedy. No man does. That's his" (*Plays* 108, 270). And opening moments in acts 3 and 4 of *An Ideal Husband* are rewritten in act 1 of *Earnest,* in which Lord Goring's dialogue with Phipps becomes Algernon's wittier exchange with Lane, and Lord Caversham's greeting to Lord Goring—"Wasting your time as usual, I suppose?"—becomes Jack's disdainful "Eating as usual, I see, Algy!" (*Plays* 205–6, 226, 253–54). All this revisionary artifice enters a form that has been enhanced, as Shaw explicitly recognized (*Works* 23:44–45), by stylized debates and duets that often recall the Savoy operas.

As it summarizes the tradition of wit, *Earnest* does not, like earlier Wilde plays, confine its epigrams to a single dandy. Now the entire script offers the modulations of one voice, whose shrewd absurdities and knowing non sequiturs turn all the characters into paradoxical and translucent masks. That is why it is so hard to say just who is being deliberately witty. If the often childish Algy is a self-conscious wit, so is his laconic man-servant Lane . . . or is he? And can the shrewd Lady Bracknell really be, as critics often assume, the unconscious butt of her own remarks? Gwendolen may seem yet more oblivious of her own wit, but she wields a verbal rapier quite skillfully in her duel with Cecily. And Cecily amply demonstrates, there and in her earlier chats with her "Ernest," an ironic subtlety that seems to belie her innocence. Even Prism and Chasuble, those versions of the pedant and senex of comic tradition, speak witty truths that may or may not be beyond their understanding. "The good ended happily, and the bad unhappily," says Prism. "That is what Fiction means" (*Plays* 275). Is she really, as Patricia Hern has assured us, "unconscious of the humour" of that remark? (Wilde, *Earnest* xxxiii). The question can hardly be answered. As Stoppard obviously knew when he revised those lines for the Player in *Rosencrantz & Guildenstern Are Dead*—"The bad end unhappily, the good unluckily. That is what tragedy means" (80)—their real speaker is the playfulness that articulates our shared game. Such pervasive masking is further complicated in the plot, of course, by Jack's and Algy's claims to be "Ernest" and by the final revelation of Jack's identity as Ernest. But, because that revelation rests on a farcical coincidence already embedded in earlier documents, Jack's assertion that he must always have been speaking the truth gives another spin to the whirligig of trivial seriousness and serious triviality.

In the mid-nineteenth century the *Edinburgh Review* had noted that it is to Matthew Arnold that "we owe the substitution of the word 'earnest' for its predecessor 'serious'"—a remark that has been preserved in the amber of the *Oxford English Dictionary*. Arnold was emphasizing the moral intensities of what he called "Hebraism" in contrast to the readiness to explore "things as they really are" that he found in Hellenism. *The Importance of Being Earnest* employs its spoofs and ironies to transpose Arnold's Hellenism, by way of Pater, into more completely aesthetic terms. The truth of life is that life is art. And yet the art of drama remains inherently social. Enacting that puzzle, Wilde's game of masks leads us dancingly through patterned oppositions and complementarities toward a hidden consanguinity and a triple marriage. Algy's opening volley with Lane prepares us for the more complex contest in which that self-consciously trivial seeker of truth engages the self-deceptively serious "Ernest," or Jack. The sophisticated Gwendolen and the innocent Cecily, each also sharing in her counterpart's dominant trait, will expand that pattern and prepare us for a double courtship, with Lady Bracknell and Jack then ironically paired as blocking parental figures. These symmetrical possibilities are developed in acts 2 and 3, with stylized doublings and reversals and balletic effects that Katharine Worth has admirably described (*Oscar Wilde* 172–75). In act 2 Algy now poses as Ernest, Cecily now receives a proposal, and the women move to a stylized Gilbertian confrontation. After the simultaneous exposure of Jack's deception and Algy's, the women pit themselves against the men, and the action moves through increasingly echoing speeches toward the moment in act 3 when the men enter whistling "some dreadful popular air from a British Opera" (*Plays* 300) and the women speak together their common mind, with Gwendolen beating time—a sequence almost as operatic as the finale of Gilbert and Sullivan's *The Yeomen of the Guard* or Mozart and da Ponte's *Così Fan Tutte.* When Lady Bracknell arrives, there are two announcements of each engagement, and the blocking parental figures reach a stalemate that can be broken only by the arrival (both required and fortuitous) of Prism. Jack then discovers that he has always been Ernest and that—though Prism is not his mother, as he thinks for a moment—Algy is indeed his brother, Lady Bracknell his aunt, and Gwendolen his cousin. The young couples embrace, and, when Prism and Chasuble almost unexpectedly join them in doing so, our stage picture seems all in the family.

What is the meaning of our musical masking? John Russell Taylor has said that the plot is there only "to hold up a glittering display of epigrams" (90). Eric Bentley has called the epigrams "serious relief" in "ironic counterpoint with the absurdities of the action" (*Playwright as Thinker* 144). Morton Gurewitch, turning those views upside down, has argued that the farce neutralizes the satire "so that our mental delight in detecting idiocy is subordinated to the joys of unreason" (118). In performance, however, the play is not so double-minded as those comments suggest. Our game of masks is integrally connected with the running critique of a moneyed, fashionable, and intellectually pretentious society. Speaking from within what Lady Bracknell calls "an age of surfaces" (*Plays* 304), these masks embody both the superficiality criticized and the act of criticism, which is quite aware that it must deal in surfaces. For Wilde even the "truths of metaphysics are the truths of masks" (*Artist as Critic* 432). We must therefore choose between an unconscious or hypocritical social mask, which seems serious but is really trivial, and a self-conscious artistic mask, which through its seeming triviality offers a serious assessment of the world of appearances.

Should we complain of the play's agnosticism, its refusal or inability to penetrate appearances? I think not, for the masking also brings a complementary recognition. The play has led us into a sprightly community of performance in which appetites and aggressions are transformed into a shared miming of muffin eating, cake serving, and scintillating conversation and in which each absurd and witty mask can be worn with delight and profit. Like Bunbury, the alienated individual has been exploded, at least for the moment, and we glimpse the ordered freedom and gaiety of a hidden identity that plays through us. Both the social criticism and the farcical music of *Earnest* point us toward that end.

III

The revisionary artifice of *You Never Can Tell* is yet more striking than that of *Earnest*. Although not one of Shaw's most famous plays, it is surely among his best. Its most perceptive admirers, beginning with Shaw himself, have resisted the popular tendency to consider it a farce. It is for A. M. Gibbs "Shaw's festive comedy" (91), for Frederick P. W. McDowell "a masterfully executed comedy of manners" (81), and for Stanley Kauffmann "the greatest high comedy in the English language after Sheridan" (cited in Crum 34). And yet—as Gibbs and McDowell have recognized, along with Martin Meisel (249–59), Margery M. Morgan (83–99) and Daniel J. Leary (in introducing the facsimile of Shaw's manuscript)—the humane comedy in this play results from an expansion and deepening of farcical strategies.

Although it may seem original to begin a play in a dentist's office, Labiche had used that setting in 1874 for *The Gladiator's Thirty Millions.* (By 1938, of course, Clifford Odets could set an entire seriocomic play, *Rocket to the Moon,* in the waiting room of a New York dentist.) The seaside hotel of Shaw's remaining acts was almost de rigueur in the farcical comedy that he here aimed to "humanize"(*Plays Pleasant* 10). The typical masks of that genre here gain some new traits: a sharper intellect, a fuller awareness of their moment in social history, and reservoirs of untapped, repressed, injured, or generous feeling. The dentist Valentine is a boyish version of the volatile hero bent on sexual conquest. Gloria Clandon, who admits Valentine's charge that she is a "feminine prig" (270), discovers behind her mask as "New Woman" an emotional vulnerability and power. Both Mrs. Clandon, the bluestocking who has written extensively on modern manners and morals, and Mr. Crampton, her curmudgeonly former husband, are concealing emotional wounds. And the comic waiter, whom the younger Clandons call William, dispenses the balm of a perceptive and melodious equanimity. He is an English waiter of Norman ancestry, a kind of Shavian natural aristocrat, but his generous waiterly manners are pure Irish. This scheme of masks overlaps with another that is drawn from the commedia dell'arte, a tradition that (as James Fisher has shown) strongly interested Gordon Craig, J. M. Barrie, and Harley Granville-Barker as well as Shaw. Crampton recalls Pantaloon, Valentine and Gloria recall the young lovers, and Mrs. Clandon's old socialist friend, McComas, recalls the learned doctor. More boldly, and by act 4 more explicitly, the Clandon twins Dolly and Philip are stylized as an asexual Harlequin and Columbine. And William's son Bohun, the intimidating Q.C., enters in a grotesque mask as a pragmatic deus ex machina. Shaw may not have known the Italian commedia dell'arte scenarios except in their corrupted music-hall form, but there is one such scenario called "The Dentist" in which Arlecchino tricks Pantalone into letting him pull four sound teeth (*Scenarios* 85ff.). George Fitzmaurice, an admirer of the music hall, may have based his grotesque farce *The Toothache* (which Matthew Coughlin has discussed) on some Dublin version of that skit. Appropriately enough, Valentine's gagging and gassing of Crampton in order to pull a broken tooth without pain succeeds in replaying the old trick with humanizing reversals. Martin Meisel has said that "to humanize Farce was in a sense to destroy it" (267), but surely this play maintains a delicate balance between its farcical music and the emotional depths it explores.

The eclectic style gains coherence partly through the Shavian voice that expresses the paradoxical life of each farcical but feeling mask but also through an insistent response to *The Importance of Being Earnest.* In January 1895, when reviewing *An Ideal Husband,* Shaw had praised Wilde as "our only thorough playwright. He plays with everything: with wit, with philosophy, with drama, with actors and audience, with the whole theatre" (*Works* 23:10). That aim was surely Shaw's own. But a month later he objected to *The Importance of Being Earnest* as an updated farcical comedy of the 1870s that relied on "inhuman" Gilbertisms and mechanical humor. He wanted "to be moved to laughter, not to be tickled or bustled into it." He thought the play's devices "could only have been raised from the farcical plane by making them occur to characters who had . . . obtained some hold on our sympathy (23:44–45). By August he had begun a play of the kind he thought Wilde should have written. Anyone with *Earnest* fresh in memory who now attends a first-rate performance of *You Never Can Tell*—like that at New York's Circle in the Square in 1986 with Philip Bosco (Waiter), Amanda Plummer (Dolly), Victor Garber (Valentine), John David Cullum (Philip), Uta Hagen (Mrs. Clandon), Lise Hilboldt (Gloria), and Stefan Gierasch (Mr. Crampton)—can watch many of Wilde's meanings being transformed into Shaw's.

"Come, old boy," says Wilde's Algernon when he is trying to learn the identity of Cecily, "you had much better have the thing out at once." "My dear Algy," retorts Jack, "you talk exactly as if you were a dentist. It is very vulgar to talk like a dentist when one isn't a dentist" (*Plays* 258). Shaw's Valentine, of course, talks like the "five-shilling dentist" he is—even though Phil Clandon thinks *dentist* an "ugly word" (*Plays Pleasant* 270, 224). Valentine specializes in having the thing out, which Dolly tells Crampton is very like plucking from the memory a rooted sorrow (231). Dental therapy in this play is one metaphor for the healing process of farce. Valentine also echoes Lady Bracknell's demand that Jack produce at least one parent before the season is over: "in a seaside resort," he tells Dolly and Phil, "theres one thing you *must* have before anybody can afford to be seen going about with you; and thats a father, alive or dead" (217–18). Our masking is already making clear its desire for a family reunion. Gloria, who inclines toward a more intellectual version of Gwendolen's pretentiousness, soon uses this

Wildean argument herself, telling her mother that a "woman who does not know who her father was cannot accept" an offer of marriage (226). But her effort to learn her father's identity collapses when it turns out—with a wink at Gwendolen's and Cecily's dispute over the proposal by "Ernest"—that Gloria, her sister, and her mother have all received proposals from the same ship's officer.

The play continues to have serious fun with Wilde's premises in act 3, when Mrs. Clandon interrogates Valentine. Reversing the position taken by Lady Bracknell when interrogating Jack, Mrs. Clandon says that she cares little about money and that Valentine has a right to amuse himself. But then, out-earnesting *Earnest,* she asks: "On your honor, Mr. Valentine, are you in earnest?" "On my honor," he replies, "I am in earnest . . . Only I always have been in earnest; and yet—! Well, here I am, you see!" (277). Soon McComas will rebuke Dolly by saying, "I insist on having earnest matters earnestly and reverently discussed" (286). Then Gloria will rebuke Valentine by saying that if he were really in love it would give him "earnestness." And, when she turns her back on him, he will retort: "Ah, you see you're not in earnest" (291). The word is regaining the emotional force that Wilde's play had drained from it; and by act 4 that force has shown itself to be more than personal. Valentine explains that he has been tempted to awaken Gloria's heart, to stir the depths in her. "Why was I tempted? Because Nature was in deadly earnest with me when I was in jest with her" (311). The earnestness of Nature, at work below our merely personal jests and grievances, supports the play's references to the "heart" or "depths" or "feelings" of a "common humanity" (289, 311–12, 288). In Crampton's plea to Gloria—"I want you to feel: thats the only thing that can help us" (263)—we recognize what must be our plea to ourselves.

As a game of masks, *You Never Can Tell* is less symmetrical than *The Importance of Being Earnest* but no less musical. Dolly and Phil, with their swift completions of each other's thoughts, soon establish the presence of a transpersonal choric music. The other pairings of Valentine and Gloria, Mr. Crampton and Mrs. Clandon, and William and his son Bohun invite us to discern behind opposed but complementary masks a ground of imperfectly acknowledged feeling. And the avuncular odd-man-out, Mrs. Clandon's old admirer McComas, joins Crampton, William, and Bohun to make a variously tempered series of father figures for the Clandon children. As Martin Meisel has shown, Shaw often equipped his plays with an operatic quartet of soprano, alto, tenor, and bass (47–50). But the quartet of Gloria,

Mrs. Clandon, Valentine, and Crampton is here supported not only by the twins (soprano and counter-tenor in allegretto duets) but also by the Shakespearean William (a baritone with an andante melody that, as Meisel remarks, follows precise musical directions [58–59]). Shaw called himself "a pupil of Mozart in comedy much more than any of the English literary dramatists" (Meisel 54), and his operatic devices here prepare for a finale that is choreographed, thanks to the hotel's fancy ball, as a bold Harlequinade.

Irritated by the reductive terms on which the play achieved popularity, Shaw wrote to Harley Granville Barker: "It has always seemed merely a farce written around a waiter. It ought to be a very serious comedy, dancing gaily to a happy ending round the grim-earnest of Mrs. Clandon's marriage and her XIX century George-Eliotism" (*Letters to Granville Barker* 45). That mixture of tone is crucial—but, despite Shaw's continuing deprecation of farce, the "serious comedy" results here from an emotional deepening of farcical ingredients. Beneath the rigid Shavian masks of our inexperience, wounded vanity, old-fashioned proprieties, and so-called modern ideas, the music of this quite serious farce repeatedly invites us to discover a common humanity. It never asks us, however, to indulge ourselves in a warm bath of feeling. William's buoyant equanimity includes a witty alertness, and the characters' rhetoric of sentiment is always suspect. The deus ex machina is appropriately William's sardonic son. "It's understood that self is put aside," says the overwhelming Bohun with dead-pan irony. "Human nature always begins by saying that" (302). After Phil Clandon finally addresses Crampton as "dad," he bends the harlequin's gilt hat he is wearing into a halo and says, sotto voce: "Did you feel the pathos of that?" (309). And Shaw himself points toward the witty emotional balance that characterizes his reversal of Wilde's *Earnest* when he has Valentine at a late moment speak with "ludicrously genuine earnestness" (310). Precisely because *You Never Can Tell* avoids the sentimental, "what passes for a happy ending" has disappointed those who, like Arthur Ganz (118–19), have wanted a more Shakespearean reconciliation of all the parties. Although this musical masking breaks the spell of individuation and lets us glimpse the shareable wisdom of the heart, it keeps our usual needs and confusions before us to the very end. That is why the waltzing and whirling exit of the Clandon-and-Crampton retinue can leave Valentine—whose bids for a dance have been rejected by Gloria, Dolly, and Mrs. Clandon—collapsed disconsolately and farcically on the ottoman, already enduring the pains of marriage.

IV

What the Butler Saw is set in a private clinic equipped with the several doors and windows required by the mix-ups of a marital farce in the tradition of Labiche and Feydeau. And the clinic is run by a philandering psychiatrist-and-husband whose evident line of ancestry runs back through Feydeau's Molineux in *A Flea in Her Ear* to the unruly doctors and beleaguered husbands of the commedia dell'arte. Interviewing at the outset a young woman who has applied to be his secretary, Dr. Prentice poses a question that may strike us as bizarre: "Who was your father?" Her reply—"I have no idea who my father was"—recalls Jack Worthing and the Clandon twins. The play's revisionary artifice is already in motion, as Prentice's response makes clear: "I'd better be frank, Miss Barclay. I can't employ you if you are in any way miraculous. It would be contrary to established practice. You did have a father?" (Orton 363). The sly non sequiturs and cobbled clichés of *The Importance of Being Earnest,* which Orton had called "much more earthy and colloquial than people notice" (qtd. in Lahr, *Prick Up* 106), become yet stranger when uttered by the unmannerly masks of an age without butlers. Geraldine Barclay continues: "Oh, I'm sure I did. My mother was frugal in her habits, but she'd never economize unwisely." And Dr. Prentice, Bracknell-like, returns to the attack: "If you had a father why can't you produce him?" (Orton 364). Prentice soon learns that Geraldine's mother, whom she hasn't seen for many years, had been raped in a linen cupboard at the Station Hotel. After remarking that he had stayed there himself once as a young man, he swiftly leads the compliant Geraldine to his curtained couch for a physical examination that seems a prelude to a kind of employment she has not foreseen. His plan, however, is frustrated by the sudden return of his wife, who soon reveals that *she* has just been raped by a page boy in a linen cupboard at the Station Hotel. The arrival of that boy, Nicholas Beckett, provokes the Prentices into a frenzied sequence of hidings, disguisings, and mix-ups, which are further complicated by the plodding Sergeant Match, who is looking for a missing part of Sir Winston Churchill's statue, and the manic Dr. Rance, who declares himself to be an inspector of lunacy from Her Majesty's government. Before we are through Geraldine and Nick will have swapped and re-swapped costumes and identities, Match will have been stripped, drugged, disguised in Mrs. Prentice's leopard-spotted dress and wounded by gunfire, and Rance will have performed some brutal psychiatric examinations and offered some juicy elucidations of the action—for this outrageous version of the doctor-*raisonneur* that Ibsen and Chekhov so often employed wants very much to write a best-seller that will combine psychoanalytic science with soft porn.

Finally, while Rance and Prentice are attempting at gunpoint to certify each other as insane, Rance presses an alarm, metal grilles fall in place to turn the clinic into a locked cage, and the electric power goes out. After being thus trapped, our masks of contemporary lunacy find that Geraldine and Nick possess the two halves of a single brooch that proves them to be the twins conceived in that linen cupboard during an earlier power-cut, when Prentice had anonymously assaulted the hotel maid who later became his wife. Geraldine's would-be seducer is in fact her father, and Nick has seduced his mother. After this literalizing of the oedipal theme of New Comedy, which Synge's *The Playboy of the Western World* had treated in its own startling way, Geraldine appears also to be a strange kind of Miss Prism. On Prentice's desk, unnoticed through all the confusion, is an unopened box that she had brought with her to the interview. To her surprise, and ours, Sergeant Match now discovers in it a larger-than-life replica of Churchill's penis, which had been embedded in her foster mother's body by the gas explosion that killed her and which Match has been seeking in order to reassemble the statue of Britain's leader.

What the Butler Saw manages to combine elements of *The Importance of Being Earnest* with much that is drawn from *The Menaechmi, The Comedy of Errors, Twelfth Night,* Feydeau's farces, Ionesco's absurdism, and Pinter's comedy of menace. But to this eclectic game, about which Maurice Charney (*Joe Orton* 107–10) and John Lahr (*Prick Up* 233) have made very useful observations, Orton brings a new realism. While writing the play, he watched the National Theatre's televised production of *A Flea in Her Ear* and "hated it," he said, because it was "directed and acted with great speed and no reality." All the "externals" in farce, he maintained, must be "believed" (qtd. in Lahr, *Prick Up* 143). The violence of *What the Butler Saw,* if properly performed, should cut through the blockage of emotions often ascribed to farce: the bleeding wounds of Nick and Match are as "real" as any theater (Orton 443). But, when Match descends a rope ladder from the skylight, "the leopard-spotted dress torn from one shoulder and streaming with blood" (446), finds the misplaced phallic image and holds it up for our startled and admiring view, and then leads the entire cast—"weary, bleeding, drugged and drunk" (448)—up the ladder into the blazing light, Orton is leading our community of realistic farce into the classical tradition. Like Pentheus, the persecutor of Dionysos in Euripides' *The Bacchae,* Match has been trapped, in drag, among the celebrants of the god. But the *sparagmos* of Euripides' play has been displaced to Churchill's exploded statue, and Match elevating the phallus becomes a mime fool or classical satyr figure presiding over a Golden Bough–ish reaffirmation of Dionysiac fertility on the other side of repression and destruction.

The "tradition" here evoked, toward which the play's last speech ironically directs our attention (Orton 448), is real enough. Anthony Caputi's book on "vulgar comedy," which comments shrewdly on elements of madness and rebirth in Plautine farce (159ff.), reproduces a photograph of just such a Roman statuette with elevated phallus (178). (Peter Brook will later attempt the same climax at the end of his version of Seneca's *Oedipus*.) Albert Bermel has noted important relations between *The Bacchae* and farce (39–40). And Orton's diary notes make clear his own awareness of "a 'Golden Bough' subtext" in this play, with castration of the father figure and descent of the god (cited in Lahr, *Prick Up* 21). In effect, *What the Butler Saw* moves through Wilde and the Plautine tradition to become a Nietzschean satyr play. Orton's comments on his vacillation between Dionysian and Apollonian impulses as a writer are but one indication of his familiarity with *The Birth of Tragedy* (15). "Farce is higher than comedy," he could also say, "in that it is very close to tragedy." It differs, he thought, "only in the *treatment* of its themes—themes like rape, bastardy, prostitution" (quoted in Lahr, *Prick Up* 187).

That is why the music of this play articulates the truths of Dionysos. Its pattern of aggressive interrogations discloses beneath these farcical masks our unacknowledged, forgotten, or unrecognized sexual impulses. It begins with a farcical dance of opposites—the probably impotent Prentice and his aggressively bisexual wife, the invitingly compliant Geraldine and the nastily forward Nick, the stoic Match and the manic Rance. But, as the dance proceeds, its disguises and transformations break down not only those opposites but all our assumptions about personal and sexual identity. At one point, when Geraldine is pretending to be Nick but cannot prove her gender, Rance says brutally: "Take your trousers down. I'll tell you which sex you belong to." Her response is pitiful, hilarious, and thematically central: "I'd rather not know!" (Orton 413). Tearing our social masks to shreds, the play's rising frenzy discloses a polymorphous sexuality for which the madly projecting Rance can give only melodramatic pseudo-explanations. "The ugly shadow of anti-Christ stalks this house," he declares, when he thinks the unfindable Geraldine has been murdered. "Having discovered her Father/Lover in Dr. Prentice the patient replaces him in a psychological shuffle by that archetypal Father-figure—the Devil himself . . . The final chapters of my book are knitting together: incest, buggery, outrageous women and strange love-cults catering for depraved appetites. All the fashionable bric-a-brac . . . As a transvestite, fetishist, bi-sexual murderer Dr. Prentice displays considerable deviation overlap. We may get necrophilia too. As a sort of bonus" (427–28).

When the dénouement forces Rance to revise this Gothic Freudianism, he is not dismayed but delighted: "Double incest is even more likely to produce a best-seller than murder—and this is as it should be for love *must* bring greater joy than violence" (Orton 446). In a sense beyond his understanding, he is right about this play: its perverse violence is in the service of love. But the Freudian notions that seem to shape its action can provide only a parodic and incomplete account of the action of performance that brings all this to light. The music of this savage farce discloses beneath our ridiculous, defensive, and bloody masks a perpetually torn and reborn sexuality that is beyond sentiment, moralism, or rational analysis—and prior to our cherished individuality. It has been called a celebration of "moral anarchy" (Bigsby 56–58) and "formlessness" (Lahr, *Prick Up* 273). But such judgments ignore the play's own commitments to form. Katherine Worth had already noted "a faint sense of poignancy as the chase works up to its desperate climax" and "a real longing for the alluring, hermaphroditic wraith that has been created out of the hopeless confusion between Gerald and Geraldine" (*Revolutions* 154). And she had concluded that *What the Butler Saw* is "a great id-releasing experience and a reassuring demonstration of the power of wit to control it" (*Revolutions* 156). Maurice Charney has admirably, if somewhat roguishly, summarized the ways in which Orton has combined "the virtues of Old and New Farce," offering "a mirror of manners, and a model for how the rational man can conduct himself in an irrational world." Orton, as he says, "did not make any tedious and artificial distinctions between earnestness and levity" (*Joe Orton* 107, 109). One need only add that the play's elaborate form brings actors and audience together in a witty dance that celebrates our intuition of unity beyond violence—an intuition that Nietzsche had attributed to the tragic chorus. We can therefore hear in the closing lines—whether spoken by Prentice as in the manuscript or by Rance as in the post-production text (Lahr, *Prick Up* 273)—a meaning beyond the speaker's intent. "I'm glad you don't despise tradition," says one of our masks to another. "Let us put our clothes on and face the world" (Orton 448). And so they climb for us into the blazing light.

V

We have moved from one play that invites us into the music of self-conscious mask wearing to another that historicizes our masks and discloses their common heart and on to a third that psychologizes our masks and discloses their primal sexuality. From this vantage point the Wildean playfulness and panache of *Travesties* may seem a step backward. Stoppard's play brings this sequence, however, to an appropriate climax. Not only does it vastly increase the amount of serious material that farce now seeks to encompass and assimilate, but it also discloses behind the masks of art, politics, and history the workings of one imperfect but inventive mind, gives that mind a local habitation and a name—the paradoxical figure of Henry Carr—and allows him to stand for our entire community of farce. The play's intuition of restored oneness in the midst of the fragmentary, fallible, and confused is in fact a scintillating many-in-one.

The music of *Travesties* retraces the plot of *The Importance of Being Earnest* through a theme-and-variations form that makes possible an astonishing literary, political, and historical expansion. Basing itself stylistically on both Wilde and Joyce, it incorporates procedures from Dadaism, Absurdism, Brechtian theater, the Irish limerick, and Irish-American vaudeville. It includes moments of Shakespeare and Beethoven and a 1974 big band version of "The Stripper." Its dialectical impulse, moreover, is Shavian. Somewhat in the manner of *Man and Superman* or the discussion scenes in *Saint Joan,* it leads us through the interaction of three articulate spokesmen for revolutionary art or politics—Joyce, Tzara, and Lenin—each of whom has farcical or poignant limitations. Except for a prologue that states the leitmotifs (as does the prologue to the Sirens episode in Joyce's *Ulysses*) and an epilogue that provides a dialogical critique, the action seems to take place in the mind of Henry Carr, an acquaintance of Joyce later travestied in *Ulysses,* who is recalling and embellishing his experiences in Zurich. The play manages to give historical and biographical specificity to its characters, reduce them to a kaleidoscopic whirl of changing masks, and locate them in the mind of a sympathetically and ironically portrayed narrator—to whom John Wood, in the first production at the Aldwych Theatre in 1974, brought a stage presence of bravura versatility. But Stoppard's musical masking also expands that versatile mind beyond its realistic capacities to include the playwright's own historical knowledge and stylistic resources, and it renders that expanded mind through the shared action of our community of farce.

Perhaps the most remarkable effect of this musical masking is its transformation of Carr's memories, which stammeringly shape themselves in partial accord with the plot of *Earnest,* into a world beyond his talents and understanding. The prologue implies that Joyce, Tzara, and Lenin are creating their world visions out of bits and pieces. Carr will do the same, but his vision soon acquires a strangely independent life. It is as though Carr were the protagonist of an expressionistic farce that begins by projecting onstage the contents of his egocentric reveries and then proceeds to play with him, call him into question, and sweep him into a world beyond his initial comprehension. *Travesties* plays with Carr as it plays with us, leading us toward a comprehensiveness that had not seemed possible in this dramatic mode. Carr's initial conversation with Bennett (the Lane to his Algernon) suggests through "time slips" and replays a potentially endless process of reinterpretation and expansion. The arrival of Tzara, Joyce, and Gwendolen as nonsense versions of themselves, speaking not in Wildese but in shared limericks, lets us know that a mind more agile and poetic than Carr's is immanent in the action. The replay of their entrances in the style of *Earnest* leads to a debate between the philistine Carr and the Dadaist Tzara and soon thereafter to an interrogation of Tzara by Joyce (modeled on Lady Bracknell's interrogation of Jack but in a catechetical form drawn from *Ulysses*) that elicits the history of Dada as it is documented by contemporary and even later sources. By the end of act 1 both Tzara and Joyce have given eloquent expression to their aesthetic doctrines. Although Carr remains the ostensible narrator, he is now quite evidently but one mask among several through which a more comprehensive imagination is shaping its world.

That impression is further complicated in act 2, which renders Lenin and his wife, Nadya, through a documentary realism that seems to make no concession either to *Earnest* or to what we may have identified as the Stoppardian imagination. Just as act 1 moved beyond Carr, so act 2 seems to move beyond Stoppard. The paradigm of serious farce is calling up its own antithesis for a dialectical engagement. And yet, if Lenin's political urgency offers a critique of our playfulness, the play also shows Lenin to be the dangerous victim of a deadly earnestness. No less a philistine than Carr, he is unaware of the fact that, as *Travesties* itself is demonstrating, art can include a more richly sensitive dialectical process than political theory. After disclosing Lenin's limitations with some poignancy, *Travesties* can return to a lighter music that we will not mistake for the whole truth. Our masking now translates Wilde's symmetries into heightened form. Gwendolen and Cecily debate their amorous, aesthetic, and political differences in stanzas composed in imitation of "Mr. Gallagher and Mr. Shean," a patter song from the (not yet produced) Ziegfeld Follies of 1922. As the dénouement approaches, the women echo that Gilbertian moment in act 3 of *Earnest* by a sustained passage of speaking and moving in unison. The play's complex dissonances are moving toward a final consonance, which seems reached when Gwendolen and Cecily regain the folders they had mixed up in the prologue. There is a rapid but formal climax, with appropriate cries and embraces. The epilogue, however, turns away from that closure to restate the fragmentary and the fallible: Old Cecily criticizes the accuracy of Old Carr's memories, and Carr himself confesses in effect that he does not understand or even quite remember the play's main issues. He forgets the "third thing" that might be the dialectical transcendence of art and revolution (99).

All masks in this game seem to be one mask, and that mask we all wear in our different ways. At one point Tzara has demanded the "right to urinate in different colours," and Joyce responds: "Each person in different colours at different times, or different people in each colour all the time? Or everybody multi-coloured all the time?" (61). Cecily later translates the phrase into "ruminate in different colours" (71)—and with that amendment the answer to Joyce's question as it applies reflexively to *Travesties* must be: all of the above. This "multi-coloured micturition," to use Carr's yet later sardonic translation of the phrase (83), suggests that the grounding unity of our earnest play is one multiform player—not Carr, though he seems our main representative, nor even Stoppard, though he is our primary agent of imagination, but the player constituted by our community of performance. The play's scrappy unity-in-multiplicity and its prismatic effects—for Miss Prism is here our symbolic producer of the multicolored—constitute a living model of the community mind without which the larger worlds of art and history could not exist. We are not far, of course, from the ground-bass of *Finnegans Wake* and more specifically its "Anna Livia Plurabelle" section, in which each of seven dams has seven crutches and every crutch has seven hues and each hue has a differing cry and in which the riddle runs: "howmulty plurators made eachone in person?" (215). In mirroring that prismatic mind, which seems both the mind of persons-in-community and that of community-in-each-person, this play exemplifies what I have called the "mystery doctrine of farce" in a way that also fulfills Schiller's prescription for artistic form. "The most frivolous subject matter," he said in the letters *On the Aesthetic Education of Man,* "must be so treated that we remain disposed to pass over immediately from it to the strictest seriousness. The most serious material must be so treated that we retain the capability of exchanging it immediately for the lightest play" (106). Such playing in earnest is for *Travesties* the wisdom of art.

These plays by Wilde, Shaw, Orton, and Stoppard are complementary intimations of a oneness that grounds our community music of serious farce. Histrionic through and through, they may seem in accord with Wilde's dictum that even the "truths of metaphysics are the truths of masks." But, as we share their disclosures of a unity that must exceed all formulations, we may suspect the adequacy of that one, too. Should we play Wilde's own game of reversals against him? Should we entertain the hypothesis that the truths of masks must finally point toward the unformulable truths of metaphysics?

Chapter 3

Communities of Heartbreak: From Chekhov and Shaw to Friel and Smith

I

Although Chekhov's plays blend farce with comedy and pathos, they are far from a brisk dancing of masks that whirls us toward a recognition of our fundamental unity. Instead, they offer a subtle counterpoint of echoes and reversals, abortive talk and shared silence, explicit heartbreak and implicit community. At the end of *The Cherry Orchard* the distant sound of a breaking string sums up the heartbreak that reverberates through these plays—and through their successors in our century. But Chekhov's dramaturgy also serves to answer that heartbreak. Combining an intimate penetration of "real people" with a clarifying and panoramic distance, it leads us toward a nuanced awareness of the community life in which we participate.

The characters in *Three Sisters,* for example, often relate to one another through oblique responses, unacknowledged echoes, and tacit resistances. They can imagine themselves to be solitary, but they are intermittently aware of a reciprocity from which they avert their attention. An agonized or gratifying self-regard shields them from recognizing that their private troubles are part of the music of yearning, evasion, and passivity in which we find them immersed. We can easily isolate the most distinctive notes in that music: Masha's hysterical indecisiveness, Olga's sick anxiety, Irina's numb exhaustion, the self-pity of Andrey and Chebutykin, the fatuous if self-ironic verbosity of Vershinin, Tusenbach, and Kulygin, and the cruel petulance of Natasha and Solyony. But the play's emotional life is extraordinarily various. The vitality we feel in the drift of its events, even in its apparently static moments, comes in part from the subliminal intensity with which those characters resist being present to one another. But it comes also from something very different: the detailed attention that actors and audience must devote to each character in relation to all the others.

That is why we can so easily feel them turning away from the community in which they have their being. Chekhov's plays invite and require of us, through a panoramic focus and a counterpointing of disjunctive but analogous speeches, gestures, and attitudes, exactly what the characters resist: that we open ourselves to the full music of our existence in mutuality. We must listen to the jagged texture and wry harmonies of the composition formed by these self-isolating dreams of shared need. Hence the defining paradox of this paradigm of playing: as we mime an array of characters who seem fixed in egocentric and self-isolating patterns, we move toward a widening of attention and an ironically qualified sympathy that hold the solution to their predicament. Their inadvertent or unconsciously willed failures elicit from us in performance a response that is both diagnostic and potentially curative. The heartbreak of Nina in *The Sea Gull,* Sonya in *Uncle Vanya,* Masha in *Three Sisters,* or Varya in *The Cherry Orchard* is transmuted by the playing that discloses it. What seems a pathetic destiny within the play's world is a personal and social condition that we are in the very act of overcoming. Len Jenkin, in his 1995 production of *Uncle Vanya* at the Yale Repertory Theatre, highlighted that double aspect of our playing by a simple but perhaps too bold contrast: the self-conscious longueurs of the play's action were separated by sprightly scene changes carried out by the actors themselves.

Plays that acknowledge the most obscure desires, pretensions, and pains of such characters do more, of course, than elicit in us a balanced and clarified attention to the community onstage. They also direct at least our subliminal attention to the array of analogous subpersonalities in each of us that clamor for recognition. A Chekhov play is therefore a kind of dream landscape for those who participate in the performance. That has been effectively recognized by directors who have broken free from the somewhat claustral realism of the early productions. Georgy Tovstonogov's account of his *Three Sisters* at the Gorky Theatre in 1965 (*Anton Chekhov's Plays* 326–39), which dissolved walls and ceilings and used both the revolving stage and small moving platforms, describes one way in which a performance can be subtly transformed into cinematic dreamwork. That dimension of *Three Sisters* was made yet more explicit by Otomar Krejca in his Prague production of 1967, in which, as Siegfried Melchinger has described it, there was "a dismantling of the spoken words through that which happens behind, between, and beyond them." The "sounds thicken, jelling into surrealist music. The gestures, the walking, swing in its rhythm, and the constant play of movement and expression that underlies the dialogue becomes high-tension choreography" (*Anton Chekhov's Plays* 400–401). A somewhat related effect was attained by very different means in Jonathan Moscone's production of *The Sea Gull* at the Yale Drama School in 1992, which used a raked stage, an open and abstractly suggestive set, and an acting style that moved flexibly between the realistic and expressionistic. Chekhov did not become Strindberg, but Nina's exclamation at the end of act 2—"It's a dream!" (*Anton Chekhov's Plays* 28)—became a leitmotif for both the community onstage and our community of performance.

What happens to that community dreamwork, with its themes of absence and presence, heartbreak and the answer to heartbreak, when it enters the English, Irish, and American theater? There have been many extensions and transpositions, and of course Stanislavsky and the Moscow Art Theatre have had a major impact on the acting style brought to realistic and nonrealistic drama of many kinds. In much British and American drama an Ibsenite plotting has been developed through the poetics of Chekhovian conversation. Harold Pinter has further transformed such a mixture by depriving it of the specification that would allow us to verify our inferences about the characters' motives or their pasts and by turning Chekhov's conversation into an array of defensive and offensive strategies. John Lahr has commented perceptively on the "bond" between these two playwrights (Ganz 60–71). Indeed, *The Homecoming,* which often recalls Chekhov's dramaturgy, repeats, distorts, or negates a number of crucial images from *The Cherry Orchard.* But we should note that its pattern of territorial warfare and self-closure provides a much sharper antithesis to our community of performance. Although less claustral than *No Man's Land,* it is closer to the ironic paradigm I shall describe in chapter 5. Many other playwrights, however, even when subjecting the Chekhovian paradigm to stylistic transformation, have depicted panoramas of isolation, blockage, and waste in such a way that we seem to relearn, in and through the action of performance, something like a precarious faith in community.

We can see how this has occurred if we consider a remarkable gamut of Chekhovian inheritors. Shaw transformed Chekhov into a world of histrionic surfaces in *Heartbreak House* (1919); Granville Barker redoubled the Chekhovian depth and subtlety in his little-known masterpiece *The Secret Life* (1923); and Sean O'Casey in *The Plough and the Stars* (1926) and Clifford Odets in *Awake and Sing!* (1935) transplanted that paradigm to Ireland and the United States. Later writers have simplified or truncated the paradigm with more sharply ironic or nostalgic effects: Lillian Hellman in *The Autumn Garden* (1951), David Storey in *The Contractor* (1969) and *Home* (1970), and Eduardo Machado in *Broken Eggs* (1984). Others, by transgressing the limits of the paradigm, have moved more explicitly beyond the vision of heartbreak: Lanford Wilson in *Fifth of July* (1978–80) and Brian Friel in *Dancing at Lughnasa* (1990) and *Wonderful Tennessee* (1993). This music of heartbreak has also been transposed into performance art by Anna Deavere Smith in *Twilight: Los Angeles, 1992.* As these plays take us through a variety of disillusioning crises for families, communities, and nations, they also suggest how the community of performance, in responding to its own projected desires, blockages, and anxieties, can rediscover its recuperative powers.

How Chekhovian is the play that Shaw himself subtitled "A Fantasia in the Russian Manner on English Themes"? Michael J. Mendelsohn and Charles Berst have argued for a deep affinity between *Heartbreak House* and Chekhov's *The Cherry Orchard.* Martin Meisel has seen an affinity in subject matter but not dramatic method. Arthur Ganz, finding that "there is very little about it that is Chekhovian," calls it "a disquisitory play like *Misalliance* . . . deriving ultimately from act 3 of *Man and Superman*" (190). The Shavian derivations, of course, are undeniable: indeed, the conversational sprawl of *Heartbreak House,* like that of *Misalliance,* is punctuated by the arrival of an unlawful intruder and an aircraft. But Shaw's interest in Chekhov is also undeniable. In 1911, as Anna Obraztsova has noted, he professed himself a "fervent admirer" of Chekhov's plays, and he was the driving force behind the Stage Society's production in that year of *The Cherry Orchard* (Miles 43). *Heartbreak House* contains many Chekhovian traits: a panoramic focus; a dissolving of linear plot; a banishing or subduing of overt action; a dreamy mix of nostalgia, unrequited love, romantic idealism, the declared need to work, and the effective refusal of work; a multitude of analogous predicaments not recognized as such by characters who talk past one another or soliloquize in public; an engaging of our sympathy for people unable or unwilling to attend to the crises that shape their own lives; and a quasi-musical form that leads us both to participate in their predicament and to transcend it. And yet these traits of Chekhovian dramaturgy have all undergone a Shavian sea change.

The playing style of *Heartbreak House* seems to offer a cheerful burlesque of drawing-room comedy. Indeed, its aggressive and self-reflexive rhetoric locates the play not just in a Sussex country house but in the theater itself. From every part of the stage the Shavian ventriloquism—more suitable, one might have thought, to serious farce than to the poetic realism of a Chekhovian play—suggests a world of masks or puppets. The early duels and duets—Hesione Hushabye's chat with Ellie Dunn about a British

Othello who is really Hector Hushabye on the make, Captain Shotover's attempts to persuade Boss Mangan that he is much too old for Ellie, Hector's knowingly empty flirtation with Lady Utterword—all have the force of comic demonstration and unmasking. Indeed, as Ellie's swift disillusionment, Mangan's hysterical defensiveness, Randall Utterword's collapse, and Shotover's riddling complexity will suggest, these characters are "layered" or plural. Each is a schizoid embodiment of theatricality itself, a stitching together of stock company "lines" that are also operatic parts, dream figures, semi-allegorical personages, and sometimes the voice of Shavian wisdom. Actors in such a play can hardly ask us to attend to the personal depths and the subtle interactions of characters who themselves turn away from awareness of such things. Rather, they invite us to enjoy the exposure of the brittle multiplicity of roles in the most sympathetic characters—in Shotover's apocalyptic bombast and defensive joking or Ellie's breakdown and self-transcendence. Our own histrionic multiplicity finds here its mirror.

That exposure of the histrionic proceeds not only in the characters' encounters but also, self-reflexively, on the level of the play's own formal strategies. Its sequence of events, far from having the realistic inevitability of *Three Sisters* or *The Cherry Orchard,* is a mocking sign of rhetorical arbitrariness and excess, forcing us to proceed from conversation to conversation by surprising turns, and from act to act by leaps into the dark—or into the light. And its gestures toward the dramatic and literary traditions conflate Shavian antecedents (the burglar of *Misalliance* becomes Billy Dunn, and Shotover is a wry extension and reversal of the Undershaft of *Major Barbara*) with the Chekhovian and the Shakespearean. Ellie Dunn, Hesione Hushabye, and Ariadne Utterword are a reworking of Chekhov's three sisters in a country house haunted by an alcoholic British captain instead of the deaf servant Firs of *The Cherry Orchard*. But Shotover is also a version of King Lear, with three modern daughters. Hector Hushabye, like Shakespeare's Albany and Chekhov's Gaev, remains chronically passive before historical catastrophe. And Ellie, of course, is also a dreaming Alice lost in this British wonderland. Calling attention to its own mocking theatricality, the play also leads us toward a distrust of Shavian rhetoric, the brilliant but potentially self-canceling power of argumentation here at the service of so many interests, which by act 3 has exposed an emptiness or postwar disillusionment that cannot be transcended by even the most sympathetic or insightful of the characters.

Nevertheless, it is not enough to say with Bernard Dukore that the play offers a panorama of "existential damnation" (231) or, with Charles Berst, that its "Tolstoyan, Christian, Shavian judgment" is colored by "the playwright's profound agony at his own insignificance and powerlessness in the face of the brutal realities of World War I" (251, 254). Those verdicts seem to overlook our amused sympathy for a wide range of characters—Hesione, Ariadne, Hector, Shotover, Ellie, Mazzini Dunn, even Boss Mangan and Randall Utterword at moments—who disclose a vulnerable and touching childishness behind the frail masks of pseudo-adulthood. Focusing on the performed action, such verdicts bypass the exhilarating celebration of theatricalist community that inheres in the action of performance. For actors and witnesses join together here in a playful deconstruction of our most characteristic "poses" and roles, a last judgment upon the educated and moneyed triviality of so much English life, a dark reflection upon our destructive impulses, a playwright's own self-anatomizing, and a replaying of *King Lear* and *Alice in Wonderland* as a Chekhovian fantasia about British society during World War I. In *Heartbreak House* the paradigm of playing that Chekhov developed through poetic realism, with its interior dialectic of presence and absence, is sustained through a self-reflexive comedy of negation, for which our histrionic nature is at once a chronic disease, a diagnostic tool, and a cause for celebration.

That, in brief, is the precarious answer to heartbreak in which Shaw invites us to participate. Its distinctive themes and strategies may be highlighted by comparison with Granville Barker's still largely unappreciated masterpiece, *The Secret Life.* Barker had produced many of Shaw's plays and had played Marchbanks in *Candida,* Tanner in *Man and Superman,* Cusins in *Major Barbara,* Frank Gardner in *Mrs Warren's Profession,* Valentine in *You Never Can Tell,* and Keegan in *John Bull's Other Island* (Kennedy 66). Although he had never directed a Chekhov play, his own earlier work contains what Jan McDonald has called "strong Chekhovian echoes" (Miles 33). And in *The Secret Life* he directly answers *Heartbreak House* as he takes the Chekhovian paradigm toward a subtlety that has much in common with the fiction of Henry James.

II

For much of this century the very existence of Granville Barker as a master of the theater seems to have been a secret rather well kept from reviewers and producers alike. When his *Waste* was revived by the Royal Shakespeare Company in 1985, some London reviewers were surprised to find there a combination of theatrical skill, political intelligence, and articulate compassion that they could not expect from even the best of more recent British playwrights. Nevertheless, what may well be Barker's finest play, *The Secret Life,* had to wait until 1997 for a major production on a reasonably adequate thrust stage—at the Shaw Festival in Niagara-on-the-Lake. (Sam Walters had directed it in 1988 in what Margery Morgan calls "the cramped conditions of the old Orange Tree pub theatre" in Richmond, England [*Plays: One* xxix, 240].) As Eric Salmon has said, "there is everything about the text of *The Secret Life* to suggest that it would live triumphantly in the theatre, given the right handling" (308). Its difficulties, which have too often led both theater folk and academics to regard it as a closet drama, are for the most part those of a subtle score for performance. Perceiving that fact, Dennis Kennedy suggested that Barker was "frankly writing for the national theatre to be" (201). Indeed, there are now a number of national and regional theaters in Britain, Canada, and the United States that could give this play the "right handling": ensemble acting, a style of evocative realism, and a delight in both wit and passion. But it was appropriate that the Shaw Festival, which has been doing Barker in recent years—*The Voysey Inheritance* (1988), *The Marrying of Ann Leete* (1993), *Rococo* (1994), and *Waste* (1995)—should rise to the occasion. Anyone who brought to this production of *The Secret Life* a vivid memory of Shaw's *Heartbreak House* was able to share in one of the most notable dialogues in modern British drama.

The Secret Life looks back on the first two decades of the century through a panorama of lives that have been touched by romantic, political, and philosophical disillusionment. And here again the transformation of a paradigm has been mediated through an intense personal presence. For Barker himself the play was clearly a midlife assessment. He began it in 1919, the year after he divorced Lillah McCarthy, married Helen Huntington, distanced himself from Shaw, and virtually ended his active life in the theater. He began it, moreover, in the year that finally saw the publication of *Heartbreak House,* a play on which Shaw had been working during the period in which Barker seems to have treated Shaw's house as his own. Barker finished *The Secret Life* in 1922, soon after what to Shaw was the heartbreaking failure of his own play on the London stage. Once *The Secret Life* had been drafted, Barker addressed his theatrical father as some prophetic Jacob might address his youngest son: "Confound you, Benjamin," he said, "your Heartbreak House. In *matter* for the theatre it may be 50 years before its time. But the actors of 50 years hence may equally find its *manner* abhorrent to them. It sets them no artistic problem" (*Granville Barker and his Cor-*

respondents 158–59). *The Secret Life* clearly proposes to do just that. Taking up the issues and motifs of Shaw's comedy of negation, it translates them into what Barker called "a tragedy of negation." And its appropriately "negative technique" also provides an answer to Shavian dramaturgy (*Granville Barker and his Correspondents* 102). Barker's play is therefore able to undertake a subtler and more realistic analysis of romantic idealism, postwar disillusionment, parliamentary democracy, the relations between *eros* and *polis,* and the deep anxiety of a social order that has lost its bearings. "The life of the mind is a prison in which we go melancholy mad. Better turn dangerous . . . and be done away with" (*The Secret Life* 78). If Captain Shotover had made that remark, we would laugh uneasily. When we hear it from the politician and historian Evan Strowde in the context of Barker's social panorama, we register a more chilling despair.

That despair, however, is not the play's last word, nor is realistic pathos its only response to the desperate verve of Shaw's most problematic comedy. In order to understand the complex nature of Barker's answer to heartbreak, we need to look closely at its dramatic mode and its orchestration of details. William Archer complained in 1923 that the play lacks "outward & visible" drama. "Perhaps thirty years hence," he said, "audiences may be purged of all lust for the event, & may have their faculties sharpened & speeded up to the sort of salmon-spearing by torchlight which the apprehension of your dialogue demands. But the theatre of thirty years hence leaves, & will leave, me strangely cold" (*Granville Barker and his Correspondents* 86). But that same objection could have been made to much of Chekhov, even though Barker's characters are often shrewder, more intellectually alert, and more precisely articulate. Barker's retort was firm: "I protest I never have—I *cannot*—write an unactable play: it would be against nature, against second nature anyhow. I act it as I write it. But"—he acknowledged—"there is no English company of actors so trained to interpret though and the less crude emotions, nor, as a consequence, any selected audience interested in watching and listening to such things" (96). That hint of professional heartbreak should remind us that Barker's directorial work had often paralleled that of Stanislavsky, whom he visited in Moscow in 1914 (Salmon 109). Indeed, just as he was finishing *The Secret Life,* he also published *The Exemplary Theatre,* a call for a national theater and school that would take the British some distance toward the Russian achievement. In 1937 he would write to John Gielgud: "I pinned my faith in the *theatre* solution; and finding it—with a war and a 'peace' on—no go, I got out." He urged Gielgud to establish, if not a "National" Theater, then "such a one as

Stanislavsky's or even Rheinhardt's of 30 years back" (*Granville Barker and His Correspondents* 410). Today, thanks in part to those who have carried on the emphases of Stanislavsky and Chekhov, we are more than ready for *The Secret Life.* Barker was wrong, of course, in thinking that late-twentieth-century actors would find the "manner" of *Heartbreak House* "abhorrent": its self-conscious theatricalism, though harking back to nineteenth-century opera and playing styles, more than holds its own on our stage. But we are now also schooled in other possibilities. In an essay first intended as a preface to *The Secret Life,* Barker declared that "the natural speech of the people" often contains "that power of expression and concentration of meaning which is the essence of poetry, even though the form be prose" ("Heritage of the Actor" 71). Such a language of the theater, through which "natural speech of the people" can even attain moments of Shakespearean or biblical elevation, is surely not strange in the age of Beckett and Pinter.

The script of *The Secret Life* therefore asks for an attentive rereading. When St. John Ervine complained of bafflement after two readings, Barker retorted: "I am mischievously tempted to tell you to read it *twice* more and to read it as you would read—if you could—an orchestral symphony" (*Granville Barker and His Correspondents* 500). Shaw would have grasped that point. "A first-rate play," he had said in 1906, pointing to Barker's *The Voysey Inheritance* and to plays by Ibsen and Galsworthy, "seems nowadays to have no situation, just as Wagner's music seemed to our grandfathers to have no melody, because it was all melody from beginning to end" (*Shaw on Theatre* 110). Such a play is all situation, and it therefore requires, as Shaw said in 1910, the repeated reading or hearing that we would give to a Wagner opera or a Beethoven symphony in order to possess its themes. "Familiar as I am with Mr. Granville Barker's methods and ideas," he added, "I find that until I have been through his plays at least six times I have not fairly got hold of them" (114). But, as musicians of the theater, Shaw and Barker were in many respects antithetical. Barker's style and taste, said Shaw in his memorial tribute of 1946, "were as different from mine as Debussy's from Verdi's" (266).

Although *The Secret Life* is no *Pelléas et Mélisande* in answer to a Shavian *Rigoletto,* both the musical comparison and the invocation of Debussy's setting of Maeterlinck are apt. Indeed, Eric Salmon has justly noted the early influence of Maeterlinck's manner of interweaving several different strands into the groping conversation of his characters (56). But of course a rather similar interweaving also enters into Chekhov's dialogues. The opening moments of *The Secret Life* in fact sound Shavian leitmotifs by way of Wagner (whom Shaw had praised to Barker in 1918 as the model of motivic development [*Letters to Granville Barker* 198]), but they are already translating the ironic agitation of *Heartbreak House* into a more Chekhovian music.

Before us is a house that faces the sea. A piano has been moved out onto its loggia. From behind the parapet of the loggia we hear a male voice, punctuated by ironic remarks from others, "coming to the end of a curious, half-sung, half-spoken performance of 'Tristan and Isolde'" (*Plays: One* 241). The group has been evoking with wry nostalgia an operatic passion of their student life more than two decades ago. Indeed, a bit later this performer, the politician Stephen Serocold, will recall an occasion when an Italian with a guitar "offered to pass the time for us by singing 'Rigoletto' right through for three lire" (257). But in these opening moments we have also seen on the moonlit steps of the house a solitary figure in white—not a young girl like Ellie Dunn but the mature Joan Westbury, in effect the Mélisande figure of Barker's play. Her stillness, as we shall soon learn, hides a bitter exhaustion. Eighteen years ago she had rejected the proposal of her Tristan, Evan Strowde, and had settled for marriage with a diplomat appropriately named Mark. Since then she has lost two sons to the war and lost her house to a fire. These opening moments should recall to us act 2 of *Heartbreak House,* in which Hesione Hushabye draws Mangan to the garden door saying, "There is a moon: it's like the night in Tristan and Isolde" (123)—and also act 3, in which Shaw's company gathers in the now moonless garden to assess its shared heartbreak. "It is a curious sensation," Ellie Dunn has said in act 2: "the sort of pain that goes mercifully beyond our powers of feeling. When your heart is broken, your boats are burned: nothing matters any more" (123). Both Joan Westbury and Evan Strowde have experienced just that sense of heartbreak. When he compares the moon to a ship on fire, she answers: "Burnt out" (244). And she prays to the moon "as one burnt-out lady to another" (251). Strowde soon begins to suggest the larger meanings of Shavian heartbreak: "When the war came," he says, "my beliefs about men and things were an enemy the more. I fought against them and beat them . . . and they're dead" (269). And he says later to Oliver, his unacknowledged son by the Countess of Peckham, "You cease to suffer . . . you cease to hope. You have no will to be other than you are" (343).

Neither play suggests an easy transcendence of this self-conscious apathy. "Heartbreak?" asks Shotover. "Are you one of those who are so sufficient to themselves that they are only happy when they are stripped of everything, even of hope?" And Ellie answers: "I feel now as if there were nothing I could not do, because I want nothing" (131). Strowde, too, says that one who ceases "to hope" becomes "extraordinarily efficient" and can therefore "ruthlessly" be something (344). But both plays recognize that such acceptance of heartbreak leaves the heart open to the devils of destruction. Shaw's Ellie calls for the return of the zeppelin that has blown Mangan and the burglar to bits. Barker's Oliver, having lost an arm in the war, flirts with anarchism, though it is characteristic of Barker's quieter wit that Oliver abjures bombs because he does not see enough difference between a dead prime minister and a live one (279). Lady Peckham says, "I don't want any more killing." And her engagingly fractious daughter Dolly, "radiant in the sunshine by the window," gives a response that makes quite clear the implications of Ellie's longing for the zeppelin: "I tell you though . . . women are going to fight in the next war. And if we hurry up I can be in the Air Force. Susan, I'll come and bomb your little head off, first thing." To which Susan responds ("with 'New England' seriousness—as it is called elsewhere"): "Please do" (303). But in a vein quite beyond such dry levity Barker concludes his panorama of botched statecraft and maimed lives by disclosing that Joan Westbury—whose desire that love remain unattainable has shielded her secret self from intimacy (357)—suffers a fatal tumor of the brain.

In both plays the chief philosophic spokesmen also find it hard to transcend heartbreak. Shotover rails through his nonsense at those who will not learn to navigate the ship of state. Mr. Kittredge, the elderly American who shares Joan Westbury's last moments, says that "we're all driven to talk nonsense at times . . . when no other weapon is left us against the masters of the world . . . who have made language and logic, you see, to suit their own purposes" (300). But Shotover seeks through the seventh degree of concentration a weapon that will explode all the explosives of the world, while Kittredge, aware that "doing defeats itself" and poised between a necessary ignorance and a difficult faith, follows a very different course. He moves through a somewhat Shavian confidence in an experimental life force (307) and a gentle acceptance of the Buddhist prayer for release from "the need to know by name or form" (360) toward an affirmed distinction between "flesh" and "spirit" (361) that recalls Saint Paul's disquisitions on those rich concepts *sarx* and *pneuma* to the Galatians (5.16–26) and the Romans (8.9): "But ye are not in the flesh, but in the Spirit if so be that the Spirit of God dwell in you." In *Heartbreak House* action turns against itself in comic negation. In *The Secret Life* a tragic negation of action leads toward a difficult detachment that opens the self to the resources of the transcendent.

That difference says much about Barker's answer to heartbreak. But, before turning to its implications, we should glance at two ways in which *The Secret Life* is a yet broader retort to Shaw. As early as *Candida,* Eugene Marchbanks had turned his back upon happiness because he had "a better secret than that" in his heart and had walked out into what Shaw later told James Huneker was "Tristan's holy night" (Huneker 255). Quite probably Shaw told the same thing to the young actor who played Marchbanks for him in 1900—Harley Granville Barker. Nearly twenty years later (just the span of time that has elapsed since Joan Westbury's rejection of Evan Strowde), Barker began to explore the ironies that might lurk in Candida's rejection of Marchbanks and Marchbanks' rejection of love, in "Tristan's holy night," and in that "secret" in the poet's heart. "I feel," says Strowde when Joan again rejects him, "like a boy crossed in his first love affair" (334). But *The Secret Life* was also, in effect, a response to a play that Shaw had not yet written. Joan Westbury, who is "of a very still habit," makes her presence felt at first mainly through her silence (259). When in 1924 Barker wrote to Shaw about *Saint Joan,* he objected to what he called its characters' habit of always beginning at *A* and speaking straight on to *Z.* That Shavian obsession seemed to him "hardest" on Joan herself. "Because it must have been what she quite silently *was* which impressed people—oh, far more than anything she said" (*Granville Barker and His Correspondents* 160). Shaw's Joan had already been answered by his own as he set new problems for the post-Stanislavskian actor and director.

Heartbreak House articulates its critique of romantic idealism, self-deceptive poses, and political incompetence mainly through set dialogues that display the Shavian genius for rhetorical dialectic and demolition. The only real political force, Hastings Utterword, is called a numskull but is kept safely offstage (60). We see the ineffective idealist Mazzini Dunn, the hollow businessman Mangan, the lapdog Hector, the rotter Randall Utterword, and an array of charming, touching, and rather strong but also rather useless women. *The Secret Life,* however, orchestrates in more genuinely Chekhovian fashion, through densely contrapuntal dialogue, a world in which the poetry, pathos, and intellectual brilliance seem attributable less to some playwright-puppeteer than to its real and complex people. (John Galsworthy once said that Shaw "creates characters who express feelings which they have not got," whereas he created "characters who have feelings which they cannot express." Granville Barker here, like Henry James in his late novels, follows a middle road of highly articulate yet realistic feeling.) Barker's politicians and men of affairs—Strowde, Serocold, Sir Geoffrey Salomons, Sir Leslie Heriot, Lord Clumbermere—have undeniable talents that have been compromised, deflected, or wasted in the process of parliamentary government. Heriot, who thrives in this milieu, has become a vulgarized and ragbag image of the electorate (328). He has accommodated himself to political heartbreak: statesmanship, he says, "is the act of dealing with men as they most illogically are, and with the time as it nearly always most unfortunately is" (322). Clumbermere, who is partly based on the soap manufacturer William Hesketh Lever, first Viscount Leverhulme (*Granville Barker and His Correspondents* 104n), is a self-made man of the old school, nourishing his soul on such inspirational verse as John Burroughs' "My Own Shall Come to Me" (367)—a much shrewder, solider, and more genuinely touching figure than Shaw's Mangan. And Barker's women, though less scintillating than Shaw's, have more ethical, emotional, and intellectual substance. Probing Joan Westbury's confession that she has "treasured a secret self . . . oh, an ego, if ever there was one," Kittredge remarks with "a certain dispersive briskness" that he "once knew a promising young man possessed of the same devil. He fell in love, had his heart broken . . . broken into. Ego came out to fight and could never quite get back again." But Joan says of her own secret self: "No, I could never flatter it into being a heartbreaker. It was never half so human" (357). So much for the simpler vanities of Shaw's Hesione and Ariadne. The Countess of Peckham, closer to those characters, combines their worldly passions with sound judgment and maternal solicitude. Strowde's sister Eleanor, who seems beyond romantic heartbreak and is now entering the political field in her own way as a fundraiser for social action, nonetheless stoically endures another kind of heartbreak when the brother she has assisted for years with his multivolume history project now abandons it for an attempted return to politics. And Kittredge's granddaughter Susan—the Ellie-like image with which Barker's play finally leaves us—is a New England girl of grave simplicity who can ask, "What's to happen to this world if people won't choose their duty and stick to it though their hearts break?" (371). It is Susan who earns the right, in the play's motivic development, to become the healing Isolde to Oliver's wounded Tristan.

That realistic complexity deepens what Barker called "the tragedy of the barrenness of idealism" and also lets it pose what he called the "larger" and "very dreadful" question, "How to propagate spiritual goodness?" (*Granville Barker and His Correspondents* 102–3) We see the evasions, the acceptances of the second best, that have led Joan Westbury and Evan Strowde to such barrenness. We also see the limitations of Salomons's cynicism, Heriot's pragmatism, Clumbermere's equating of righteousness with profit, and Susan's simplicity. The play confronts us with a poignant spectacle of death and judgment, redeemed only by a few highly qualified gestures toward new life. That is why, after the penultimate scene has shown us Joan's approach to death, attended by the sympathetic Kittredge, the play finally brings together Susan and Oliver. Here *The Secret Life* moves beyond the spiritual marriage of Ellie and Shotover and beyond the ironically sketched romance of Anna and Trofimov at the end of *The Cherry Orchard,* toward a realistic rethinking of Ibsen's *When We Dead Awaken.* Susan has commonsensically said that, if Joan loved Strowde, she should have married him. "Love isn't all of that sort," responds Oliver. "Sometimes it brings Judgment Day." "But that's when the dead awake . . . isn't it?" asks Susan. "Yes . . . ," says Oliver, "to find this world's done with." Susan persists in her optimism, declaring that Strowde, because he has loved Joan to the last, will "be born again . . . in a way." And a moment later, after Oliver has teased her for believing in miracles, she challenges him: "Wouldn't you want to be raised from the dead?" "No, indeed," he says. To which she responds, "You'll have to be . . . somehow." Oliver, who is on the point of leaving, stops at the door and considers her—his willful despair threatened by her confidence in what Barker calls "an honest mind and her unclouded youth." Then he says, "Do you wonder I'm afraid of you, Susan?"—and goes out (373–75).

In leaving us with that question, and with that image of tacit spiritual power, the play suggests why, despite its Chekhovian texture of analogous and contrapuntal situations, Barker could say to William Archer, "The later Ibsen is my master." He added at once, however, a circuitous qualification: "I don't name Tchekov. But (or 'for' or 'though') it was when I saw the Moscow people interpreting Tchekov that I fully realised what I had been struggling toward—and that I saw how much actors *could* add to a play" (*Granville Barker and His Correspondents* 102). Barker's emphasis on performance has important relations to the play's psychological and ethical substance. What finally *is* "the secret life"? Eric Salmon, who sees in the play an unreconciled conflict between the "ultimate unreality" of doing and the "ultimate reality" of being, says that in the story of Joan Westbury and Evan Strowde, "Being merges in loving and loving in death, the perfect unactivity." A "perfection reached only in death" is here "the supreme sublimation of all mortal passion" (303–4). But surely the play looks with a rather cool irony on the *Liebestod* of Tristan and Isolde, and it also effectively transcends the duality of doing and being. In fact, just as it has offered a range of meanings for *heartbreak,* so it has offered several meanings for the *secret life.*

One, of course, is Susan's simplicity. Others are expressed by Strowde, by Joan, and by Kittredge. Strowde, who first uses the phrase, says that men's strength "must spring from the secret life . . . and what is it, as a rule, but the old ignorant savagery?" (266). For Joan, however, the secret life has been a "sacred self that cannot yield to life," an empty and agonizing freedom of questionable worth (358). Kittredge, speaking of neither the savagery that may impel action nor the aloof freedom that refuses action, offers yet another understanding of the secret life. He recognizes that we must "keep nothing of our own" and "abandon everything but hope." We will then find hope itself to be a "lure" that leads to a secret that is "well known, and disbelieved" (306–7).

Kittredge later expounds that secret to Joan on her deathbed, in terms that conflate Pauline and Buddhist spirituality: "This I can believe," he says. "The generation of the spirit is not as the generation of the flesh . . . for its virtue is diffused like light, generously, unpriced. Doing and suffering and the work of thought must take its toll of us. And all that life corrupts death can destroy. Then we may cease to know. But, freed from self's claim upon it, scattered, dissolved, transformed, that inmost thing we were so impotently may but begin, new breathed, the better to be." Then Joan moves beyond his voice into "light and silence" (361). Barker himself told Archer that he inclined toward Kittredge's answer (*Granville Barker and His Correspondents* 103), which transcends the conflict between doing and being by an understanding of "spirit" as a selfless and nonacting action that can move through us. That answer is manifest in Kittredge's continuing physical and spiritual presence to the dying Joan.

A similar answer also inheres in the secret life of any convincing performance of this script, for a performance is committed to a realm of interpersonal doing that will disclose being. Barker's awareness of that fact is clear in his comments on the Moscow Art Theatre and on modern theater generally. When the people in Moscow showed him "how much actors *could* add to a play," they were not adding the arbitrary or adventitious but were finding and giving emotional reality to the subtext implicit in Chekhov's lines. They were doing so, as Barker emphasizes in *The Exemplary Theatre,* through a collaboration that brings unity of understanding out of a diversity of viewpoints. The play's substance can then become for the audience a sharing not just in the characters' actions but also in the actors' finding of the characters in themselves and of themselves in the characters. As members of the audience, we clarify a shareable secret life by witnessing onstage and in ourselves that double and reciprocal action.

Awareness of that shared life tends to resolve here and now, at least for the moment, the problems of love, idealism, self-definition, and social and political life with which the world represented by the play is so urgently and often pessimistically concerned. Barker was quite certain of that. "Acting," he said in *The Exemplary Theatre,* is "the art of sympathy," and the theater is "the epitome of social life itself" (248). The "key to government," he also said, is "self-understanding, which . . . must mean, in terms of a community, mutual understanding"—and in that mutual understanding we find "the knowledge of our souls" (284). Implicitly, Barker was bringing us back to the symbolic import of Kittredge, who gives himself to the generous "light" that abandons all self-concern in hope for the community. In sum, dramatic art is the "working out" of "the self-realization . . . of society itself" (53). The diverse talents and points of view that have been brought to the script join in a "genuine reconciliation" in which the audience can participate (49). Barker summed up this doctrine in sentences that must have been written with *The Secret Life* at least in the back of his mind: "Unity in diversity must be our social ideal, and it is this that the drama in its very nature does expound and, through the sympathetic power of impersonation, interpret. This is the drama's secret" (128).

And this, finally, is Barker's answer to heartbreak. In responding to *Heartbreak House,* he pointed toward the secret life of drama itself. "A play is material for acting," he said in what he planned as an introduction to *The Secret Life.* "It may be far more, but it must be that to begin with" ("Heritage of the Actor" 53). *The Secret Life* is indeed far more—one of the most intricately and beautifully *written* plays to come out of England in this century. Because the script is "material for acting" in a far more Chekhovian way than Shaw's "Fantasia," it demands that readers begin by searching for the subtexts that actors would realize together onstage. There *The Secret Life* can lead us toward a sympathetic and yet detached identification with its remarkably various characters. *Heartbreak House,* in its brilliantly and self-consciously histrionic mode, throws us back upon ourselves with an unanswered challenge: how, beneath all our poses, are we to live our lives? Taking up that challenge and exploring it deeply through maimed characters who have been drawn deathward, *The Secret Life* lures us into the mutual understanding in which life itself may find an answer.

Such is the dialogue with Shaw that was given theatrical presence by Neil Munro's fine production of *The Secret Life* at the Shaw Festival in 1997. His "Director's Notes," while not developing this dialogue, gave us a clue in their prefatory quoting of Shotover's statement: "When your heart is broken . . . nothing matters any more. It is the end of happiness and the beginning of peace." Munro, who had shaped the previous Barker productions at the festival, chose here to emphasize the hidden continuities that tie together the characters' "elliptical thinking and poetic intention," which create "a world of mystery and unknowing." "Can the practical socio-political beast ever be brought into harmony with the secret life of the soul?" he asked. And he offered a shrewd summary of the performed action: "Barker shows us how the power of thought, spurred on by emotional intensity, can do palpable damage to the life of the everyday, while at the same time offering us palpable faith in the goodness which resides at the centre of the spiritual self."

Excellent ensemble acting and directing gave us yet more, however, inviting us into a panorama of various characters and situations in which similarities were heightened not only by echoing phrases but also by repeated images and groupings. The rendering of hidden continuities relied to some extent on music (Prokofiev's *Sonata for Cello and Piano in C Major opus 119,* Malcolm Forsyth's *The Swan Sees His Reflection,* Arvo Pärt's *Mirror in a Mirror,* Benjamin Britten's *Sonata in C opus 65*) and on a realistic-expressionistic staging (influenced by Mark Rothko, in particular his *White Band No.27*) that grounded us in historical particularities but allowed a gradual and cumulative merging of environments. Despite the modest dimensions of the stage, we moved easily from group scenes and intimate dialogue to panoramic implications. The initial stillness of Joan Westbury (played with intensity if not grace by Fiona Reid) at the seaside villa carried forward, as an image, to the stillness of her last moments amid New England snows, in a scene that conflated overturned furniture and fragmentary statues from earlier moments. The political shrewdness, romantic yearning, interior disarray, and almost hopeless frustration of Evan Strowde (played quite brilliantly by Christopher Newton) came through with great intensity as set off within the play's interweaving of a gamut of political and semiphilosophical types. And the final moments, with a Susan Kittredge (Lisa Waines) who was herself so frequently a still image, the youthful and hopeful complement of Joan Westbury, and an Oliver Gauntlett (Mike Shara) who translated into his youthful desperation the blockage so complexly rendered by the older characters, gave us indeed (especially with the realistic-expressionistic staging) a strong suggestion of what the late Ibsen meant by the possible awakening of the dead.

One might have been apprehensive that Neil Munro's directorial and design choices would turn *The Secret Life* into a theatrical dream, a distanced mirror of our playing. In a larger theater or on a proscenium stage that might have happened. But the intimacy of the thrust stage at the Court House Theatre at the Shaw Festival provided the opportunity for a necessary balance. We never lost our sympathetic identification with these characters, whose predicaments were ours and whose passionate thinking aloud could enter the realm of our own secret thoughts, or with the actors, whose power of becoming those characters provided us with a tacit clue to their predicaments. The production amply demonstrated the viability of *The Secret Life* upon our contemporary stage. Appropriately enough, the play shared the season not with *Heartbreak House* but with Chekhov's *The Seagull.* And Christopher Newton—the festival's artistic director as well as an actor in both plays—rightly linked them: "In masterpieces like *The Seagull* and *The Secret Life,* great writers probe deeply into the human heart."

III

The Secret Life may well be the most subtle and poignant development in this century of the Chekhovian paradigm of acting and witnessing. But other plays have offered different strategies for depicting an often comic panorama of disillusionment and heartbreak while inviting the actors and witnesses toward a self-realization of community. Most notable is O'Casey's *The Plough and the Stars*—a play that, like Synge's *Playboy of the Western World,* led to riots at the Abbey Theatre.

Whereas *Heartbreak House* and *The Secret Life* offer panoramas of English middle-class disillusionment against the backdrop of a Great War that is offstage or in the past, *The Plough and the Stars* gives us Irish working-class dreams, dissipations, frustrations, and courage amid a patriotic uprising during that war. Disillusionment here takes the form of a love-hate relation with Irish politics, Irish temperament, and the universal pathologies of self-deception and violence. O'Casey said in 1943 that he had been acquainted with Chekhov's works for thirty years (Kosok 71), and his use of Chekhovian dramaturgy in *The Plough and the Stars* has been outlined by Robert Hogan. The "exterior action" is signaled by the four acts—the intimations of conflict, the military preparations, the Easter Rising of 1916, and its aftermath. Within that, Hogan notes eight "interior actions"—the attempts of Nora Clitheroe, Jack Clitheroe, Bessie Burgess, Fluther Good, Peter Flynn, the young Covey, Mrs. Gogan, and her child Mollser to cope with the circumstances that render them powerless. In each act O'Casey gives some development to the interior actions and then brings certain of them together in counterpoint to form "a Chekhovian chorus" (45). Like most dramatic analysis, however, Hogan's account abstracts the represented action from our action of performance. It therefore cannot show the striking ways in which O'Casey has modified the paradigm of acting and witnessing that Chekhov, Shaw, and Barker had explored.

What links does *The Plough and the Stars* establish between its onstage panorama and the action of performance in which we participate? Unlike *Three Sisters* and *The Secret Life,* it seems not to require a sustained attention to tacit relations, psychological nuances, and the complexity of subtextual life. Its counterpoint of speeches and actions is cruder than Chekhov's or Barker's, often broadly comic or melodramatic. At least two characters, however, Fluther Good and Bessie Burgess, are far from simple, and Heinz Kosok has rightly argued that the play organizes an extraordinary complexity of attitudes (71–86). Nor does this play invite us, like *Heartbreak House,* to share a self-conscious theatricality that is both a social disease and its means of diagnosis and partial cure. O'Casey's characters are as obsessively rhetorical and histrionic as Shaw's—but more naively or melodramatically so. Although we may regard them with condescending irony or amusement, we are drawn into the pathos of their situations. And by the play's end we have discovered in its pattern of blindness, infatuation, rage, and violence a fractured image of the wholeness of community that we experience in the performance itself. Three main strategies combine to produce that effect.

In visual terms the play invites us to imagine that we are virtual inhabitants of the onstage world. In act 1 we view from the rear of its back drawing room the tenement home of the Clitheroes, which other residents temporarily occupy, repairing a door (Fluther Good), snooping about (Mrs. Gogan), or claiming proprietary and familial rights (Peter Flynn and the Covey). Our vision penetrates through the back and front drawing rooms and through a window onto a lamplit street where workmen are engaged in repairs. After Nora and Jack return, their domestic scene is invaded by Captain Brennan, who brings orders for Jack to lead a reconnaissance attack on Dublin Castle. And, when Jack leaves with Brennan, the consumptive Mollser invites herself in, the departing regiment of Dublin Fusiliers is singing outside, and the antagonistic Bessie Burgess appears at the door. This porous domain is a thoroughfare, and we seem invisible visitors, both inside and outside of the action. In act 2 the public house, with its counter extending across two-thirds of the stage and passing out of sight, and its back wall almost filled by a huge window, creates a yet greater effect of openness and vulnerability. Through the window we can see silhouetted the Man (in historical actuality, Padraic Pearse, on that November day in 1915) who addresses a gathering crowd. He will move in and out of our vision, watched also by the Barman, the prostitute Rosie Redmond, and the residents and officers who pass through the pub, his Voice a frequent presence among us. The arguments, seductions, and intoxications inside the pub will counterpoint, and partly explain, the hypnotic call of that Voice to military action. In this place without solid walls we seem again both to share and to transcend the points of view of characters who are engaging in self-blinding and violent attempts to maintain their own psychological walls. Act 3, now using a convention as old as Roman drama, gives a frontal view of the Dublin tenement, moving us into the street itself, along with the characters who participate in the looting and violence that accompanies the Rising. And in act 4 we are in the most claustral but most vulnerable of the play's locations, Bessie Burgess's attic room. Again viewing this space from the rear, we watch as Bessie is killed by rifle fire when she pushes the hysterical Nora away from the small upstage window. O'Casey has brought us to inhabit a series of dangerous spaces within which a familial, civic, religious, and political community seems determined to implode upon itself.

We are not simply immersed, however, in the characters' bickering, religious and political antagonisms, and military violence. O'Casey's second and rather Chekhovian strategy is to provide an array of contrasting but complementary characters, none of whom is denied sympathetic understanding: the fussily defiant Peter and the volatile but solid Fluther, the would-be Marxist Covey and the defensively ironic prostitute Rosie, the querulous and hysterical Mrs. Gogan and the disdainful Bessie, the sentimental Nora and the bluff but inexperienced officers. We see rhetorical patriots and nearly inarticulate victims. And finally, of course, we see Dublin tenement dwellers set against British Tommies who are, at bottom, very much like them. The surface diversity leads toward a subtextual unity, for behind all the angry self-justifications and self-dramatizations we can feel lives of pinched circumstances, denied opportunities, limited freedoms. Neighborhood and international strife are the projections of shared discontents. And, though men dominate the military action, our feelings are finally held by the women, who are both melodramatic victims and unexpected heroines. In the play's ironic climax the dying Bessie, once the ominous antagonist, curses the Nora whose life she has saved, and the rueful Tommies, having killed that mother of one of their own, drink the tea she was keeping warm on her fender as they sing of their own home fires. That sequence of poignant images suggests both our potential community and the passionate blindness through which we destroy it. Both acting and witnessing the meaning of that sequence, we participate in a social unity that the characters cannot bring to consciousness.

Those strategies might be insufficient without a third: O'Casey's use of moments of group intoxication and entrancement that are as double-edged as the self-conscious theatricality of *Heartbreak House*. His characters are vulnerable to a gamut of inflated rhetoric and seductive song in the service of anger, eroticism, nostalgia, patriotism, and religion. Fine language and old tunes are powerful agents of human solidarity—and of self-deception and divisiveness. When used onstage they can therefore sweep us into ironically complicated versions of the characters' feelings. Reckless hyperbole and dancing rhythms are O'Casey specialties, his Dublin elaboration of the resource that Synge had explored in *The Playboy*. Here, in moments of low comedy, wry pathos, or savage irony, the intoxicating language makes us feel the force of those other intoxicants that drive it—Fluther's bibulous rage, the Covey's proletarian contempt, the Man's patriotism, Bessie's scriptural faith. Although this language mainly seduces those who use it, the songs work their magic on all who listen. Those in act 1 are tinged with ironies that distance us from the characters but not from their own lyric burdens. The Covey's renditions of "Dear harp of me counthry" (146) and "Oh, where's th' slave so lowly" (152) are means of taunting Peter, but we recall more poignant renditions. Jack's self-conscious if reluctant performance of "Th' violets were scenting th' woods, Nora" (155–56) means more to her than to him—and what it means to us is a function of that irony. And, when the Dublin Fusiliers sing "It's a long way to Tipperary" as they depart for the front to support the British, the political ironies do not cancel the nostalgia (159). In each instance the melodies evoke for us a harmony that is being denied. At the climax of act 2, when Rosie sings "I once had a lover, a tailor," as she marches the drunken Fluther offstage in counterpoint to Clitheroe's commands to the Dublin Battalion of the Irish Citizen Army, the song keeps us with the randy spirit of pub life even as it dramatizes its self-defeating intoxication (179). Act 4, reversing the those tactics, now employs song to lead us past the dramatized conflicts and acknowledged ironies into realms of feeling that we can more fully share. As Bessie tends Nora, she sings the poignant "Lead, kindly light, amid th' encircling gloom" (206–7). Then Nora sings an Ophelia-like reprise of Jack's song, "Th' violets were scenting th' woods, Nora" (214). As the action reaches its catastrophe, we hear from Bessie, who has now become the suffering protagonist, the climactic "I do believe, I will believe / That Jesus died for me" (216). And finally the British soldiers, nostalgically identifying themselves with the British civilians whom they have left behind, sing "Keep the 'owme fires burning / While your 'earts are yearning" (218). For us the pathos widens to include all who are caught up in a military conflict produced by their own obscure desires and vulnerabilities and beyond their understanding

Because our responses are more complex than the speakers or singers would understand, each verbal or musical flight asks us to feel the powerful emotions that can both separate us and bring us together. Through such entrancement, as through the visual organization and the patterning of complementary characters, *The Plough and the Stars* leads actors and witnesses into a lyric-ironic doubling of its action, allowing us to participate emotionally in the tragicomic Dublin dreamworld while keeping at bay its temptations to violence. We need not translate that sharing of feeling into explicit propositions about human community. Its experience in performance is itself an answer to heartbreak.

Clifford Odets's *Awake and Sing!* arrives at a very different way of setting forth a panorama of heartbreak that is transcended through our action of performance. There has been much debate over the ancestry of this play. For some the young Odets is an American Chekhov, for others an American O'Casey (Weales 77). But important distinctions need to be made in both directions. Although Odets's dialogue is often shaped from surface irrelevancies and subterranean connections, its tone, pace, and rhetorical strategies are entirely different from those in *The Cherry Orchard* or *Three Sisters*. Even when remarks seem oblique or out of the blue, they are sharp, vivid, rapid-fire, and often heightened by metaphor both colloquial and winningly fresh. The seeming irrelevancies result not from a shared evasion or withdrawal but from a habitual abrasiveness that does not wish, or dare, to recognize its object or admit the full meaning of its emotion. No doubt the Berger family, working-class with middle-class aspirations, recalls the counterpoint of economic frustrations, defensive tactics, and escapist desires in O'Casey's Dublin tenement. We see the domineering Bessie, whose insistence on control reflects her anxieties about the family's future; her passive husband, Myron (one of the more Chekhovian of these characters), who lives in his memories of the past; the passionate daughter Hennie, caught between defiance and fear, who is trapped into marriage with Sam

Feinschreiber but finally persuaded to go to Havana with the crippled racketeer Moe Axelrod; Uncle Morty, the successful businessman; the grandfather Jacob, a dreamer and talker whose prophetic but evasive conflations of his beloved Caruso ("Oh paradise on earth"), communist economics ("Marx said it—abolish such families"), and Isaiah ("Awake and sing, ye that dwell in dust") (51, 55, 83) can make him seem rather like a Jewish Shotover; and the rather unfocused son Ralph, who inherits Jacob's insurance and wants to have his own life. But these characters are caught in a tighter mesh of mutual relationships than those in *The Plough and the Stars* and are portrayed within one rather claustral fourth-wall set. Nor does Odets offer us anything like the rhetorical and lyric modes of intoxication or entrancement through which O'Casey brings us into the action.

Like both Chekhov and O'Casey, Odets can use melodramatic premises and solutions (Hennie's pregnancy and forced marriage, Jacob's suicide and insurance, Moe and Hennie's escape to Havana) that are effectively undercut by irony. Whatever Odets's conscious intentions in revising the last act of the play's earlier version, *I Got the Blues,* the terms in which Moe now imagines a Cuban paradise ("The whole world's green grass and when you cry it's because you're happy") and those in which Ralph now imagines his new maturity ("I want the whole city to hear it—fresh blood, arms. We got 'em") (99–101) inspire no greater confidence than Anya's "Fare thee well, old life!" and Trofimov's "Welcome, new life!" at the end of *The Cherry Orchard* (210). For the most part, however, *Awake and Sing!* does not condescend to the language of its characters. It can afford to let us take its closing gestures of hope (or, if you like, factitious political optimism) with some irony because the Bergers' language, with its habitual abrasiveness, displays an unquenchable vitality. That vitality seems for them an unconscious resource, often a weapon, in which they take little mutual comfort. They hardly appreciate one another's eloquence. But actors and audience can participate in their verbal skirmishes as in some delightful music. The digressions and non sequiturs are part of its texture. We relish such things as Bessie's "He opens his mouth and the whole Bronx could fall in" (55). And the pregnant Hennie's response to her mother's "Tell me what happened": "Brooklyn Bridge fell down" (53). And Hennie's response to Sam's "Why should you act this way?": "Cause there's no bones in ice cream" (91). We delight also in Moe's articulation of his fury: "What the hell kind of house is this it ain't got an orange" (58). And in his colloquial encouragement of Ralph: "I wouldn't trade you for two pitchers and an outfielder" (101). Most important, we recognize—as the characters themselves apparently do not—the intrinsically social nature of such language.

It was Odets's theatrically heightened version of Bronx English that most impressed Alfred Kazin on the occasion of the first performance:

> How interesting we all were, how vivid and strong on the beat of that style! Words could do it . . . Sitting in the Belasco, watching my mother and father and uncles and aunts occupying the stage in *Awake and Sing* by as much right as if they were Hamlet and Lear, I understood at last. It was all one, as I had always known. Art and truth and hope could yet come together—if a real writer was their meeting place . . . The excitement in the theater was instant proof that if a *writer* occupied it, the audience felt joy as a rush of power. (81–82)

That tribute and Gerald Weales's detailed analysis of the "happy surprise" given us by the play's idiom and metaphor point toward the most important aspect of its participatory meaning (80–82).

A shared linguistic vitality is the key to Odets's version of the Chekhovian paradigm of acting and witnessing. The play's real answer to heartbreak resides not in its forced and ironic conclusion but in the buoyancy of its discourse. Margaret Brenman-Gibson has shown that *Awake and Sing!* was most deeply for Odets not a play about a struggle for life amid petty conditions (as his later notes formulated its spine) but a "family play" that puts onstage his internal "gallery of characters" (249). Its impact "derives not from its social protest . . . but from the potency of spirit in its people" (259). But the primary manifestation of that potency of spirit is surely a creative language to which actors and audience bring a conscious appreciation that the characters do not. Weales has remarked that the Group Theatre, for whom the play was written, "was a family of sorts for Odets" (78)— but, in fact, the extended family of *Awake and Sing!* consists of all those who participate in its performance and so in its language. That is true even if we do not have Kazin's upbringing or Odets's, Clurman's, and Carnovsky's relations to the Group. The play's events suggest no real solution to the Bergers' economic or familial problems, but its expressive utterance is for us just such a solution, a participation in shared linguistic creativity. We experience that solution, with a delighted awareness for which the hard-pressed and often heartbroken characters quite literally find no time, whenever a performance of *Awake and Sing!* invites us to join in its familial celebration.

IV

What happens to the Chekhovian paradigm when the playwright simplifies the contrapuntal texture, or heightens verisimilitude, or emphasizes negative aspects of the dramatic situation and seems therefore to provide no ready stylistic means through which the community of performance may transcend heartbreak? The depicted panorama may then evoke a sharper irony, an ambiguous poignancy, or a wry nostalgia. And we must look more attentively to the performance itself for assurance of a vitality that somehow responds to that predicament.

The Autumn Garden, which Brooks Atkinson described in his opening night review as "boneless and torpid" (Rollyson 308), is probably Hellman's strongest play. In 1960 Marvin Felheim would call it the most "completely Chekhovian" play in the American theater (191). And, indeed, *Autumn Garden* recalls Chekhov's *Platonov* in several respects. Here Hellman moved beyond her usual Ibsenite and melodramatic plotting to engage an array of middle-aged characters, summer guests in a house on the Gulf of Mexico in 1949, who find that they have frittered away their lives. The play's tonal ambiguity and detachment from its characters have invited a range of interpretations, from Felheim's reading of it as a "modern tragedy" to Katherine Lederer's response that it is a "serious comedy." (Stanislavsky and Chekhov, we may recall, had similar arguments about genre.) The play's first director, Harold Clurman, who in rehearsal often found himself debating Hellman on matters of detail (Rollyson 303–5), described its tone as "unsentimentally expressed *regret*" (Clurman 197). He told Hellman that, "while the whole tenor of her play was an ironical presentation of its characters, she had not made them as 'forgivable' as they might be," pointing out that "though Chekhov's characters were often foolish and feckless, one ended by loving them." "True," retorted Hellman, "but I'm not as good as Chekhov" (50). Unconvinced by that retort, Clurman wrote in the *New Republic:* "She will not embrace her people. She does not believe they deserve her (or our) love. Love is present only through the ache of its absence. Miss Hellman is a fine artist; she will be a finer one when she melts" (qtd. in Wright 238). Lee Strasberg later suggested, however, that the "inherent humaneness of the characters" might have been brought out in performance by a more "Chekhovian" environment than Clurman's production had offered, with a setting open enough "to permit action to go on while other people were speaking, and thus to create a kind of symphonic orchestration of the behavior and attitudes of the people" (19). Although Clurman thought Hellman would not have accepted a different set (47), Strasberg was surely right. Arvin Brown's revival of the play in 1976 on the arena stage of the Long Wharf Theatre made that clear. Praising the production for its fresh recognition of the "qualities" and "nuances" of *The Autumn Garden,* Walter Kerr said the play "emerges, at long last, as one of Miss Hellman's very best" (qtd. in Lederer 89).

In order to evoke our sense of potential community-life, Hellman's crisply ironic style must rely a great deal upon what Barker had discovered in Moscow—"how much actors *could* add to a play." The older characters—Mrs. Ellis, her daughter Carrie, General Griggs, his wife Rose, Constance Tuckerman, the failed artist Nick Denery (who had jilted Constance years ago for a wealthy woman), Nina Denery (who repeatedly rescues Nick after each bout of obsessive philandering), and Edward Crossman (for whose declaration of love Constance has been waiting, much as Chekhov's Varya awaits a declaration from Lopakhin)—all move toward the conclusion that it is now too late to change habitual patterns that have long been ignored or disguised. The painful "heart trouble" that Rose has refused to acknowledge for fifteen years constitutes one metaphor for the play's many "denials" of continuing heartbreak (540). (Other metaphors may be found in Nick's insistence on painting a second portrait of Constance to demonstrate his and her maturity, in Constance's failure to speak to Crossman of her feelings, and in his refusal to admit that his alcoholic silence has contributed to her predicament.) Griggs finally articulates—in a speech that Clurman asked Hellman to write (Lederer 76–77) and that Dashiell Hammett finally licked into shape for her (Rollyson 299–301)—what seems to be the shared recognition toward which these characters variously move: "So at any given moment you're only the sum of your life up to then. There are no big moments you can reach unless you've a pile of smaller moments to stand on. That big hour of decision, the turning point in your life, the someday you've counted on when you'd suddenly wipe out your past mistakes, do the work you'd never done, think the way you'd never thought, have what you'd never had—it just doesn't come suddenly. You've trained yourself for it while you waited—or you've let it all run past you and frittered yourself away. I've frittered myself away, Crossman" (542–43).

Hellman insisted, however, that the play was not "meant to say that people can't do anything about" their lives. "It is meant to say the opposite—they can do a great deal with their lives . . . I don't like cheerless plays" (qtd. in Lederer 77). As she knew, Chekhov had made similar comments.

Their validation always requires that the performance itself generate in its actors and witnesses a sense that we remain in touch with some potentiality for fresh decisive action and some basis for genuine community. We see the potentiality for action, of course, in the dénouement of the characteristic Hellman plot that emerges from this panorama, as Sophie Tuckerman breaks off her engagement with Frederick Ellis and "blackmails" Nick because of his sexual aggression. (In a parallel but lesser movement Frederick breaks off his ambiguous attachment to Mr. Payson, an offstage figure of dubious morals whose interest in him has turned out to be merely pecuniary.) But any more general optimism must rely upon the performance. Given a sufficiently Chekhovian production, as at Long Wharf, Sophie's realism and determination will be complemented by our own sympathetic inhabiting of the panorama of more blocked or self-blocking characters. The play's ironists—Mrs. Ellis, Crossman, and Briggs—provide a negative critique of wasted lives. But our shared action of performance opens a way out from that blockage, enacting for the moment a community that those characters have refused to imagine.

Only in that play did Hellman approach the Chekhovian paradigm for which David Storey has had a more natural affinity. *The Contractor, The Changing Room,* and *The Farm,* as William Hutchings has said, constitute "in effect if not by design, a late flowering of the Chekhovian tradition" (*The Plays of David Storey* 3). And even *Home,* which Hutchings relates to Beckett rather than Chekhov, is a remarkable instance of this paradigm. Storey takes Chekhovian qualities toward an extreme that renders them nearly invisible. *The Contractor* and *The Changing Room,* as Hutchings has noted, give us what Allott in Storey's *Life Class* will call "invisible events." As in Chekhov's plays of indirect action, the obviously significant events occur before the play begins or between the acts. In *The Contractor* we do not see the wedding of Ewbank's daughter or the actions that have shaped the lives of his family, his foreman Kay, and his various workmen. The performance focuses on the routine construction and dismantling of the large and beautiful tent that the contractor has ordered (from himself) for that occasion and on the random but characteristic interactions of those involved in, or tangential to, this labor. (In *The Changing Room* the action will undergo a further reduction—to the routine of "changing" before, during, and after a Rugby game.) But the real significance of the onstage event is itself virtually "invisible." As Hutchings argues (165–80), the erecting of the tent, the collaborative routine of work, constitutes a kind of secular ritual that provides a temporary but repeatable social bond for an otherwise fragmented microcosm of English society—a tenuous bond, no doubt, but one that is firmer than the Ewbank family ties or the marriage bonds that are celebrated between the acts. Although the play concludes with what Hutchings calls a "prevailing tone of melancholy" (179), it seems to celebrate a ritualized version of the "work" for which the characters in *Three Sisters* and *The Cherry Orchard* often yearn.

The Chekhovian invisibilities, however, are more comprehensive than Hutchings's account suggests. This is a panorama of heartbreak more systematically evaded, more deeply repressed, than that in *The Autumn Garden*. Despite the appearance of social bonding, as William Free has noted in "Space, Language, and Action in *The Contractor*," the Ewbank family and the workmen persistently refuse to confront the missteps and failures, the alienations from any possible community, that are evident in their jokes, irascibilities, and moments of regret (Hutchings, *David Storey* 205–10). Ewbank's family seems to be breaking up; his university-educated son is a drifter; his daughter and her aristocratic fiancé are probably heading for trouble. The foreman Kay has a criminal record; the workmen lack faith in marriage or education—and the only one "that doesn't hold a grudge" is a stammering mental defective (*Plays: One* 40). Ewbank says bitterly that he employs "anybody"—"Miners who've coughed their lungs up, fitters who've lost their fingers, madmen who've run away from home" (30–31). The play's main event, moreover, as Lois More Overbeck has noted in "What It Is to Be a Woman' in the Plays of David Storey," must leave all the parties with a sense of relative emptiness and futility (Hutchings, *David Storey* 144–46). Ewbank describes to Kay his reaction upon seeing the tent reduced to a shambles by the riotous celebration: "I came out here, you know, this morning . . . Saw it all . . . Damn near broke my bloody heart." And he implicitly extends that observation to cover the events of his own life and that of his family. "A lot of bloody misfits. You could put us all into a string bag, you know, and chuck us all away, and none'd be the wiser" (Storey, *Plays: One* 105, 106). From that point of view the construction and destruction of the tent sum up a pattern of futility. We can understand why Storey, looking back on this play and others from the vantage point of 1983, should call them "plays of despair" (Hutchings, *Plays of David Storey* 129). The detailed texture of *The Contractor,* its pattern of reactions and evasions, points to a pervasive condition of isolation, aimlessness, and heartbreak for which the Chekhovian ritual of "work" seems at best a temporary palliative.

This play offers, nevertheless, a fuller answer to heartbreak, by means of other Chekhovian qualities that Storey has rendered nearly invisible. *The*

Contractor, like *The Changing Room,* is no naturalistic slice of life but an example of what Storey has called his "poetic naturalism" (*Plays of David Storey* 3). Lindsay Anderson, Storey's major director, has commented on a complex "choreographic element" that must integrate action and dialogue. "The action-scenario is rather like the pretext of a ballet" (*David Storey* 10, 15–16). In other ways, too, this script is a score for a delicate Chekhovian music of performance. Its verbal texture, replete with echo effects in the banter of Marshall and Fitzmaurice and the stammering of Glendenning, often recalls the more antiphonal passages in *Waiting for Godot.* It can support a semilyrical tone even when the meanings conveyed are laced with bitterness or aggression. Our participation in this verbal and physical music of performance therefore doubles, in an affirmative key, the erecting and dismantling of the tent that Ewbank has ordered from himself. (And, of course, it more obviously doubles the game that is the main offstage event of *The Changing Room.*) The acting ensemble and the audience come together in a theatrical ritual more richly insightful and satisfying than the ritual of work that they are miming. Storey himself in recent years seems to have appreciated this tacit answer to heartbreak more than his comments of 1983 would suggest. Participation in rituals of shared performance has become the explicit subject of his plays of 1992, *Stages* and *Caring,* which were provoked by his reflections upon the lifelong process of "negotiating roles we would like to have ourselves as well as those by which we would like to be surrounded." It is a process, he says, to which "mutual regard" is integral: "if I love you will you love me?" And he recalls how, as a nine-year-old boy, he "had watched sceptically one character on a stage at the Grand Theatre in Leeds 'pretending' to search for another—unready, at that age, to accede to the scenario being offered—but now, a lifetime later, acceding to little else—and, in the theatre in general, and in these plays in particular, inviting everyone out there to join him" (*Plays: One* xii).

In Storey's *Home,* which approaches the more claustral "playing hell" of Beckett and Pinter, these elements of the Chekhovian paradigm of acting and witnessing are nearly invisible. The set: four metal garden chairs and a table. The panorama: five characters who come to stand for others within their "home" and, indeed, for all of us beyond its imagined walls. The onstage action is here more fragmented, the community more precarious, for Chekhovian self-absorption has become an alienation that we gradually conclude must be pathological. Conversation results from physical propinquity, random or devious mental associations, and the slithers of obsessive role-playing. The middle-class Harry and Jack, who disingenuously evade questions of sexual behavior, sustain an eerily genteel manner. They ride what Richard Dutton has called a "fine line between polite but aimless conversation and a tacit game of verbal chess, with every feint matched by an appropriate challenge, though neither player feels confident enough to launch a forthright attack" (153). Their little fictions, their probes and defenses, anticipate the more aggressive duels of Spooner and Hirst in Pinter's *No Man's Land.* Kathleen and Marjorie, on the other hand, are working-class Cockneys immersed in bodily pains and desires and in salacious gossip, who send the talk lurching into the rough, bawdy, and blasphemous. And the monosyllabic and probably lobotomized Alfred, who plays a kind of Lucky to these naturalized and doubled echoes of Beckett's Vladimir and Estragon, expresses his feelings through acrobatic and ritualized struggles with chairs and a table.

Home has been called by Carol Rosen "a theatrical dead end," "a play about listless people who no longer want things to happen," "a study of psychic hibernation" (135). But her often sympathetic account, which amply recognizes the wider reverberations of Storey's symbolic naturalism, abstracts from a remarkably dynamic play its surface passivity, "a seemingly neutral environment that is, finally, a void," "an image of human despair" (137, 143). Such formulations miss the fact that these people very much want things to happen—and fear their happening. They also miss the fact that, in a variety of ways, our participation in their despair must alter its meaning. We gradually attune ourselves to a subtext of heartbreak—the sexual proclivities, uncontrollable aggressions, emotional failures, and inexplicable losses that have brought these people to a home away from home that may be an asylum but seems more like Britain or the world. Beneath an utterance that veers away from specific problems, they are responding with a kind of locked interior struggle to their failure, helplessness, panic, and paralysis. Tears are never far below the surface of the often amusing and even quite lyrical dialogue, which repeatedly gestures toward our more comprehensive stage.

Late in the play their literal and psychological twilight becomes that of "this little island," England itself:

> *Jack:* Empire the like of which no one has ever seen.
> *Harry:* No. My word.
> *Jack:* Light of the world.
> *Harry:* Oh, yes.
>
> (*Plays: One* 173)

And very soon Jack will suggest that their shared burden has cosmic import:

> *Harry:* See the church.
> (*They gaze off.*)
> *Jack:* Shouldn't wonder He's disappointed. (*Looks up.*)
> *Harry:* Oh, yes.
> *Jack:* Heart-break.
> *Harry:* Oh, yes.
> *Jack:* Same mistake . . . won't make it twice.
> *Harry:* Oh, no.
> *Jack:* Once over. Never again.
>
> (175)

A moment later they are quietly weeping.

Storey has resisted the notion that *Home* is "about a nuthouse," for that is "not the material of the play itself and to say it's a mental home is a way of distancing the critics and audience from the play. It sets you away from the emotion, from the suffering, whereas the characters, I would think, are what you might see in the street any day. I mean they really are with us, rather than apart from us" (Hutchings, *Plays of David Storey* 119). Indeed, what is insanity? These characters are certainly with us, and yet a performance of *Home* enables us to transcend their heartbreak. We take our cues from their oblique and muted caring for each other, from our less restricted ability to empathize and understand, and from the richly antiphonal qualities of Storey's poetic and echoing dialogue. What the characters will not or cannot express becomes amply articulated in our shared performance. As we act and witness encounters built from refusals to encounter, listen to revelations that never quite reveal, and delight in incongruities and analogies to which the characters remain oblivious, we transform their world from the inside. Although the dominant tone is the pathos of centers of consciousness closed in upon some frightened reduction of themselves, the music of performance allows us to participate in that condition with an awareness of the harmonies that link these predicaments. As an extreme version of the Chekhovian paradigm, *Home* invites us to inhabit and so transform a pathological community that offers a hyperbolic image of ourselves.

Very different from Storey's condensation of Chekhovian strategies is Machado's expansion of them into an epic and nostalgic tetralogy on revolution and family displacement. *The Floating Island Plays,* which trace the history of the Ripoll, Hernandez, and Marquez families over three generations, translate Lyubov Ranevskaya's loss of her beloved cherry orchard into their loss of the Cuban homeland. Set in 1928 and 1930, *The Modern Ladies of Guanabacoa* (1984) shows middle-class manners, business, and politics in transition. It focuses on the Ripoll family, whose daughter Manuela will marry the young entrepreneur Oscar Hernandez, a character apparently based on Machado's grandfather of the same name. *Fabiola* (1985), which moves from 1955 to 1967, deals with more catastrophic changes encountered by the upper-class Marquez family into which Oscar's daughter Sonia has now married. *In the Eye of the Hurricane* (1989), set in 1960, depicts Oscar's encounter with the revolution and the resulting family betrayals and business disaster. And *Broken Eggs* (1984) picks up the story of Sonia, her mother, Manuela; her children, Oscar, Lizette, and Mimi; her ex-husband, Osvaldo; his sister, Miriam; and their father, Alfredo, on the occasion of Lizette's marriage in 1979 at a country club in a Los Angeles suburb.

Perhaps the most powerful rendering of familial and political disintegration occurs in *Fabiola,* in which the ghostly presence of the title character, Pedro Marquez's dead wife, becomes a haunting image of a lost Cuba, and a hidden corruption overcomes the delights of sensuality and revolution. In act 1, as Pedro carries on a sexual affair with his younger brother Osvaldo, Sonia's husband, she rejoices in Castro's victory and the departure of Batista. "Now we will be free," says Pedro's mother, Cusa (79). By the latter part of act 2, however, after the Bay of Pigs, Osvaldo has escaped to Miami Beach with their baby son, Oscar, and Sonia is planning to follow him. Cusa has learned to say, "Fidel wants a country where we don't belong" (101). Pedro has sunk into alcoholism, and he commits suicide as the Castro *milicianos* evict the family from their home. But the previously written sequel, *Broken Eggs,* is of greater interest here. As it depicts the exiled family members still locked in quasi-incestuous relations of love and hate, it offers a bitterly nostalgic version of the Chekhovian paradigm of acting and witnessing.

During a January day, in a waiting room off the country club's main ballroom, we observe the members of the partially sundered family as they take part in a wedding celebration suffused with resentment, mutual accusations, and longing for their Cuban home. Eliding the wedding itself (as in Storey's *The Contractor*), the two acts move from uneasy preparations, reencounters, and reminiscences to more violent arguments, final breaks, recriminations, and a nostalgic close. The morning events of act 1 include Mimi's disclosure of her pregnancy; Osvaldo's attempt to maintain a romantic relation with Sonia, who still loves him, while yielding to the whims of his new Argentine wife; and a violent confrontation, with mutual accusations of homosexuality, between Osvaldo and Oscar. The disillusioned Oscar, who will gradually become the main reflector of the action, is sent by Sonia to tell the Argentine that Osvaldo is posing for a portrait with "his past family." Returning to the now empty stage, he offers this assessment: "The family portrait? This family . . . My family. The Father, Jesus Christ his only son and the Holy Ghost (*Crossing himself*) . . . why the *fuck* did you send me to this family" (194).

In act 2, as an offstage orchestra plays in the ballroom, the afternoon events heighten our sense of lives that continue halfheartedly in the present while still anchored in the past. To Osvaldo's passionate kiss Sonia responds:

> *Sonia:* Dance with me. Tell them to play a danzón.
> *Osvaldo:* Let's dance in here.
> *Sonia:* She'll get angry? It's our daughter's wedding.
> *Osvaldo:* She's my wife.
> *Sonia:* I was first.
> *Osvaldo:* You're both my wife.
>
> (196)

Miriam, after making a phone call to Cuba, says, "I sometimes think that I live at the same time there as here. That I left a dual spirit there . . . A while ago I looked out at the dance floor and I thought I was in the ballroom back home" (198). Reminiscences of love, revolution, and death lead toward a climax in which Osvaldo finally breaks away from Sonia ("I'm starting fresh. You should too"). She agrees ("I should, yes, I should") but insists on one last toast for the bride, giving him then a drink to which she has added Manuela's recipe to produce diarrhea. Oscar and Miriam recognize that they too are addicted to "revenge." And the revenge may be a drug. "Everyone in this family's got a drug," says Miriam, and she gives Sonia some of her valium—a ticket back to Varadero Beach. Miriam retreats dreamily into the past as Oscar, now in the offstage ballroom, sings over the microphone the haunting "Isla."

> En una isla
> Lejos de aquí
> Dejé
> La vida mía
> Madre mía
> Isla mía

Sonia, however, resists that retreat: "Sonia is not coming back. Cojimar, Sonia will never be back." And, in a final gesture toward the future, she accepts Mimi's invitation to dance to Oscar's song (214–18).

This bitter, nostalgic, and tenuously optimistic panorama opens out for us with greater specification, of course, if we recall the other three plays and so share more fully the characters' memories. It may be yet more suggestive if we recognize in Oscar a quasi-autobiographical figure and see the parallel, quite strong in the closing drug-induced retreats, with Eugene O'Neill's transformation of Chekhovian and Ibsenite paradigms into a family tragedy of mutual recrimination, *Long Day's Journey into Night.* But *Broken Eggs* has its own integrity. With faster pace and more emotional violence than Chekhov would allow, it invites us to share a gamut of overlapping and highly ambiguous objectives: to return and yet escape, to cling and yet take revenge, to evade the truth and yet recognize it, to repeat the past and yet start afresh. The reveries, the song, and the dancing of the closing moments recapitulate that music of ambivalence. Helped by what the actors bring to that music, we can reach an understanding beyond the awareness of any character—except, perhaps, the tacit awareness of an Oscar who has yet to write the play.

V

What happens when the playwright approximates this paradigm, with its community of heartbreak and its responding community of performance, but blends it with other paradigms or reverses its import? This has occurred in an extraordinary range of plays, from Tennessee Williams's *The Notebook of Trigorin* (1980–83), a free adaptation of *The Sea Gull* that gives poetic voice to Chekhov's buried conflicts, to yet more extreme departures.

Some, of course, remain fairly close to the main Chekhovian stream even when under the influence of Tennessee Williams. Like *Broken Eggs,* Lanford Wilson's *Fifth of July* (1978–79) first appeared as the anticipatory sequel of a family saga—one that includes *Talley's Folly* (1979), *Talley & Son* (1980–86), and plans for at least one other play (Zinman 17). Wilson, whom Mel Gussow has called "one of the most Chekhovian of American playwrights" (Barnett 138), has given us a conversational and lyrical translation of *Three Sisters* (1984) and has more recently been working on *Uncle Vanya.* His director and collaborator through many years, Marshall W. Mason, has sought onstage an American version of Chekhovian conversation. Comparing the task of his Circle Repertory Company to that of Stanislavsky and the Moscow Art Theater, Mason said that his actors know that Wilson "doesn't want the line to be played 'on the line.'" They "have developed an approach to the work that is very useful for doing Lanford's plays, which is, in the acting style, glancing instead of direct, so that the play can be more bold and stand on its own" (Williams 118, 119). Although James Martine has described *Fifth of July* as a bad play written under the sway of Tennessee Williams (Bryer 49), this is surely Wilson's most Chekhovian play—and perhaps one of his best. The pattern of characters, the intercutting of digressive conversations, and the specific issues suggest a transposition of *The Cherry Orchard* and Hellman's *The Autumn Garden* into the rural Missouri of 1977. And yet *Fifth of July* quite systematically reverses the Chekhovian paradigm.

Ted Talley, an English teacher who lost his legs in Vietnam and now cannot quite face a job at the local high school, plans to sell the small farm that he inherited and on which he lives with his lover, Jed Jenkins, a passionate horticulturalist who has rediscovered a "lost" variety of English rose and has been planting a formal garden that will require twenty years in which to mature. In the present action Jed will quietly step in to assist Ted at crucial moments. Reworking Lyubov Ranevskaya's situation to include reminiscences of the 1960s, Wilson presents a homosexual relationship more sustaining than Frederick Ellis's ambiguous attachment to Mr. Payson in *The Autumn Garden*. As Philip Middleton Williams has noted in his study of the revisions made by Wilson and Mason (49–58), in *5th of July* (the version of 1978) that relationship gradually emerges to view, but in the revised and retitled text it is established from the outset, with a kiss, as the center of the play. Wilson has wryly observed that, though his "realistic view" of a "gay relationship" might lead one to consider this "the ultimate gay play," a published catalogue of such plays omitted it because homosexuality is "so not a problem in the play that it's really not a gay play at all" (Williams 148).

The prospective purchasers of Ted's house and land are two friends from the 1960s who seem always on the go, the devious John Landis—whom Ted had once loved—and his rich wife, Gwen. In some respects John is a darker version of Lopakhin, but this pair is also an updating of those obsessive travelers, the devious Nick Denery, who had jilted Constance, and his rich wife, Nina. Late in the play Ted discovers that John had betrayed him years ago, when he thought to evade the draft, by leaving him behind when he went to Europe with Gwen. (As in *The Autumn Garden*, several of the characters must confront information about themselves or others that has been hidden or suppressed.) Gwen, who wants to become a country music star, and Weston Hurley, her guitarist, are also American versions of Chekhov's flamboyant image of rootlessness and emotional isolation, the entertainer Charlotta—with a touch of Gayev's chronic disconnection, perhaps, in Weston. The fourth member of Ted's 1960s group is his resentful sister June, another erstwhile lover of John Landis, who has refused to acknowledge that he fathered her vivacious fourteen-year-old daughter, Shirley. In effect, Wilson here reworks both the abandoned Constance and her niece Sophie, from *The Autumn Garden,* into post–1960s versions of Varya and Anya. (More articulate than either, Shirley also echoes the naive idealism of Trofimov—but with the justification of adolescent verve.) The prime agent in the Chekhovian plot is Ted's aunt, Sally (Talley) Friedman, an eccentric but shrewd woman who has planned to move to a retirement home in California after scattering the ashes of her late husband Matt in the nearby river. At different moments her behavior recalls both Hellman's ironic commentator, Mrs. Ellis, and Chekhov's amusingly preoccupied Firs. But, after surviving a mild stroke and deciding to scatter Matt's ashes over the farm, she reverses Lopakhin's coup in *The Cherry Orchard* by bidding successfully for the property against John and Gwen Landis and so keeping it in Talley hands.

Through those transpositions and reversals the play reverses the ambiguous or bleak expectations of Chekhov and Hellman. Jed will keep his garden; Ted will accept his past, conquer his fears, and resume his vocation as a high school teacher; and Sally will remain in Missouri. Only Shirley, prevented by her mother from going with John and Gwen to Nashville, is brought to tears. But she bounces back with an élan both touching and amusing:

> *Shirley:* I don't care. The important thing is to find your vocation and work like hell at it . . . You do realize, though, the terrible burden.
> *Ken:* How's that?
> *Shirley:* I am the last of the Talleys. And the whole family has just come to nothing at all so far. Fortunately, it's on my shoulders . . . I won't fail us.
>
> (*Fifth of July* 75)

Those lines, as Gene Barnett has noted (115), evoke Sonya's "courageous speech" at the end of *Uncle Vanya:* "We shall work for the sake of others, now and when we are old, never knowing peace or rest" (*Anton Chekhov's*

Plays 95). But Shirley is far from Sonya's pathetic reiterations, and the difference in tone amounts to a comic reversal of Chekhov's finale.

Fifth of July accords with Wilson's vow of 1970 to abandon the "easy" pessimism of his early plays: "To be solidly optimistic and find moments of hope and reason to live is more difficult" (Williams 31). That note becomes explicit when Ted reads aloud from the science fiction being tape-recorded by his brilliant but pathologically shy student, Johnny Young: "After they had explored all the suns in the universe, and all the planets of all the suns, they realized that there was no other life in the universe, and that they were alone. And they were very happy, because then they knew it was up to them to become all the things they had imagined they would find" (74). Wilson himself, shy about the obvious and preferring a Chekhovian obliqueness, included those sentences only when urged by Mason to do so (Williams 118). Implicitly, however, the buoyant dialogue everywhere in *Fifth of July*—especially when given the "glancing" interpretation on which Mason has insisted—has already enacted an answer to heartbreak. Ted's self-ironic wit, Aunt Sally's eccentricities and good sense, Gwen's hyper-loquacity, Weston's hip naïveté, and the many absurd conversational collisions offer a playfulness that transcends from the outset the temporary blockage and pain. We inhabit with sympathy or amusement all the characters in this Chekhovian reversal of Chekhov. But our most serious onstage representative—and also the representative, no doubt, of the playwright-horticulturalist, whose avocation will provide material for the later short play, *A Betrothal* (Barnett 138)—is the taciturn, loving, and rather acerbic Jed, the observer as player, who has found his own double vocation and will continue to tend the gardens for which he has accepted responsibility.

More profoundly Chekhovian, and yet more innovative, is the work of Brian Friel, whom Richard Pine has called the "Irish Chekhov" (1). *Living Quarters* (1977), *Aristocrats* (1979), and *Translations* (1980) have made various use of Chekhov's themes and dramaturgy. (As Alan Peacock has noted [116–19], *Living Quarters* also revises Euripides' *Hippolytus*.) Friel has more recently translated and adapted *Three Sisters* (1981) and written a Chekhovian adaptation of Turgenev's novel *Fathers and Sons*. Richard York in "Friel's Russia" has summarized the traits shared by *Aristocrats* and *Three Sisters:* desultory conversation, bleak monologues, echoing recurrence of obsessive subjects, moments of half-understood intensity, and emotions that unpredictably rise to consciousness and expression (164). Those traits also enter *Dancing at Lughnasa* (1990), a play that nonetheless radically transforms the Chekhovian paradigm of acting and witnessing—in part by crossing it with Williams's *The Glass Menagerie* and Synge's *The Playboy of the Western World*.

Dancing at Lughnasa depicts the five Mundy sisters of Ballybeg—Kate, Maggie, Rose, Agnes, and Chris—who are coping with loneliness, unemployment, the idiosyncrasies of their brother Jack (an ailing and disoriented missionary priest who has been converted to pagan ways by his Ugandan servant and parishioners), the seduction of Chris by Gerry Evans, who has a legal wife and child in Wales, and the seduction of the simple Rose by the offstage Danny Bradley, who leads her back in the hills. This bleak cottage panorama, with its signs of suppressed vitality, is recalled by an autobiographical narrator who, like Tom Wingfield in *The Glass Menagerie,* frames the story and also plays himself. Tom offers us a guilt-laden reminiscence of his sister Laura, who has been abandoned by her father, by the Gentleman Caller, and by Tom himself. Friel's Michael, the son of Chris Mundy and Gerry Evans, leads us into the story of the five sisters from a greater historical and moral distance. Both narrators dwell on historical contexts that seem at first to be major themes—the wartime 1940s in the United States, the depressed 1930s in Ireland—but that soon yield in importance to family relationships and more broadly psychological and symbolic issues. The Mundy sisters, however, whose stolid inhibition, suppressed desire, and gutsy determination elicit admiration and amusement as well as sympathy, have less in common with Laura Wingfield than with Synge's tough-minded, lyrical, and poignantly abandoned Pegeen. As in *The Playboy,* our response to the women's predicament is complicated and partly transcended by an uneasy delight in histrionic male behavior. *Dancing at Lughnasa* selects three forms of role-playing from the tonal and archetypal richness of Christy Mahon. Gerry Evans is the fast-talking, fast-dancing, rootless seducer whose blarney can repeatedly win a woman's heart against her better judgment. Father Jack is the demented transgressor of cultural norms, the joyful participator in polygamy and ceremony, the ironic representative of a quasimythical realm (a leper colony whose traits are borrowed, as Pine has noted, from Victor Turner's Ndembu [227]) that offers a critique of Ireland's repression and stagnation but retains its most disturbing social illness: a pattern of male dominance and evasion. And the narrator Michael embodies an elegiac and exploratory playing that reaches out to us in its effort to overcome the loneliness and loss of the past in a present celebration. That third kind of histrionic behavior may be hard to glimpse on the page. According to Friel's stage directions, the seven-year-old Michael is an invisible presence, and his lines are spoken by the adult Michael, standing to one side, "in his ordinary narrator's voice" (7). But in diction, syntax, and cadence, those lines are clearly a child's—and Gerard McSorley, who played the role in Patrick Mason's production for the Abbey Theatre, appropriately gave an adult version of a child's voice. The forceful but understated effect was a Brechtian "third-person" rendering of the character, by another character who is simultaneously playwright, actor, and audience. Through strategies more complex than those used in the creation of Williams's Tom or Wilson's Jed, Friel here dramatizes the dimensions of our shared playing.

The most original aspect of Friel's play is its half-passionate, half-ironic commitment to the nonverbal and the ceremonial. In Father Jack that commitment takes the form of amnesia, near-dementia, and obsessive behavior. He has forgotten much of his English—including the word *ceremony* itself.

> *Jack:* Ceremony! That's the word! How could I have forgotten that? The offering, the ritual, the dancing—a ceremony! . . .Coming back in the boat there were days when I couldn't remember even the simplest words. Not that anybody seemed to notice. And you can always point, Margaret, can't you?
> *Maggie:* Or make signs.
> *Jack:* Or make signs.
> *Maggie:* Or dance.
>
> (40)

Dance has already erupted among the sisters, provoked by an intermittently operating radio and thoughts of the festival of Lughnasa—a contagious nonverbal language that gave voice to a suppressed subtext: the defiance, sensuousness, grace, and chthonic vitality smothered by their daily existence (21–22). At the end of act 1, as Michael recounts what would soon happen to Jack, and to Rose and Agnes, Jack beats out a tattoo on the boy's kite sticks and begins a shuffling dance. Michael then recalls the "ritual circles" in which his parents danced—"No singing, no melody, no words"—before Gerry went off to fight with the International Brigade (42). In act 2, just after the bloody death of Rose's pet rooster, Jack will stage an elaborate ritual in which he exchanges his plumed tricorn hat for Gerry Evans's straw hat, whereupon Gerry does a Chaplin walk across the garden, singing a snatch from Cole Porter's "Anything Goes" (68–69). The rituals of animal sacrifice and masculine exchange are inseparable here from their degradations, even as the celebratory dancing and the community activity up in the hills—fires, the sacrifice of a goat, a boy badly burned, a woman seduced—

suggest pathetic remnants of fertility rituals that might have been found in the pagan festival of Lughnasa before it was denatured by Irish Christianity.

The play's ambivalence toward the nonverbal and the ceremonial involves a tension between the Dionysian and the ironic that is central to Euripides' *The Bacchae* and that haunts *The Playboy* as well as Williams's *Orpheus Descending* and *Suddenly Last Summer.* Michael's final speech sums up his ironic nostalgia, the pain of what is recalled and the transcendence of that pain, in the image of dancing to "a dream music that is both heard and imagined":

> Dancing as if language had surrendered to movement—as if this ritual, this wordless ceremony, was now the way to speak, to whisper private and sacred things, to be in touch with some otherness. Dancing as if the very heart of life and all its hopes might be found in those assuaging notes and those hushed rhythms and in those silent and hypnotic movements. Dancing as if language no longer existed because words were no longer necessary. (71)

Even as Shirley's closing speech in *Fifth of July* reversed that of Sonya in *Uncle Vanya,* so Michael's closing speech more subtly transposes that of Olga in *Three Sisters.* Friel had already translated Olga's "as ifs" in these words:

> Just listen to that music. It's so assured, so courageous. It makes you want to go on, doesn't it? . . . Yes, of course we will die and be forgotten—everything about us, how we looked, how we spoke, that there were three of us. But our unhappiness, our suffering, won't be wasted. They're a preliminary to better times, and because of them the people who come after us will inherit a better life—a life of peace and content and happiness. And they will look on us with gratitude and with love. But our life isn't over yet. By no means! We are going to go on living! And that music is so confident, so courageous, it almost seems as if it is about to be revealed very soon why we are alive and what our suffering is for. If only we knew that. If only we knew that. (113–14)

Michael now invites us to join him in becoming Olga's "they," a later generation that may remember five sisters. Although less content than Olga imagines us, more chastened by reality, we can also enter more fully into this music, which is not the paradoxically cheering air of a departing military band but haunting strains, half-remembered and half-imagined on the edge of silence, that express the otherwise inarticulate heart of life itself. And yet for us, as for Olga, the meaning of those visionary strains is no more than partly revealed. *Dancing at Lughnasa* has led us into a theatrical music that seems on the edge of such remembered dancing and its chthonic prototype, a music that speaks to us and within us of heartbreak and its healing.

Friel's *Wonderful Tennessee* (1993) is entirely written in terms of such music. As a play of atmosphere and moods, it manages to cross the Chekhovian paradigm of heartbreak with a Beckettian paradigm, which Friel will explore more fully in *Faith Healer,* of infernal blockage and waiting. A detailed commentary would require a kind of musical analysis. Like David Storey's *Home,* this play is largely composed of brief exchanges—here among the three couples who have come to a pier on the remote coast of Donegal in the expectation of sharing Terry's birthday voyage to an island he claims to have purchased. But *Wonderful Tennessee* is laced with music, and its conversation is a quasimusical interweaving of themes. As the couples spend the night in fruitless expectation of that voyage, the Beckettian waiting and game-playing unfold by implication both their frustration and their paradoxical fulfillment. The Chekhovian frustration is manifest: the failure of Terry's birthday outing, the suicidal fantasies and actions of his wife, Berna, his secret love for Frank's wife, Angela, Frank's uncompleted historical study, and the unfulfilled musical promise and imminent death of George. The countervailing fulfillment-in-failure is evident not only in the haunting music that George plays and the others share and elaborate, but also in the game devised by Angela, who tosses lobster pot weights at an empty bottle placed close to a lifebelt stand. "It's called: how close can you get without touching it?" (55). The play's action amplifies that game on many levels as the six characters seek to approach, and yet not to approach, some fulfillment—ecstasy, magic, passion, or death. Classical and Irish references to the distant past and references also to a more recent tragedy make the unattainable island an image of both a lost paradise and a potential disaster. The play's paradoxical music is summed up by Frank, who recognizes that the end of our desire, our "rage for the absolute," is "beyond language," because "there is no vocabulary for the experience" (41). *Wonderful Tennessee* invites us into a theatrical music that articulates both the heartbreak and the healing of that experience.

The Chekhovian paradigm, with its alienated artists of monologue into whose lives our community of playing may enter with sympathy and humor, has recently been taken by Anna Deveare Smith in a surprising direction. She has combined journalistic interviews, Studs Terkel's kind of oral history (as in *Hard Times* and *Working*), and performance art. A high point of her continuing project, *On the Road: A Search for American*

Character, is *Twilight: Los Angeles, 1992,* in which many confessional monologues shape for us a meaning of the Los Angeles riots to which no single speaker can bring full understanding. The published text does not make fully clear the Chekhovian effect of this one-woman performance, which is supplemented by multimedia effects. Arvin Brown has justly said in a Long Wharf Theatre program note:

> She is a profound interpretive artist in the guise of a reporter. We know, of course, of her process: The countless interviews, the ability to engender trust in all of her subjects so that they unburden themselves with an almost startling ingenuousness. The understanding that forces those she talks with to reveal the very thing they often least wanted to expose: their human fragility. But the process for Ms. Smith yields up only the common clay of her art. What she sculpts from little individual confessions becomes a monument to the complexity of the human experience. She never imitates, rather she uncovers essences: the tilt of a head here, the telltale stammer there, that like the pointillist's dots of color become a full painting only when one takes a step or two back from the canvas . . . She creates her characters from a photographic recall of how they move, how they sit, how they use their hands, how their eyes look when they lie. But her characters live on the stage because the photoplates she has so carefully collected are dipped in her own compassion, the only developing fluid she would ever consider worthy of her final prints.

But we must also acknowledge Smith's humor—a quality that makes her performances positively exuberant onstage, even when shot through with pathos. Strangely enough, she does not mention this quality in her introduction to *Twilight: Los Angeles, 1992.* And in her lectures she rather hesitates to acknowledge it. Her tone is more Chekhovian than she may wish to admit, given the desperate and immediate social issues to which she addresses herself.

There are further clues to the presence of the Chekhovian paradigm in the most recent Berkeley Repertory Theatre version of her piece. Expanding, rearranging, and cutting material in the published text and adding yet other monologues, she has shaped this version to give a sense of a "non-conversation" among those who cannot or will not understand each other, a blocked exchange that finds its coherent meaning in the person of the performer and, through her, in us. Smith has also split up some of the monologues, so that we have a more Chekhovian sense of a repeated return to the voices of those who are closed within their own perceptions. Act 1 is now framed by the sweet, rather condescending and narcissistic, and yet sympathetic and horrified observations of Jessye Norman, who from her distance can see no way of coping with this situation. Its other monologues give us, through Smith's swiftly changing persona, a series of socially and racially diverse but often unwittingly similar perspectives—first briefly on the backgrounds to the riot, then on the stories of Latasha Harlins and Rodney King, and then more fully on the riot itself. By the closing frame, we can measure the distance between Norman's horror-struck aloofness and Smith's intimate participation. In effect, Smith has taken the Chekhovian sense of a playing community that enters and so transcends the limitations of the characters and focused that community for us within a single player.

Her awareness of this strategy becomes clear in act 2, which now opens with a statement by Cornel West that is serious in intent and dead-right in its perceptions but, as it comes through this performer with astonishingly photographic accuracy, also hilariously mannered. As West develops his belief not in "optimism" but in "hope," he pays tribute both to Chekhov and to John Coltrane. "Brother Anton," as West calls him, becomes a presiding spirit for the whole production. Act 2, moreover, has a yet more explicitly Chekhovian shape. One section, "To the Table," is subtitled "A Conversation about Race That Never Happened." Actual words by Alice Waters, Paul Parker, Jin Ho Lee, Bill Bradley, Elaine Brown, and Rudy Salas Sr., people who "have not, to date, been in such a room together," suggest through the performer the possibility of a conversation that our social distance and self-involvement have thus far precluded. Another section includes "AA Meeting," in which Maria, Juror #7 at the Federal Trial of the officers who beat Rodney King, recounts the jury process. She, too, is a natural actor, who can enter into the disparate rages, fears, and needs of all the jury members. Theatrically, Smith creates here a pyramid effect, as she plays the player who presents the other jurors. Through some rich comedy this piece suggests that we all may have the capacity to move beyond our self-produced blockages to enter playfully into genuine community. The closing frame for act 2 and the entire performance is provided by Twilight Bey, organizer of the gang truce, whose voice is that with which Anna Deveare Smith seems most fully to sympathize. She makes that point theatrically at the very end. Without any pause in Twilight Bey's monologue—

> I am a dark individual,
> and with me stuck in limbo,
> I see darkness as myself.
> I see the light as knowledge and the wisdom of the world and
> understanding others

—she discards the bits of costume that have suggested Twilight's identity, allows her own concerned voice and quiet presence to emerge from behind his homeboy persona, and affirms his final lines as hers, and ours:

> and in order for me to be a, to be a true human being,
> I can't forever dwell in darkness,
> I can't forever dwell in the idea,
> of just identifying with people like me and understanding me and mine.
> (Smith 255)

Twilight: Los Angeles, 1992 both expands and condenses the Chekhovian paradigm. The performed action includes an entire city, indeed an entire nation, in distress and heartbreak; and our action of performance, which holds the potential for resolving that distress, is now focused for us within one performing self who is also a community. Each of us is invited to become that community.

Chapter 4

Playing Hell: Sartre, Beckett, Genet, and Pinter

I

In Pinter's *No Man's Land* we move through increasingly ambiguous verbal battles to a moment when, by more or less common consent, "there is no possibility of changing the subject." A parasitical littérateur then steals his host's own earlier words to pronounce upon him a dubious judgment: "You are in no man's land. Which never changes, which never grows older, but which remains forever, icy and silent" (95). And the host drinks to that.

Stalemate or collusion? It is hard to say. But that exchange might almost be taking place between audience and actor-playwright—as, indeed, it may have seemed to do when Pinter himself appeared in the role of Hirst in a London production of 1992. Its moment of frozen violence, however, does more than bring to a self-conscious climax Pinter's own exploration of feared or willed sterility. It also provides an image of our theater's most obsessively unchanging subject. In recent years that subject has informed the range of stylistically various plays set in "confining institutions" by Pinter, Peter Nichols, John Arden, Arthur Kopit, Peter Weiss, Friedrich Dürrenmatt, David Storey, Kenneth Brown, Brendan Behan, Jean Genet, Arnold Wesker, David Rabe, and Samuel Beckett that Carol Rosen has termed "plays of impasse." More fundamentally, it has generated throughout this century an extreme paradigm capable of endless transformation. Life is hell, a sinister conspiracy, a cold mechanism, a hall of mirrors, a closed room, a quicksand of language. And hell is theater. Or, perhaps, life is theater, a spectacle of masks, a script of life lies, an endless regression of plays-within-plays, an empty game. And theater is hell. Play it either way, or both ways, as tragedy, farce, *teatro grottesco,* naturalist *tranche de vie,* symbolist dance-play, surrealist myth-play, expressionist dream-play, absurdist anti-play, and you could run through half the modern repertory.

Think of Ibsen's Rubek in *When We Dead Awaken,* contemplating his sculpted image: "He must stay for ever in his Hell." Think of Pirandello's nameless man in *Henry IV,* after he has killed Belcredi and condemned himself to the appearance of insanity: "here we are . . . together . . . forever!" Think of Yeats's desire to create a theater reminiscent of Mallarmé's Hérodiade, "dancing seemingly alone in her narrow moving luminous circle" (*Autobiography* 193), and of his Old Man in *Purgatory,* who has killed his own son in a futile attempt to free the spirit of his mother from its purgatorial dream:

> Mankind can do no more. Appease
> The misery of the living and the remorse of the dead.
>
> (*Collected Plays* 436)

It is but a step to the recognition of Sartre's Garcin in *No Exit:* "For ever, and ever, and ever" (47).

The Daughter of Indra in Strindberg's *A Dream Play* descends to just such a realm of empty and repetitive self-entrapment. The spirit of Jonathan Swift in Yeats's *The Words upon the Window-Pane,* caught in such a dream, utters through an uncomprehending medium the curse of Job: "Perish the day on which I was born!" (*Collected Plays* 388). And play after play suggests that there is no escape from such a predicament. In Maeterlinck's *The Blind* the beggars wait in ignorance, fearfulness, and resignation for the return of a priest who has cared for them, only to discover that he is among them, quite dead. In Ionesco's *The Chairs* an apocalyptic deaf-mute can bring to an empty world nothing but an unintelligible message. Beckett's Godot fails to keep a putative appointment. "Use your head, can't you, use your head," expostulates Hamm in *Endgame,* "you're on earth, there's no cure for that!" (68). From their depths or jungles or machines or bars, such characters as Gorky's Satin in *The Lower Depths,* Brecht's Garga and Schlink in *The Jungle of Cities,* Cocteau's Oedipus in *The Infernal Machine,* and O'Neill's Larry in *The Iceman Cometh* enact their agreement. And in Brian Friel's *Faith Healer,* the faithless Francis Hardy speaks to us from beyond the living of his own dark destiny.

We know, of course, that these instances of living death onstage are part of a history of theatrical change. When Pinter the actor played Hirst, Pinter the playwright had already moved beyond *No Man's Land* to such quite different plays as *Betrayal, One for the Road,* and *Mountain Language.* And when, in the New York production of 1994 Christopher Plummer and Jason Robards played Spooner and Hirst, no reviewer could avoid comparisons with John Gielgud and Ralph Richardson in those roles in the London production of 1975. And yet the plays themselves have often appeared to suggest that any change must be part of a dialectic that proceeds inexorably toward some dehumanized end. The third act of Shaw's *Man and Superman* could offer a rather easy escape from the hell of romantic self-deception to a heaven of philosophy. Sartre's *No Exit,* deriving from an ironic vision of confinement that was central to Ibsen's dramaturgy but rejected by Shaw, must maintain a more purely negative rigor. And the theatrical confinements of Beckett's *Krapp's Last Tape, Happy Days, Play,* and *Not I* are yet more claustral, transforming the condition of Yeats's heroic and disembodied Swift into theatrical hells of deliberate banality. Beckett's apparent minimalism can accommodate, nevertheless, a subtle musicality, an interior spaciousness, and a wide field of reference. Perhaps in major art every reduction in scope must be matched by some complementary intensity or magnification. Indeed, Genet's *The Screens* also provides an astonishing spectacle as it speeds the living and the dead toward nothingness. By comparison with those extremities of invention Pinter's *No Man's Land* may seem an uneasily retrospective distillation of our obsessive theme, as if we in the theater were now like Spooner and Hirst, darkly choosing to imagine that the subject can never be changed. The less sympathetic of the early reviewers charged, in fact, that the play was merely a Pinter pastiche of Pinter.

Why insist on playing hell? Critics and playwrights have often attributed our obsession to the anguished clarity of our disillusionment. A truly modern mind, they have said, can accept no ontological ground for any predications of truth or value. It must recognize that our world is a blind energy, an absurd chaos, or a meaningless flux, that the self is a will to power, a set of determined responses, or a mere nothingness, and that language is a misleading convention, a subtle means of coercion, or a tangle of ambiguous games. Such a mind, they assure us, can seriously imagine its own existence as occurring nowhere but in some fiction of a hell in which it cannot actually believe. The incredible has seemed to become the inevitable. That paradox has a certain plausibility, but it issues from self-contradictions of the kind that always arise when we forget the necessary conditions of our own thought—and of the theater. Each of those negative or reductive statements relies on the presence of what it explicitly denies. A world that provided no ground for cognitive relations could not be known as meaningless or absurd. A mere will to power or set of determined responses could never understand itself. An essentially misleading, coercive, or ambiguous language would be unable to convey its own attributes.

Within such infernal fictions we could not begin to imagine or perform an infernal fiction. A fashionable and self-contradictory pessimism or nihilism can tempt us toward our theatrical hells, but it can hardly explain the meaning or value we find there.

Why should we play hells that seem to deny our ability to play them? We cannot answer that question without keeping in mind the fact that a play's full meaning always resides in the relations between its represented world and our action of performance. Those relations, as I have suggested in previous chapters, are freighted with analogies, complementarities, and apparent contradictions. They enable our participation in a musical and intellectual transcendence of worlds of farce. They provide tacit assurance that our communities of heartbreak are not without healing remedies. But the disparities between the represented world and our action of performance become especially striking when we play hell. Every performed hell is caught in two sets of contradictions. It is in crucial respects a negation or denial of the world of performance that founds and discloses it. And, because it must derive its principles of intelligible action from that negated or denied world, it is also internally inconsistent. Those contradictions, however, are not mere logical confusions. They inform our theatrical event much as they do the narrative world of Dante's *Inferno,* in which the pilgrim descends through self-closed circles of the living dead who have denied the principle of such exploratory movement. Whenever we enact an extreme image of entrapment, inauthenticity, blindness, or violence, we take to the point of evident absurdity certain tensions in our experience. When our playing seems to lead us into the static and closed, the isolate and repetitive, it also points to some actual transcendence of that realm of self-reflecting illusion. In doing so, it sheds a penetrating light on the paradoxical field of polarity and reciprocity that grounds our shared experience.

Each play, however, can illuminate only certain aspects of that field. We may probe more deeply the various relations they posit between the actions represented on stage and our actions of performance, if we imagine a descent through four circles of hell. Sartre's *No Exit,* Beckett's *Play,* Genet's *The Screens,* and Pinter's *No Man's Land* are diverse enough to serve as instances of the many ways in which playwrights have shaped this theatrical paradigm. They set before us infernal images that have invited rather easy labeling: existential inauthenticity, self-consciously theatrical isolation, lyrical nihilism, and ambiguously frozen violence. But they also invite us to play such images and, so, to discover their necessary conditions and complements. Each play therefore leads us to experience a reversal that may recall that remarkable moment near the end of the *Inferno* when Virgil, who has been bearing Dante downward along the icy flanks of the ruler of despair, turns upside down and begins to grapple as one who mounts.

II

Of these four circles beyond apparent hope, *No Exit* most obviously gives us a self-contradictory negation of the authentic life it must assume. Not that it merely illustrates certain arguments in *Being and Nothingness.* Our playing of what Sartre had called "a dead life" requires participation in a mode of dialogue that the characters persistently corrupt and that Sartre himself was never able or willing to describe. But what we most easily see at first is the predicament in that closed room.

"It has happened *already,* do you understand?" taunts Inez at the play's end. "Once and for all. So here we are, forever" (47). As Estelle and Garcin echo her sardonic laughter and as all three then collapse on their sofas in hysterical recognition, they seem extreme images of the "triumph of the Other" that Sartre had declared to be the meaning of death (*Being and Nothingness* 545). Each has grudgingly relinquished the realm of earthly life. Inez has heard the whispering of lovers on what was once her bed and then has failed to hear even that. Estelle, before a similar fading of all earthly sounds, has heard Peter and Olga enliven their dance with gossip about "Poor Estelle." Garcin, whose reputation is longer in dying, has heard himself denounced by Gomez as a coward. But each is also an image of a subtler triumph of others that had begun long before the time of physical death. Estelle, a narcissist who complains that she has no sense of existing unless provided with some visible self-reflection, depends on the mirroring gaze of others to make her seem a valued object. Inez, a self-declared sadist, needs the suffering of others in order to maintain herself. Although it has been said that she entered hell with "self-knowledge" (Cohn, *Four Contemporary French Plays* vii) or "represents Sartre's point of view" (Thody 82), she clearly exhibits—as Hazel Barnes has noted (102)—what Sartre had called sincerity in bad faith, the self-deceptive attempt to identify oneself with the content of previous acts (*Being and Nothingness* 65). And Garcin, who is narcissist and sadist by turns, a confused idealist with a self-deceiving will to self-sufficiency, finally sees that one who identifies consciousness with any role or ideal must submit to the unpredictable validating judgment of others. "Hell is—other people!" (47). So it is for those who depend in principle on an alienating and objectifying look. At every moment they will have *already* lived.

No doubt the torture in this room (where Garcin needs Inez, who needs Estelle, who needs Garcin) is increased by the fact that no one or two can withdraw or establish some gratifying relation without being interrupted by another who has been left out. But could earthly life release them from such ironic blockage into anything more than self-stultification or *folie à deux?* Did it ever do so? As the play closes, its entire form threatens to become an image of the human condition as nothing but a dead life of which "the Other makes itself the guardian" (*Being and Nothingness* 541). For theatrical "realism" here discloses itself to be an instrument of our inauthentic self-objectifications. What is the box-stage? A claustral space posited in a void and supplied with props in derivative bourgeois styles: Second Empire furniture, a bronze by Barbedienne. Within that setting, recognized by Garcin as appropriately bogus, three melodramatic characters fill up their quasi-eternal stage time by going through the motions of a sexual power struggle as they gradually expose their past lives (shades of Ibsen and Strindberg?). But they can be "characters" for us only because they are frozen in their own grotesquely self-contradictory effort to freeze themselves as characters (shades of Pirandello?). And their useless self-recognition, punctuated by an attempt to murder the dead that recalls the climax of *Six Characters in Search of an Author,* has been decreed by a script that seems itself the "design" of the omnipotent "they" of whom Inez repeatedly speaks, a "they" whose many "eyes" Garcin finally feels are devouring him (a foretaste of Beckett's *Happy Days* and *Play*!). But those eyes belong to us. Who are we, in fact, but the spectator-gods of this hell to which we have condemned the images of our actual lives? Have we not become the "look" of the "Other"? In engineering this exposure of the self-alienation that pervades our lives in and out of the theater, Sartre has covered much of the distance from Ibsen to Beckett.

"Authenticity" here seems as unlikely as the "radical conversion" and the "ethics of deliverance and salvation" that Sartre had notoriously relegated to a footnote in *Being and Nothingness* (412n). But the self-contradictions in this performed action are patent. A dead life is a living death, which can be nothing but life that continually negates itself. When critics say that *No Exit* lacks what is ordinarily called action, that its "acts" are "in the past" (Guicharnaud 137), that its characters "had surrendered" their "freedom" before death (Kern 11), or that its "existence after death lacks the essential condition which time possesses for Sartre" (Barnes 101), they simply forget what Sartre knew quite well most of the time: that the theater "represents the act and can represent nothing but the act" (*Sartre on Theater* 91). The stage, then must represent that process whereby we continually create ourselves through a series of undertakings (Worthen 154–55). But even Sartre was quite capable of oversimplifying his own earlier texts. He could therefore say: "There is no alternative in *No Exit*" (*Sartre on Theater* 303). But, surely, no more than *Rosmersholm* or *Six Characters in Search of an Author* can this play be *merely* retrospective. Its irreversible action manifests itself in every exchange of speeches, for, as Sartre also knew, in the theater "language is action" (*Sartre on Theater* 62). Each character is here trying to become a self-conscious object. Each therefore wants and fears to be defined by others. And as the three interact, they move toward the mutual blockage that will ironically heighten both the want and the fear. The import of their shared action, which proceeds through unique choices in a realistic time that is simply out of phase with the accelerated time they glimpse on the offstage earth, becomes explicit when the door of the room flies open and all nevertheless insist on remaining inside. In that moment of truth Sartre challenges the characters with the opportunity to abandon the known and enter the void of the uncreated. Who can say what would happen if someone walked out of that open door? The moment is reminiscent of the Son's refusal in *Six Characters* to leave the family on which his loftily histrionic self-definition depends and of the lifelong passivity of the petitioner in Kafka's *The Trial,* who simply accepts the gatekeeper's denial of his right to pass through the Gate of the Law. Commenting on that parable in *Being and Nothingness,* Sartre concluded that "each man makes for himself his own gate" (550). Because Inez damns herself quite self-consciously, she can articulate, though without grasping its full meaning, what is also true for Garcin and Estelle: "I prefer to choose my hell" (23).

We can sympathize, of course, with their refusal to risk an exit from the hell of attempted self-objectification. But just such an "exit" would begin to appear even within this room if Garcin relaxed his grip on his claimed moral identity or Inez let her painful self-image lapse toward oblivion or Estelle contented herself with being nothing. Such transformations are unimaginable only because they seem formally precluded by the self-contradictory field of this "design," which is both free and determined, planned in advance but also generated before our eyes by the shared efforts of self-isolating wills that are ostensibly past the point of willing. Through our own predictable but quite un-Sartrean desire to fix those three as intelligible characters who would not violate their given "motives," we have collaborated in that design. But we must nevertheless admit that precisely when Garcin says, "Well, well, let's get on with it," the curtains must close upon this hell. For "getting on with it" is also unimaginable. The characters' action of mutual discovery and entanglement could hardly be repeated, and any continuation of this blockage would now be for us a formless and meaningless bore. In reaching its moment of endless closure, the play has actually completed its illuminating trajectory. Sartre himself later said, "there is no art which is not a 'qualitative unit' of contradictions" (*Sartre on Theater* 136). The world of authenticity, it seems, would have to be a very different world.

Or would it? *No Exit* has seemed to cast us, its witnesses, in the role of bodiless subjects who observe as object the doomed attempt of subjectivity to turn itself into an object. But that self-contradictory model of the performed action is itself a negation of our action of performance, which requires that the actors be *with* one another, their roles, and their witnesses in the imperfect mutual inclusion that always characterizes the reality among human beings. Here we must firmly set aside a number of Sartre's own objectifying and therefore reductive pronouncements. A character, he could say, "is always definitely someone else, someone who is not me and into whose skin I cannot slide" (*Sartre on Theater* 9). But that half-truth would make acting impossible and would reduce witnessing (our mediated participation in the actor's discovery of the role in himself and himself in the role) to the merely external vision that Sartre's philosophy requires. In the theater, he could say, "I no longer exist except as pure sight." Hence "the real meaning of theater is to put the world of men at an absolute distance" (*Sartre on Theater* 12). That half-truth would indeed turn us into the spectator gods of *No Exit* and deny our ability to perform the play. We must here trust the performance and not the philosopher, whose Cartesian assumptions—of which Marjorie Grene has provided a lively account—have always prevented him from explicitly recognizing the inter-human dimension of his own plays and their dependence on the expressive reciprocity of our bodily existence. They have also prevented him from acknowledging the reciprocity inherent in the actor's relation to the role, and enabled him to treat the actor as the very image of the inauthentic, "a medium for nonbeing" (*Sartre on Theater* 165). As I have suggested in the introduction, we would have to turn from Sartre to Merleau-Ponty in order to find an account of our embodied subjectivity that would more adequately ground an understanding of the actual complexities of performance.

What happens if we trust the performance? Moment by moment we attend to the contradictions between "staying dead," the self-isolating action never to be understood by Estelle, Inez, Garcin, or any Medusa-eyed spectator-gods, and "playing dead," the analogous but antithetical action that we share in the theater as we move toward understanding. Through the expressive forms that mediate for us those "dead lives," we live each character's attempt to be an unchanging reality and also live the implications of exploring our undefined selves by lending them to that self-deceptive attempt. We live each character's insensitive use of others as mirror, victim, or judge, and also our sensitive collaboration in the heuristic miming of such use. As we render the characters' self-defeating insistence that each subject must become an object, our intersubjective play is for us a nonobjectifiable and participatory act, not some Sartrean project for a fleeting "We-subject" that might dream itself "master of the earth" (*Being and Nothingness* 425) but the unfolding of a reciprocity that is prior to every individual "I." And as we play the script's apparent reduction of the world to a Cartesian dualism of subject and object trapped in an instant of lucidity that ironically closes on itself, we inhabit a moving field of mutual disclosure in which our shared action emerges prior to any dualism and in which the play's style can therefore declare itself the symbolic form of the blockage it portrays.

Finally, of course, *No Exit* invites us to exit through the open door of the theater in which we have played it. And Sartre himself readily asserted that this hell need not be for "me" unless "I" choose it: "No matter what circle of hell we are living in, I think we are free to break out of it. And if people do not break out, again, they are staying there of their own free will" (*Sartre on Theater* 200). But, though critics have often found Sartre's plays to illustrate his philosophy, the meaning of *No Exit* does not consist of the conceptual contradiction between the inauthenticity of its characters and the hypothetical authenticity of some arbitrary and agonizing creative choice to be made by the solitary consciousness posited in *Being and Nothingness*—a choice that, according to Robert Champigny, Sartre could never adequately portray in fiction or drama (197ff.). That meaning lives in the enacted and witnessed contradictions of our performance, as we commit ourselves in dialogue to realizing the values implicit in a script that seems to deny the possibility of such commitment. Because authenticity, like art, inhabits a world of paradox, it requires a lived dialectic with the images of the inauthentic. We approach it here by playing hell.

III

Let us descend a little lower. Before us, three grey urns about a yard high. Protruding from each, a head: woman, man, woman, the three impassive faces lit from below by a triple spot. And in toneless chorus:

> "One morning as I was sitting—"
> "We were not long together—"
> "I said to him, Give her up—"

Lines we have heard before, twice in chorus, twice severally. Will they play a third time, *da capo, da capo* . . . ? Blackout for five seconds. Spot on the man's face alone:

> "We were not long together—"

Blackout again, five seconds. *Fine* (*Collected Shorter Plays* 158).

There can be little doubt that the claustral and infernal framework of *Play* descends in part from Ibsen by way of Sartre. The Cartesian isolation of the subject in Beckett's work has been documented by Hugh Kenner, John Pilling, and Steven Rosen, and Vivian Mercier has noted that "*Godot, Endgame, Play* are all offspring of *Huis clos*" (84). We have seen it before: action that seems sheer retrospection, existence frozen into a repetitive design, a triangle of histrionic objects, and spectator-gods who are pure sight and hearing. But Beckett refuses half-measures. What now seems too inevitable, arbitrary, and pointless to be called bad faith must be yet further reduced. Melodrama must be more banal and pretentious, characters more interlocked and isolated, time more instantaneous and endless, consciousness more bodiless and materialized, the actors more like funerary puppets, the witnesses more like inhuman inquisitors. And the theatrical perspective must be reversed. Instead of a "realistic" action that gradually reveals itself to be a fantastic prison of self-conscious images, we apprehend just such a prison, which implies its basis in what we may call the real. Instead of the prolonged approach of a radical journalist, a lesbian postal clerk, and an empty flirt to their climactic moment of endless closure in a drawing-room hell, we have a brief three-part sequence that is played twice by anonymous heads and an inscrutably directorial spotlight. The fragmentary speeches of the heads—memories of cliché infidelity, responses to present interrogation—come to us in a formal (but unintelligible) chorus, intercut narratives, and intercut reflections on the hellish present. This action on a bare stage is offering simultaneous images of life, death, and the theater itself.

Beckett focuses those images through a style that also descends in part from the Japanese Noh, as translated by Ezra Pound and explored by W. B. Yeats—with accents and emphases, as I shall argue in the next chapter, that descend in part from Byron. Although Beckett told Yasunari Takahashi that he was "not consciously" influenced by the Noh, he "had a great admiration for Yeats's later poetry and plays" (68). In several Noh plays a wandering priest meets spirits who unfold the issues of their past lives and the effective suffering of their disembodied existence. In *Nishikigi,* for example, the priest meets the ghosts of long-dead lovers who remain "tangled" together in a "dream" that yet prevents their union: "We had no meeting together" (Pound, *Translations* 286–87, 289). In Yeats's *The Dreaming of the Bones* the priest has been replaced by one of the rebels of Easter 1916, fleeing Dublin for his life. And he encounters in the mountain landscape the long-dead Diarmuid and Dervorgilla, who brought the Normans into Ireland, and who must remain separate and accursed unless they are forgiven: "Seven hundred years our lips have never met" (*Collected Plays* 281). The rebel remains unforgiving, and Diarmuid and Dervorgilla remain in their hell. That modernization of the Noh was also partly behind Yeats's rendering of the séance encounter with Jonathan Swift in *The Words upon the Window-Pane* and the predicament of the Old Man who sees the ghost of his Mother in *Purgatory.* Beckett's *Waiting for Godot,* too, is in this respect a frustrated Noh encounter, or what Takahashi calls an "anti-Noh" (70), in which the spiritual manifestation does not occur. Partly deriving from the failed quest in Yeats's *At the Hawk's Well* it makes a riddling use of the conventional tree painted on the background of the Noh stage as "the symbol of unchanging green and strength" (Pound, *Translations* 246)—a tree that had reappeared in Yeats's *Purgatory* as an ironic image of the Old Man himself. Beckett, one should acknowledge, said that the visual conception of this play was inspired by a painting by Caspar David Friedrich—though accounts differ as to which one (Knowlson, *Damned to Fame* 142). But any number of "sources" may flow together in an artist's mind. In *Play* the separated but entangled spirits of *Nishikigi* and *The Dreaming of the Bones* have become an adulterous triangle, somewhat like that of Cuchulain, Emer, and Eithne Inguba in Yeats's *The Only Jealousy of Emer.* "We were not long together," says M, and they do not have the slightest hope for reunion. The traveling priest has become, in effect, an inquisitorial spotlight, the implications of which we begin to grasp only late in the performance.

Life, death, and the theater have now become aspects of a triple emptiness. What is life as remembered here but a constantly interrupted monologue before the mirror of one's imagination as one exhausts oneself in trying to satisfy the woman one says one loves or fights like a moralistic cat to keep the philanderer who wants more than the security one has to offer or tries with futile irony to remove that man from the clutches of the nagging wife who claims him? What is death as experienced here but such a *monologue à trois,* continued after some suicide, traffic accident, or fire in yet deeper ignorance of the presence of others, in which one failingly recapitulates what has never ceased to obsess, fights off the light of consciousness as if it were an unwanted lover, a scorching sun or an impersonal eye, wonders if anyone is listening or looking, and hopes for darkness, madness, or peace? And what is theater as reflexively imaged here but this life, this death, the blindly conscious players stammering their routines in solitary togetherness, the observed minds forever separate from the obsessing bodies, the soliciting eye lusting mechanically to know the secret of dead lusts, in a collective monologue that reflects the triviality of one's own imagination?

Some of the bizarre self-contradictions in this performed action are bolder than any in *No Exit.* But others may not strike us until *Play* has been continuing *da capo, da capo,* in our heads after we have left the theater. How does life here negate itself? These nonpersons seem to have lost their formerly affluent lives in the banal rhetoric of erotic escapism and also in suicide or accident. But who, knowing only what reaches us through the grid of darkness imposed by the controlling spotlight, would care to fix responsibility? In *No Exit* a continuous present action, producing its own entanglement and blockage as it mirrors the past, can clarify the genesis of hell. But in *Play* every impulse to action is cut off by darkness, a blockage that *can* be repeated ad infinitum, either without change or (as Beckett has suggested after the experience of productions in London and Paris) with variations that imply an entropic loss of form or the directorial spotlight's arbitrary reshuffling of temporal order (160). During *Play's* narrative movement the disruptions of each head's attempt to shape a self-deceptively gratifying story seem mainly to heighten the wry bathos of impotent inauthenticity and appropriate accident. But in the reflective movement, as the heads face their present condition, what is disrupted is more often the eerily toneless response of sheer agony ("Like dragging a great roller, on a scorching day" [155]) or desperate hope ("Is it that I do not tell the truth, is that it, that some day somehow I may tell the truth at last and then no more light at last, for the truth?" [153]) or defiant yet apologetic challenge ("Why not keep on glaring at me without ceasing? I might start to rave and—[*hiccup*]—bring it up for you. Par—" [156]) or hinted reconciliation: "Dying for dark—and the darker the worse. Strange" [157]; "There are endurable moments" [152]"; "All this, when will all this have been . . . just play?" [153]). What renders such impulses without issue?

In Sartre's language: the Other. But here an obsessively verbal consciousness itself has become the Other, actively decreeing its own affirmation and negation. The spotlight that generates and kills reflective speech in these heads is an interrogator both whimsical and rigidly programmed, the slow strobe eye of an occasionalist spectator-god who may be "no less a victim of his inquiry" (Knowlson, *Samuel Beckett* 92) than the heads, and the playwright's cruellest instrument in filing, cutting, and distancing *Play* into a shape silhouetted against nothing. The principle of life here seems the principle of death, the will to verbal light a dying for dark, and the darker the worse. Far more unremittingly tyrannical than the staring eyes in the hell of *No Exit,* the blinking eye of this ambivalence made absolute seems to declare authentic play to be *hors jeu.*

Which is nonsense, of course, for who performs this action? Not M, W1, W2, and the spotlight. The action of performance requires that we attend to qualities that do not exist for those mental objects: continuity, wit, grace, verbal music, humane understanding. Playing *Play,* we apprehend the discontinuity of its self-closed speeches, discern the comic juxtapositions of incongruous (or unexpectedly congruous) remarks, and follow the illuminatingly obsessive transformations of such verbal motifs as *give up, out, pardon, thing, bitch, smell, darkness, looking, I, you, can't, play, yes,* as they pass from speech to speech and speaker to speaker. Only gradually can we begin to experience the blockage of these heads, as their own verbatim repetition enables us to move onward to a more coherent image of their condition. On second hearing we appreciate the nuances of their lofty self-pity and their undisguised pain, suspect the spotlight's silent cruelty or blind self-victimage, and begin to wonder at our own ability to be simultaneously with them and with ourselves, one consciousness and many, in the words and attending to the words, not disembodied heads but members of an embodied consciousness without which the remarkably lyric orchestration of this piece would be impossible. If the stylized world of the played here exhibits the theater as a Cartesian model of our blocked situation, a consistent Beckett would have to say of that model, as he did of the sundering of subject and object in *Film,* "No truth value attaches to above, regarded as of merely structural and dramatic convenience" (*Collected Shorter Plays* 163).

For our stylized world of playing includes the urned heads, the spotlight, and the proscenium stage—and, indeed, the analogically evoked and undeniably *present* playwright, actors, and spectators—in a field of shared attention that transcends the harsh antitheses that seem the frustrating substance of Beckett's art.

That is why the most probing comments on *Play* have come from critics oriented toward performance rather than philosophy. Ruby Cohn has shown how its "theatereality" is organized according to complex narrative, quasi-dramatic, and verbal patterns (*Just Play* 28, 53–54, 125–27). And she has noted that Beckett directed it with heightened attention to its essentially musical effects (198, 274–76). Enoch Brater has argued that Beckett's late drama gives us "not so much the voice of the character, but rather the voice of the playwright." The "strongest actor in this drama is the playwright himself," for this is "not drama in the shape of poetry, but poetry in the shape of drama" (17). And yet William Worthen has emphasized the fact that Beckett forces actors and characters "to share the painful and apparently arbitrary circumstances of their common stage." By requiring the actors to remain impassive and undeviatingly frontal in confining urns while overcoming the demands of the fragmented but formally organized text, *Play* "reifies the conditions of stage acting." It invites us to see M, W1, and W2 "simultaneously as attenuated characters and as constricting yet evocative dramatic roles" (203–4). From this double perspective *Play* is about the "complex interplay between text and performer" (210). Jonathan Kalb has summed up one consequence of such interplay by distinguishing Beckett sharply—indeed, somewhat too sharply—from Brecht. "One could say that all Beckett's plays are concerned with the impossibility of recognizing clean subject/object distinctions like the ones Brecht wanted to emphasize. He uses performance circumstances to dramatize the impossibility of escaping the proscenium frame, and hence of transcending life's theatrical circumstances . . ." The "ideal path" to "understanding the metaphorical relationships between spectators and characters/actors" entails our recognizing that we are, "to use Robbe-Grillet's phrase, as 'irremediably present' as the actors" (47). When describing what Billie Whitelaw, David Warrilow, and others have brought to Beckett's roles, Kalb adds that it is "the live actor, the fact of life in the actor, that finally animates Beckett's stage pictures and amplifies the impact of their disturbing, melancholy beauty—even though that animation gains expression only through the most highly calculated sounds and movements" (66).

Far from being mutually exclusive, such comments provide complementary insights into the multidimensional nature of Beckett's participatory theater, in which the playwright, his depersonalized text, the actors, and the spectators join in an action that variously reflects their condition. In effect, the playwright who has most fully dramatized the Cartesian alienation of subject from object has done so through a marvelously inclusive and boldly anti-Cartesian art. It would be hard to find a more misleading description of such art than that on which critics have often relied, Beckett's own wittily reductive formula in "Three Dialogues" for Bram van Velde's painting: "The expression that there is nothing to express, nothing with which to express, nothing from which to express, together with the obligation to express" (*Disjecta* 139). If we must play the dubious game of finding the implicitly self-referential in Beckett's comments on painters, a better choice might be his tribute to Jack Yeats as one who "brings light, as only the great dare bring light, to the issueless predicament of existence" (Pilling 24). In any conceptual formulation, that bringing of light must seem as contradictory as the nihilism it overcomes. But the sheer possibility of light (no inquisitorial spotlight but the light that can play both spotlight and heads, the light that animates playwright, actors, and spectators) testifies to an issue from the predicament. We begin to live that actual though strictly inconceivable issue as we play the apparent inadequacy of our apparent medium, or what Beckett in "Three Dialogues" paradoxically called "the presence of unavailable terms." Finally, *Play* invites us to hear among our empty nonheads, *senza fine,* a music of human defeat that implicitly celebrates the transfiguring power of our playful and shareable attention to our always failing means of expression.

IV

Our downward course here opens out as if to tempt us with the illusion that the worst is past. The objectifying closure inherited from the realistic Ibsen and the Westernized Noh drama has given place to panoramic vistas, progressive "stations," expressionistic costumes, and self-conscious maskings that recall another line of descent, from *Peer Gynt* through such works as Strindberg's *A Dream Play,* Kaiser's *From Morn to Midnight,* and Brecht's *The Caucasian Chalk Circle.* We have reached the conclusion of Genet's seventeen-scene masterpiece. Surely this is no "play of impasse"? The theater? Open to the sky. Enclosed by irregular board fencing, our tiers of seats face four tiers of screens.

On the second floor, near a right-hand screen painted with fireplace and vase, the Husband holds his bicycle and cries: "He's arriving! Come and see" (*The Screens* 186). Lalla, who has been drawing on the screen a huge and thorny rose stem, turns toward center stage, where a screen suggests the village square. At the left, before the brothel screen, Malika and Djemila also turn to look. Above them the Cadi and Guard look down from the prison screen, the Grocer and Clerk from the shop screen. Below them the Europeans in their decorative rags stand up in front of their gilt armchairs and long black screen, make a half-turn, and gaze upward. And from the fourth floor, with its three white screens, the dead peer down: Kadidja, the Mother, Warda, Pierre, and the Sergeant. The square fills with cripples. Ommu arrives: black shoes and dress, white greasepaint, a corpse propped by two canes. All await Saïd, who has committed himself to thievery, gratuitous cruelty, and treason as the shortest road to the void.

It is a world of multicolored violence and degradation that is unvexed by the enclosures and reductions of *No Exit* and *Play*. Europeans and Arabs, outsides and insides, bodies and minds, objects and symbols, actors and witnesses can communicate with force even across stylized distances that heighten their apparent incompatibility. Time is not only episodic but also anachronistic, overlapping itself. Space is multiple, kaleidoscopic, with reversible directions. When costumes can be a century out of date and Pierre can hear the General "rolling down the depths of time" (123) some moments before he falls (127), when characters expected from the right can enter from the left and events occurring above can be observed below, the action speeds toward an omnipresent nowhere. Some characters, of course, have already met their violent deaths, have passed through the series of white screens, and have entered upon an affably spectatorial transcendence. Now the living and the dead, all masked or grotesquely made up, await the diabolical advent of the unmasked Saïd who is going farther than anyone. As they face our tiers of seats, these tiers of gazing role-players seem a perverse reflection of our own image. For, unlike *No Exit* or *Play, The Screens* does not pretend to exclude the values of its own action of performance. It incorporates, inverts, and seems to annihilate them. Openness, participation, movement, being, uniqueness, dialectical transcendence: what are they here but screens masking the abyss?

No wonder Genet has been called "the master of ceremonies of a frenzied plunge into annihilation" (Guicharnaud 259), or, "in the plainest sense of the word, a nihilist" (Coe 308). But, if he seems so here, that is because *The Screens* follows a negative dialectic that remains shrewdly but self-contradictorily closed. Beginning in a satirical negation of the ethic of bourgeois colonialism, that dialectic proceeds (rather like some parody of Buddhist logic) to negate its own negation by self-destructive violence or contemptible betrayal and then to de-realize all negations in an aesthetic of dispossession that informs the play's style. Both the Mother and Ommu, in their ravings about "truths that are false" (155) and "truths that must never be applied" (195), articulate versions of that negative dialectic. And it variously unfolds before our eyes as we watch the Mother turn endless trouble into explosive and suicidal laughter, Leila turn ugliness and suffering into the "great adventure" of masochistic sanctity (62), Kadidja turn political revolt into hysterical murder and mayhem, the Arabs and Frenchmen move from violent death into a gently humorous shrugging off of life's myopic passions, the Sergeant elaborately mime the defecation of the world, and the quietly haunted Saïd travel through the essence of evil toward the emptiness of possible song.

The play's knowing rejection of ethical alternatives to that movement is hinted in its witty if unfair retort to Brecht's *The Caucasian Chalk Circle*. The Dutch planter, Mr. Blankensee, after uttering a tribute to the rose as if he were reciting Mallarmé, proceeds to preempt the moral of Brecht's parable: "In a German operetta, I forget which, a character says: 'Things belong to those who've known how to improve them . . .' Who is it who's improved your orange groves, and my forests and roses?" (74). Outlined against that fatuous conflation of left and right, Saïd can seem a stoic anti-Grusha, the plain man determined to evade by negation a world of grotesque masks. And the Cadi, whose whimsical verdicts often recall those of Brecht's lord of misrule, Azdak, can reverse the Brechtian ethic of possession to fit Genet's aesthetic of dispossession: "Things cease to belong to those who've been able to make them more beautiful" (141). That proposition has a certain Sufi or Buddhist beauty—but does it register for this play a charming detachment, a thievish rationalization, or a nihilistic aestheticism?

Certainly the self-conscious diabolism of *The Screens* coexists with some contradictory values that the play never overcomes or cancels. If this play is the "final gesture of defiance" by a "man who chooses evil purely for its own sake" (Thody 207), it remains scandalously committed not only to liberty, equality, and fraternity but also to kindness, gentleness and good humor. Saïd's obscene blinding of Leila intensifies our sympathy for that lonely dreamer, who has admired the gentle and kind appearance of a burnt match (109). Although both Leila and Saïd earn the right to disappear, the others who die during this action remain onstage to constitute a nonpossessive, humorous, and egalitarian community. Pierre's meeting with the Mother who has killed him, Kadidja's education in the art of dying "more and more" (145) to one's violent earthly imagination until one "drains oneself. Of oneself" (169), a process quite beyond the characters of *No Exit,* and Brahim's recognition of the astonished gentleness of the freshly dead soldiers (159) are all signs that point toward no decadent beauty or meaningless void but a horizon where detachment and friendliness can reconcile warring passions. Increasingly free of time, place, and separative self-identifications, these dead suggest the more complex mode of awareness that the action of performance invites us to live.

We can see why Genet told Roger Blin that everything in a production of *The Screens* "should work together to break down whatever separates us from the dead. We must do everything possible toward creating the feeling that we have worked for them, and that we have succeeded" (*Letters to Roger Blin* 12). For, if the performed action commits itself to deliberately outrageous ethical contradictions, the action of performance can move toward luminous clarity only as actors and witnesses detach themselves from the desire to possess, arduously de-realize the play's demonic dialectic, and so find themselves most truly reflected in the celebratory common life of the dead. Do we doubt that an "aesthete" or "nihilist" would be interested in such meanings? If so, Sartre's *Saint Genet, Actor and Martyr,* that biographical reading of the early work that influenced Genet himself, may prepare us for that understanding. Sartre comments astutely on "the secret place where Evil, engendering its own betrayal, is metamorphosed into Beauty" (192), on a self-canceling moralism (567), on a contrapuntal and Mallarméan absence in the words, a verbal symphony in which the only temporality is the "vibratory disappearance" of the universe (576–77), and on the possibility of ethical values being contained in Genet's aesthetic (578). But Sartre holds that "Genet's ethical attitude cannot yet go beyond the stage of generosity" (579). And, when he suggests that "the only way out of hell" for Genet's reader is the proper use of "the horror with which Genet inspires you" (586), his position is more applicable to *No Exit* than to *The Screens.*

We should turn, then, to Genet's own comments on the theater. In 1954, before writing *The Balcony, The Blacks,* or *The Screens,* he could attack Western acting as a complacent "exhibitionism." Nothing can be expected, he said "of a profession that is practiced with so little gravity or self-communion." To elaborate an ethic or an aesthetic would require "courage and renunciation" ("Note on Theatre" 38). He later modified the severity of that judgment but not its ethical criteria. In his letters to Blin he distinguished between the apparent ethical content of *The Screens* and its actual meaning: "My play is not an apologia for treason. It takes place in a realm where morality is replaced by the esthetics of the stage" (21). But for him the stage, that collaborative realm of "liberty" and "death," was not without ethical obligations: if the actors are "unencumbered by any social responsibility, they will assume another, with respect to another Order" (12). He therefore urged that they put aside mere "cleverness," approach "the most secret depths of their being," and become true devotees of the patron saint of actors, Saint Tiresias, "aware that they are a presence constantly beset by femininity or its opposite" but ready to play that given opposite "to the point of abasement" (63). He praised the "theatrical meticulosity" and the vulnerable "strength and delicacy" of Jean-Louis Barrault (58), and the "attentive" presence and great "courage" of Maria Casarès (68, 72). Such actors were giving themselves to this shared work for the dead. Those are not, surely, the views of a "nihilist" or a man "who chooses evil purely for its own sake."

Nor did Genet think the play's witnesses exempt from such imaginative labor. Demonstrators who interrupt the performance, he said, "give into the lazy side of their nature when they see on-stage a dead French officer sniffing the meticulous farts of his soldiers, whereas they ought to be seeing actors playing at being or seeming" (62). And he had asked Maria Casarès to find, in her "new uglified face, a beauty that every spectator—not the public but every spectator—could find within himself in some faltering way, buried but capable of rising to its own surface" (72). What then happens if, as alert spectators, we see, in and through the performed action with its negative dialectic, the remarkable playing of that action? Not only the characters and events but the actors and witnesses will become screens through which we may glimpse what is disturbingly and refreshingly distant from surface appearance. For this playing of "truths that must never be applied" constitutes a living system of what Genet had called "signs as remote as possible from what they are meant first to signify" ("Note on Theatre" 38). The proper style of playing therefore includes an extreme tension between gesture and tone, the expected and the actual, the mimed and the miming. Abjection must be rendered with an astonishing elegance and obviousness, chaotic noise with a difficult and precise silence (*Letters to Blin* 36, 37). "The Arabs' quaking in the presence of Sir Harold's son," said Genet, must not only provide "a painful vision of fear." The actors "will tremble from head to toe, from their shoulders to their hands, and the trembling should be carried to trancelike lengths but should, in passing, evoke the image of a field of rye swayed by a strong wind, or the flight of a flock of partridges" (61). And yet Genet was not asking for a false poeticizing of the action. He urged that the actor playing Ommu be less declamatory when asserting that useless ideas must live through the song they have become. "This should be said very softly. While she runs" (52). And her declaration at the end that "it's the unimportant things that have to live" should be delivered "with impatience, anger, clarity, irritation. Not the pompous way Merleau-Ponty would have said it" (56). In so rendering a multiple negation, the actors and the witnesses become expressive masks not of a meaningless void but of a plenum prior to our culturally conditioned opposites. The performed action suggests a luminous de-objectifying of the real. Our playing becomes the positive equivalent of Saïd's dubious end: the self-negating and self-transcending words of a shared song.

We can begin to see why *The Screens* became so important to the director Peter Brook during his experimental season of 1963–64 and why his encounter with this mode of attaining a kind of theatrical communion through the playing of hell could have such a profound impact upon his next major production, Peter Weiss's *Marat/Sade,* in which the dialectic between Marat's revolutionary vision and Sade's pessimistic interrogation was transcended by just such outrageous, exuberant, and carefully controlled playing. We can also begin to see why *The Screens* could have a no less profound an influence upon Brook's later productions of *A Midsummer Night's Dream* and *The Mahabharata*—plays that might seem the very opposite of what Genet is usually said to stand for but that also lead us through playful detachment to understand the world as dream or illusion. For Genet's play is a dramatic rite in which a nihilistic mimesis is the apparent substance of a language of playful gesture—a language that is exploring the intense "presence" of "an extraordinary emptiness" (*Letters to Blin* 14). Through participation in that language, Genet urged, each actor would cast "light" on the others, and the stage would become "a site not where reflections spend themselves but where bursts of light meet and collide." The mimetic reflections of life would here enable an illumination that proceeds from our acting and witnessing. It was no mere flippancy that caused Genet to add: the stage "would by the same token be a site where Christian charity amused itself" (49). Such a dramatic rite asks us to abandon our possession of the physical or moral goods, our pretension to be a solid someone, justified in warring against all others. It asks us to experience ourselves instead as screens or masks for a "void" or "no-thing" within which the opposites of our usual world can luminously collide. Its aim is far from being "quite simply nothingness" (Guicharnaud 259). As we let go of our variously one-sided and self-blinding selves, there comes into being a fresh attentiveness like that of Genet's dead. The immediate goal of such playing, in his own words, "is to reveal and make heard what generally passes unperceived." And beyond that? "Its real goal, of course, is a new joy, a new festivity, and God knows what besides" (*Letters to Blin* 72).

Surely that goal was at least approached by Joanne Akalaitis's extraordinarily fine production of *The Screens* in 1989 at the Tyrone Guthrie Theatre in Minneapolis. The physicalization of the play used epic theater devices reminiscent of Brecht—voice-overs of FLN announcements and visible stage lights. A circus acrobats' net was stretched over the light grid, and in the second half of the play it became the land of the dead, with actors bouncing around or sleeping in the net. (Could one feel as if one were looking back at a Brechtian *Screens* through Peter Brook's *A Midsummer Night's Dream,* in which offstage actors watched the production from aloft?) Music by Philip Glass and Foday Musa Suso complemented the sex-and-power driven action. Those who could take the five-and-a-half hour production (counting the dinner break) had, according to one witness, an appropriately double experience of "the horror of the world Genet depicts and the joy of the actors performing it" (Parham 251).

V

Can we climb down the flanks of despair to a yet colder and more truly geocentric point? No doubt. We can play "absolutely as it is" (15), without Cartesian reduction or fantastic translation, our anxious attempt to maintain a powerful or invulnerable "I" in the dissolving field of theatrical and linguistic consciousness. We can enter no-man's-land, which "never changes, which never grows older, but which remains forever, icy and silent." "I'll drink to that" (95). Seated in his straight-backed chair, the curtains drawn against the light of a summer morning near Hampstead Heath, "our host" raises his glass to the assembled company: his two protectors or "oldest friends," who have explicated his order that the subject be changed for the last time; his ingratiating and threatening guest ("Mr. Friend"), who has just now echoed his stammering phrases of the night before; and those of us seated in the dark theater that almost seems an extension of the closed room—thanks, in Peter Hall's first production at the National, to John

Bury's incomplete oval of gray-curtained windows flanked by two columns, which managed without violating the fourth-wall convention to suggest the equivalence of stage and house. Here we are . . . together . . . forever. A slow fade.

Although we have seen two acts in which none of the plausible, witty, devastating, or agonized speeches has established for any speaker an unambiguous identity, we know clearly enough what is at stake and for whom. Our host? A taciturn alcoholic who has locked himself into the past with his "true friends" (45), the dead, and is haunted by a guilt-laden dream of drowned love. Neither he nor anyone else onstage ever speaks his name. The subtle brute called Briggs or Denson or Albert (who says he's written a letter to the *Times* on "Life At a Dead End") speaks of his boss as "a man of letters" (67). Briggs's mate, the probably bisexual "poet" called Jack Foster, refers to the host as his "father" but also tells of being recruited as secretary and housekeeper (35). And the guest? Seedy, glib, with elaborately factitious Edwardian speech, he claims to derive his strength from never having been loved (27), calls himself by the name of Spooner (though the host later uses another name), and says he is a poet with a checkered career and a house in the country (though Briggs says he collects beer mugs at a pub in Chalk Farm). If the host drowns love and evades identification by retreating to the changeless land of his photograph album—"In my day," he says, "nobody changed" (78)—the guest fends off love by remaining in the "truly unscrupulous present" (20) in which he can keep an "objective" distance from such "matter" (19) as other people, interpret the past "to suit your taste or mine" (20) and be assured "that I am as I think myself to be, that I am fixed, concrete" (17).

Pirandello and Sartre knew what to make of such attempts to found a solid essence on the void, as does our host, who recognizes the guest as his double: "And so I say to you, tender the dead, as you would yourself be tendered, now, in what you would describe as your life" (79). The guest offers to go through the host's album, with its "ghosts" of trapped emotions, putting names to the faces and making possible a "proper exhumation" (83–84). But he has already made himself the equivalent of those whom Briggs calls the "blank dead" (79), for every claim to be someone in this play—"I am I," he declares (89)—is an anxious attempt to dominate the present by substituting for its unpredictable life a verbal form drawn from the unverifiable past. The host's evasions, the guest's aggressions, and the protectors' variations on those moves all come to the same thing.

The name of their game is Naming the Dead. That is why the names here are all ironic jokes. Although the program, of course, tells us that our host is Hirst, that name is almost irrelevant unless we happen to know that Hirst, Briggs, Foster, and Spooner are names of four skilled but long-dead players of cricket, Pinter's favorite game (Gale 203–4). That is also why the lines often suggest a faded album of literary faces to which every Spooner in the audience is invited to put names. When the guest urges, "Let me live with you and be your secretary," the host, who has bragged of seducing Emily and has been accused of seducing Stella, replies: "Is there a big fly in here? I hear buzzing" (88). (The answers to those implicit riddles run a gamut from Marlowe through Swift to Dickinson.) And that is why the play invites us to join the characters in an unpredictable present that becomes more perplexing, empty, and loveless with every attempt to freeze and control it through names drawn from the past.

We share the initial sparring over drinks as the guest tries with suspiciously candid chatter to entice the host into self-revelations. We grasp for clues as Spooner trades memories of bucolic life, savors the host's discourse on virgin death, and proposes the subject of absent wives. And we watch astonished as he swiftly attacks—"Her eyes, I take it, were hazel?" (31)—forces the now drunken and shaken host to declare his icy condition and then comments with jingling irony (partly drawn from T. S. Eliot's "Portrait of a Lady") on his ignominious exit (34). Do these antagonists who have apparently just met know each other better than we know either? But our suspicion is at once deflected by Briggs's claims to recognize Mr. Friend as the pintpot attendant, and our sense of reality is unsettled by some strangely literary anecdotes. Can Spooner, with his knowingly impressionist portrait of *The Whistler* by the Amsterdam canal, be a British version of Jean-Baptiste Clamence in Albert Camus's *The Fall?* Does Foster come back from some unwritten Conrad novel of the Far East to tell of the coin that disappears into thin air? When the host returns, half-soliloquizing about his album, his dream, his past—"It's gone. It never existed. It remains" (46)—we are prepared to resume interpretation on a somewhat loftier plane. Yes: almost a Jamesian version of Beckett's Hamm! But we are making the same demand for cognitive control that Spooner makes when he says: "It was I drowning in your dream" (47). As the protectors resist his attempt to become master of the undefined game, we are forced with him back to a minimal grasp of farcical melodrama. Briggs removes the host, who now declares that he knows the guest from somewhere, and Foster—asking, "You know what it's like when you're in a room with the light on and suddenly the light goes out?"—turns out the light on all of us (53).

The second act sucks us further into a world where the past is unknowable, the future unpredictable, the present a room of loveless wills constructing themselves out of fictions, and each fiction a mocking symbol of that world. No sooner does the guest learn that the host is a "man of letters" than the host names the guest as "Charles" (and Briggs as "Denson"). The ensuing reminiscences, fabricated by bluffing players who are trying to enclose each other in increasingly outrageous versions of the past, led half the New York reviewers in 1976 to say that Hirst had seduced Spooner's wife. But Ibsen is here being parodied by the compound ghost of Oscar Wilde and Joe Orton. The play flashes its cards with a rapidity that is deliberately confusing: the host says he seduced Charles's wife "Emily" (69), the guest (forgetting his identity as Charles, or risking another gambit?) refers to the seduction of "Emily Spooner" (76), and the host finally contrasts the "lout" he is addressing with the "Charles Wetherby" he had known (78). What is the truth of the past? An album of nameless faces, midsummer gullies filled with lost tennis balls, a dream of a body floating in the water, words that name the blank. The host's request for an explication of his order that the subject be changed for the last time, a most whimsical conclusion to this systematic teasing of our lust for knowledge, appropriately sums up a hell in which every season of the soul seems a verbal maneuver.

It is no wonder that *No Man's Land* itself seems a pseudorealistic blend of situations drawn from Pirandello's *Henry IV* (in which a nameless role-player fences in the dark with role-playing intruders who probe his fixation on the past) and Beckett's *Endgame* (in which four players whose past is a tangle of grotesque stories enact the self-reductive gambits of a single consciousness) with themes and phrases that often recall Eliot: the neurotic self-analysis of "The Love Song of J. Alfred Prufrock" and "Portrait of a Lady," the evasive rhetoric of "Gerontion," the paralyzed force of "The Hollow Men," the laconic nihilism and echoing stichomythia of *Sweeney Agonistes,* the muffled guilt of *The Family Reunion,* the language of the dead in the zero summer of *Little Gidding*—"now and in England and in Hampstead and for all eternity" (17). Like Spooner's quite probably nonexistent "Homage to Wessex" in terza rima and the Dantesque section of *Little Gidding* that it brings to mind, this play finds its infernal substance in a stylistic encounter with "a familiar compound ghost / Both intimate and unidentifiable." Hardy, Marlowe, Dickinson, Swift, Milton, Coleridge, Wordsworth, Shakespeare, Dickens, the Brontës, Auden, and Williams: these and other ghosts namelessly haunt the stage. "All we have is the English language," says the yahoo-disdaining and Wessex-loving Mr. Friend. "Can it be salvaged? That is my question" (18). Existence has become words, words, words—a present instance of what Spooner will call "the wittiest and most subtle systematic withdrawal known to man" (20–21)—and Hamlet has become a failed poet who mirrors a playwright on the dump of last year's language.

That is why this very literary hell, with its burned-out writer, failed writer, would-be writer and subtle thug, also parodies the development and refinement in Pinter's work from *The Room* through *The Collection* to *Old Times* of just such a perplexity of givens: the struggle for dominance in a closed room, the unverifiable past as the aim of present action, the agons that shift from banal realism into eerie near-symbolism, the antagonists who appear out of nowhere and make themselves up as they go along, the language of pastiche that eloquently betrays its own evasiveness, the tableaux of frozen violence, and the dramatic form that implies not our objective transcendence of the presented world (as in *Ghosts* or *No Exit* or *Play*) but our half-knowing complicity in its ambiguities (as in Kafka's *The Trial* or Camus's *The Fall* or Beckett's *The Unnameable*). Briggs knows his Pinter. He can frame his account of Foster with a flat formula of unverifiability: "I should tell you he'll deny this account. His story will be different" (62). Our host's talk of shadows echoes that of Beth in *Landscape* (Gale 209). Spooner seems an emasculated Goldberg from *The Birthday Party,* an educated Davies from *The Caretaker,* a not-so-dumb waiter. "I have known this before," runs his archly Eliotic cadence. "The command from an upper floor" (68; Gale 216). The game of Nostalgia with popular songs in *Old Times,* a play in which three characters almost share a single consciousness, has here become a four-handed game of solitaire with tags from the literary and theatrical past. And our real host is not Hirst but the playwright who recently spent the "best working year" of his life as a kind of filmic secretary to a famous writer who had enclosed himself with his album of memories in a cork-lined room (*Proust Screenplay* x). It is only an ironic step from Proust to Hirst.

As a self-parodying enactment of our will to verbal and formal power over a world that must respond by assuming the name and form of our death, *No Man's Land* is a true descendant of Ibsen's *The Master Builder* and *When We Dead Awaken.* It invites us to join characters and playwright in the hell of echoing absence that is constructed by every self-defining and self-perpetuating "I." What is the alternative to that deathly no-man's-land? Not "manliness" as usually understood but a nonverbal, nonwillful, and anonymous presence: being no man. We might gather from Pinter's critics that such an alternative is impossible or irrelevant. They usually assert that Pinter's plays depict a problematic reality that is being explored, evaded, or negotiated by characters who are known to be essentially "selfish" or necessarily "coercive." And it is true that the performed action of *No Man's Land* could not include for more than an instant a noncoercive and nondeceptive presence without causing the play to explode. If the serenely sitting émigré at Jack Straw's Castle emerged from the words of Spooner's story, he would have to become a defective like Aston in *The Caretaker* or a zombie like Barnabas in *A Slight Ache.* Even Hirst's momentary waking to the "sounds of birds" (94) must yield at once to a retrospective deafness and so remain a mere hint of an apparently unrealizable alertness to new life. What endures is the meaning of his Hamm-like assertion: "Today I shall come to a conclusion" (86).

But surely the contradictions in this performed action (the surprising and refreshing pastiche, the ambiguities that disclose their aggressive or defensive intent, the evasive anecdotes and solipsistic mutterings that deftly render a shared meaning, and the illusions of unverifiability and unpredictability that arise from a firmly inconsistent narrative progression) should warn us that the play's closure is knowingly factitious. Each contradiction tacitly acknowledges the possibility of a noncoercive alertness to the paradoxical beauty of what is perceived to be false. Indeed, Pinter knows quite well that no good playwright can act in accord with the psychological "necessities" that critics have found in his plays. Aggression? Deception? Anxious selfishness? "Given characters who possess a momentum of their own," he has said, "my job is not to impose upon them . . . The relationship between author and characters should be a highly respectful one, both ways" (*Complete Works: One* 14). An author should avoid the "cheating" involved in a claim to know what cannot be known (Gale 254). Although reality may be a "quicksand," it is "no worse or better for that" (*Complete Works: One* 12). And though language arises from the "evasion" of communication and builds "a prison of empty definition and cliché," writing plays can confront the "nausea" induced by language, can "move through it and out of it," and can therefore be "a kind of celebration" (13–14, 15). In short, Pinter cannot claim to inhabit a simply Pinteresque world. But neither do the actors and witnesses of *No Man's Land,* for here, as in *No Exit, Play,* and *The Screens,* though more precariously, the action of performance transforms the hell of the performed action.

As we act and witness this chillingly comic exposure of our effort to freeze the problematic flux of experience, we are not merely tempted to understand what cannot be understood: we are also forced back toward an ignorant yet strangely fruitful attention to the present. We begin to see why Pinter could say that any attempt to guess what "really" happened in the "past" of *Old Times* is a mistake, that "the past is not past, that it never was past," that we should attend to the "ever-present quality in life" (Gussow 132–33). We begin to see why he asked not for some conceptual or symbolic identification of his characters but for a painful "recognition," an "active and willing participation" (*Complete Works: One* 11). And we may suspect that Ruth in *The Homecoming*—that ironic counterpart of Ranevskaya in *The Cherry Orchard*—is not just being seductive when she says: "My lips move. Why don't you restrict . . . your attention to that? Perhaps the fact that they move is more significant . . . than the words which come through them" (*Complete Works: Three* 69).

Merely watching and listening, allowing the unpredictable present to flow through us, observing without explanation or condemnation the movements behind the words, sharing the anxious silences that the words fail to cover, we become increasingly alert to that naked vulnerability that is always trying through yet another verbal maneuver to constitute itself as a controlling "I." But who is alert? Who inhabits this constantly renewed interval between perception and naming, between the perception of vulnerable life and the self-naming that must always name the already dead? Not "I" or "we." Just before the end of our playing this interval of shared awareness seems fleetingly evident within the performed action, as our host hears the early sounds of birds: "Sounds I have never heard before" (94). Just so the same interval must have been repeatedly evident to the playwright nauseated by clichés who listened so attentively for the previously unheard sounds of this play. And suddenly it is clear (but to whom?) that the curtained and coercive room of *No Man's Land* is a trap of "timeless moments" in which every sentence is for the "I" an ironic "step to the block," that in playing these moments we may descend towards a freshness of life "heard, half-heard, in the stillness" (Eliot, *Collected Poems* 208, 209), and that no speaking of such playing can ever be more than a self-contradictory sign of its geocentric reversal . . . an ending in which no man begins. In what may seem the nadir of modern theatrical representations of human life, in the most powerful evocations of our willed absence, we may experience the irrefutable signs of our shared presence.

Do we need "biographical" evidence that entering into such a static and frozen ending—as actor, as member of the audience, even as playwright—can be a fresh beginning? That dramatizing our self-blockage may provide an unblocking experience? While Pinter himself was playing Hirst, between Christmas 1992 and the end of January 1993, he was impelled and enabled to complete his first full-length play in fifteen years, *Moonlight,* a play that more deeply and echoingly explores whatever light is left in the dark. As he put it to an interviewer, "acting . . . every night, saying those words every night . . . I was stimulated . . . and one day while I was still acting at night, I started to scribble away and so something was released by saying all these damned words." Describing this "mysterious process" to another interviewer, he began sounding very much like Hirst: he had found "pools within it that I hadn't known were there: as if the light hit it. I just see that image, I don't know why, of light hitting dark pools and illuminating those pools." As Ronald Knowles put it succinctly: "By way of re-entering his own play with such imaginative projection and immersion, the author found seven characters waiting in 'moonlight' for their story to be told" (119). We may take that, I think, as one version of the new life that opens before us when we play hell. Other versions will become apparent as we turn to the presences of Byron and Beckett in our theater.

Part 2

Presences

Chapter 5

The Presence of Byron

I

As we have often had occasion to see, theatrical paradigms are mediated and transformed by the presences who help to shape the mirrors of our playing. The contributions of four quite different presences can more fully suggest that mediating and transformative power. George Gordon, Lord Byron, an often neglected ancestor of the ironic, self-lacerating, and self-negating modern sensibility, has informed a variety of modern paradigms. Samuel Beckett, who carried that sensibility toward its apparent vanishing point in "playing hell," has paradoxically nourished in others some very different modes of theater. Wole Soyinka, one who has learned from Beckett to do otherwise, has restlessly sought to relate the paradigms of European theater to his Nigerian understanding of individual and community transformation. And Peter Brook, a director who also learned much from Beckett, as from Genet, Brecht, and Shakespeare, and who has increasingly made the world theater his province, has sought through several paradigms to identify the transformative process inherent in play itself.

When we think of ancestral presences in the theater today, we most easily fasten upon Shakespeare. We find him looming behind playwrights from Shaw and Brecht to Beckett, Bond, and Barker, and in contemporary productions by Peter Brook, Kenneth Branagh, and others he may himself be the most important of "modern" playwrights. But the distinctive accents of our theater—from Wilde and Shaw to Williams, Brenton, and Stoppard—owe as much to the more elusive presence of another poet and dramatist, Lord Byron. Although sometimes mentioned in studies of individual dramatists, Byron has usually escaped the attention of historians of modern drama. Denis Donoghue in *The Third Voice: Modern British and American Verse Drama* saw little need to refer to him. Tom Driver in *Romantic Quest and Modern Query: A History of the Modern Theater,* finding the English Romantic poets important "only insofar as they show that romanticism of the dream can seduce even the best of talents," concluded that Byron was "perhaps the epitome of dream-romanticism, with its adulation of the heroic quester," one who "did not put much reality into his *Manfred*" and whose *Marino Faliero* and *Sardanapalus* "are best forgotten" (16). Nor do Robert Brustein in *The Theatre of Revolt* and Austin E. Quigley in *The Modern Stage and Other Worlds* add to our understanding of a presence that seems almost invisible, like the air we breathe.

For fuller understanding we must look to the critics of romantic drama, from G. Wilson Knight to Martyn Corbett, and to those who have related it to modern culture. George Steiner in *The Death of Tragedy* praised the "range of technical audacity" in Byron's plays and found "preliminaries to some of the most radical aspects of modern drama" (202). He said of *Heaven and Earth,* a "kind of dramatic cantata," that it "is only in the contemporary theatre that such effects have been fully realized" (209–10). Alan Richardson in *A Mental Theater: Poetic Drama and Consciousness in the Romantic Age* noted that the modern theater, when freed from naturalist dramaturgy, has been able to render through lyric poetry and poetically charged prose the themes of intellectual seduction, divided self-consciousness, and repetition that are prominent in romantic drama (188–89). And Jeffrey Perl in *The Tradition of Return* has described *Manfred* as preparing the way for "all the antitheater drama that succeeds it" (116). In fact, Byron should be evident yet more generally as an archetype of the self-ironic and self-destructive Prometheanism at the heart of modern culture. Just as "Byronism," Europeanized and then Americanized, has engendered or influenced poetry from Alexander Pushkin's *Eugene Onegin* to John Berryman's *Dream Songs,* so it has helped to shape a protean "mental theater"—lyrical, argumentative, expressionistic, or naturalistic—that combines personal, social, historical, and philosophical themes as it moves through a variety of paradigms.

Mental theater meant to Byron something much more vigorous than "closet drama" (*Letters and Journals* 8:187). As David Erdman argued years ago, we cannot take at face value Byron's insistence that he refused to write for the stage. William Ruddick has shown how Byron's historical tragedies are "plays addressed to the ear and to the inward eye"—though he too cautiously suggests that our age "offers a new possibility for their successful performance through the verbal resources of radio drama" (94). Such theater, as Byron knew, has classical antecedents and can draw upon the poetic richness of Shakespeare and other Elizabethans (Ruddick 83–85, 93). But other forms of Byron's mental theater derive from liturgical traditions: to both

Cain and *Heaven and Earth* he gave the subtitle "A Mystery," and he called the latter "a kind of Oratorio on a sacred subject" (*Letters and Journals* 9:81). Interpreted most broadly, *mental theater* points to Byron's emphasis on a variously styled drama of often suppressed intellectual passions and exacerbated self-consciousness. Such theater has had other nineteenth-century exemplars: Goethe, who applauded *Manfred* and recognized its affinity with *Faust,* Shelley in *The Cenci,* Kleist in *Penthesilea* and *The Prince of Homburg,* Büchner in *Danton's Death,* and Ibsen in *Peer Gynt* and *When We Dead Awaken.* Prominent in the ancestry of our own mental theater, too, are medieval mysteries and moralities and major works of Calderón. With all these in mind Strindberg revitalized the "station-play" in *A Dream Play, To Damascus,* and *The Great Highway.* Hofmannsthal, who adapted *Everyman,* also adapted Calderón's *The Great World Theater* and turned *Life Is a Dream* into *The Tower.* Jerzy Grotowski "confronted" Calderón's *The Constant Prince.* Claudel's experiments in mental theater included not only *Break of Noon,* which reworks the guilty and self-involved Manfred's encounter with the vision of Astarte and the spirits, but also *The Satin Slipper,* which recalls Calderón's understanding of "world theater," and *Tobias and Sara,* which approaches biblical material through the dramatic form of the "mystery." In the English-speaking theater of our century we will often encounter such repetition, transformation, and partial reversal of Byron's themes and modes.

His defiant and desperate accents have had special importance in our own mental theater. Although his plays, including an adapted *Manfred,* were successfully produced in the nineteenth century (Taborski 152–345), not until later was the stage dominated by his alienation, exacerbated self-consciousness, and self-lacerating passions. The paradigm of "playing hell" in our mental theater has focused on the blocked situations of alienated characters, haunted by disillusionment, guilt, or fatality, who confront death and judgment in some closed room or indefinite void. Translating the consciousness of isolated characters into the forms of social art, such plays can explore the tensions between hidden suffering and the need for public display and between the experienced alienation in the "performed action" and our freshly discoverable community in the "action of performance." They run a gamut of styles—from Ibsen's *When We Dead Awaken,* Chekhov's *Uncle Vanya,* Strindberg's *The Ghost Sonata,* and Shaw's *Heartbreak House* to Kaiser's *From Morn to Midnight,* Brecht's *Baal,* and Pirandello's *Henry IV* and on to Sartre's *No Exit,* Beckett's *Endgame,* Pinter's *No Man's Land,* Shepard's *The Tooth of Crime,* and Mamet's *Edmond.* Drawing upon naturalism, symbolism, and expressionism, the Byronic mental theater can incorporate lyrical drama, the symposium, drawing-room comedy, and forms derived from Greek tragedy and the medieval morality play.

Such mental theater is symptomatic of a strain of Byronism in modern culture that is no less virulent when unconscious, disguised, or repressed, but Byron's own work has surfaced in important ways. At the Moscow Art Theatre, long after having explored the self-regarding plangencies of Chekhov's Vanya, Stanislavsky translated Byron's *Cain* into two different scenic designs. One, unproduced, was an elaborate medieval cathedral in which "the illusion of stars in the Abyss of Space was created by the countless lighted candles carried by the monks." The other, produced in 1920, employed black velvet to give the illusion of suspension in midair and huge statues to represent the "mighty phantoms of earlier beings" (Magarshack 354; Taborski 341–49). Forty years later Grotowski opened his Theater Laboratory with an adaptation of *Cain* in which the text was subjected to parodistic transformations and the actors entered the ranks of spectators implicitly cast as Cain's descendants (Taborski 351–64; Tempkine 82; Wiles 55). It is not surprising that James Joyce, who had imitated the late Ibsen in his only play *Exiles* and the expressionistic Strindberg in the Nighttown episode of *Ulysses,* should try in 1930 to turn *Cain* into an opera (Steffan 472–73). It is more significant, however, that a number of English-speaking dramatists have engaged quite directly, if with some resistance, their Byronic heritage. These responses, which testify to an imposing presence, may remind us that what Peter Szondi and Andrew Kennedy have called the "monologic" language of modern drama is, at a deeper level, a complex conversation within the romantic tradition.

II

We could easily start with Oscar Wilde, whose conflation of Byron's aristocratic, histrionic, and self-ironic observer with rake figures drawn from Restoration comedy was important for such various playwrights as Shaw, Yeats, O'Neill, and Stoppard. Yeats understandably put Wilde and Byron in the same "Phase" in the metaphysical, historical, and psychological system of *A Vision* (148–49). But the most important mental theater of this century in English is that of Shaw. Reworking the elements of romantic comedy, melodrama, farce, and opera into his own "rhetorical drama of impassioned ideas" (Meisel 431), Shaw became an avant-garde playwright a generation ahead of his contemporaries (Weintraub, *Unexpected Shaw* 223–33). His discussion plays drew upon Ibsen, but his dream plays developed independently of Strindberg, and his dialectical history plays and absurd fantasies preceded those of Brecht and Beckett. Everywhere Byron was a presence to be imitated, rebutted, and half-denied.

One value of Byronism in Shaw's mental theater was its stress upon the histrionic. "All Shaw's memorable characters," as Maurice Valency noted, "have a latent Byronic image, firmly and often comically suppressed, which is eventually developed into visibility" (115). We can easily think of Charteris in *The Philanderer* (1893), Sergius in *Arms and the Man* (1894), Valentine in *You Never Can Tell* (1896), Dick Dudgeon in *The Devil's Disciple* (1897), Tanner in *Man and Superman* (1903), and Hector Hushabye in *Heartbreak House* (1919). But there are touches of Byron also in Marchbanks at the end of *Candida* (1895), Caesar in *Caesar and Cleopatra* (1898), Brassbound in *Captain Brassbound's Conversion* (1899), Shotover in *Heartbreak House,* and even Joan in *Saint Joan* (1923). In the preface to *Great Catherine* (1913) Shaw admits that he has followed Byron's conception of Catherine in *Don Juan.* And in *Back to Methuselah* (1920), a revisionary biblical drama that relies on Byronic examples, the romantically dashing Cain echoes some of his precursor's arguments (Nethercot 46).

Fascinated by the character types, settings, and themes in Byron's plays, Shaw complicated and undermined them. The romantic and self-indulgent cynicism in *Heartbreak House* leads toward personal and political paralysis. Deliberately reversing what Byron had called "the whole effect and moral" of *Manfred* (*Letters and Journals* 5:257), Shaw's preface alludes with irony to the end of that poem: "In truth, it is, as Byron said, 'not difficult to die,' and enormously difficult to live" (*Complete Plays with Prefaces* 1:474). The exploitation and transcendence of the Byronic had been yet more explicit in *Arms and the Man,* in which Raina suspects "that perhaps we only had our heroic ideas because we were so fond of reading Byron and Pushkin, and because we were so delighted with the opera that season at Bucharest" (*Complete Plays with Prefaces* 3:127). Shaw describes Sergius as a "clever, imaginative barbarian" whose "acute critical faculty" has been "thrown into intense activity by the arrival of Western civilization," with the same result that the advent of nineteenth-century thought had produced in England—"to wit, Byronism":

> By his brooding over the perpetual failure, not only of others, but of himself, to live up to his imaginative ideals; by his consequent scorn for humanity; by

> his jejune credulity as to the absolute validity of his concepts and the unworthiness of the world in disregarding them; by his wincings and mockeries under the sting of the petty disillusions which every hour spent among men brings to his sensitive observation, he has acquired the half tragic, half ironic air, the mysterious moodiness, the suggestion of a strange and terrible history, by which Childe Harold fascinated the grandmothers of his English contemporaries. (3:150–51)

Just such a Byronism, purged of remorse and half-purged of despair, committed to an ideal called "realism" and supported by a comic sense learned in part from *Don Juan,* became for Shaw's mental theater an animating force.

No doubt Shaw could deny that fact, as in his most interestingly disguised response to Byron. The third act of *Man and Superman* thrusts a Platonic symposium—Tanner's dream of being Don Juan in Hell—into the middle of a farcical romantic comedy. Shaw's prefatory epistle acknowledges that the protagonist and his dream self are in the tradition of Molière and Mozart. But it also purports to explain why Byron has nothing to do with this play. After the "completed works" of Molière and Mozart, "Byron's fragment does not count for much philosophically." (A fragment of sixteen cantos in almost sixteen thousand lines!) Byron's hero, says Shaw, is "not a true Don Juan at all" but a young man whose behavior was much as Shaw's own might have been at that age, had he been given such European advantages. Like Peter the Great, he says, Byron is an instance of "that rare and useful, but unedifying variation, an energetic genius born without the prejudices or superstitions of his contemporaries." Although the "resultant unscrupulous freedom of thought made Byron a bolder poet than Wordsworth," that was "only a negative qualification," for it did not enable him "to become a religious force like Shelley." "Let us, then," Shaw concludes, "leave Byron's Don Juan out of account" (*Complete Plays with Prefaces* 3:490).

What would a twentieth-century Byron be like if he *could* become a "religious force"? No doubt he would be Bernard Shaw, the seriocomic exponent of the Life Force itself. This dialectic of rejection, transformation, and incorporation is similar to that through which Shaw absorbed Shakespeare. Although he knew many versions of Don Juan's story (Crompton 91), he has disarmingly portrayed himself here as covering his own Byronic traces. Already in the 1880s he had described Mozart's Don Giovanni in proleptic terms as "the first Byronic hero in music" and had written a short story, "Don Giovanni Explains," in which the protagonist is no aggressive philanderer but a man trapped by the amorous designs of others. In those preludes to *Man and Superman,* as Stanley Weintraub has said, Shaw was attracted by "Byron's irresitibility to, and his pursuit by, the opposite sex, and his ironic inversion of, and sardonic comments upon, conventional values" (Weintraub, "Genesis" 25). But Shaw's dramatic strategy in *Man and Superman* involves a double transformation that enables us to participate in these Byronic impulses with both rueful delight and philosophical admiration.

As part of a complex theatrical paradigm, act 3 of *Man and Superman* transposes the music of farce, just before the final cadence, into a philosophical cadenza that seems to distance the performed action even as it more firmly locates it in our own minds. In generic terms this Platonic symposium is a dream version of the dialogue with spirits that Byron had already used in *Manfred* and again in *Cain,* in which the protagonist was also taken to Hades. In acts 1, 2, and 4 of *Man and Superman* the verbally agile but often comically defeated Tanner is an updated and intellectualized version of Byron's passive young Juan, who "had no idea / Of his own case, and never hit a true one" (1.682–83). In act 3 Tanner's archetype, Don Juan, exhibits a dialectical brilliance that can rival that of Byron himself. More knowledgeable than Byron's Cain and more paradoxically Luciferian than his Lucifer, Shaw's Don Juan vanquishes the rather bourgeois Shavian Devil and proceeds to the heaven of philosophers. In act 4, however, the twentieth-century embodiment of Don Juan is then vanquished in the sexual comedy of the Life Force. Byron had confessed in *Don Juan:* "If I have any fault, it is digression; / Leaving my people to proceed alone, / While I soliloquize beyond expression" (3.858–60). Shaw knew that temptation very well—and often passed it on to his characters. At the end of *Man and Superman* the young woman who has trapped Jack Tanner invites "universal laughter" by indulgently encouraging him in what now seems an entertaining minor vice: "Go on talking" (3.686).

III

Other kinds of Byronic mental theater were developed by Yeats and Eliot. Yeats drew upon French symbolism, Irish heroic myth, and the Japanese Noh, and Eliot upon Greek tragedy, medieval drama, Christian liturgy, and drawing-room comedy. For both, Byron was a presence to be imitated, transformed, and transcended—and they helped to transmit that presence to the yet more important mental theaters of Beckett and Pinter.

Yeats at seventeen, climbing along the narrow ledge at Howth Castle, liked to imagine that he was "Manfred on his glacier" (*Autobiography* 39). The tower in which "night after night, for years," Manfred "pursued long vigils" assumed for the adult Yeats the form of Thoor Ballylee (3.3.1–2), called in "Ego Dominus Tuus" that "old wind-beaten tower, where still / A lamp burns on beside the open book" (*Poems* 160). Certainly he was as interested as Manfred in raising spirits and studying spells (1.2), and he learned to translate Manfred's endurance into a Nietzschean delight in recurrence. Alone upon the cliffs of the Jungfrau, Manfred had said:

> There is a power upon me which withholds,
> And makes it my fatality to live;
> If it be life to wear within myself
> This barrenness of spirit, and to be
> My own soul's sepulchre . . .
>
> (1.2.23–37)

In "A Dialogue of Self and Soul," which turns a Byronic doubleness of mood into a sharp debate, the Yeatsian Self resists the Soul's desire for deliverance from life in words that echo this formulation:

> I am content to live it all again
> And yet again, if it be life to pitch
> Into the frog-spawn of a blind man's ditch,
> A blind man battering blind men . . .
>
> (*Poems* 236)

Yeats's poetic and dramatic theory made much of a distinction between mere "character," a bundle of socially determined accidents, and "personality," which he defined as "the individual form of our passions." Manfred, he said, has such a personality, but "we do not necessarily know much about his character" (*Letters* 548). The poet-heroes of Yeats's early plays, the mocking Seanchan in *The King's Threshold* (1904) and the romantic Forgael in *The Shadowy Waters* (1911) are quite un-Shavian, but, like Marchbanks, Tanner, and Shotover, they are self-conscious outsiders in a partially Byronic mode. And Yeats's major Irish hero, Cuchulain, becomes in the cycle that runs from *On Baile's Strand* (1904) to *The Death of Cuchulain* (1939) increasingly identifiable as a mind that, like Manfred's, is turned in upon itself in pride, guilt, solitude, and confrontation with death.

Adaptations from the Japanese Noh enabled the stage figure of Cuchulain to approach the "tragic image" evoked for Yeats by the dancing of Michio Ito, in which the human figure "seemed to recede from us into some more powerful life" but only "to inhabit as it were the deeps of the mind" (*Essays and Introductions* 224). Aesthetic distance and intimate participation become one in that stylization. The musician's song that opens *At the Hawk's Well* (1917) posits just such a mental theater:

> I call to the eye of the mind
> A well long choked up and dry
> And boughs long stripped by the wind,
> And I call to the mind's eye
> Pallor of an ivory face,
> Its lofty dissolute air,
> A man climbing up to a place
> The salt sea wind has swept bare.
>
> (*Collected Plays* 136)

That description of Cuchulain's face suggests Byron's Giaour: "Though young and pale, that sallow front / Is scath'd by fiery passion's brunt" (ll. 194–95). But except for the "sea wind" we might as easily be imagining Manfred on the Jungfrau just before his encounter with Astarte, for Yeats's Cuchulain will here soon encounter the spirit-woman who diverts him from the well of immortality. In *The Only Jealousy of Emer* (1919), a play that is on one level an autobiographical masquerade, the Ghost of Cuchulain will meet that spirit again. The ironic climax renders the decision of Emer (a wife as long-suffering as the queen Zarina in Byron's *Sardanapalus*) to renounce Cuchulain's love in order to save him from the fatal attraction of the spirit Fand but in full knowledge that he will resume his affair with his mistress Eithne Inguba. The Noh provided a paradigm—an aesthetically distanced encounter of spirits in which both actors and witnesses participate in the depths of their minds—through which Yeats could engage his personal version of the erotic and guilt-laden encounter with spirits that was a major Byronic scenario.

The outlines of *The Only Jealousy of Emer* dissolve on inspection into such an amazing web of ironies that critics have often settled for some partial reading. Cuchulain turns and yet does not turn from Fand: his speeches and the choric comment stress his remorse, but the dramatized agency of change is Emer, operating externally and magically upon him. But Emer's choice is forced by the spirit Bricriu. She will lose Cuchulain no matter how she chooses, and her renunciation in favor of Eithne Inguba not only brings him back to life but also expresses her only jealousy—of Fand. But the death toward which Fand draws Cuchulain is also a transcendent consummation, and yet she is more than either a symbol of death or a spirit called up by his desire: she is herself a yearning and suffering soul. In symbolic terms, she is both the sea against which isolate souls must battle and also a statue of solitude, one of the victims and products of the sea's fertile violence. The opening choruses define the play's major focus as the mysterious correlations between the chaotic matrix of the sea and the beauty of the soul. White shell and white wing are at one with the waters without end and the wind that blows. This identity beyond enmity is expanded by the dramatic action, in which solitary passions are imposed by cosmic pattern and yet felt, in pain or remorse, to result from individual will. Solitude both fated and chosen, passions both suppressed and accepted: those Byronic themes are central to the play, as, in its first version, Cuchulain's address to Fand made explicit:

How could you know
That man is held to those whom he has loved
By pain they gave, or pain that he has given,
Intricacies of pain.

(*Variorum Plays* 559)

Other plays also transmute Byronic themes and forms. *The Dreaming of the Bones* (1919) evokes among the desolate rocks of the Clare-Galway hills the long-dead lovers Diarmuid and Dervorgilla, betrayers of Ireland, to whom the Young Man escaping from Dublin after the Easter Rising refuses to extend forgiveness. *Calvary* (1920) and *The Resurrection* (1931), condensing the biblical mode of *Cain* and *Heaven and Earth,* shift boldly to the New Testament and take Byronic pride toward a Nietzschean consummation. In *Calvary* both Lazarus and Judas defiantly escape Christ's love, and *The Resurrection,* employing a mythological equivalence already present in the climax of Byron's *Sardanapalus,* gives us Christ as a reborn Dionysos.

Yeats's mental theater, however, was not entirely a lyric evocation of a world of myth. *The Words upon the Window-Pane* (1934), a realistic play in prose, uses a spiritualist séance conducted by a Mrs. Henderson to create an auditory version of mental theater as a play-within-a-play in a Dublin lodging house. As the guests assemble they are told by the evangelist Abraham Johnson of an "evil" spirit that has "destroyed our séances" (*Collected Plays* 379). Mrs. Mallet says: "He would not let anybody speak but himself" (382). What we soon hear—as the Cambridge student John Corbet recognizes—

is the half-mad, physically chaste, but remarkably Byronic spirit of Jonathan Swift, trapped by guilt and fate, addressing Vanessa and then Stella, soliloquizing obsessively. His arrogance of intellect seems paramount. He speaks of his Pygmalion-like use of Vanessa: "When I rebuilt Rome in your mind it was as though I walked its streets" (383). But Vanessa acknowledges that "no man in Ireland is so passionate." We glimpse his resistance to the temptation of love and mutuality and his fear of solitude. "Can you face solitude with that mind, Jonathan?" asks Vanessa. To which Swift responds: "My God, I am left alone with my enemy. Who locked the door, who locked me in with my enemy?" (384). Monologue itself seems here to have constructed its own purgatorial prison. "Have I wronged you, beloved Stella?" asks Swift, after a hymn has been sung to bring what the "control" Lulu calls "good influence." "Are you unhappy?" (385). And then: "Yes, you will close my eyes, Stella" (386). But in response to that pleading intimacy, Stella's silence, her absence, speaks most eloquently. After the séance is over and the visitors have left, a *coup de théâtre* provides something like a closing chorus. Through the weary medium crouched by the hearth—and therefore, as it seems, through the actress, and through us as we share the action—erupts the self-dramatizing voice of the dirty old man of her trance: "Five great ministers that were my friends are gone, ten great ministers that were my friends are gone." As Mrs. Henderson prepares tea, she suddenly lets a saucer fall and break, and Swift speaks again from the depths of her mind and ours: "Perish the day on which I was born!" (388).

But it is with *Purgatory* (1939) that Yeats most fully adumbrates our mid-century Byronic mode of playing hell. Its Old Man, enraged by the family "pollution" that has destroyed his heritage, has killed his dissolute father and now kills his son in a futile effort to free his mother's soul from the continual reenactment of her complicity in his father's crime. Yeats dramatizes this situation in a flexible four-stress verse that recalls the rhythms and the antithetical motifs of *Isaiah:*

> We wait for light, but behold obscurity;
> For brightness, but we walk in darkness . . .
> We are in desolate places as dead men . . .
> We look for judgment, but there is none;
> For salvation, but it is far off from us.
>
> (59.9–11)

At the Hawk's Well had drawn upon that passage in its final chorus—

I have found hateful eyes
Among the desolate places . . .

(*Collected Plays* 144)

—but now Yeats has transformed that style, in part through study of Byron's example.

In 1926 he had written to H. J. C. Grierson: "I am particularly indebted to you for your essay on Byron" in *The Background of English Literature.* "My own verse," he said, "has more and more adopted . . . the syntax and vocabulary of common speech. The passages you quote [from *Childe Harold's Pilgrimage* and *Don Juan*] . . . are perfect personal speech." The "natural momentum in the syntax," said Yeats, is "far more important than simplicity of vocabulary." Byron, he thought, constantly allows such momentum "to die out in some mind-created construction" but "is I think the one great English poet—though one can hardly call him great except in purpose and manhood—who sought it constantly" (*Letters* 710). *Purgatory* sustains just such "natural momentum" in its four-stress lines. The driving yet flexible rhythm clarifies the antitheses and discontinuities of the Old Man's world, with their repetitions and evasions, in a way that prepares for the antiphonal conversations (and, of course, the tree) of Beckett's *Waiting for Godot:*

Boy: So you have come this path before?
Old Man: The moonlight falls upon the path,
The shadow of a cloud upon the house,
And that's symbolical; study that tree,
What is it like?
Boy: A silly old man.
Old Man: It's like—no matter what it's like.
I saw it a year ago stripped bare as now,
So I chose a better trade.
I saw it fifty years ago
Before the thunderbolt had riven it,
Green leaves, ripe leaves, leaves thick as butter.

(430)

With the boy's murder that rhythm becomes a repeated beat that at first signals apparent success—

My father and my son on the same jack-knife!
That finishes—there—there—there—

(435)

—and then, with the return of the visionary horses, actual failure:

> Hoof-beats! Dear God,
> How quickly it returns—beat—beat—!
>
> (436)

The beat of the verse is the fundamental gesture of the Old Man's consciousness, the repeated knife thrust of his soul.

T. S. Eliot would say of Yeats: "It was only in his last play *Purgatory* that he solved his problem of speech in verse, and laid all his successors under obligation to him" (*On Poetry and Poets* 82–83). And more recently Eric Bentley has said:

> In *Purgatory* . . . whatever he does *not* do, Yeats has arrived at a style of dramatic utterance superior to anything he had written in his life before and therefore inferior to nothing in modern English drama. If, from some viewpoints, it is anti-theatrical, from the professional viewpoint it is pure theatre—a play, not to produce, but to act. And it calls for pure acting— . . . the speaking of great words and the discovery of the positions, moves, and gestures that go with them.
>
> (97)

Through that style, developed partly in response to Byron's "personal speech," Yeats has given us a character who seeks like Byron to become his own dramatist, stage manager, protagonist, and chorus.

The fundamental subject of *Purgatory* is neither the degeneration of Ireland nor the psychology of the supernatural, but the spiritual dynamics that underlie our mid-century desire to play hell. That is why, as in Byron's *Manfred,* Beckett's *Endgame,* and Friel's *Faith Healer,* the protagonist's consciousness is closely examined but his "objective" referents are reduced to a minimum. The play's power is enhanced by an austere set—like the Noh-influenced cloth and tree of the original Abbey production. Stage directions indicate that the lighted window is in some sense "there" for the audience, but the Boy cannot see it—"There's nothing but an empty gap in the wall" (433)—until the moment before his own death (435). Yeats had often recognized that ghosts may be projected or molded by living minds. "Sometimes," he said, "our own minds shape that mysterious substance, which may be life itself, according to desire or constrained by memory, and the dead no longer remembering their own names become the characters in the drama we have invented" (*Explorations* 55). As the Old Man enacts and interprets his own drama, drawing the Boy into it, he constructs a psychological prison through an evasion of relationship and a self-deceptive appeal to the power of history and the cosmos. Others exist as images of what he is and is not, images upon which he projects his self-pity and self-hatred. With conscious heroics and witty madness, he clings to a vision of tradition, community, learning, and purity from which he feels alienated—and which he can only further subvert through violent action in its name. Like the young rebel of *The Dreaming of the Bones* he is among the unforgiving consequences of the past; like the maddened Swift he would reduce the future to an impossible purity and certainty. And the play mirrors his incoherence and self-contradictions with a lucidity beyond his awareness.

The man who resents his father's unsuccessful denial of education has yet more successfully deprived his own son, who asks: "What education have you given me?" The sudden answer focuses the Old Man's self-hatred, grievance, and guilt:

I gave the education that befits
A bastard that a pedlar got
Upon a tinker's daughter in a ditch.

(*Collected Plays* 432)

This hatred of his own degradation, which with irony he can both recognize ("No good trade, but good enough / Because I am my father's son, / Because of what I did or may do") and deny ("Hush-a-bye baby, thy father's a knight") (433, 435), underlies the swift violence of his punishing and self-punishing gestures. Vacillating between uncontrolled action and maundering recollection, he is a degraded victim and avenging minister posturing before the mirror of his own imagination:

to kill a house
Where great men grew up, married, died,
I here declare a capital offense.

(432)

Having stuck his father with the knife that cuts his dinner and left him in the burning house, he will now murder his own son with that same knife.

His self-deception shapes the ironic speech that follows the murder:

I am a wretched foul old man
And therefore harmless. When I have stuck
This old jack-knife into a sod

> And pulled it out all bright again,
> And picked up all the money that he dropped,
> I'll to a distant place, and there
> Tell my old jokes among new men.
>
> (435–36)

The lines reverberate with symbolic reenactments—knife, sod, brightness, money, jokes, and men. "I finished all that consequence" (435): no, his own speech has prepared us for the returning hoofbeats. That self-description—"I am a wretched foul old man"—evokes King Lear's moment of release from his purgatory: "I am a very foolish fond old man . . . You must bear with me. Pray you now, forget and forgive" (4.7.60, 84–85). But this Old Man has a very twisted understanding of purgation.

T. S. Eliot said of *Purgatory:* "I wish he had not given it this title, because I cannot accept a purgatory in which there is no hint, or at least no emphasis upon Purgation" (*On Poetry and Poets* 302). We might better describe the hints as richly ironic. The Old Man says of the dead:

> they know at last
> The consequence of those transgressions
> Whether upon others or upon themselves;
> Upon others, others may bring help,
> For when the consequence is at an end
> The dream must end; if upon themselves,
> There is no help but in themselves
> And in the mercy of God.
>
> (431)

But the necessary help "in themselves" drops from the Old Man's mind, and his ending of the "consequence" rationalizes his rage against his own degraded image. Although he fails to understand his self-produced hell, the play invites its participants to do so. As we act and witness it together, letting it reverberate in the deeps of the mind, its import for us can be purgatorial.

In his last play, *The Death of Cuchulain* (1939), Yeats recapitulated his versions of the Byronic mental theater. He split himself, more schematically than Byron did in *Don Juan,* into the self-ironic "producer," the symbolic protagonist, and the wry ballad singer, with each of whom we may partially identify. In the opening frame, as a "very old man looking like something out of mythology" who has been selected to produce this play because he is "out of fashion and out of date like the antiquated romantic stuff the thing is made of," Yeats vents his burlesqued contempt for "this vile age" (438). In the main action, as Cuchulain, he brings to ironic completion the imagined heroic life with its erotic entanglements. As in *Manfred,* this requires a series of encounters with the past: first Eithne Inguba, then the crow-headed Morrigu, war goddess, and then Aoife, the spirit of the Hawk's Well, who bore his son and intends to kill him. But he meets death instead at the hands of the Blind Man of *On Baile's Strand,* who will get twelve pennies for the deed. Manfred had said, "'tis not so difficult to die." Cuchulain says:

There floats out there
The shape that I shall take when I am dead,
My soul's first shape, a soft feathery shape,
And is that not a strange shape for the soul
Of a great fighting-man?

And, as the Blind Man reaches for his neck, he adds:

I say it is about to sing.

(444)

After Emer's Noh-like dance before a black parallelogram that represents Cuchulain's head, we hear "in the silence a few faint bird notes" (445). But then the stage is taken over by a ragged street singer whose ballad—"the tale that the harlot / Sang to the beggar-man" (446)—emphasizes the elusive "reality" of heroic life in the degraded images of the present. A mixture of dramatic modes has turned what Tom Driver deprecated as Byron's "dream-romanticism, with its adulation of the heroic quester," into a tautly ironic and lyric instance of the modern stage.

The Byronic mental theater also held Eliot in thrall. His first poetic "enthusiasm," at sixteen, was for Byron (*On Poetry and Poets* 223). His first appearance in print, in secondary school, was a Byronic exercise in ottava rima. Although soon complicated by the presence of Baudelaire, Byron's influence persisted, as Grover Smith has said, in poems whose characters, though "seldom heroic," share a "burden of blight and guilt" (3). When the protagonist of *The Waste Land* tells us that he sat down and wept by the waters of Leman (*Collected Poems* 60), he substitutes for Babylon the lake that warned Childe Harold "to forsake / Earth's troubled waters for a purer spring" (3.799–800). So too in Eliot's most spirit-haunted plays. *The Family*

Reunion (1939) combines drawing-room conversation with motifs and machinery taken from Aeschylus' *Eumenides;* but its protagonist, Harry, Lord Monchensey, obscurely responsible for his wife's death and haunted by figures in the alcove whom others cannot see, might well say with Manfred:

> My solitude is solitude no more,
> But peopled with the Furies.
>
> (2.2.130–31)

As Northrop Frye has recognized, "Harry, prig or not, is as Byronic a figure as contemporary drama affords" (99).

Strangely enough, Eliot's *Murder in the Cathedral* (1935) reflects the same heritage. Basically, this liturgical play is an analogical elaboration of the paradigm of the Christian Mass: a ritualized presentation of death and new life in which the witnessing participants can deeply share. Exploring Thomas Becket's problematic decision to take the way of martyrdom, Eliot draws an audience of tenuous or minimal religious commitment into the action through devices borrowed from Greek tragedy, Milton's *Samson Agonistes, Everyman,* and *Saint Joan.* As Martyn Corbett has noted, however, Byron's *Heaven and Earth,* which mixes "the choric form of Greek tragedy with the prosody and poetic diction derived from Christian liturgy and the Bible," anticipates Eliot's "much more considered and rigorously worked innovations." Corbett finds it "remarkable that Eliot's celebrated 1937 essay on Byron should have neglected his attempt to do in the 1820s that which Eliot himself achieved in the 1920s" (*Byron and Tragedy* 188). That neglect, however, reflects Eliot's persistent disguise of his theatrical ancestor. The reversals seem calculated. In *Heaven and Earth,* Byron's Chorus of Mortals voices its anguish over an impending watery destruction:

> And where:
> Shall prayer ascend,
> When the swoln clouds unto the mountain bend
> And burst,
> And gushing oceans every barrier rend,
> Until the very deserts know no thirst?
>
> (ll. 1115–19)

Eliot's Chorus of Women, in similar anguish, hopes for the purifying effect of just such a destruction:

Clear the air! clean the sky! wash the wind! take stone from
stone and wash them.
The land is foul, the water is foul, our beasts and ourselves
defiled with blood.
A rain of blood has blinded my eyes.

(*Collected Plays* 47)

Eliot's archbishop, too, absorbs and reverses the Byronic. Childe Harold looked upon the world as a place

Where for some sin, to sorrow I was cast,
To act and suffer.

(3.689–93)

Becket says of the women of Canterbury: "They know and do not know, what it is to act or suffer" (17). A trivial echo? There is more. Like a clerical version of Manfred, Becket must have his climactic "strife with shadows"—a conversation here stylized to evoke *Everyman*. The fourth and unexpected Tempter urges him to proceed toward his vision of martyrdom. "Who are you," asks Becket, "tempting me with my own desires?" And he erupts in a quasi-Byronic manner:

Can sinful pride be driven out
Only by more sinful? Can I neither act nor suffer
Without perdition?

The Tempter responds with Becket's own words: "You know and do not know, what it is to act or suffer." That exchange rewrites the moment when Manfred cries out to the tempting spirit:

Must crimes be punish'd but by other crimes,
And greater criminals?

—and declares:

Thou didst not tempt me, and thou couldst not tempt me;
I have not been thy dupe nor am I thy prey—
But was my own destroyer . . .

(3.4.123–24, 137–40)

Manfred had earlier claimed:

> I have ceased
> To justify my deeds unto myself—
> The last infirmity of evil.
>
> (1.2.27–29)

Becket, however, moves beyond self-justification in a very different way:

> The last temptation is the greatest treason:
> To do the right deed for the wrong reason.
>
> (30)

He will therefore "no longer act or suffer, to the sword's end."

Eliot's mental theater was a repeated attempt to purge the Byronic. He called Byron "an actor who devoted immense trouble to becoming a role that he adopted," a man who was "so occupied with himself and with the figure he was cutting nothing outside could be altogether real" (*On Poetry and Poets* 238, 226). He might have been describing the predicament of Thomas Becket, or Harry, Lord Monchensey, or even Edward Chamberlayne in *The Cocktail Party* (1950), who says, almost as if he were an inhabitant of Sartre's hell in *No Exit:*

> There was a door
> And I could not open it. I could not touch the handle.
> Why could I not walk out of my prison?
> What is hell? Hell is oneself,
> Hell is alone, the other figures in it
> Merely projections.
>
> (*Collected Plays* 169)

Eliot told E. Martin Browne that the lines are a retort to Sartre (233), but Edward's predicament is Byron's, and Manfred's (1.1.251), as Eliot had already diagnosed it. In *The Elder Statesman* (1958), which is partly a cross between *Oedipus at Colonus* and *Everyman* (Hay 144, 151), the scenario is again a revision of the Byronic. Lord Claverton, in certain respects another autobiographical character, also encounters visitors who are ghosts from the past. Choosing to expiate his guilt and pride by an abandonment of all roles, he says to his daughter, "I've been freed from the self that pretends to be someone; / And in becoming no one, I begin to live" (*Complete Plays* 354).

Some years earlier, in *Little Gidding,* Eliot had encountered another ghostly visitor, who arrived near "the ending of interminable night" and who, in the voice of the aging Yeats, pointed toward a now somewhat moralized Byronic prospect:

> the rending pain of re-enactment
> Of all that you have done, and been; the shame
> Of motives late revealed, and the awareness
> Of things ill done and done to others' harm
> Which once you took for exercise of virtue.
>
> (*Collected Poems* 204)

Eliot was rewriting the *Manfred* scenario all his life.

W. H. Auden also wrote in the shadow of Byron. Early poems, with a laconic outsider's uneasily satirical responses to the social scene, revise the Byronic heritage. In his early plays Auden often aimed to combine symbolic intensity and extravagant burlesque (*Plays* xiv). *The Ascent of F 6* turns the difficult saint of Eliot's *Murder in the Cathedral* into a mountain-climbing artist destroyed by his messianic fantasies (Sidnell 186–92). Michael Ransom's allegorized climb conflates important elements from Ibsen's *Peer Gynt* and *Brand,* on which Auden would later provide insightful comment ("Brand *versus* Peer"), but some of its details—Ransom's obscure guilt, his encounter with an Abbot from the mountain monastery, and his confrontation with a series of spirits—also suggest *Manfred* (Mendelson 251).

By 1966 Auden would call *Manfred* "dead and a big bore" ("Byron: The Making of a Comic Poet" 12). But in the meantime he had transformed his own style with the help of the later Byron. Soon after completing *The Ascent of F 6,* he took a copy of Byron with him to Iceland, read *Don Juan* with great relish, and wrote a brilliantly chatty "Letter to Lord Byron," in which he exclaimed:

> Byron, thou should'st be living at this hour!
> What would you do, I wonder, if you were?
>
> (*Collected Poems* 86)

What Auden did, as playwright, was to turn toward a more evidently "mental" though still stageable theater, which gives prominence to the serious comedy that in "Don Juan" he would describe as Byron's great achievement. Byron had called *Heaven and Earth* "a sort of Oratorio on a sacred subject." Auden's *For the Time Being* (1942), subtitled "A Christmas Oratorio," runs closer to that musical form and to the comic vein of *Don Juan*. Like Eliot's recent essay on Byron, it recognizes the danger of being deceived by our own role-playing:

> I mean that although there's a person we know all about
> Still bearing our name and loving himself as before,
> That person has become a fiction; our true existence
> Is decided by no one and has no importance to love.
>
> (*Collected Poems* 273)

But its comic climax is provided by a Herod who seems both a modern liberal and, at one point, a travesty of the Byronic Lucifer. Agonizing over the need for a Massacre of the Innocents, he complains that, if the story of the Nativity is true, "it would mean that God had given me the power to destroy Himself. I refuse to be taken in. He could not play such a horrible practical joke. Why should He dislike me so?" (304).

Yet more inward in its concerns, more involuted in its cerebration, *The Sea and the Mirror* (1944), a dramatic commentary on Shakespeare's *The Tempest,* treats the nature of art as a reflection of the human predicament. But a fundamental note here is once again a Byronic alienation. That note is not sounded by Caliban, who in pseudo-Jamesian style points like Eliot's characters beyond our condition as "born actors" toward a "restored relation" with a "Wholly Other Life" (340). At the echoing periphery of the drama, however, the self-absorbed Antonio maintains his isolation:

> *Your all is partial, Prospero;*
> *My will is all my own:*
> *Your need to love shall never know*
> *Me: I am I, Antonio,*
> *By choice myself alone.*
>
> (318)

It is not surprising that, when beginning work on the opera *Elegy for Young Lovers,* in 1959, Auden imagined the main character (who later became a poet modelled on Yeats and Goethe) as an eccentric actor who is under the fixed delusion that he is Byron's Manfred (Carpenter 399).

More important to modern drama than Auden are the lines of descent that lead through Yeats's passionate and claustral plays to a further deflation of the heroic and accentuation of ironic blockage in the mental theaters of Beckett and Pinter. Jeffrey Perl has said, "Beckett takes up precisely where

Yeats left off in *Purgatory,* the most apocalyptic of modernist dramas" (*Tradition of Return* 280). But here, too, we may discern the mediated presence of Byron. The histrionic Hamm in *Endgame* has become like Manfred his proper Hell, listening to a dripping in his heart as he imagines a world in ashes. Krapp in *Krapp's Last Tape* obsessively reviews his file of annual soliloquys, approaching but censoring an account of a painful love affair. In Beckett's later work the stage action yet more succinctly embodies an agonized lyric—reaching in *Not I* (1972) the condition of a Mouth and an Auditor. Although Beckett had studied Byron (Pilling 136), he absorbed such Byronism partly from Yeats. Not only does *Waiting for Godot* use the tree that Yeats first used in *At the Hawk's Well,* but Winnie in *Happy Days* (1961) also quotes from the opening song in that play. Up to her waist in the earth, tortured by some offstage deity, she defines her own infernal mental theater through Yeats's line: "I call to the eye of the mind" (58).

Yeats, Eliot, and Beckett prepare for the lyric-ironic dreamwork of Pinter's middle period: *Landscape* and *Silence,* with their cross-cut monologues, *Old Times,* with its retrospective and ambiguous erotic triangle, and *No Man's Land,* with its frozen male landscape. From Manfred, with his half-divulged passion and guilt, and his self-laceration, we proceed to Yeats's Cuchulain and Old Man, to Beckett's Krapp, and to Pinter's Hirst. In *No Man's Land* the image of the blighted and retrospective protagonist is doubled, rendered sordid and sexually ambiguous, and amplified through an enigmatic language echoing Eliot and other writers. Spooner and Hirst, ostensible poets, confront each other as tempters and challengers, evoking guilt-laden memories of pasts that may well not exist. By the play's end Manfred's glacier on the Jungfrau has become a "winter" wasteland in a Hampstead drawing room, "icy and silent," where the "there is no possibility of changing the subject" (*No Man's Land* 92–95). In Pinter's shared lyrics of solitude, reverberating in the deeps of the mind, as in other versions of playing hell, Byron remains the invisible master.

IV

On occasion that master has become more clearly audible or even visible in the theater to which he has contributed. Again the paradigms are various. Eugene O'Neill and Tennessee Williams, working with poetic naturalism and expressionism, were steeped in Byronic feelings of guilt, isolation, fatality, and defiance, but each dramatized those feelings without reference to Byron except in one revealing play.

O'Neill's young autobiographical characters in *Ah, Wilderness!* and *Long Day's Journey into Night* are devoted to more lushly pessimistic writers from later in the century, including Oscar Wilde, but O'Neill himself knew many passages from *Childe Harold's Pilgrimage* by heart and could recite them "interminably" when drunk (Gelb 88; Bogard 367). And several of his plays approach the *Manfred* scenario of an agonized protagonist and his uncanny tempters. *The Emperor Jones* (1920), which may also recall *Peer Gynt* (Bogard 136–37) and Strindberg's station plays, translates *Manfred* into very different cultural and geographic terms. The protagonist, a self-made military man with "typically negroid" features, has "something decidedly distinctive about his face—an underlying strength of will, a hardy, self-reliant confidence in himself" (*Complete Plays* 1:1033). The scene is not the Alps but a Great Forest on an island in the West Indies, where Jones encounters spirits who represent his shapeless fears, his personal guilts, his heritage of violence, and finally the tribal "forces of evil" that drive him to his death (1:1058). In *The Great God Brown* Dion Anthony combines Byronic and Dionysian traits, and in *Lazarus Laughed* (1926), that grandiose "play for an Imaginative Theatre" (*Complete Plays* 2:537), Lazarus mocks Caligula by saying gaily: "Tragic is the plight of the tragedian whose only audience is himself! Life is for each man a solitary cell whose walls are mirrors!" (2:572). He resolves that Byronic predicament by his Dionysian and Nietzschean choice of death. O'Neill said that he knew of "no play like 'Lazarus' at all" (Bogard 279), but he may have known Byron's biblical plays and Yeats's *Calvary,* which had already included Lazarus in its transformation of the Byronic into the Nietzschean.

Manfred also hovers behind the seeming naturalism of *The Iceman Cometh* (1939). Here the paradigm is a "community of heartbreak" permeated by betrayal and guilt, in which semi-expressionistic stylization asks us to find ourselves reflected in an otherwise "naturalistic" scene. The social panorama, drawn from O'Neill's youthful experience, suggests Gorky's *The Lower Depths;* the theme of the life lie recalls Ibsen's *The Wild Duck;* the deployment of three main characters and a chorus derives from Greek tragedy (Bogard 414–15); and the salesman of death, Hickey, is a reworking of Lazarus in a darker mood (Chabrowe 73–99). But the contrapuntal orchestration of voices—the triple rumination of Hickey, Parritt, and Slade with choral accompaniment—constitutes a vast inflation of

Manfred's progression through hidden guilts toward death. Manfred had said, "'tis not so difficult to die." O'Neill's massive orchestration invites us to share that temptation from a vantage point of both sympathy and horrified detachment.

Only in *A Touch of the Poet,* a more conventionally romantic play written between 1935 and 1942, before and after the composition of *The Iceman Cometh,* did O'Neill refer directly to Byron. In a village near Boston in 1828, Cornelious Melody is a tavern keeper down on his luck, with "a ruined face, which was once extraordinarily handsome in a reckless, arrogant fashion." It is "the face of an embittered Byronic hero" (*Complete Plays* 3:197). Still posing as an aristocratic military man, Melody recites histrionically to his image in the mirror:

> I have not loved the World, nor the World me;
> I have not flattered its rank breath, nor bowed
> To its idolatries a patient knee . . .

And so on to the proud declaration: "—I stood / Among them, but not of them" (*Complete Plays* 3:203; *Childe Harold's Pilgrimage* 3.1049–55). It is one of the many passages that O'Neill himself loved to recite.

Although Tennessee Williams's life has been called Byronic (Spoto 98, 223), his plays exorcized a more puritanical fear of sex than Byron seems to have known. Elements of a conflicted Byronism, with its secret guilts and its penchant for satire, appear everywhere in this world of Southern Gothic: in the drifter Val Xavier and the nymphomaniac Cassandra Whiteside of *Battle of Angels* (1940), later revised as *Orpheus Descending* (1957), in the rueful Tom Wingfield of *Glass Menagerie* (1944), fixated on the memory of his innocent sister, and in the pseudo-aristocratic Blanche DuBois of *A Streetcar Named Desire* (1947), whose nymphomania seems driven by her guilty secret, a horror of homosexuality that has provoked her husband's suicide. The guilty secret in *Cat on a Hot Tin Roof* (1955) is Brick's homosexuality, in *Suddenly Last Summer* (1958) the horrifying story of how Sebastian's homosexual cruising led to his cannibalistic murder and to the threatened lobotomy of his cousin Catharine, and in *The Night of the Iguana* (1961) the sexual and religious missteps of the defrocked Reverend Shannon.

Williams did approach his invisible master obliquely in *Lord Byron's Love Letter* (1945), the premise of which recalls Henry James's *The Aspern Papers* and looks forward to Tom Stoppard's *Arcadia.* A Spinster and an Old

Woman in late-nineteenth-century New Orleans pick up a few dollars from tourists by showing a letter to the Spinster's grandmother, who allegedly had met Byron in Greece in 1827. After the tourists' departure, we gather that the Old Woman herself is the grandmother and that the Spinster is in fact Byron's granddaughter. But only in *Camino Real* (1953) did Williams bring Byron himself onstage. This somewhat Strindbergian dream play, an expressionistic "community of heartbreak," says much about Williams's uneasy relations to the sources of his poetic imagination. And its version of Byron, inserted at the play's midpoint, its fulcrum, has a moral intensity remarkably different from the Byronic figures of Shaw, Yeats, Eliot, or O'Neill.

The ostensible dreamer of this play, in whom we are nominally to find ourselves reflected, is Don Quixote, who has followed the road of romance until it has become the sordid road of contemporary culture. He has arrived at a walled town (with a luxurious Siete Mares Hotel, a Skid Row, and a plaza where the fountain no longer flows) under the control of a Mr. Gutman, whose behavior suggests the Nazi-like tyranny and commercial corruption of a vaguely Latin country. There is only one direction of possible departure, an archway leading to "Terra Incognita," a wasteland that stretches toward the distant snow-topped mountains. Quixote's dream of sixteen scenes, or "blocks," which contains an array of Mexican and Near Eastern types, features four aging romantics drawn from history and fiction—Casanova, Marguerite Gautier or "Camille," the Baron de Charlus, and Lord Byron—and also a young American vagrant named Kilroy. Unlike the other romantics, the Byron whom we meet in Block Eight wants to return to sources of inspiration from which he has been distracted. Into this expressionistic panorama of blockage, impotent nostalgia, and despair, Williams has introduced a histrionic character with the moral power to become once again an exemplar of romantic heroism. Williams based this episode, moreover, on a documentary source that he revised and expanded to strengthen Byron's exemplary vision and moral fiber.

Byron enters as one made "soft" by luxury, who intends to depart from his "present self" to find himself as he "used to be." Gutman remarks: "*That's* the *furthest* departure a man could make! I guess you're sailing for Athens?" Byron affirms that the struggle for "freedom" still means something to him, that he has not forgotten his "old devotion to the—" But then he seems to lose the thread. "—To the *what,* Lord Byron?" taunts Gutman. "You can't remember the object of your one-time devotion?" Byron limps away from the terrace, toward the fountain. "When Shelley's corpse was recovered from the sea," he begins. "—It was burned on the beach at Viareggio.—I watched the spectacle from my carriage because the stench was revolting . . . Then it—fascinated me!" Proceeding with his oblique answer to Gutman's question, he advances upon the stage apron toward us, delivering what is in effect (though overheard) a bravura soliloquy:

> I got out of my carriage. Went nearer, holding a handkerchief to my nostrils!—I saw that the front of the skull had broken away in the flames, and there— . . . And there was the brain of Shelley, indistinguishable from a cooking stew!—*boiling, bubbling, hissing!*—in the *blackening—cracked—pot*—of his skull! . . . —Trelawney, his friend, Trelawney, threw salt and oil and frankincense on the flames and finally the almost intolerable stench— . . . was *gone* and the burning was *pure*!—as a man's burning should be . . .
>
> A man's burning *ought* to be pure!—*not* like mine—(a crepe suzette—burned in brandy . . .)
>
> *Shelley's* burning was finally very *pure!*
>
> But the body, the corpse, split open like a grilled pig! (73–75)

That speech is taken from Edward John Trelawny's account in his *Recollections of the Last Days of Shelley and Byron* (2:221–24), but with crucial changes. Williams omits Byron's request that Trelawny preserve Shelley's skull for him ("but remembering that he had formerly used one as a drinking cup, I was determined that Shelley's should not be so profaned"), omits also the wine poured over Shelley's dead body ("more . . . than he had consumed during his life"), transferring that notion to Byron's own guilty reference to a "crepe suzette." After heightening Trelawny's description of the cooking brain ("the brains literally seethed, bubbled, and boiled as in a cauldron"), Williams omits the declaration that "Byron could not face this scene, he withdrew to the beach and swam off to the *Bolivar*." In fact, only in Leigh Hunt's presence did Trelawny then perform the action that Williams's Byron now describes as a prelude to his own renewed dedication:

> —And then Trelawney—as the ribs of the corpse unlocked—reached into them as a baker reaches quickly into an oven! . . .
>
> —And snatched out—as a baker would a biscuit!—the *heart* of Shelley! Snatched the heart of Shelley out of the blistering corpse! —Out of the purifying —blue flame . . . .
>
> —And it was *over!* I thought—

And here he turns to face Casanova and Marguerite:

> —I thought it was a disgusting thing to do, to snatch a man's heart from his body! What can one man do with another man's heart?

Casanova rises, strikes the stage with his cane, and contemptuously demonstrates with a loaf of bread how one can twist such a heart, tear it, crush it, and kick it away. To which Byron responds that "a poet's vocation, which used to be my vocation, is to influence the heart in a gentler fashion . . . He ought to purify it and lift it above its ordinary level. For what is the heart but a sort of— [*He makes a high, groping gesture in the air.*]—A sort of—*instrument!*—that translates *noise* into *music,* chaos into—*order . . .*—*a mysterious order!*" The speech risks the bathetic, and Abdulla and Gutman stifle their mirth. But Byron then begins a self-castigating account of how his vocation had been "obscured by vulgar plaudits," "lost among gondolas and palazzos" and "the visible grandeur of marble, pink and gray marble, veined and tinted as flayed corrupting flesh," so that he now listens "to hired musicians behind a row of artificial palm trees instead of the single—pure-stringed instrument" of his heart (75–78).

Williams offers here his own version of an important nineteenth-century romantic theme: Shelley's literal and figurative heart. After retrieving the heart from the fire, Trelawny gave it to Leigh Hunt, who gave it to Shelley's wife, Mary. It was finally buried in 1889, with the body of Shelley's son, Sir Percy Florence Shelley. The nineteenth-century literary treatments of that heart, according to Sylvia Norman, had been "slightly absurd, a trifle vulgar, wholly sentimental—which is not to be wondered at, since, after leaving Shelley's body, it was handled by no one free from fanaticism, exaltation, misery, or some such *abnormal feeling* towards Shelley" (12). At this moment in *Camino Real* we are not far from such feelings, and Byron's incantatory speech may also contain the coded homoeroticism that Eric O. Clarke has detected in earlier Shelley worship. But Williams goes further. What can one man do with another man's heart? This Byron is recalled by his vision of Shelley's heart to a renewed awareness of his own. He decides to sail to Athens, where in the "absolute silence" the "old pure music" (78) may come to him again. As he limps across the plaza and crosses toward the archway into the desert, others mutter apprehensively. Kilroy starts to follow but loses his nerve. Only Byron will risk death in order to enter Terra Incognita, and his heart, moving from a fascination with corruption to a reassertion of purity, is obviously that of Tennessee Williams. The play invites us to participate in a multiple enactment of the route through histrionic identification and projection toward a vision of poetic authenticity. Indeed, *Camino Real* not only attributes to Byron something like the Shelleyan religion that Shaw had found lacking in him; it is at this point also a confessional rewriting of Shaw's dream fable in *Man and Superman* about Don Juan's decision to leave the deceptively paradisal realm of the Devil. As this expressionistic "community of heartbreak" draws to a close, Kilroy will be killed and an autopsy will remove *his* heart, which will prove to be solid gold. The fountain will then flow, and the violets in the mountains will break the rocks. But, despite that deliberate vulgarizing of romantic motifs, which consorts with the often carnival-like atmosphere of Quixote's dream, the agonized and determined figure of Byron remains in our minds—a powerful image of self-betrayal and turning, of poetic continuity and rediscovered authenticity.

V

Three contemporary playwrights, born too late to be hypnotized in adolescence by his poetry and personality and at home in several mental theaters, have nonetheless evoked Byron as an important liminal presence. In a time of self-conscious relativism they invite us to seek the "imagined" Byron through a "history" that is our own construct. Romulus Linney's *Childe Byron* (1977–81) brings Byron to life as a hallucinatory presence for his daughter Ada on the day of her death in 1852. Howard Brenton's *Bloody Poetry* (1989) encounters him through a Brechtian and phantasmagoric vision of the Shelley circle in 1816–22. And Tom Stoppard's *Arcadia* (1993) approaches him, but never quite reaches him, through some fictitious friends and acquaintances in 1809 and some literary detectives in the present day. These plays give us three late moments in the long conversation with Byron and romanticism that may now be drawing to a close: a passionate re-engagement, a sardonic identification, and a farcical-elegiac farewell.

From this side of the Atlantic, Linney has kept an eye on the British historical play ever since Robert Bolt's *A Man for All Seasons* (1960). His early play *The Sorrows of Frederick* (1967) connects with an attenuated Goethean and Byronic tradition. *Three Poets* (1989), a boldly syncretic instance of mental theater, revises the tenth-century biblical drama of

Hrosvitha, lets the love poems of Komachi speak through a Noh mask, and evokes Anna Akhmatova's "Requiem" through a Soviet interrogation. As a historical dramatist, Linney seeks a "point of entrance" through some "cathartic emotional experience" that he can share. He has said that *Childe Byron* was inspired by an aspect of the poet's life he understood all too well, "the pain of a divorced father who can't reach his daughter" (Paikert 5). But the play's actual strategy is just the reverse. Giving us a Byron imagined by his adult daughter, it dramatizes Linney's effort, and our own, to bridge the distance that separates us from an ancestor whose lineaments we must reconstruct. And it requires us to face—in Ada and in ourselves—the implications of our effort to approach the past.

The play is founded on two incontrovertible facts: Ada, the daughter of Byron and Annabella Milbanke, was a brilliant mathematician who translated and annotated a French monograph on Charles Babbage's Analytical Engine, a clockwork ancestor of the electronic computer. And she died, like Byron, at the age of thirty-six. We are asked to share the effort of this determined woman, now dying of stomach cancer, drugged with laudanum, and hallucinating, as she evokes the presence of "that dreadful man who died when he was thirty-six, and I was eight" (13). Ada seeks to marshal everything she has learned about her father during the past year and so discover the "real" Byron. "What is the problem? I lived my life without you. What is the solution? I don't know. Therefore I must tabulate my data. I must become my own Analytical engine, and discover what you really were. Logically. Without regret, or sentimentality" (14). His life appears to her in dreamlike and playlike scenes that are linked by music of Hector Berlioz that, as she tells Byron, is "based on your poems" (15). But, as she enters that life, she becomes unable to maintain her stance of dispassionate analysis.

The prologue discloses Ada in her London bedroom, a dark shadow lit by an upstage spot. Set against Berlioz's music and the noise of an electronic computer, we hear an antiphonal arrangement of voices. Byron's voice speaks passages that frame the third canto of *Childe Harold's Pilgrimage* (from st. 1, 117, and 115), ending with:

> My daughter! With thy name this song begun.
> My daughter! With thy name thus much shall end.
> I see thee not, I hear thee not, but none
> Can be so wrapt in thee: thou art the friend
> To whom the shadows of far years extend.

Ada's voice responds with passages from her own work that expound the structure of Babbage's Analytical Engine (10). The quasimusical prologue has established certain oppositional themes: the viola entrance from Berlioz's *Harold in Italy* and the driving sound of electronic computation, paternal love and filial analysis, romantic passion and modern mathematics.

When the lights come up on Ada, who is beginning to write her will, the thirty-six-year-old Byron appears, a romantic figure in cloak and collar, and the two begin their preliminary sparring. Ada imagines Byron's youth with the help of his early verse, a scene from *The Deformed Transformed,* and conversations between a Boy and a Woman who play young Byron and his mother. The older Byron then advises his younger self and (after we hear snatches from the contemptuous reviews of *Hours of Idleness*) trains him to box, while the Boy composes a version of lines 1050–51 and 1057–59 from *English Bards and Scotch Reviewers!* The Boy soon becomes the choirboy with whom, at Cambridge, Byron had fallen in love—"a creature like the animals I took home all my life . . . All my helpless, wretched, lonely things. Myself, when young." Embracing him, Byron speaks "Stanzas for Music" ("There be none of Beauty's daughters . . ." [26–27]). In quick succession, with the help of several actors who step in and out of the roles, we move through Byron's departure on the Lisbon Packet in 1809 (with "Lines to Mr. Hodgson"), the travels of Childe Harold (with well-known bits from st. 179 of canto 4, st. 73, 113, 6, and 114 of canto 3, and st. 4 of canto 1), the return to England and fame, the womanizing, the continued loneliness, and the sustaining relation with his half-sister Augusta Leigh. Through all of these scenes runs an undercurrent of defiant and projected narcissism. Of the affair with Augusta a woman comments: "It's one more way of loving himself" (35). Then, as Augusta tells Byron that she is pregnant with his child and as others clamor for his erotic attention, he exclaims: "I must free myself from this gigantic wing of love that o'ershadows me. I must find a wife!" (36). Ada now steps forward into the story that she has been imagining: "I am here, Lord Byron. Waiting." "You? Waiting for what?" "To become my own mother" (37).

Act 2, which opens with "She Walks in Beauty," makes of our imaginative and analytic agent an intimate participant in Byron's marriage. As Ada plays her mother, we begin to see the import of our shared desire to imagine Byron himself. Ada's conscious orientation, like that of Annabella Milbanke, seems antithetical to that of Byron: mathematics, not emotion, is for them "the language of reality" (40). And yet Ada's quest increasingly seems as erotic and narcissistic as Byron's own. We move inexorably toward her willed identification with her father, which blends romantic attraction, passionate hatred, filial possession, self-affirmation, and self-love. The courtship of Annabella, as played by Ada, balances Byron's passion for a moment with the "strong woman" he says he needs (42). But the equilibrium of country girl and rake, mathematician and poet (43), is lost after the birth of the child. When the marriage founders and Annabella charges Byron with brutality, homosexuality, incest, and sodomy, Ada voices her mother's outrage and then, in her own person, accepts Byron's self-exile from England. He recounts his later time abroad, with Teresa Guiccioli and her husband, with Shelley and his wife and sister, concluding with his increasing dissipation, the death of Shelley, and what this Byron calls the deliberately suicidal decision to return to Greece.

The play now embarks upon a complex dance of love and hate, identification and withdrawal. Ada imagines with Byron what might have happened had he returned to England: "There we'd be, father and daughter. I would put you to bed, tuck you in, kiss you on the cheek, and then, no doubt, like the vampires you wrote about, sink my teeth into your throat—" (57). She throws herself into his arms, embraces him fiercely, weeps, and then just as fiercely tears herself away from him. The conversation turns to her own book, and Byron reads out her claim that "mathematical truth is that superb language through which alone we may adequately express the great facts of the natural world, and what is written there . . . This language alone, spoken by a great engine, may finally trace . . . the unceasing changes of mutual relationship, far too complicated for the human mind." His curiosity aroused by analogies with propositions in *Childe Harold,* Byron now seeks to learn what had happened to Ada. But Ada resists his interrogation, raging at her own previous emotions: "Hating my mother and loving you? My God, you are a vampire, after blood" (58). They swiftly move into mutual recrimination. "I wish to God you had never been born!" he shouts. "So do I!" she retorts. Refusing to leave, he forces her to admit her gambling, her indebtedness, her madness. Ada throws her books and notes on the floor and declares that Byron is "dead, dead, dead!!!" (61).

But there is one more reversal. Byron approves her defiant act of freeing herself from him. "And I must say," he adds, "you became an astonishing creature." "Like you," says Ada. "Like you." "Yes," he answers, "like me." That recognition of fundamental identity in and through opposition—reminiscent of Synge's strategy in *The Playboy,* with its repeated "You're like me, so"—also catches up by implication those who act and witness

Childe Byron. From that mutual recognition emerges the "answer" to the problem Ada has set herself: She completes the writing of her will, even as Byron speaks to her a lyric pastiche of *Childe Harold's Pilgrimage,* canto 3, stanza 117, and then reads out her injunction that her body be placed in "the vault containing the body of George Gordon, the Sixth Lord Byron," just as Byron says, "Though the grave / Closed between us / 'Twere the same—." His closing line, "I know that thou wilt love me," she answers with a revised version of the lines from canto 3, stanza 115, with which the Prologue had ended, now directed to him:

My father. With thy name this song began.
My father. With thy name this song shall end.
I see thee not, I hear thee not, but none
Can be so wrapt in thee. I am the friend
To whom the shadows of far years extend.

(62)

Childe Byron is a remarkable study of imaginative obsession and historical exhumation, which draws us into an articulate disclosure of the rage and love—in large part rage against ourselves and love for ourselves—that drive us to recall, possess, reject, and identify ourselves with an ancestral presence. Moving indeed for any who can respond at some level to Byron's poetry, the play has yet greater depth and complexity for those already acquainted with the Byronic imagination.

For a more comprehensive approach to the grand pathology of that imagination, however, we must turn to Howard Brenton's *Bloody Poetry* (1984), which emerged from the same British tradition of history plays. Brenton had earlier explored this vein in *Hitler Dances* (1972), *The Churchill Play* (1974), and translations of Brecht's *The Life of Galileo* (1980) and Büchner's *Danton's Death* (1982). Janelle Reinelt has perceptively commented on the Brechtian strategies of *Bloody Poetry* (34–39), which is a far more complex and insightful play than some London reviewers thought. Indeed, it is a brilliant instance of the transmutations to which modern playwrights have subjected Byron's seething brain and self-conscious impurity of heart. That is so despite the fact that its phantasmagoria, pitched between dream play and memory play, traces from 1816 to 1822 the course not of Byron's life but of Shelley's.

The play's program features a sentence from Richard Holmes's biography, *Shelley: The Pursuit:* "Shelley's life seems more a haunting than a history." And the play follows Holmes's account with revisionary freedom.

The opening scene in Switzerland is a coach-borne meditation by Bysshe Shelley that proleptically includes passages from "Mont Blanc" and "England in 1819"; the penultimate scene is another meditation, on the Gulf of Spezia, in which he moves from "The Mask of Anarchy" to a broken rendering of the conclusion of *Prometheus Unbound.* Other scenes lead us, through the poet's consciousness, to a wider circle. We witness the meeting with Byron at Lake Geneva, debates with him about Wordsworth's "Immortality Ode" and Plato's Allegory of the Cave, the fit induced by Byron's recitation from Coleridge's "Christabel," and the visit with Byron to a madhouse near Venice that Shelley wrote up in "Julian and Maddalo."

We also see the network of loves, deceptions, and painful consequences that bind him to Mary Godwin Shelley, Claire Clairemont, Harriet Westbrook Shelley, George Byron, and others. Bysshe leaves England with Mary and Claire, half-sisters whom he calls his wife and his friend, but whom Byron will recognize as "concubines" (44). Because Claire is also having an affair with Byron, she can arrange the meeting of Bysshe and Mary with "England's greatest living poet." (12) After Bysshe's legal wife Harriet drowns herself, at the outset of act 2, she continues to haunt him as a visible "ghost"—as natural in appearance as the Ghost of the Gravedigger's Boy in Edward Bond's *Lear.* We hear of Bysshe's love for Fanny Godwin and Jane Williams and of Byron's love for his half-sister Augusta Leigh, for Countess Guiccioli, and for others of both sexes. And we also hear of children: two children of Bysshe and Harriet, custody of whom Bysshe and Mary seek after Harriet's death; two children of Bysshe and Mary, one of whom—in Brenton's most notable violation of chronology—dies as Bysshe is reacting to the Peterloo Massacre; and the child of George Byron and Claire, who dies in a convent only after Claire's and Bysshe's unsuccessful attempts to gain possession of her. These complications, arising from sexual freedom, egocentricity, and parental responsibility, are set forth with sympathy for all concerned—a task made easier by Brenton's inclusion of Byron's physician and "official biographer," William Polidori (18), an envious, sycophantic, and hypocritical spy who may sometimes remind us of Old Carr in Stoppard's *Travesties* or Salieri in Shaffer's *Amadeus.*

Byron's centrality in this play becomes clear as we begin to grasp how its themes of haunting, drowning, and blindness are developed through a post-Shavian and rather Brechtian dialectic of compelling and often quite sympathetic voices that explore the costs of a romantic vision. For Byron, and implicitly for Brenton, the Platonic allegory of the cave has matters exactly reversed. It is the visionary poet, Bysshe Shelley, who is blinded, haunted, and finally drowned, because he will not or cannot focus on the bloody realities about him. Although his indictment of English tyranny and moralism is unanswerable and his verbal evocation of "love" and "life" is persuasive, his recognition of his own egotism is minimal. He can say that his "worst ghost" is not that of Harriet but "a phantom that is exactly myself" (42). But that recognition leads to no further insight because it is so speedily translated into an abstraction: "We haunt ourselves. With man-made tyranny . . . We haunt ourselves, with the ghosts of what we could be, if we were truly free!" (42). No doubt Bysshe understands the need for self-knowledge. "Let's peel open our brains," he says to Byron, "find the soul itself! Let's . . . cut ourselves open, wreck ourselves, turn ourselves inside out! To find out what we are, what we can be!" (45). By a circuitous historical route, he is echoing the Marat of Peter Weiss, who in the English version staged by Peter Brook, had said with visionary intensity—and impotence:

> The important thing
> is to pull yourself up by your own hair
> to turn yourself inside out
> and see the whole world with fresh eyes.
>
> (*Marat/Sade* 27)

Neither Bysshe's poetry nor his speechifying, however, can accomplish that task, which is precisely the aim of Brenton's play.

Two other voices in the dialectic of *Bloody Poetry* are those of Claire and Mary. Claire, with her ready sexuality and buoyant optimism, has a naive faith that free love can be reconciled with the claims of marriage and motherhood. Mary, the most soberly perceptive and sardonic member of this family of romantic love, alludes to the monster in the story she is writing as a "figure" for the lovelessness of Bysshe and George (27). She knows that such men "in love with life" can "cause only pain for those around them" (43). Claire speaks to her of replacing Augusta Leigh in Byron's imagination: "I will tangle him. I will wrench him. Are we not always saying to each other, the world is yet to be made, we are changeable, we will invent a new society and a new human nature?" And Mary answers: "A new human nature? Out of George Byron?" (44). Later, after she has proposed to Bysshe—for "somehow we are going to have to domesticate all these grand passions" (54)—and he has left the scene, she charges him with self-deception if not duplicity:

> Oh, you can do the words, can't you, Bysshe. Quote—
> Never will peace and human nature meet
> Till, free and equal, man and woman greet
> Domestic peace.

And she adds in mockery: "Now how about doing the life . . . ?" (55).

The most complex participant in this dialectic of voices is Byron, through whose sensibility the play comes to a sharp focus. This Byron is arrogant, restless, witty, cruel, brilliant, silly, self-dramatizing, alcoholic, and ostensibly despairing. He is given over to lusts that he disdains to justify yet able to acknowledge the "home truths" that Mary offers (32). He knows that he and his friends are indulging in the freedom of upperclass renegades (24), that he cannot judge the honesty of his own work (31), that Bysshe is addicted to abstraction (39), and that the poet in a madhouse must be "a lesson to us all" (71). Against the visionary claims of love and life Byron points to the bloody real on which this play is also founded: "All your idealism, revolution in society, revolution in the personal life, all trumpery! The practice of it, sir, the practice doth make us dirty, doth make all naked and bleeding and real!" (44). He is, in effect, a Brenton version of Weiss's Sade, pitting himself against a Marat-like naïveté. He puts it straight to Bysshe as they lounge in the Venetian gondola: "You poor sod, y'believe in love, y'do, poor bastard. Yet you harm as many as I, you would-be 'moral immoralist.' You shred and tear lives around you as much as I, the cynic, the libertine" (68). When they reach the madhouse it is Byron who gives voice to the madman. And when Bysshe utters the words left in Julian's mind by Count Maddalo—

> Most wretched men
> Are cradled into poetry by wrong,
> They learn in suffering what they teach in song
> ("Julian and Maddalo" ll. 544–46)

—we hear behind them a mad laughter that is also Byron's.

When Richard Holmes said that Shelley's life "seems more a haunting than a history," he meant that we too should be haunted by its implications (xiii). Brenton, whose plays have often vented a Shelleyan outrage against the evils of modern society and who has great sympathy for Shelley's vision of love, understands that necessity. The framing of the play's action by Bysshe's poetic meditations helps to make *Bloody Poetry* just such a haunting for the audience. But after his meditation on the Gulf of Spezia there is a final scene. Byron stands on the beach at Viareggio, behind him the ghost of Harriet, before him, furled in a sail, the body of Shelley. We are now beyond the kind of romantic self-purgation in which Williams's Lord Byron could indulge when remembering this beach in *Camino Real.* And we are beyond the romantically suicidal impulse to which Linney's Byron confesses in *Childe Byron.* The rather Brechtian dialectic of *Bloody Poetry* demands a more difficult turning, which must take place in the minds of the audience after the performance. Now is the time for a passionate and sweeping outcry that is also, in the light of the entire play, a nuanced judgment. And this Byron, who was dismissed by some reviewers of the 1984 London production as an unedifying spectacle, has earned the right to utter that judgment:

> We'll burn the body on the beach.
> I loved him.
> And in the name of all the mercies, look what the sea did to his flesh.
> *He shouts.*
> Burn him! Burn him! Burn him!
> Burn us all! A great big, bloody, beautiful fire!
>
> (83)

The Byron of *Bloody Poetry* is a larger, more difficult, and more self-condemnatory image of the romanticism with which *Childe Byron* is still enamored. Outrageous antihero and abrasive mentor, he finally becomes our choric mask, a self-impeached judge. This essentially conservative play by a radical dramatist, which blends vision and reality in a way that demands a passionate Brechtian acting, is among the most probing reinventions of Byron's mental theater.

In sharp contrast Tom Stoppard's *Arcadia* is an extraordinarily complex farewell to the matter of Byron. This successor to the serious playing with philosophical, historical, and scientific ideas in *Jumpers, Travesties,* and *Hapgood* further expands the paradigm of serious farce to include both the romantic and the elegiac. Its alternating and interconnected story lines, one nineteenth-century, the other modern, elaborate themes already associated with Byron's presence in the theater: the strengths and dangers of the romantic imagination, the relations between feeling and thought, the ironies of cultural transmission, and the efforts to understand nature and reconstruct history.

Like *Childe Byron* and *Bloody Poetry, Arcadia* is anchored both in Byron's biography and in a wider intellectual history. The biographical anchor is Byron's letter of April 16, 1809, to John Hanson: "If the consequences of my leaving England, were ten times as ruinous as you describe," he wrote, "I have no alternative, there are circumstances which render it absolutely indespensible, and quit the country I must immediately." The editor of Byron's letters has commented: "What Byron's urgent reasons for leaving England were at this time has never been revealed" (*Letters and Journals* 200–201). In *Arcadia* a modern Sussex don, Bernard Nightingale, who quotes both letter and comment (53), convinces himself that he has discovered those reasons: Byron must have killed the minor poet Ezra Chater in a duel. The anchors to a wider intellectual history are provided by the changing style of English landscape gardening, from classical order to romantic wilderness, and the later change in the mathematical "language of nature" from classical science to "chaos theory." At least since 1989 Stoppard had been interested in James Gleick's *Chaos,* an elegant account of the recent development of mathematical and scientific models of how interactions between the determined and the random enable simple systems to produce complex behavior and order to emerge from chaos. Certain that "there is a play in that somewhere" (Delaney 224), Stoppard found it by combining a satirical treatment of Nightingale's effort to pin down the historical presence of Byron with a serious imagining of the "prehistory" of chaos theory. *Arcadia* suggests that the abandonment of classical systems of order was both a capitulation to romantic feeling and a prelude to the discovery of new cognitive models for the chaotic. Although careful in interviews not to commit himself to a belief in "Classical mathematics" and "Romantic mathematics" (Delaney 267), Stoppard did not simply add that cultural metaphor to Gleick's account. Gleick had already correlated the shift from classical science to the new "science of chaos" with that from the eighteenth-century hostility to wild nature (and sympathy for cultivated and paradisal gardens) to a "peculiarly modern feeling for untamed, uncivilized, undomesticated nature" (117–18). But Stoppard knows that this feeling is not so "peculiarly modern." Byron had said in *Childe Harold's Pilgrimage:* "High mountains are a feeling" (3.72). To Harold the mountains, ocean, desert, and forest "spake / A mutual language" (3.8). He found "a pleasure in the pathless woods," and, mingling with the Universe, felt what he could "ne'er express" (4.178). Hence the appropriateness of Stoppard's focus upon both romantic landscape gardening and the romantic prehistory of chaos theory. *Arcadia* shares the Byronic sensibility not through direct mimesis but as mediated through cultural history.

It is a play about several modes of knowing—carnal, introspective, historical, and scientific. Its nineteenth-century story line begins in 1809 with thirteen-year-old Thomasina Coverly's question to her tutor: "Septimus, what is carnal knowledge?" (1). In the twentieth-century story line the literary archaeologist Hannah Jarvis, confronted by the failure of all attempts to know, will say, "Comparing what we're looking for misses the point. It's wanting to know that makes us matter" (76). But *Arcadia* is also a play about transience, about death (by bird shot, dueling, monkey bite, and fire), and about the "doom" foretold by the second law of thermodynamics (65). From the vantage point of the twentieth-century characters and ourselves, the play's nineteenth-century characters are already dead—a fact that is repeatedly emphasized. Thomasina's mother, Lady Croom, resisting the transformation of her eighteenth-century garden ("nature as God intended it") into the new picturesque and Gothic style, declares with passion: "I can say with the painter, '*Et in Arcadia ego!*'" As her precocious daughter knows, she is unwittingly identifying herself with the voice of Death: "Yes, mama," she answers, "if you would have it so" (12). Thomasina, having "grown up in the sound of guns like the child of a siege," knows that her bird-shooting Papa "has no need of the recording angel, his life is written in the game book." "A calendar of slaughter," says her tutor Septimus Hodge. "'Even in Arcadia, there am I!'" (13). But this witty play is also about sexual and elegiac pathos. Sexual desire, which drives the more farcical goings-on, is seen by the modern Chloë Coverly as counter-deterministic force, or, in her brother Valentine's phrase, "the attraction Newton left out" (74). Thomasina will later conclude (which is to say, has already concluded) that Newton's deterministic machine "leaves the road at every corner" because of the "action of bodies in heat" (84). *Arcadia* moves through such seriocomic analogizing to a conclusion that deflates Nightingale, the literary detective and caddish seducer ("Sorry one and all . . . sorry, Byron") (95), brings Hannah to the limits of her knowledge and the threshold of her suppressed sexual feeling, and leads Septimus and Thomasina into a birthday waltz—for us, a touching dance on the very edge of death that is doubled in time by Hannah's awkward acceptance of the invitation to dance offered by her young admirer, the silent Gus Coverly.

The two stories take place in the same rather bare room at Sidley Park, the Derbyshire home of the Coverly family, a "long day's ride" from Byron's Newstead Abbey (53). As the play shuttles back and forth between Byron's time (sc. 1, 3, and 6) and our own (sc. 2, 4, and 5), objects from both periods accumulate on a central table. We follow the twentieth-century attempts to reconstruct events that we have just witnessed or will soon witness, through an action that mysteriously synchronizes with the action that it would interpret. Situations and bits of conversation often reappear in a new guise; Augustus and Gus, nineteenth- and twentieth-century adolescents, are played by the same actor; an apple given by Gus to Hannah is then eaten by Septimus in 1809; and Septimus has a pet tortoise, Plautus, that seems identical with Valentine's twentieth-century pet, Lightning. Hannah notes that the hermit who lived in Sidley Park grotto from about 1812 to 1834 had a tortoise, too. "Perhaps," she says, "they go back to the first garden" (76). Certainly they go back, in theatrical terms, to George's pet in Stoppard's *Jumpers*. In scene 7 all the parallels converge upon the same space in the same stage time. As the twentieth-century characters don Regency costume for an annual dance, the plots alternate more briskly, begin to overlap, and then conclude in that waltz hauntingly doubled across the centuries.

The nineteenth-century story, after its rather Wildean conversation between Septimus and Thomasina about "carnal embrace," discloses that the tutor, who has anonymously and contemptuously reviewed Ezra Chater's first book, "The Maid of Turkey," has been seen in just such an embrace with Chater's wife. Chater challenges him to a duel, but he is mollified by Septimus's hypocritical praise of that book and his promise to write a laudatory review of a second book, "The Couch of Eros," a copy of which Chater now gratefully inscribes. Later, on learning the identity of the contemptuous first reviewer, Chater will again challenge Septimus, who this time will vow to kill him. These farcical complications are the occasion for three elliptical letters, which Septimus tucks into "The Couch of Eros" and which—nearly two centuries later, after being found in Byron's library—will constitute evidence of a sort for Bernard Nightingale. We learn from Thomasina that "Mama is in love with Lord Byron" (36). Lady Croom has been "paying attention," off stage, to Septimus's friend from Cambridge, who is another guest at Sidley Park (37). She tells Septimus that Byron intends to include Chater in the second edition of *English Bards and Scotch Reviewers* and wants to borrow "The Couch of Eros" for that purpose, and she carries off the book forthwith. By the end of scene 3 Septimus has been provoked into agreeing to duels with both Chater and Lady Croom's brother, Captain Brice, who is acting as Chater's second. Confident of success, Septimus plans to be "off to the Malta packet," leaving his "penurious schoolfriend" Byron to tutor Thomasina (42). We are left with the strong impression, reinforced by the sound of a pistol shot at the end of scene 4, that Septimus must have killed Chater in the appointed duel. The shot is reprised at the beginning of scene 6, when we return to the story of 1809 and discover that the duel did not take place (Septimus has just shot a rabbit) because the guests had departed before dawn. During the night Lady Croom had made the unsettling discovery that Mrs. Chater was visiting Byron's room. Byron has been banished—and has taken "The Couch of Eros" (and its epistolary baggage) with him. "Lord Byron is a rake and a hypocrite," says Lady Croom, "and the sooner he sails for the Levant the sooner he will find society congenial to his character" (69). The Chaters have been packed off to India with Captain Brice, who had long been conducting a passionate affair with that rather accessible lady. At the end of scene 6 we see that Septimus himself will manage to console Lady Croom for the loss of Byron.

In scene 7, as the nineteenth-century story advances to 1812, it focuses upon the relation between Septimus and the now sixteen-year-old Thomasina, who fancies that she might marry Lord Byron. With the up-to-date naïveté of Wilde's Gwendolen Fairfax she tells her brother: "He is the author of 'Childe Harold's Pilgrimage,' the most poetical and pathetic and bravest hero of any book I ever read before, and the most modern and the handsomest, for Harold is Lord Byron himself to those who know him, like myself and Septimus." Septimus remarks that Byron is not aware of her existence (79). By this time, however, we have realized that Thomasina must be a mathematical genius. Whether or not Stoppard knew Linney's *Childe Byron* or intended through Thomasina to evoke Byron's daughter Ada, the parallels are striking. Ada had written that "mathematical truth is that superb language through which alone we may adequately express the great facts of the natural world," a language that, "spoken by a great engine, may finally trace among the agencies of our creation, the unceasing changes of mutual relationship" (Linney 58). Thomasina at age thirteen has imagined the necessary existence of the algebraic "formula for all the future" (5). She shares with Septimus the belief "that nature is written in numbers" and so declares, "I will plot this leaf and deduce its equation. You will be famous for being my tutor when Lord Byron is dead and forgotten" (37). The possibility of just such an equation through "the global construction of fractals by means of iterated function systems" would be demonstrated by Michael Barnsley in this century and has been described and illustrated by James Gleick (236–40). In a parody of Fermat's famous note about the proof for his last theorem, Thomasina writes that she has found a "New Geometry of Irregular Forms," a "method whereby all the forms of nature must give up their numerical secrets" (43). Inspecting her notebook, Valentine Coverly will discover that she was graphing an iterated algorithm—precisely the method he is using, "from the other end," in hope of finding the equation of the fluctuations of grouse population on the estate (43–45). In effect, Thomasina anticipates the work of Stephen Smale and James Yorke on biological populations and Benoit Mandelbrodt and others on fractal geometry (Gleick 59–69, 90–118). Valentine will also discover, as he pushes her equations through the computer "a few million times further than she managed to do with her pencil" (76), that they give strange images, "Structure building itself in the rubble and mush," "Islands of order emerging in oceans of disorder." But he resists thinking about that counter-entropic mystery (79). In this century Robert Shaw would show that "strange attractors were engines of information" and that, despite entropy, chaos is "the creation of information" (Gleick 257–62). At the end of scene 7, on the eve of her seventeenth birthday, this precocious mathematician is prepared for carnal knowledge. As she waltzes with Septimus, she invites him to her room that night. He cannot, may not, will not. They dance once more, for her birthday, and we know that she will die this night in a fire. And we also must infer, with Hannah, that Septimus will become the grief-stricken hermit of Sidley Park, driven to insanity by his effort to complete Thomasina's equations and so restore "hope" in a world that seems otherwise destined for extinction (65).

The twentieth-century story, which introduces the Coverly descendants and their visitors, focuses with seriocomic intensity on three investigations. Hannah Jarvis has written a book on Lady Caroline Lamb, whose attentions drove Byron into marriage with Annabella Milbanke (Marchand 364–65) and who later put herself and Byron into a novel *Glenarvon.* Hannah now seeks to trace the changes in the Coverly garden as an index of the lamentable fall from rationality into romantic feeling. The hermit in the Sidley Park grotto, she thinks, will be her central image, "a mind in chaos suspected of genius" (27). But the more she learns about that image, the less certain is her own understanding. Bernard Nightingale, who has contemptuously reviewed Hannah's earlier book, now suspects that the Coverly estate holds the answer to the question as to why Byron left for Lisbon. Although the play does not broach the "Byron connection" (29) before the middle of scene 2 and does not confirm Byron's presence at Sidley Park until scene 3, it makes clear that Nightingale's version of events is ludicrously in error. The third investigator, as we gradually discover, is Valentine Coverly, who is searching for an equation that, if iterated, would graph the changes in the estate's grouse population (45) and who finds that his search is astonishingly parallel to the mathematical interests of Thomasina and Septimus. Nightingale's theory is exploded by the discovery that Ezra Chater lived to discover a dwarf dahlia in India. Hannah's theory is shaken by her inference that Septimus is the hermit. And Valentine, despite his confidence in computers, turns away from the hopeful images that have been generated by Thomasina's equations. The play's remarkable orchestration of quests and uncertainties then closes with that waltz doubled in time, a moment of harmony that somehow remains on the other side of knowledge.

As Paul Delaney has said, "However intricately it embodies scientific theory, *Arcadia* may itself be imbued with a sense of mystery that does not yield all its answers even as it invites us to join in the dance" (266). The music of serious farce moves in this play toward a moment of elegiac reflection on human finitude amid the unknowable. And where is Byron in this music? He is more than the offstage occasion for a satire against literary detection. We might imagine him, as Hannah had imagined the hermit, as the very "genius of the place" (28). He is there precisely to disappear as a specific character or image, to be unfindable yet generalizable, to be glimpsed behind a field of analogies, to be inhabited through parodic, satirical, or poignant substitutes, to stand therefore as an evasive sign of the romantic passion and imagination whose import has pervaded one hundred eighty years of cultural history. "I live not in myself, but I become / Portion of that around me," Childe Harold had said (3.72). In retrospect, we may extend his flamboyant declaration to cover the multiple inheritance of that passionate, histrionic, and questing figure and his doomed and satirical siblings. *Arcadia* sums up and invites us to inhabit, in a spirit of amusement, sympathy, and intellectual excitement, certain of the outermost ripples of that widening inheritance. In doing so, it suggests much that the elusive presence of Byron has meant as it has shaped or informed the paradigms of modern English-speaking theater.

Chapter 6

Wham, Bam, Thank You Sam

I

In examining certain of our theatrical paradigms, we have had occasion to note that apparent chaos in the performed action can disclose in the action of performance a harmonious order, that apparent isolation can disclose a various community, and that apparent absence can disclose the liveliest presence. Those paradoxes are nowhere more evident than in the work of Samuel Beckett. And there they have engendered another: Beckett's work, after taking the Byronic inheritance to a self-consciously dying end, has continued to nourish some quite different paradigms.

As Jonathan Kalb has noted, we may discern Beckett's presence in "the best work of the contemporary avant-garde"—the Wooster Group, Robert Wilson, Richard Foreman, Joseph Chaikin, and others (144). Beckett, Kalb has argued, offers a novel blending of "presentational and representational action" (3) that makes "the actor's denuding a part of his subject matter" (146) and leads "the spectator to be conscious of spectating" (159). Sooner or later, he suggests, the antitextual avant-gardists will have to recognize "that one of their guiding spirits actually turns out to be a classic author" (162). That would indeed be a pleasant irony. But what Ruby Cohn has called Beckett's "theatereality" (*Just Play* 28) is only one way of blending presentational and representational action and so recognizing our shared presence in the theater. For Kalb, Beckett is "the last best hope of the Author in the theater" (162), but in fact a text-based theater is far from dead. Peter Brook, who has assimilated Artaud, Grotowski, Beckett, and Brecht, said as early as 1968, "Shakespeare is a model of a theatre that contains Brecht and Beckett, but goes beyond both. Our need in the post-Brecht theatre is to find a way forwards, back to Shakespeare" (85–86). Sam Shepard, whose importance Kalb ignores, has not only called Brecht his "favorite playwright" (Marranca 202) but has also brought Beckett's theatereality into the practice of the American avant-garde. And a good many playwrights, by translating Beckett into other modes of imagining a participatory space, have illuminated his way of "playing hell."

Critics have often thought Beckett the reductio ad absurdum of an age in which the mind, having lost its illusions of a divine source, an order of values, or a sustaining world, finds itself trapped in the arbitrary, incoherent, and meaningless. One has summed up Beckett in the phrase "zero identity." The "declining vitality of the self," he has said, here "reaches its low point," and human existence is "suspended over a void made palpable" (Langbaum 7, 137). Another, for whom Beckett's subject is "the imminent collapse of being itself," has found in his plays "a theatrical metaphor for man suffering an existence which is in the process of continuous devaluation" (Schwarz 354). Yet another has argued that Beckett's canon consists of efforts to find a shape for "the proposition that perhaps no relationships exist between or among the artist, his art, and an external reality" (Dearlove 3). And yet another has said that for Beckett the stage becomes "a model of consciousness, which, if it creates order, does so only to discover that order has no ontological ground." With this "theatrical positivism," devoting itself to self-canceling games and routines, the modern theater reaches its epitome and "seems also to come to an end" (Driver 387–89).

Nevertheless, the writing and performing of Beckett's plays rest upon the possibility of reliable perception, communicable ideas, and informed action. One critic has argued that *Not I* achieves an extreme condition of human absence by providing minimal details about an "uneventful life," depriving the present of "immediacy," avoiding any image of "consciousness," and offering "only the text that repeats itself within it" (Lyons 155, 157–59). At Lincoln Center in 1972, however, audiences found Jessica Tandy's rendering of that old woman's blighted, bitter, and yearning life—articulated through the hysterically detached medium of her mouth—a poignant and searing experience. In theater there can be no serious question of zero identity, the imminent collapse of being, or theatrical positivism. Any reduction of characters to comic types, partial persons, and disembodied voices derives its theatrical force from the fact that it both requires and resists the medium of actors not so reduced. No performance of *Endgame* could take place in the world represented by that play. The roles of the confused and enervated pair who wait for Godot require the precision and brio of skilled comedians. The trapped Winnie is a rich part for an artist of that oblique form of dialogue with an audience that we call dramatic monologue. Through apparent negations Beckett invites us to relish a sparkling allusiveness, a precise articulation of uncertainties, and an arduous miming of incapabilities. Every apparent separation of mind from body, as William Worthen has argued, offers a challenge to the actor's discipline (203–14). Every apparent loss occurs within a world of literary and theatrical plenitude without which this performance would be impossible. And every image of solipsism reaches us through a collaboratively shaped event. If the performed action seems to imply despair or vertigo on the edge of the abyss, the action of performance requires of director, actors, and audience the full stretch of our sympathetic and interpretive powers. Through the shared imagination of absence such plays as *Endgame, Happy Days,* and *Not I* open themselves to the fullness of human presence.

Beckett surely knew all this. When directing his own plays, he emphasized their quasimusical forms. His assistant director in Germany, Walter Asmus, has said of *Waiting for Godot:* "You get a longing to experience it as mere music, not in terms of tones but in terms of relationships between people. That's ultimately what Beckett wants, I think" (Kalb 183). In 1957 Beckett had written to his first American director, Alan Schneider, warning against journalistic attempts to interpret *Endgame:*

> My work is a matter of fundamental sounds (no joke intended) made as fully as possible, and I accept responsibility for nothing else. If people want to have headaches among the overtones, let them. And provide their own aspirin. Hamm as stated, and Clov as stated, together as stated, nec tecum nec sine te, in such a place and in such a world, that's all I can manage, more than I could. (*Disjecta* 109)

He also wrote a young playwright, Keith Johnstone, that a "stage is an area of maximum verbal presence, and maximum corporeal presence." Johnstone, who was teaching improvisation at the Royal Court Theatre, was especially delighted by that "corporeal" (*Impro* 24). And two years after *Not I,* when thinking about *That Time,* Beckett jotted down this note: "to the objection visual component too small, out of all proportion with aural, answer: make it smaller on the principle that less is more" (Knowlson and Pilling 219). Such craftsman's remarks are worth far more than Beckett's talk about the expression that there is nothing to express. Only if we recognize him as an ironic artist of "maximum presence" can we understand how this playwright of stasis, sterility, and absence has become such a fertile presence in a theater that still declines to come to an end.

II

Throughout the decade or two after *Waiting for Godot* and *Endgame* Beckett's presence in British plays was already quite evident. In 1962 Peter Brook's *King Lear,* influenced by Jan Kott's essay "*King Lear* or *Endgame*" (*Shakespeare Our Contemporary* 127–68), incorporated what Kott called a grotesque "clown's play" performed on "Job's stage." That was one attempt to "find a way forwards, back to [a] Shakespeare" already signaled in *Endgame*'s echoes of *Hamlet* , *King Lear,* and *The Tempest.* Brook's production rediscovered Shakespeare on what Kenneth Tynan called a stage "empty and sterile, a bare space of hostile earth" (D. Williams, *Peter Brook* 26). But the reduction and exclusion were means of intensifying our own presence. Charles Marowitz, who assisted Brook, said that in giving up the play's conventional appeals to sympathy, "we prepare ourselves for the profounder emotionalism which comes from understanding the merciless logic of the play's totality; the realization that the tragedy is not Lear's but ours" (D. Williams, *Peter Brook* 19). A cold mirror of often grotesque role-playing became a partial vehicle for a participatory redefinition of tragedy.

During these years Harold Pinter sought a different way forward, back through a Chekhov who is also evident in Beckett's circling dialogues of inaction, pregnant but abortive silences, and interlacing of failed pathos and uneasy laughter. From *The Birthday Party* (1959) to *The Caretaker* (1960) and *The Homecoming* (1965) Pinter translated those effects into plays that seem to mime ambiguous events in our own sordid and potentially violent world. Within that illusion Pinter's stylization of words, gestures, and silences, and his refusal to supply answers to our questions about past action and present motivation, establish what often seems a self-sufficient realm of poetic role-playing. With *Landscape* and *Silence* (1968) Pinter took that realm yet closer to the retrospective theater poetry of the later Beckett, in which "action" is yet more exclusively verbal, actors become more fully the vehicles of the play, and audiences are both more detached from its "world" and more fully involved in its imaginative cocreation. In *Old Times* (1971) his retrospective theater poetry regained the fuller semblance of a lost "world," now as differently imagined by three characters animated by Pinter's territorial aggressions and defenses. And in *No Man's Land* (1975), as I have shown, Pinter recapitulated his Beckettian trajectory within the extraordinarily self-conscious role-playing of a hellish cul-de-sac. Like Beckett, but without the rigors of his minimalism, Pinter asks us to participate in miming a necessary absence that is mysteriously open to the richness of literary and theatrical history, a dark comedy of manners that can offer a bravura role to John Gielgud or Ralph Richardson. Meanwhile, David Storey found in *Home* (1970) another way forward from both Beckett and Pinter, back through Chekhov, by retaining Beckett's ambiguous location, as in *Waiting for Godot* or *Endgame,* and a Beckettian and Pinteresque ambiguity of past action, but deftly "naturalizing" those effects, and inviting us to share a role-playing that remains more delicately poised between realistic illusion and symbolic poetry. Our participatory presence in *Home* can therefore lead us to a gradual recognition of historical and psychological pressures that have resulted in our condition of "absence" in contemporary Britain.

Several other playwrights were seeking a way forward from Beckett, back through Pirandello—a Pirandello who also already lurks in the shifting relations that obtain between Beckett's disturbingly "empty" characters and the roles they play. For these playwrights our paradoxical absence amid presence was yet more starkly a function of a human nature both abysmally and resourcefully histrionic. One was James Saunders, whose *Next Time I'll Sing to You* (1963) contains a character named Rudge who is fascinated by existential questions of being and nonbeing, and who turns out to have "written" the play in which he and others appear. Another was Charles Marowitz, whose conversations with Peter Brook after seeing Lionel Abel's *A Little Something for the Maid,* in which the female character becomes by turns "everybody in the male character's life" (D. Williams, *Peter Brook* 39), led him to consider ways of "conveying theatrical meaning without reliance on narrative" (*Marowitz Shakespeare* 11). That partially Beckettian aim led to a collage *Hamlet,* presented in London by Brook and Marowitz during their "Theater of Cruelty" season in early 1964, in which a continual "transmutation of character as a result of jumps in time and location" (*Marowitz Shakespeare* 12) summarizes the disintegration of Hamlet into his repertory of roles. Later in 1964, Saunders, Marowitz, and Tom Stoppard were at a playwrights' colloquium in West Berlin, where Stoppard's verse burlesque, *Rosencrantz and Guildenstern Meet King Lear,* was staged. Although Marowitz did not like the sketch, Saunders urged Stoppard to expand it into a full-length play. And that play of 1967, *Rosencrantz and Guildenstern Are Dead,* manages to turn Hamlet inside out by combining it with modes of role-playing drawn from *Waiting for Godot, Six Characters in Search of an Author,* and *Next Time I'll Sing to You.* As I have shown elsewhere (*Tom Stoppard* 37–67), it is an attempt to go forward from Beckett, back through both Pirandello and Shakespeare. Although critics complained that Stoppard drew on *Waiting for Godot* without taking its existential predicament quite seriously, he was turning to his own uses a paradox in Beckett's work that they had missed. *Rosencrantz and Guildenstern Are Dead* plays self-consciously with the notion of ontological "absence" as a means of establishing a lively theatrical presence.

Stoppard's next major play, *Jumpers* (1972), seems unlike Beckett's work despite the fact that its comic hero, the bumbling moral philosopher George Moore, makes an academic career out of Vladimir's talent for worrying over the uncertain grounds for ethical action while ignoring nearby calls for help. Brashly eclectic in style, *Jumpers* uses Orton and Feydeau, Shaw and the circus, Joyce and the TV sitcom to explore the ambiguities of our philosophically rootless condition. Only at its end does Beckett's submerged presence declare itself. When the exasperated and exhausted George falls into a Joycean dream and delivers a passionate and absurd speech in defense of ethical certainties despite the fact that "nothing is certain" (87), he is answered by the suave and amoral philosopher, Sir Archibald Jumper, who suddenly becomes Stoppard's ironic *raisonneur.* Archie's jazzy speech plays with yet more specific memories of *Waiting for Godot:* Vladimir's interest in the two thieves, only one of whom was saved (9b); Pozzo's dark summary of how "they give birth astride of a grave, the light gleams an instant, then it's night once more" (57b); and Vladimir's celebration of that vision: "Astride of a grave and a difficult birth. Down in the hole, lingeringly, the grave-digger puts on the forceps. We have time to grow old. The air is full of our cries" (58a–b). Seeming to remember these things, Archie begins with a riff on the theme of the two thieves:

> Do not despair—many are happy much of the time; more eat than starve more are healthy than sick, more curable than dying; not so many dying as dead; and one of the thieves was saved. Hell's bells and all's well—half of the world is at peace with itself, and so is the other half; vast areas are unpolluted; millions of children grow up without suffering deprivation, and millions, while deprived, grow up without suffering cruelty, and millions, while deprived and cruelly treated, none the less grow up. No laughter is sad and many tears are joyful.

Then, impudently reversing Pozzo's and Vladimir's dark reflections on the birth astride of a grave, he adds: "At the graveside the undertaker doffs his top hat and impregnates the prettiest mourner. Wham, bam, thank you Sam" (87). With that arch translation of death into fertility and *ma'am* into *Sam,* Stoppard drives home his play's complex irony. Archie has reason enough to be grateful: the world portrayed in *Jumpers* seems almost as devoid of ontological grounding as that in *Waiting for Godot,* and this sinister Dr. Pangloss is its apologist. But Stoppard himself is also grateful: he has found in Beckett not solipsistic games but a precise and inclusive wit, an acute ethical sensibility, and a wry sympathy with the foibles and anxieties of our common humanity. The world represented in *Jumpers* may seem to deprive our ethical judgments of ontological grounds, but it would be unintelligible without its complex reliance on our imperilled capacities for such judgments (Whitaker, *Tom Stoppard* 85–107). Like *Waiting for Godot,* it is an ironic work that establishes its center of dramatic understanding not in the world it represents but in the relations between that world and the community that plays it.

III

Beckett's continuing ethical and even metaphysical presence, and his ability to inform a range of theatrical paradigms, may emerge most clearly in the distinctive work of two African dramatists. The country road of *Waiting for Godot,* which runs across a bare stage from nowhere to nowhere, has had special resonances for both Athol Fugard and Wole Soyinka. The South African road through the great Karroo, that "awesome landscape of nothing" in which Fugard was born (Honegger 38), became an insistent motif in his work as early as 1961 with *The Blood Knot* (*Boesman and Lena and Other Plays* 75–76). And the hazardous Nigerian road, littered with carrion and automobile parts, has long been for Soyinka a place of both accidents and essence, ruled by Ogun, the god of death and creativity and the first actor (*Myth, Literature and the African World* 140–60). Although Fugard and Soyinka learned much from Beckett, they did not let his reputation as playwright of absence distort their own understandings of the theater. Fugard has remained a poetic naturalist who agrees with Albert Camus that a literature of despair is a contradiction in terms. Soyinka has sought to balance his work between satire and tragedy, even as it approaches ritual theater. And both playwrights have understood that Beckett's road of ontological insecurity must somehow become in the theater a road of ethical and even metaphysical transformation.

During the 1960s Beckett was central to Fugard's attempts "to understand the possibility of affirmation in an essentially morbid society" (*Boesman and Lena and Other Plays* xi). Rehearsing a nonwhite production of *Waiting for Godot* in 1962, he told the cast that "Vladimir and Estragon must have read the accounts of the Nuremberg trials—or else they were at Sharpeville or were the first in at Auschwitz. Choose your horror—they know all about it." And he thought that the often unemployed man who was playing Lucky "had his fingers on the pulse" of the action because "*Godot* was all about what had been happening to him as long as he could remember" (*Notebooks, 1960–1977* 62–63). But, if Fugard could say that Vladimir and Estragon "are Man in a state of Anguish" (102), he did not find the play itself a depressing sign of that condition. Everything of Beckett's that he had read made him want to work. "I suppose," he said, "it's because I really understand, emotionally, and this cannot but give me power and energy and faith" (67). He rejected a critic's argument that Beckett's writing is an extension of the thought of Descartes. And he defended that writing against a friend's charge of "despairing futility." What did he find in it that was positive? "Love and compassion." But for what? "Man's absurd and bruised carnality" (68).

In producing *Godot,* Fugard learned once again that a play is fundamentally "an actor before an audience" and that its production may be even more important for what it does to the actors than for what it does to the audience (*Notebooks, 1960–1977* 65). The "audience's awareness of the actors and the living moment," he said, is matched by "the actor's awareness *within* that moment." And he added: "My wholeness as a playwright is that I contain within myself both experiences—I watch and I am watched—I examine the experience and I experience" (89). Partly because Beckett could elicit and confirm such insights into the participatory nature of theatrical events, Fugard thought him a greater "poet in the theatre" than T. S. Eliot "has been or ever will be" (78). In a note to a published extract from *The Blood Knot* he defined "the pure theatre experience" in quite Beckettian terms. Its ingredients, he said, are "the actor and the stage, the actor *on* the stage. Around him is space, to be filled and defined by movement and gesture; around him is also silence to be filled with meaning, using words and sounds, and at moments when all else fails him, including the words, the silence itself." And he added significantly: "Externals, and in a sense even the text can be one, will profit nothing if the actor has no soul" (*Statements: Three Plays* intro.).

Several years after his production of *Godot,* Fugard began writing a play about a "colored" and Afrikaans-speaking couple who, having been reduced to "rubbish" by their society, face each other "across the scraps and remnants of their life" (*Notebooks, 1960–1977* 181, 155). Like Vladimir and Estragon or, indeed, like the Morris and Zach of Fugard's *The Blood Knot,* Boesman and Lena are "tied" together, "victims of a common predicament—and of each other" (168). And, like Beckett's pair, they cling to each other in antagonism, uncertainty, and fidelity. But the level at which their predicament fascinated Fugard was finally, as he said, "neither political nor social but metaphysical . . . a metaphor of the human condition which revolution or legislation cannot substantially change" (168). Like Lena, we are all burdened by those "unanswerable little words: Why? How? Who?" (167). And our ontological insecurity leads us, as it leads her, to ask that our "life be witnessed" (173).

Boesman and Lena is shot through with variations on familiar Beckett themes. "I asked you when we came here last," says the muddled Lena, staring about the empty stage. "Is that nonsense?" "Yes!" snaps Boesman. "What difference does it make? To anything? You're here now!" (*Boesman and Lena and Other Plays* 246). But Lena will not let the question drop. "From where to where?" she later asks. "All mixed up. The right time on the wrong road, the right road leading to the wrong place" (265). She would understand Estragon's complaint: "I sometimes wonder if we wouldn't have been better off alone," he says to Vladimir, "each one for himself. We weren't made for the same road" (35a). But Lena's husband is not just a South African Vladimir. In his arrogance, disgust, self-hatred, and secret dependence he is also a Pozzo and a Hamm, just as Lena, in her confused passivity and hard resistance, is also a Lucky and a Clov—and, in her final claim to be worthy of being witnessed, another Vladimir and a Winnie. *Boesman and Lena* therefore contains a synthesis of Beckett situations, but it produces a rather different effect. Fugard the naturalist, always concerned with the "intimacy of experience" (Honegger 36), has found for these compound characters a rich subtext. "Only a fraction of my truth," he could say, "is in the words." His "statement"—"the 'action' of the piece"—was "in the sub-text" (*Notebooks, 1960–1977* 171, 184). Any performance therefore brings into the open, to a degree impossible in the more stylized action of *Godot, Endgame,* or *Happy Days,* the implicit positives that Fugard found in Beckett's bleak verbal comedy. The New York production of *Boesman and Lena* on the open stage of Circle in the Square in 1970, with powerful performances by James Earl Jones and Ruby Dee, made very clear the fact that, though its major characters seem tied to each other by hatred, abuse, and acceptance, the play is really about their hidden love and their imperfectly acknowledged value. Indeed, Lena's demand to be witnessed by Outa, the dying old black and the ultimate Lucky of this play, constitutes a major clue to the ethical and metaphysical implications of both Fugard's and Beckett's drama.

Vladimir, we recall, says to the Boy, "Tell him . . . tell him you saw us" (*Waiting for Godot* 35a). And in *Happy Days* Winnie fastens her eyes on the audience and says: "Someone is looking at me still . . . Caring for me still . . . That is what I find so wonderful . . . Eyes on my eyes" (*Happy Days* 49–50). Fugard's Lena says to Outa: "You be witness for me" (*Boesman and Lena and Other Plays* 260). And again: "I'll tell you what it is. Eyes, *Outa*. Another pair of eyes. Something to see you" (262). And she proceeds to share with him her mug of tea and piece of bread. She realizes that the rudimentary witnessing provided by a sick and outcast black who can repeat only one word in her language—"Lena"—can provide the present goal for all her wanderings. "The walks led *here,*" she says to Boesman. "Tonight. And he sees it" (278). But Outa is not Lena's only witness, nor are she and Boesman left on an empty stage as witnesses for each other. Fugard's understanding of the participatory dimension of Beckett's theater and his own implies that the playwright, actors, and audience are also witnesses to this situation, which is also theirs, and that such mutual witnessing is finally more important than the represented deprivations. When Vladimir hears the cries of the blind and fallen Pozzo, he says: "To all mankind they were addressed, those cries for help still ringing in our ears! But at this place, at this moment of time, all mankind is us, whether we like it or not" (*Waiting for Godot* 51a). And a few minutes later Estragon says of Pozzo himself: "He's all humanity" (54a). For Fugard the comedy of that situation does not obliterate its primal truth. In 1971 he could look back on the writing of *Boesman and Lena* as the time when he "moved from 'artifice' to 'witnessing'—with all the compulsion, urgency, moral imperative of that role" (*Notebooks, 1960–1977* 195). And on many occasions—in South Africa in 1969 with Fugard and Yvonne Bryceland as Boesman and Lena, in New York in 1970 with James Earl Jones and Ruby Dee, in London in 1971 with Zakes Makae and Bryceland, and even in Paris in 1976 with a cast directed by Roger Blin, the first director of *Waiting for Godot*—actors and audiences have found their various walks leading *here, tonight,* for a renewed awareness of our human solidarity.

Although never again following Beckett so closely, Fugard has continued to turn the road of emptiness, isolation, and repression into one of mutual understanding. And he has continued in surprising ways to suggest Beckett's presence while going beyond the paradigm to which Beckett was committed. *The Road to Mecca* (1984), for example, seems firmly in the Ibsen tradition. The action takes place in a provincial and Calvinist town. The set is a livingroom. The dialogue is freighted with retrospective analysis. The three characters are a narrow-minded pastor, a desperate young teacher and political activist, and an eccentric widow. Gradually, however, we learn why this widow, who lives along a road that runs through the vast emptiness of the Karroo, has for years devoted herself to making a fantastic sculpture garden and decorating her sometimes candle-lit room with mirrors and bits of ground-up beer bottles. Helen has sought to transform the dark road of her life into an illuminated road to Mecca. And, in doing so, she has come to seem a bizarre and poignant image of the modern artist, an artist rather like Beckett as he is commonly perceived, who keeps a precarious hold on sanity by withdrawing from the void to create a tiny but endlessly reflecting play of lights and mirrors and grotesque figures. Having shown us this, however, *The Road to Mecca* proceeds to suggest a more adequate image of dramatic art—both Beckett's and Fugard's—one in accord with the process that its actors and audience have already begun to experience. By showing us the understanding of Helen's quest attained by the pastor and by the young teacher, Elsa, it begins to undo the ironies of isolation that both Ibsen and Beckett had underlined. Even as Fugard had found in Beckett's work an inspiriting energy and faith, so Elsa now finds in Helen's a courage that helps her to break out of her own desperate self-closure. In their moment of mutual understanding Helen resolves to learn how to blow out the candles and face the darkness—and Elsa makes the difficult leap to join her in trust. For Fugard the dominant theatrical paradigm has proved to be a stage representation of the very process—a clearly affirmative ethical and artistic process—in which the action of performance is inviting us to participate.

The partial image of Beckett as a hermetic master who withdraws from a landscape of destruction or emptiness to fashion an art almost indistinguishable from absence or death has been explicated very differently by Wole Soyinka. Unlike Fugard, Soyinka has not acknowledged Beckett's work with much sympathy. In a lecture given at Cambridge in the early 1970s, for example, he cited it as an instance of "literary ideology" taking "private hallucinatory forms." Beckett, he said, "gropes incessantly towards the theatrical statement that can be made in one word, a not-too-distant blood-relation of the chimeric obsessions of the Surrealists." He granted that, if we leave the "lunatic fringe of the literary Unilateral Declaration of Independence," we may find that "a literary ideology does occasionally achieve coincidence—and so a value expansion—with a social vision" (*Myth, Literature and the African World* 63). But he chose not to mention the fact that he himself had already expanded Beckett's "ideology" in just that way.

After studying with G. Wilson Knight at the University of Leeds, Soyinka had worked at the Royal Court Theatre in the late 1950s as play reader, writer, producer, and actor, along with a remarkable group that included Edward Bond, John Arden, Anne Jellicoe, and Keith Johnstone—the admirer of Beckett's corporeal "presence" who influenced them all through his teaching of improvisation and the use of masks to unlock the hidden and perhaps Dionysian energies of the psyche (*Impro* 9–10). During the early 1960s Soyinka was back in Ibadan, putting some of this teaching into practice as he wrote and directed Nigerian plays for several acting companies. He returned to London in 1965 to advise on Stage '60's production of his play *The Road* at the Theatre Royal, Stratford East. *The Road* makes it clear that he had come to see Beckett as a partial image of his own rather Nietzschean attempt to devise a theater in which characters, actors, and witnesses might enter something like the Yoruba "abyss of transition" and so experience both death and new life.

Just as Beckett, in Soyinka's later phrase, "gropes incessantly towards the theatrical statement that can be made in one word," so Professor in *The Road,* according to an introductory note, is engaged in a "part psychic, part intellectual grope . . . towards the essence of death" (*Collected Plays, vol. 1* 149), which he understands to be the hidden Word. A defrocked Christian minister of doubtful sanity, he approaches that essence through the accidents of the road. He runs an "Aksident Store" that recycles the parts of wrecked lorries, forges licenses for unskilled drivers, and devotes himself to a Yoruba cult of death. Like some demented *symboliste,* he goes about pulling up road signs because the word BEND, for example, sprouting from the earth, might give him a clue to the ultimate Word. The immediate result, of course, is an increase in accidents and hence in his temporal business. In his description of a nearby gorge, Professor seems to have revised Vladimir's meditation on the difficult birth astride of a grave—not, as Stoppard's Archie would revise it, into a celebration of fertility but into a yet harsher comment on sterility: "Below that bridge, a black rise of buttocks, two unyielding thighs and that red trickle like a woman washing her monthly pain in a thin river. So many lives rush in and out between her legs, and most of it a waste" (197). But Professor's grope toward the Word of absence and death is not just a wry version of Beckett's. It is also part of a serious interrogation of Ogun, the death-bringing and creative tutelar spirit of lorry drivers and actors.

The rather sprawling shape of *The Road,* antithetical to Beckett's minimalism, richly expands Professor's ideology so that it coincides with an ethically ambiguous social vision. Its comic and macabre episodes, which cover a daylong stretch of almost continuous action, acquaint us with an entire community of drivers who are haunted or obsessed by death. Drumming, choral dirges, and hypnotic dances are an integral part of the play's effect. In its first major climax in part 2, the drivers Samson and Kotonu reenact their experience during a Drivers Festival in celebration of Ogun, when a third driver, Murano, had been run down by their lorry while bearing the *egungun,* a mask of hypnotic and deathly power. Since that accident, we know, Murano has been suspended in a state of living death. He has been for us, ever since the play's opening moments, a liminal presence onstage, radiating absence: mute, limping, ready to slash out with a knife. And his incommunicable knowledge has been the most immediate object of Professor's quest. At the end of this day, after bringing the palm wine to Professor for their nightly communion, Murano disappears into the Aksident Store and then seems to reemerge as the *egungun.* The mask begins a dance of death, accompanied by drummers who are urged on by the Professor in his hope of provoking some direct disclosure of the Word. At the climax of the dance, however, a terrified driver tries to halt this "sacrilege," knifes Professor, and is smashed to death by the *egungun.* As the mask collapses into nothingness, Professor utters a dying benediction that asks us to identify with the abyss that the play has in many ways evoked:

> Be even like the road itself. Flatten your bellies with the hunger of an unpropitious day, power your hands with the knowledge of death . . . Spread a broad sheet for death with the length and the time of the sun between you until the one face multiplies and the one shadow is cast by all the doomed. Breathe like the road, be even like the road itself. (228–29)

A haunting and ironical presence, Professor embodies a death longing that is also a desire to reach a heightened and creative state of life.

His full meaning becomes evident if we place *The Road* in the context of Soyinka's notes on the theater, which outline one of the major paradigms to which Soyinka has been committed. "The stage," he has said, "is created for the purpose of that communal presence which alone defines it." A play's "essence" must therefore be found not in the "printed text" alone but in the arena of performance (*Myth, Literature and the African World* 43–44). Soyinka tells how, in Yoruba ritual drama, the actor shares "the protagonist's foray" into the "psychic abyss of the re-creative energies," the choric community shares the actor's own "disintegration and re-assembly within the universal womb of origin," and the entire event repeats the primal experience of Ogun, the first actor (30–31). Qualified by a distancing irony, that vision of participatory theater—which rather parallels Nietzsche's account in *The Birth of Tragedy*—informs *The Road.* And Beckett's expanded presence here seems finally to come to this: by way of G. Wilson Knight, Nietzsche, Keith Johnstone, and Yoruba lore, Soyinka has understood that Beckett's plays can operate rather like severe European versions of those Yoruba masks and rites of death that may unlock a subliminal and transpersonal creative energy.

Fugard and Soyinka shed light on Beckett's ironic minimalism from two sharply different angles. *Boesman and Lena* invites us to experience an ethic of mutual witnessing that is grounded in an implicit metaphysic of human solidarity. *The Road* invites us to explore an ethically ambiguous realm that threatens—or promises—to transform our social identities. That exploration is grounded in an implicit metaphysic of participation in a transpersonal energy that can support the risky journey of the ongoing community. From the paradoxical matrix of Beckett's theater of apparent absence these African playwrights have drawn two complementary modes of histrionic presence and given them a fresh paradigmatic amplification.

IV

The puzzles lurking in Beckett's theater are further unfolded by two American playwrights, David Mamet and Sam Shepard. Beckett's presence has often been mediated in Mamet's work by Harold Pinter, the American vernacular, the underbelly of Chicago, and salesmen's hype, and in Shepard's work by jazz and rock culture, Pirandellian theatricalism, Brechtian narrative acting, and the myth of the West. It is easy to find traces of Beckett's theatrical milieu in Mamet's trashed Resale Shop in *American Buffalo* and his prison cell in *Edmond,* as in Shepard's abandoned Chevy in *The Unseen Hand,* his bare room in *Action,* his cosmic throne room in *The Tooth of Crime,* and his reverberating motel room and spectral rocking chair on the edge of the Mojave Desert in *Fool for Love.* Both playwrights give us characters who seem to be lost in a pile of junk or making themselves up as they go along or ruminating in an echoing void or speeding toward an impossible absence. More important, both playwrights have also understood the theater, with Beckett, as a shareable model of consciousness that is both interpersonal and intrapersonal. They have therefore given American expression to the strange presence-in-absence or intimacy-in-isolation that gained force in Büchner, the later Ibsen, Chekhov, and Strindberg and that has dominated Beckett's work.

Several dramatic strategies, we may recall, make *Waiting for Godot* and *Endgame* not so much dialogues among distinct selves as the miming of a mind's conversation with itself. Reduced, stylized, and isolate types appear as mirroring and complementary pairs: Didi and Gogo, Pozzo and Lucky, Hamm and Clov, Nagg and Nell. Their balanced actions, stichomythic exchanges, and dreamlike echoings and reversals comprise lyric and meditative wholes beyond any individual intent. *Happy Days* and *Play* further subsume their isolate characters within a larger theatrical field: the offstage alarm clock, stage lights, and audience of *Happy Days* and the spotlight and audience of *Play* are agents within the plays that they seem to control or observe. The relations among characters and participants no longer seem to be simply external: each character, actor, and audience member can easily be imagined as a function of some waking dream, which seems both the collaborative act of several minds and the encompassing act of some larger mind or psychic field. Beckett's rigorous direction of *Endgame* as an almost musical performance (Cohn, *Just Play* 230–79) is in harmony with this notion. If a Beckett play offers us a model of consciousness, it is one in which we also participate. Within such a model the characters and participants can seem both terribly alone and inseparably members of one another.

Mamet's theater has approached that condition by way of its most distinctive attribute: the dialogue. In *The Duck Variations* of 1971, Mamet had already transferred the meditative duets of *Waiting for Godot* on isolation and togetherness, nothing and everything, to a Chicago park, where he explored their possibilities for serial elaboration. Didi and Gogo have a lovely duet on "All the dead voices": "They make a noise like wings"; "Like leaves"; "Like sand"; "Like leaves"—and so forth (40a). When the fourteenth Duck Variation has the elderly George and Emil describe the duck's death in antiphonal style—"Living his last"; "Dying"; "Leaving the Earth and sky"; "Dying"; "Lying on the ground"; "Dying"; "Fluttering"; "Dying"; and so forth—Mamet is quietly saying, "Thank you Sam" (*Sexual Perversity in Chicago* and *The Duck Variations* 121–22). By 1976, with *American Buffalo,* this verbal music, of which the characters tend to become mere functions, had absorbed some important lessons from Pinter as well as Beckett. The inarticulate mumblings, gropings, backtrackings, and outbursts of Don, Teach, and Bob combine to shape a taut, subtly nuanced, and rhythmically elaborate counterpoint of banality, aggression, evasion, and desperation. These characters—like their more glib and strident cousins in *Glengarry Glen Ross,* of 1983—are really as isolate as Hamm and Clov, though too unselfconsciously gregarious to be aware of their own predicament. They seem to have not ambiguity but vacuity as a subtext. As masks of a hollow society, they could meet us on no grounds of mutual understanding, and they seem almost beyond our pity or judgment. But, as richly modulated, interwoven, and embodied voices, they compose with us a contrapuntal celebration of the American vernacular.

The main paradoxes of Mamet's earlier theater are clarified in a very different kind of play, *Edmond,* of 1982, which recapitulates a heritage that runs from Büchner through Georg Kaiser to Beckett. *Edmond*'s twenty-three elliptical scenes follow the downward course of a wife-hating, black-hating, homosexual-hating, and implicitly self-hating man who abruptly leaps from his middle-class existence into the life of the streets. His story, like that of Büchner's Woyzek, involves the fatality experienced by an enraged and repressed loneliness. Edmond's psychotic career, which leads from a search for prostitutes, a mugging by a pimp, and the murder of a waitress, on to a prison, where he is sodomized by his black cell mate, seems to be in the cards from the beginning. But this play is also a rethinking of Kaiser's *From Morn to Midnight,* which it follows in its "station drama" form and in some details of plot and character. Kaiser's violently erupting Cashier, who tries for a brief upward mobility, meets his end in a Salvation Army Hall rather like the Mission through which Edmond passes in scene 17. Both *Woyzek* and *From Morn to Midnight* translate the inverted lyricism of isolation into a jagged scenic form in which we can participate. And for both a suggestion of fatality seems to make irrelevant the ethical judgments that their portrayals of society obviously invite. But poetic naturalism and expressionism fuse in Beckett's synthesis, as Mamet implicitly recognizes in the final scene of *Edmond,* which offers a boldly sexual reading of the male world of *Waiting for Godot.* The protagonist and his cell mate become, in effect, another Vladimir and Estragon, as their groping antiphonal meditation moves through questions of destiny, abandonment, self-degradation, and guilt to a strangely peaceful resolution. Their goodnight kiss, sentimental or outrageous if these are merely two distinct selves who have reached a dead end, resolves the play's interior or transpersonal exorcism of hatred, an exorcism of which all the characters seem to be functions. Divorced from women, the remaining psychic and physical opposites, destructive and self-destructive in their opposition, have moved to an ironic truce of intimacy and isolation within and beyond us.

In recent years Mamet has sometimes moved forward from Beckett, back toward the poetic naturalism of Chekhov, even while maintaining the sense—as in other "communities of heartbreak"—that the characters and the participants in the action of performance are both terribly alone and inseparably members of one another. In *The Old Neighborhood* (1997), a sequence of three one-act plays in which Bobby returns to the Chicago of his youth, Mamet holds to a scenic minimalism ultimately deriving from Beckett and strongly suggesting Pinter's *Old Times*. Unlike Pinter, however, Mamet depicts no attempt to dominate the memories of others: Bobby is a sympathetic if enigmatic listener to reminiscent monologues by his old friend Joey, his sister Jolly, and his old flame Deeny. What emerges from these tautly written and yet expansively obsessive and rather Chekhovian self-disclosures is the painfully cramping effect of the Jewish family and neighborhood, the insensitivity and hostility of gentile spouses, and the pathos of friendship, family love, and romantic love that has been allowed to lapse. We also see, in Jolly's husband, Carl, and more fully in Bobby himself, a sympathetic listening—indeed, the possibility of a witnessing love—that shares these predicaments. As such a listener, Bobby carries forward into Chekhovian naturalism the ethical implications of the demand and the response we found in Beckett's Vladimir ("Tell him . . . tell him you saw us") and Winnie ("Someone is looking at me still . . . Caring for me still"). Like Fugard's Lena, the friends from *The Old Neighborhood* ask that their "life be witnessed." In the paradigm at which Mamet has arrived, that very process, represented onstage by Bobby, offers a model for the participants in the action of performance. Nor does Mamet let Bobby off the hook. His marital predicament—a separation, an uncertain future—is established at the outset. And he moves in the third play to a surprised recognition of the subtext that has impelled Deeny's insistent reminiscence of their early days together: her continuing love for him. The last twist of this paradigmatic strategy is to convict the sympathetic witness of a still inadequate attention: to ask us to listen yet more intently to those we have loved and forgotten.

Shepard's theater has rendered the painful isolation and yet intimate connection of characters and participants by more various means. He has spoken of his early and rather baffled admiration for *Waiting for Godot* (Marranca 191), and David DeRose has shown in detail how Shepard's first play, *Cowboys* (1964), is "something of a *Waiting for Godot* gone western" (11). Shepard drew upon Beckett's antiphonal dialogues and self-conscious solos or arias, his portrayals of desperate and virtuoso role-playing, his obscure twinnings, reciprocities, reversals, and transformations, and the paradoxical fields of uncertainty within which they are established. Here and elsewhere, however, Shepard's transpositions of Beckett have a dramaturgical expansiveness and a rhetorical looseness that suggest an improvisatory art. Bonnie Marranca has noted that his plays "are written from the point of view of the actor, and so incorporate the notion of performance" (26). Indeed, Shepard is a major link between Beckett and avant-garde performance art. His collaborative work of 1979 with Joseph Chaikin, *Savage/Love,* is simply the most visible instance of a pervasive influence. But Marranca has made the fundamental point: "Before writer-directors such as Richard Foreman, Robert Wilson, and Lee Breuer were writing texts that broke down the structure of dialogue and elevated the solo voice—taking consciousness as subject matter—Shepard had already moved in this direction in his early plays" (23). In effect, Beckett's Hamm, the solo performer, is given the stage. *Chicago* (1965), as DeRose also shows, is a version of *Endgame,* in which, like Hamm, Stu "sits immobile, attempting to dictate reality around himself through an elaborate spoken narrative," as he is attended by his companion, Joy, who sustains him physically and emotionally but is on the verge of leaving (27–28). Here Shepard characteristically modulates Beckett's fusion of presented and represented action toward the frenetic and intoxicating. The long, hypnotic monologue at the end of the play, as DeRose says, "appears to possess the speaker," and "the character becomes a shaman who carries the audience with him into the unknown and unseen root of his anxiety" (29).

La Turista (1967) might be called Shepard's first full-length play, if Shepard had not argued in 1974 that such an understanding of *full-length* is "ridiculous, because . . . well, Beckett wrote *Come and Go* and it's five pages long but it's full length, whereas some of O'Neill's" (Marranca 199). In two acts *La Turista* replays its protagonist's double desire to go away and to go home, but it does so in the context of two settings and two groups of auxiliary characters—Mexican and American—that replicate each other. As in *Godot,* the more it changes, the more it's the same thing. The doubling plot also operates, through weird transformations, to exile Kent increasingly from the action that he already wants to escape—and from the stage itself. With the help of a swinging rope, he finally leaps from the back of the auditorium through the rear stage wall, becoming the emptiness that both he and his circumstances have wanted him to become. Or has he simply vanished from our theatrical field into the depths of our minds? *The Tooth of Crime,* of 1972, translates Hamm's bare room with its dominating chair into a center of power within some stellar void and further elaborates Hamm's histrionic virtuosity through the doomed figure of Hoss, who can say: "Ya know, you'd be O.K., Becky, if you had a self. So would I. Something to fall back on in a moment of doubt or terror or even surprise" (*Seven Plays* 225). In his "style match" with Crow, Hoss necessarily loses to that epitome of the next rock generation, whose "survival kit" is the "image" (249), who can almost always avoid talking "like a person" (230), and who can sing: "But I believe in my mask—the man I made up is me" (232). The play's rock music, as hypnotic as Soyinka's rites of death, sweeps us into a shared celebration of histrionic behavior that we understand to be driven by our suicidal fear of our own absence.

La Turista and *The Tooth of Crime,* like Beckett's *Godot, Endgame, Happy Days,* and *Play,* manage to suggest that the theater itself is both our necessary field of play and our unavoidable prison. *Action,* of 1974, is Shepard's most probing exploration of that Pirandellian ambivalence. Although written when Shepard could name Brecht as his "favorite playwright," this is also, as Stephen J. Bottoms has insisted, his most richly Beckettian play (116, 124). Jeep's first lines—"I'm looking forward to my life. I'm looking forward to uh—me. The way I picture me"—open a self-analytic and quietly hysterical meditation on the arbitrariness of histrionic action as a prison or desert (*Fool for Love and Other Plays* 169). That meditation takes place not just within Jeep—who can ask, "What's a community?" (183) or, like a baffled Method actor, "Could you create some reason for me to move?" (186)—but within a group of characters who inhabit an incoherent and incompletely specified situation, both isolate and banal, and who find it hard to convince themselves that they are other than empty but somehow animate bodies (183–84). As DeRose has noted (65), the antithetical anxieties of Jeep and Shooter, metaphorically elaborated throughout the play, suggest that we can hardly endure either an existence that is open to the indeterminate or one that is sheltered by our own fictions. And that awareness also dictates frequent ruptures in the dramatic form itself. Not only does *Action* repeatedly subvert our understanding of where, when, or how the action occurs; Shepard also "seizes every opportunity . . . to highlight the presence of the actors behind their characters by creating moments in which the illusion of rationally motivated characterization is disrupted" (69). At the cost of ordinary dramatic coherence Shepard has dared to represent in *Action* a world for which zero identity and theatrical positivism might seem to be adequate labels. But to present that world in the theater as a "problem" requires a present community that is both resourceful and thoughtful.

Shepard's American family plays, as they are commonly called, show how the formal implications of Beckett's anxieties can be used to complicate a more traditional dramaturgy. *Curse of the Starving Class* (1977) and *Buried Child* (1978) may seem for a while to return us to a naturalistic form reminiscent of Ibsen or the later O'Neill, in which family entanglements, issues of inheritance, and social transformations are prominent themes. But each play calls attention to its self-consciously fictive nature through clashes of styles, discontinuities of action, boldly mythical elaborations, and an increasing ambiguity about the status of any character or event. Here Beckett is present, much as in Albee's *Who's Afraid of Virginia Woolf* or Pinter's *The Homecoming,* on the level of the playwright's own subtext, which becomes the subtext of our performance event.

Two later plays reassert that filiation more obviously, as they continue a painful exploration of the mysteries of interpersonal relations within this problematic field. *True West* (1980) shapes a taut drama out of the shifts of power and identity between characters that seem separate but behave like aspects of a single mind. "I think we're split in a much more devastating way than psychology can ever reveal," Shepard has said (*Fool for Love and other Plays* 5–6). *Fool for Love* (1983) focuses, in its tense drama of incest, both our helpless love for those who are not finally separate from ourselves and our unbridgeable distance from them. The half-brother and half-sister, Eddie and May, are trapped in another Shepard low-rent motel—unable either to stay or to leave. And the presence of their absent father, a late addition to the script (DeRose 122), prevents us from naturalizing its action according to any rational scheme. Rocking in a chair on an extension of the stage or wandering into the midst of the action, he incarnates the isolate meditation that has either generated this drama or been generated by it. Despite the violence, anguish, and baffling entrapment here, our ethical judgment seems irrelevant. In this paradigm, as actors or witnesses, we have become clear-sighted participants in a field of multiplicity and unity, isolation and intimacy, that seems a more than Sophoclean fatality beyond our understanding. Whenever Eddie tries to break out of this claustral box and the miked door booms, the reverberations of self-conscious imprisonment within the field of our theatrical participation say, in effect: "Wham, bam." Of the playwrights who have wrestled with the psychological ambiguities of Beckett's plays, it is Sam Shepard who has invited us to realize most variously and most unnervingly their potential for trauma and hysteria.

V

Beckett's continuing presence in scripted theater may be most brilliantly evident in Brian Friel's *Faith Healer* (1979). This is, according to Declan Kiberd, "the finest play to come out of Ireland since J. M. Synge's *Playboy of the Western World*" (106) and, according to Thomas Kilroy, "the one theatrical text of our time which unmistakably takes its place with the best of Beckett or Synge or the Yeats of *The Herne's Egg* and *Purgatory*" (A. Peacock 99). *Faith Healer* might have entered into the earlier chapter on "Playing Hell," for it transforms the Beckettian hell even as *Dancing at Lughnasa* transforms the Chekhovian music of heartbreak. Translating the paradoxes of theatereality into quasinaturalistic monologues without loss of inherent mystery, it goes beyond Sartre, Beckett, or Pinter in its evocation of Dante—as if we were granted a glimpse into some ambiguously post-Christian circle of hell.

Although its four monologues—Frank, then Grace, then Teddy, then Frank again—seem quite realistic, the play's premises are not. Time here is a circuitous and evasive no-time: when could Frank (already dead, though we cannot yet be certain of that) address *us* in an empty hall, seemingly prepared for his performance? When could Grace, now clearly surviving Frank, address *us* in her London flat? When could Teddy address *us* after returning from the morgue to view Grace's body? And when could Frank once more address us, now in the courtyard where he has already met his death? These places, then, must also be nowhere—or rather here, in this very theater. We are not observing "real lives" through some invisible fourth wall; we are being addressed, in a nowhere that is now, by actors who are inhabiting and portraying not people but fictions. As the tattered poster says: "One Night Only." That is the performance in which we participate—because the audience itself is this play's absolutely necessary fourth character. Actors and audience must both must say of Frank, Grace, and Teddy—paraphrasing Grace's own statement—that they are "real enough, but not real as persons, real as fictions," *our* fictions, extensions of ourselves that come into being only because of us. Like Dante's pilgrim in hell, we encounter the essence of three lives, of our lives, abstracted from time and place, illuminated by the spotlight of eternity.

The result: a multifaceted jewel of a play that turns and turns in the imagination. It is a fable of the artist, and of the artist in each of us—for Grace and Teddy are also artists in their fashion. It is a diagnosis of what happens to gifts, especially gifts of faith, in a faithless age, to hope in an age of desperation, to love in an age that fears to acknowledge its primacy. It is a play about identity, vocation, and community, as they have been undermined by unanswerable questions. It asks, finally, how we pose those questions through a shared performance that testifies to our mutual need.

Faith Healer brings together, in effect, three modern traditions that have emphasized our search for truth through testimony that is fallible, mendacious, self-consciously fictive, or strangely transcending death. One is the dramatic monologue. Three of Browning's speakers are remote ancestors of the "Fantastic Francis Hardy, Faith Healer." "Bishop Blougram's Apology" is the devious account offered by a worldly man of faith who acknowledges that he is above all a man of doubt. "Mr. Sludge, 'The Medium'" is the self-defense offered by a highly disreputable artist in spiritualist chicanery. And, in a darkly heroic vein, "Childe Roland to the Dark Tower Came" is Roland's paradoxically retrospective account of how he approached that terrible place where he anticipated and, we may presume, found his own death. Browning's masterpiece *The Ring and the Book* , which combines seventeenth-century legal history and Victorian psychology, gives us a gamut of narrators who recount their conflicting versions of the events that led to a criminal trial. In the twentieth century T. S. Eliot's "The Love Song of J. Alfred Prufrock" gives us a modern but implicitly Dantesque figure who can speak to nobody living but speaks to us. More perplexingly conflating different historical moments, the speaker of Eliot's "Journey of the Magi" begins with a proleptic quotation from Lancelot Andrewes and then describes a landscape that contains images of Christ's passion. Likewise, the speaker of David Jones's "The Tribune's Visitation," on the occasion of that passion, anticipates in his rhetoric the Eucharistic meanings that Saint Paul would later find there. In a quite different way Geoffrey Hill's *Mercian Hymns* fuse the consciousness of the eighth-century king Offa with that of the autobiographical poet. And Seamus Heaney locates his poetic sequence, "St. Patrick's Purgatory," in a place in Ireland where, according to tradition, one may hear the speech of the dead.

Modern fiction, too, from Henry James to William Faulkner and beyond, gives us ironic narrators who may be "dead" and alive, "real" and fictive. In Faulkner's *The Sound and the Fury, As I Lay Dying,* and *Absalom, Absalom!* we approach the truth through multiple narrators who sometimes speak from beyond the grave. The narrators of Albert Camus's *The Fall* and Vladimir Nabokov's *Lolita* are both self-consciously damned and transparently fictive. And the drama, of course, has also moved from the clashing retrospective accounts of Ibsen's characters, the unreconcilable memories of

Pirandello's self-conscious fictions in *Six Characters in Search of an Author,* and the monologues of Yeats's Noh-influenced ghosts in *The Dreaming of the Bones* and *Words Upon the Window-Pane,* on through the dead characters of Sartre's *No Exit* to the clearly fictive characters of the later Beckett: Krapp in *Krapp's Last Tape,* a stagey presence who converses with his previously tape-recorded selves; Winnie in *Happy Days,* who turns her monologue on and off at the behest of the theater's alarm clock and spotlight; and the three heads in *Play,* who recapitulate their lives together at the behest of an inquisitorial spotlight. Brian Friel, whose interests have long been narrative as well as dramatic, approached this poetic, novelistic, and dramatic tradition in *Lovers* (1968), which gives us a young couple on the edge of death and then dispassionately recalled after the event, and also in *The Freedom of the City* (1973), in which three characters are given monologues that describe the circumstances of their own deaths. Now, in *Faith Healer,* he makes this multiple tradition his own.

To what end? Abstracted from any real time and place, mere functions of the playwright's imagination and ours, the characters are nevertheless dramatic vehicles of the play's major themes—the artist and the performer in each of us, and the ways in which identity, vocation, and community have been undermined by doubt and despair, fear of love, and a longing for death. Each monologue is a struggle between a desired self-conception, elaborated for an audience, and what opposes that desire in the depths of the psyche—a hidden, oppositional subtext. Each monologue is therefore potentially therapeutic—but we are the therapists, listening not so much to the alleged facts of past lives as to the maneuvers of the present telling, and the characters can hear us only within themselves.

Grace, most simply, wants to convince us and herself that she is recuperating from Frank's death. That death has devastated her because, though she sees how she has been exploited and abused, she has been utterly dependent upon him. Her pervasive distortions, the erasing of difficulties, the reversals of fact—who threatened to leave whom?—and the little fictions about Frank's attentiveness, all contribute to a pattern of self-persuasion. She wants to believe that her marriage was far better than it was, that she can survive its dissolution, that she is more than a fiction of her husband's imagination. The list of Welsh and Scottish towns repeatedly enters her monologue to cover a rising hysteria. And in its closing moments, we see her approach to hopelessness and self-destruction.

Teddy, who provides the scherzo in this four-part composition, is a very different case. I want, he says in effect, to believe that I am a professional man, that my relations to Frank and Grace have nothing to do with need or love, and that I can continue unaffected by their self-destruction. But his circuitous monologue repeatedly traps him into acknowledgments of his need, of his love—most notably in his silent moments of emotion when contemplating the deaths of Frank and Grace but also in that evocation of the evening in Ballybeg: "And suddenly she is this terrific woman that of course I love very much, married to this man that I love very much—love maybe even more" (47). But Teddy cannot sustain that recognition without collapsing: he must finally return to his speech to the "copper" and to us: "a professional relationship . . . Cause that's what it was, wasn't it, a professional relationship? Well it certainly wasn't nothing more than that, I mean, was it?" (48). And, as he stands looking at us, his silence, the silence that is necessary for Teddy as a survivor, speaks louder than his words.

Frank is a more difficult case. His action, like that of a Browning character, is to make a brilliant performance out of the very collapse of his performing career. He wants to make the willed death (sought in order to escape his uncertainties, his questions about a gift without faith, a vocation without ministry) into another kind of histrionic success—after the fact. He nearly persuades us. Imagine the baleful and hypnotic glamor that his monologues would have if not accompanied by those of Grace and Teddy. Frank is the self-doubting, world-doubting, and self-destructive hero who tries to suppress his need for Grace, his need for Teddy—those characters whose names suggest that they are the only gifts of God that he will ever know. Frank is so filled with rigidly controlled emotion about the cost of his life that he repeatedly turns others into a supporting cast. The "restoration of Francis Hardy" (20) on the return home to Ireland is in fact his self-destruction. His verbal ritual, the recitation of those village names, is part of the self-hypnosis that his continuing project requires. His second monologue ends with the debauching of a ritual death. He is his own faithless savior.

Faith Healer is itself a ritual beyond ritual, which invites us to work through all the discrepancies and shifts of emphasis in these monologues but not to arrive at any certainty about what actually happened to Frank and Grace and Teddy. Rather, we must understand, so far as we can, the present meaning of lives like theirs—lives trapped by dependency and denial, devoted to professional survival, and glamorized by despair. In doing so, we inhabit a world in which the characters' dark destinies can no longer be projected, in Beckett's fashion, upon some ambiguously malevolent or meaningless cosmos but must be accepted as functions of their own impulses. Like the monologue artist of Ralph Ellison's *Invisible Man,* those characters are speaking for us. In such ways, without moving beyond the paradigm of playing hell, *Faith Healer* brings further clarification to the self-critical and affirmative aspects of Beckett's imaginative world. The play itself, therefore, rests upon the "faith in the transforming power of the imagination" that Friel would more explicitly (if no less ironically) affirm in his 1994 play *Molly Sweeney* (Lahr, "Friel's Blind Faith" 110), a play that constitutes a kind of thematic and formal sequel to *Faith Healer*—and so a further testimony to the presence of Beckett.

Chapter 7

Soyinka's Roads to the Abyss

I

Wole Soyinka, whose work has testified to the presence of Beckett, is himself a considerable presence of the opposite kind. Whereas Beckett has refined to a minimalist death a single paradigm and yet energized a variety of work by others, Soyinka is a shape-shifter who has absorbed such variety into his own rituals of transformation. A Nobel Prize–winning playwright to be reckoned with on three continents, he is also a theorist of drama, a scholar, poet, novelist, and memoirist as well as an actor, director, producer, and political activist. And he remains the subject of intense debate. Is he fundamentally a satirist or a tragedian? Is he a Yoruba traditionalist, a romantic individualist, or a modernist who appeals to a foreign bourgeoisie? Some plays have rather clearly satirical emphases: *The Lion and the Jewel* (1959), *The Trials of Brother Jero* (1964), *Kongi's Harvest* (1965), *Madmen and Specialists* (1970) *Jero's Metamorphosis* (1973), *Opera Wonyosi* (1977), *Requiem for a Futurologist* (1983), *A Play of Giants* (1984), and *The Beatification of Area Boy* (1995). Others are predominantly tragic: *The Swamp Dwellers* (1959), *A Dance of the Forests* (1960), *The Strong Breed* (1964), *The Bacchae of Euripides* (1973), and *Death and the King's Horseman* (1975). In each, however, and especially in *The Road* (1965), the satirical and the tragic are complementary. Nor can we separate Soyinka's traditionalism from his romantic modernism. The expressionist and absurdist strategies of *Madmen and Specialists* pay tribute to Yoruba folklore. The ritual pattern of *Death and the King's Horseman* consorts with an Ibsenite realism. The revision of Euripides' *The Bacchae* into a post-Christian communion rite and the translation of Brecht's *The Threepenny Opera* into the Nigerian satire of *Opera Wonyosi* are exercises in yet bolder eclecticism. Soyinka's plays take up with relish so many theatrical styles and paradigms that they elude assessment from any narrow point of view.

The localism, internationalism, and eclecticism result from tensions in the modern world and in Soyinka's imagination. Although he understands theater as "communal presence," he also knows that all peoples are now coming into a single conversation. His imagination, as Biodun Jeifo noted when introducing *Art, Dialogue and Outrage,* is antinomic or dialectical. An early essay, "The Fourth Stage," pits the regenerative "will" against the tragic "abyss" (*Myth, Literature and the African World* 146). A more recent essay finds in Aristophanes' *Lysistrata* both a satirical verve and an "idiom of fertility rites" and behind both a "life impulse" that can be manifest in both comedy and tragedy (*Art, Dialogue and Outrage* 32).

How has that "life impulse" led him to shape and reshape various theatrical paradigms? Here we must be selective. The generative center of Soyinka's most important plays, as I have suggested in chapter 6, is a multiform "abyss" or field of transformation on the horizon of our ordinary experience, a transliminal state that promises both destruction and re-creation. He has pondered Nietzsche's *The Birth of Tragedy* and relived certain myths that our civilization would reduce to mere objects of knowledge. He sees that we must risk the appearance of death on the way to refreshed life, that the tragic protagonist's destiny of self-breaking and transcendence is normative, and that modern actors and witnesses must be led toward participation in such a destiny. He has therefore sought dramatic forms in which the community can experience a journey of disintegration and reintegration through "our inner world of transition, the vortex of archetypes and kiln of primal images" (*Myth, Literature and the African World* 36).

The roads toward that abyss, Soyinka has said, belong to Ogun, "Lord of the road" that unites gods and humans, and "the first actor" (*Myth, Literature and the African World* 27, 124). Ogun's rescue of himself from the "edge of total dissolution" is repeated by the Yoruba actor who mimes a foray into the "psychic abyss of the re-creative energies," and by the community of "choric participants" who share that miming (31, 33). Such ritual drama has been one major paradigm for Soyinka's own work, despite the immense cultural distance between the Oshun and Obatala festivals and the metropolitan performance of an English-language play by a Nigerian of Christian upbringing and British education. Hence Soyinka could say that *The Road* depicts in Murano "the passage of transition from the human to the divine essence" and in Professor a "part psychic, part intellectual grope . . . towards the essence of death" (*Collected Plays, vol. 1* 149). And he could warn that *Death and the King's Horseman* must realize a "largely metaphysical" confrontation "through an evocation of music from the abyss of transition" (*Death and the King's Horseman* 5–6).

Ogun, however, is not only Promethean and Dionysian but also an Apollonian god who enforces a "transcendental, humane but rigidly restorative justice" (*Myth, Literature and the African World* 141). He therefore leads us also through a social abyss of greed, corruption, and murder. And Soyinka is not just an admirer of ritual and tragic drama that leads to a communal celebration beyond the yes and no of simplistic moral judgments; he is also a political activist and moral absolutist, who can on occasion scorn the "enervating tragic Muse," condemn "evil," uphold "justice" and "liberty" (*The Man Died* 87, 283, 224, 95, 277, 286), and write mordant satires on those who, masked by spiritual privilege or self-deceived by identification with some principle or will, arrogate to themselves a trivial or terrifying power. Tragic ritual and satiric festival are for Soyinka two sides of the re-creative Möbius strip that, in his poem *Idanre,* symbolizes the roads of Ogun (85, 87). That is why the explorations of tragic destiny in *The Strong Breed, The Road,* and *Death and the King's Horseman* must also involve critiques of social injustice and why the satirical vision of moralized cannibalism in *Madmen and Specialists* and *Opera Wonyosi* must also suggest that, as a community, we are a tragic scapegoat. It is significant that *Requiem for a Futurologist*—a topical satire that James Gibbs has considered "out of the mainstream of his work from this period" (*Wole Soyinka* 37)—could be described by Soyinka himself (so Henry Louis Gates Jr. has told me) as the completion of the metaphysical "Trilogy of Transition" that began with *The Road* and *Death and the King's Horseman.* Indeed, Dr. Godspeak Igbehodan of *Requiem for a Futurologist* is closely related to Brother Jero, to Professor in *The Road,* and to Dr. Bero and the Old Man in *Madmen and Specialists.* On Soyinka's roads to the abyss we follow a protean figure whose Yoruba hubris can seem inseparable from European acculturation, whose death can result from religious necessity or secular alienation, and whose masks include the prophet, charlatan, tribal functionary, artist-intellectual, healer, and murderer.

Such ambiguities point toward another aspect of the multiform abyss: a modern skepticism and nihilism. Always implicit in a play's unresolvable contradictions or willed affirmations, this aspect of the abyss is sometimes explicitly evoked. *The Road* asks us to share Professor's philosophical uncertainties and finally to confront the apparent nothingness that animates the spinning *egungun* mask. *Madmen and Specialists* devotes much of its absurdist rhetoric to evoking a nihilistic abyss. A similar uneasiness lurks in the antinomies underlying the hypnotic affirmations of *The Bacchae of Euripides* and in the tension in *Death and the King's Horseman* between the Yoruba beliefs that sustain Elesin's rite of suicide and the secular "honor" and "survival" that provide his son's rationale for that act.

Attacks on Soyinka's plays as socially ambivalent or philosophically confused are therefore somewhat beside the point. Even the seemingly didactic plays are not primarily discursive statements but experimental forms of dialectical and participatory action. Their dissonances are part of a strategy that leads us toward a triple dissolution—metaphysical, social, and axiological—that we may experience as an "abyss of the re-creative energies." We cannot understand that dramaturgy if we simply regard Soyinka, with Georg Gugelberger, as a "pseudo-traditionalist" who writes in "the tradition of European modernism" (12) or, with Geoffrey Hunt, as an individualist whose "romanticism" is a function of "class-ambivalence" (Gugelberger 12, 64, 74). Nor should we accept Hunt's assumption that drama is categorically different from ritual (77) or Ketu Katrak's contrary assumption that Soyinka's plays aim at a "communal benefit" that must be found *within* the actions portrayed onstage (12, 100). Rather, we must regard those actions as part of a performance in which we participate. Soyinka has been firmly committed to the view—which is central to my account of theatrical paradigms—that the full meaning of a play inheres in the relation between the performed action and the action of performance. As he has said, "The stage is created for the purpose of the communal presence which alone defines it" (*Myth, Literature and the African World* 43). That is where we must find the communal benefit toward which his plays direct themselves.

We must understand Soyinka's ritual paradigm, however, within a broader cultural context than his polemical statements may suggest. He has said that "the supposed dividing line between ritual and theatre should not concern us much in Africa, the line being one that was largely drawn by the European analyst" and that only a "Eurocentric conditioning or alienation" would lead one to regard the "transitional realm" as mere "fantasy" (*Myth, Literature and the African World* 7, 33). Such characterizations of European thought as a reductive rationalism disguise the importance to Soyinka of Nietzsche's *The Birth of Tragedy,* which his essay "The Fourth Stage" revises, and of Jung's archetypal psychology, which it both absorbs and denigrates. They also obscure the fact that, before returning to Nigeria in 1960 to study West African drama, Soyinka had found at the University of Leeds and at the Royal Court Theatre not just "Eurocentric conditioning" but reasons to believe that a drama of ritual and masks can open us to transformative realities beyond our ordinary awareness.

Bruce King, in *The New English Literatures,* has called his work at Leeds with G. Wilson Knight, the eminent critic, actor, and director, a "meeting of like minds" (78). Soyinka's debt to Knight has been noted by Ketu Katrak (5, 6, 12, 13), James Gibbs (19, 28, 115, 125), and Ann B. Davis (Gibbs, *Critical Perspectives on Wole Soyinka* 147–48). But Knight's work has not yet been given its full due as a shaping influence upon Soyinka's dramaturgy. Knight sought repeatedly to reconcile Nietzsche and Christ, even as Soyinka would do in his adaptation of *The Bacchae.* Perhaps more important, Knight had maintained, in *Principles of Shakespearean Production,* that artistic convention is "almost one" with ritual, which is a "willed acceptance in terms of which the barriers between universal and personal, God and man, are broken." He insisted on "an almost ritualistic performance" of key moments in Shakespeare's "mystery of tragic sacrifice" and suggested that the renewal of life through such sacrifice still requires of us at least the image of royalty (219, 222, 233, 236). In a book on Ibsen that resulted from a course Soyinka took with him, Knight went on to argue that even realistic and ironic plays can lead us toward Dionysiac self-realizations, the discovery of our "super-rational powers," and an attainment of life through the experience of death. For Ibsen, he said, the "positive quality in death" must be "projected, almost incarnated, through flesh-and-blood people who dare" the "appalling step" of suicide, and "we are invited to link our subjective experience to theirs." A seeming "problem-play" like *Ghosts,* therefore, "shades through the purely tragic into a conclusion touched by a gleam beyond mortality" (*Ibsen* 50, 110, 113). Echoing that view, Soyinka would say that the stage presents "cosmic" forces larger than the "actual twists and incidents of action" (*Myth, Literature and the African World* 43). From this vantage point we can glimpse certain larger meanings in *Death and the King's Horseman,* which combines the abortive ritual suicide and final Shakespearean suicide of Elesin with the more Ibsenite suicide of Olunde. We can also glimpse such meanings in *The Road,* the closing moments of which combine a theatrical masking, a nearly suicidal blasphemy, a panic-induced murder, and a spiritual manifestation.

Nor has criticism yet taken account of what Soyinka must have learned at the Royal Court, where George Devine, William Gaskill, and Keith Johnstone were working with masks in an effort "to induce *trance* states." They drew on Japanese Noh and West Indian voodoo and on the studio work of Stanislavsky, Vakhtangov, Michael Chekhov, and others. Their work relied on the fact that a mask or role can induce in an actor a deepening of the trance states that partially shape all human behavior. "A Mask," Keith Johnstone has said, "is a device for driving the personality out of the body and allowing a spirit to take possession of it." David Cregan, who attended these sessions of mask work with Soyinka, has said that Johnstone "knew how to unlock Dionysus" (*Impro* 143, 148, 154ff., 10). Soyinka himself, as an actor and director, has gained some reputation for an ability to unlock the subliminal, and, even when his plays use not African but Greek, Brechtian, or absurdist masks, they remain close to a theater grounded in trance.

Returning to Nigeria, Soyinka began to develop this understanding of theater in his interpretation of Yoruba ritual drama, in which the "so-called audience," an "integral part" of the conflict, "contributes spiritual strength to the protagonist through its choric reality which must first be conjured up and established." Without "this communal compact whose choric essence supplies the collective energy for the challenger of chthonic realms," the "drama would be non-existent" (*Myth, Literature and the African World* 39). But how can a modern play approach that communal participation? What is needed, as Nietzsche made clear in *The Birth of Tragedy* and as Hofmannsthal, Yeats, Lorca, Eliot, and Brecht have all understood in their different ways, is some adequately mediating presence on stage: a traditional chorus, a range of choric roles, speeches or songs of choric effect, or a pervasively "choric" dimension in the "music" of language or theatrical embodiment.

Soyinka's plays suggest a restless search for mediating presences that might focus our participation and relate it to the protagonist's journey. *A Dance of the Forest* contains a kind of choric overkill: its masked commentators, turgid language, and exuberant choreography lead us in too many symbolic directions at once. *The Swamp Dwellers,* with its enigmatic Beggar, and *The Strong Breed,* with its final grouping of guilty speakers and silent observers, make more powerfully reticent use of onstage witnesses to heighten our awareness of implicit complexities. Neither play, however, lets us come close to its tensely ambivalent protagonist. Again quite different are *The Trials of Brother Jero, Kongi's Harvest,* and *Jero's Metamorphosis:* despite a variety of choric devices—Jero's wry speeches to the audience, several kinds of seductive and parodic music, even a bacchanalian feast—they subordinate our shared predicament to satirical animus or comic delight. But Soyinka's most comprehensive plays—*The Road, Madmen and Specialists, The Bacchae of Euripides,* and *Death and the King's Horseman*—constitute an array of invitations for actors and witnesses to accompany the protagonists, with varying degrees of critical awareness, toward a problematic ecstasy on the edge of the abyss.

Read in chronological sequence, these plays seem to move through negations toward affirmations and suggest a substantial progress toward greater stylistic clarity and scenic control. But they also suggest that Soyinka has somewhat retreated from the generative abyss in all its ambiguity or that the clarity of traditional forms has exacted the sacrifice of a more difficult implicit power. *The Road* and *Madmen and Specialists* treat Nigerian material through different postexpressionist idioms, offering apocalyptic ironies with tragic resonance. *The Bacchae of Euripides,* which modernizes the classical, and *Death and the King's Horseman,* which classicizes the modern, are more fully tragic celebrations. But the "communion rite" and the "threnodic essence" of the later two plays are no more genuinely affirmative or participatory than the doubtful music of the earlier two. In order to make this point, let me reverse the chronology so that the earlier plays may comment on the later ones. The most insistently euphoric play, *The Bacchae,* can then be answered by the most insistently nihilistic, *Madmen and Specialists.* And *Death and the King's Horseman,* which evokes the numinous passage of transition, can be answered by *The Road,* with its transition from the human to the divine and its grope toward the essence of death.

II

In writing *The Bacchae of Euripides,* Soyinka borrowed many lines from William Arrowsmith's translation (in the Grene and Lattimore *Complete Greek Tragedies*) but rejected its main emphases. Arrowsmith had kept what he understood to be Euripides' ironic balance between a bigoted Pentheus and an amoral Dionysus (*Euripides V* 146–53). Soyinka, however, invites us to accept a partly moralized and politicized version of that Dionysian amorality. In this respect, as in its miming of the hunt of Pentheus, his version recalls the Performance Group's *Dionysus in 69.* But Soyinka rejects the freewheeling individualism encouraged by Richard Schechner, who made thematic use of the actors' personal identities and resistances. Although Schechner described the chorus in Nietzschean terms—"the matrix of the play," "indestructible and, finally, joyful"—the Performance Group's work on character stressed the spontaneous discovery of individual feelings within the outline provided by the role. As actors elaborated on the text, lines became nakedly autobiographical, a process intended to image a Dionysian freedom. In the mortification scene "a psychic space opens between those performers who are free to show themselves and the man playing Pentheus, tied to the text as to a stake" (*Dionysus in 69* n.p.). Soyinka, who called that production a "search for the tragic soul of twentieth-century white bourgeois-hippie American culture" (*Myth, Literature, and the African World* 6f.), contents himself with adding a Chorus of Slaves, a Slave Leader whose chants draw on his own *Idanre,* and a symbolic expansion of Dionysus to include not only the earth's beneficence and the cruelty of repressed libido but also the revolutionary spirit of freedom and justice and the redemptive spirit of Christ. (The symbolic equation of Dionysus and Christ, by way of a vision of the miracle at Cana and the final crucifixion-communion imagery that substitutes for Euripides' theophany of Dionysus, may recall themes and images in Yeats's *The Resurrection.*)

The Dionysian "universal energy of renewal" (*Collected Plays, vol. 1* 143) becomes a musical presence that enchants, hypnotizes, and coerces the characters into its dance. The action is a series of pulsations that invite actors and witnesses toward choric participation in that universal energy of renewal. First, Dionysus gently leads the anxious vestals of the scapegoat rite into a dance with the Slaves; then the Slave Leader arouses the Bacchantes into a pop scene frenzy; and then the Slaves' denunciation of Pentheus modulates into a liturgical invocation. On the chaining of Dionysus, the Slaves join the Bacchantes in another invocation that becomes violent ecstasy at the moment of the god's liberation. Slaves and Bacchantes then form a fanatic front as they mime the hunt of Pentheus; the entranced Agave, returning with Pentheus's head, becomes the center of a graceful Maypole dance that soon grows frenzied; and finally the music of Dionysus wells up and fills the stage with the god's presence as a fountain of blood-wine spurts from the orifices of the head. All the characters have now been led to the acceptance on which the god has insisted. The Slave Leader, long a spokesman of the god under other names, has found his avenue of liberation. Pentheus has found the death for which his power-mad psyche subliminally yearned. Tiresias has found the true life that eluded his professional tricks. Agave has hypnotically accepted her role in a horrific pietà communion. Even Kadmos and the Old Slave, their uneasy moralism silenced by awe at earth's mystery, accept and drink. And, by the play's design of music and masking, we are brought to share in that communion.

Unless, of course, we resist. Can we accept its hasty reconciliation of opposites? "*The Bacchae,*" said Roland Joffé, who directed the play in collaboration with Soyinka at the National Theatre, "is a celebration of being and the words 'good' and 'bad' are totally irrelevant." (What, then, of the moral issues of slavery?) It is also, said Joffé, "the tragedy that Freud saw, how to reconcile the conscious limited mind with the unconscious unlimited mind." (A tragedy for which *good* and *bad* are irrelevant?) And, in confronting "those who agree with Nietzsche with those who don't," concluded Joffé, the play is "a criticism of the sort of repressive civilisation which desires to annihilate paradox" (Gilbert 24, 25). The director's attempt to justify the Nietzschean thrust of the play was certainly in harmony with its own attempt to hypnotize us into an acceptance of the moral necessity of the amoral. Pentheus is here deprived of all moral and intellectual justification; Agave need not go into penitent exile; and every symbol exhorts us to accept the blood of hysterical revolution as the earth's necessary refreshment. Many in the audience, therefore, are likely to find the "communion rite" not a reconciliation of opposites but an insistence on opposition. We can understand why John Lahr, complaining of a production that seemed a labored attempt at freedom, could say: "The tragedy is turned into a tract" (59). In willing the ecstatic, *The Bacchae of Euripides* becomes vulnerable to the criticism that its Tiresias has made of a perfunctory scapegoat rite: "Ecstasy is too elusive a quarry for such tricks" (*Collected Plays, vol. 1* 244).

In relation to this expansive but reductive version of Euripides' tragedy, the earlier *Madmen and Specialists* is like some anticipatory, and more successful, satyr play. It offers in advance a shrewd critique of the pretensions of *The Bacchae of Euripides.* In large part a product of Soyinka's months of solitary confinement as a political prisoner during Nigeria's civil war, *Madmen and Specialists* takes up each problematic theme, locates it in the backwash of an abstractly evoked military conflict, and probes it with an ironic needle. No cult of phallic and hysteric madness here liberates the repressed by assassinating a ruler. Instead, a murderous specialist in political control prevents a maternal cult of chthonic benevolence from curing the madness produced by degradation and outrage, and so brings on a miniature Armageddon. But here even the tyrant has some potential for good: Dr. Bero is an unfaithful son who has betrayed his healing vocation for the sweet taste of power over human flesh. His father, who masks himself with ironic nihilism, sees that a Nietzschean transcendence must end in a denial of one's humanity and that a human questioner is the gaping hole in every political system. No political or religious charade could escape his criticism. Instead of a Chorus of Slaves who achieve a dubious lyric freedom, *Madmen and Specialists* therefore gives us a chorus of Mendicants who find a mocking freedom within their slavery. And, as a proleptic critique of *The Bacchae*'s self-interested ecstasies and sublimated cannibalism, it gives us the religion of "the new god and the old—As" (*Collected Plays, vol. 2* 241), in which a garbled Christian doxology, a cynical *amor fati,* and a torrent of wry verbal transformations suggest the terrible ambiguity of any human interpretation of the divine. Aafaa's ecstasy here is a faked epilepsy. In wartime blood becomes more potent than wine.

And the Old Man prepares with Swiftian irony a cannibalistic feast, only to find the practice adopted by his son without moral compunctions. Even *The Bacchae's* recognition that nature's order transcends our moral distinctions appears more sanely in this play, which rejects Dr. Bero's pretensions but accepts the herbal lore of the earth mothers, Iya Agba and Iya Mate, and their final destruction of what would only be misused.

The shared movement of *Madmen and Specialists* leads us toward an ironically ecstatic foundering in the abyss opened up here (and everywhere in the world, as we know) by the arrogant separation of rhetorical and technological power from maternal wisdom and sisterly love. Crucial to that movement is the verbal and histrionic game-playing of the Mendicants and the Old Man, who mirror the game-playing of our performance. In part 1 the Mendicants locate us all as mocking players within our cultural moment of truth. They provide a cynical counterpoint to the chorus of earth mothers, whose truths seem too simple for our sophisticated desperation. And they introduce us to the music of the seemingly unbreakable cycle of As. In part 2 the games become more exuberant, and Aafaa's alphabetical résumé of As leads into the Old Man's more elaborate verbal permutations, which focus our insights into a world of murderous abstraction. Even Dr. Bero picks up the game of linking ironic barbs with alliteration, slant rhymes, and puns. Finally, the parodic orations of the Blindman, the Old Man, and Aafaa and the grotesque litany of self-righteous "practice" sweep us into the moment when, like some inquisitory Lear on the heath, the Old Man mimes with frightening realism the surgical victimizing of the questioning Cripple: "Strip him bare. Bare! Bare his soul!" (264). As he raises his scalpel, hysterical mockery and repressive hysteria become for him, and for us, a single emotion. Dr. Bero shoots him down, Iya Agba hurls the embers into the store, the Mendicants break into gleeful song, and (as the blackout cuts off the song in midword) we realize that our ironic miming of modern cannibalism has led us to inhabit each perverse or perceptive role. "A part of me," the Old Man has said, "identifies with every human being" (276). Cannibalism, therefore, is autophagy: eating others, we eat ourselves. To this dark communion of awareness we have been brought by the play's sardonically Dionysiac music.

In sum, the "negative" and rather obscure visionary action of the earlier *Madmen and Specialists,* moving through tragic satire toward an apocalyptic ecstasy, seems more complex and even more profoundly affirmative than does the clarified and willfully "affirmative" attempt in the later *Bacchae of Euripides* to move through catastrophe toward an ecstasy that is defiantly liberating. These two plays, of course, deliberately pursue extremes—and pay the price. But a similarly sobering conclusion emerges if we compare the two most capacious and most successful of Soyinka's plays, *The Road* and *Death and the King's Horseman*. Each seeks to incorporate our ordinary world of experience and the "abyss of transition" that we dimly discern on its horizon. But again the later play, despite its surface clarity, implicit affirmations, and undeniable force, has lost or suppressed much of the felt complexity with which the earlier play had grappled.

III

Death and the King's Horseman, which has been called Soyinka's finest play, is no less syncretic than *The Bacchae of Euripides,* though it may not have seemed so to its audiences in London, Chicago, and New York. Soyinka here reimagines a Yoruba folk opera with the help of Greek and Shakespearean tragedy and the Ibsenite problem play. The primary source, Duro Ladipo's *Oba Waja,* moves in five acts through a sequence based on an actual episode of 1946. That sequence includes the British District Officer's uneasy decision to prevent the Olori Elesin from following his king into death, as hereditary obligation would dictate; the stopping of the death rite; Elesin's ambivalent response to accusations by the people and by the spirit of the dead king that he has yielded to the white man's law; the decision of Elesin's son, in a Ghana bar, to return to Nigeria to bury his father; and the ironic meeting of the two, which leads first to the son's suicide and then to the father's (*Three Yoruba Plays* 53–72). As Ulli Beier has said, "Ladipo has kept fairly close to the facts" of the historical episode "except that he makes the Olori Elesin kill himself in the end, whereas he stayed alive in real life" (74). In his revisions of Ladipo's script, paradoxically enough, Soyinka has attempted to immerse this action more fully in the "Yoruba mind" even while framing it within an Anglo-African perspective. On the one hand, he has turned Ladipo's tolerant British officer faced with a "cruel dilemma" into a more easily satirized figure, has given central place to Elesin's encounter with the abyss of transition, and has provided two choric figures, the Praise-Singer and Iyaloja, who help us to understand that encounter. On the other hand, he has eliminated the spirit of the dead king, added some partly Europeanized Nigerians, made the officer's wife more sympathetic, and turned Elesin's son from a Ghana trader into a British medical student. He has even placed the episode two or three years earlier in order to enable wartime comparisons of Yoruba and British ideas of ritual and sacrifice. He has also removed from the stage both

Elesin's act of capitulation and his son's suicide and has rendered the whole through an English international style. As a result of these changes, the tribal beliefs on which Elesin stakes the meaning of his life come to seem more intense, more open to us as poetic options, but also more questionable.

A rather Shakespearean counterpoint invites us into that intensity. Scenes 1, 3, and 5 compose a nearly classic double tragedy of honor lost and honor sustained, in which moments of climactic lyricism (the story of the Not-I bird, the ecstatic death dance, and the final dirge) prepare for the "music from the abyss of transition" on which Soyinka's introductory note insists. The intervening scenes, ironic and discursive, seem designed to whip and entice the resistant European mind toward that music. Scene 1 presents a choric introduction to Elesin in his hubris, as he makes the risky if metaphysically justifiable demand for a bride on the day of passage into death. Scene 3 leads us, after the comic repulsion of Sergeant Amusa from the marketplace, into the death dance. Against the lyrical and choreographic brilliance of those scenes, scenes 2 and 4 set a world of wooden conversations and trivial festivity, in which Simon Pilkings and his wife Jane desecrate *egungun* costumes as they tango at home and waltz at a fancy-dress ball in honor of the touring prince and where Elesin's son Olunde defends to Jane the rite of voluntary death and then scornfully confronts his still-living father. Scene 5, bringing the two worlds more fully together, presents (for Simon and Jane Pilkings and for us) the tragic self-recognition of Elesin, his suicide while confronting his son's body, and Iyaloja's choric transcendence of that mixed failure and success.

That scenic counterpoint, however, also distances us from the meaning of what Soyinka has called the play's "threnodic essence" by raising questions about moments that might otherwise seem absolute in their intensity. We learn only after the fact that Elesin's trance-journey, at the end of scene 3, has been disrupted by his divided will. We learn only after the fact that Olunde's scorn for his father, at the end of scene 4, has turned into a suicidal rebuke. As often in Greek tragedies, this play denies us direct access to the most crucial turning points and so forces us to judge the protagonists from an inferential distance, But how are we to judge? In accord with what religious or cultural norms? Here the play seems to blur its focus.

At the end of scene 5, the Praise-Singer and Iyaloja eloquently place both Elesin and Olunde in terms of the Yoruba ritual tradition. But that placement has already been called into question by Olunde's conversation with Jane Pilkings. What claim have Yoruba ethics and metaphysics upon this thoughtful young man with a British medical education? If we may judge from his own remarks, he must have acted on the basis of what the Praise-Singer and Iyaloja would regard as a shockingly relativized interpretation of his father's beliefs. Although he objects to any Anglo-centric judgment, his own defense of obligatory and sacrificial suicide has rested, with occasional irony, on its congruence with British ethics. He finds the naval captain's self-sacrifice "rather inspiring," an "affirmative commentary on life," and holds that "ritual suicide" is no worse than the "mass suicide" of a "devastating war" about which he has no illusions: "I know now how history is made." And, when he maintains that his father has "the deepest projection the mind can conceive," he refers not to some metaphysical realm but to "peace of mind" and "the honour and veneration of his own people." Olunde's most trenchant statement implies a tolerant pragmatism: "I slowly realized," he says to Jane, "that your greatest art is the art of survival. But at least have the humility to let others survive in their own way." He thinks that preventing his father's death would be "a terrible calamity" for "the entire people" (52, 51, 53–55, 57–58). Already committed as a medical student to helping others survive, he sacrifices himself in his father's place without ever endorsing the metaphysical "world" on which the survival of this people is ostensibly based.

Perhaps, like Eman in *The Strong Breed,* Olunde may acknowledge some sacrificial destiny that he cannot fully explain. If so, he is an appropriate secondary protagonist in a play that, despite Soyinka's introductory note, does explore the uncertain territory between conflicting cultures. There are many signs of that troubled mediation. Although *Death and the King's Horseman* seems to indict the white man's desecration of ancestral costumes for mere entertainment, this play itself gives those costumes to white players. Although it celebrates the salvation of a "world" that "is tumbling in the void of strangers" (75), it renders that salvation in the heightened poetic idiom of those strangers. Ladipo's *Oba Waja* had repeatedly sounded the motif of a world that may be "spoilt in the white man's time" (*Three Yoruba Plays* 59, 61, 64, 68, 69, 72). *Death and the King's Horseman* evokes the precariousness not just of the Yoruba world but of the entire human world in our time of divorce from the "great origin" (18, 63). And yet, despite the inadequacy of philosophical explanations, in this play the world remains one in which the acceptance of death is intuitively understood to be the price of creative life. G. Wilson Knight would certainly applaud that understanding. And Iyaloja can therefore speak for us all as her lament modulates into confidence: "Now forget the dead, forget even the living. Turn your mind to the unborn" (76).

Just as *Madmen and Specialists* had already offered an ironic probing of the celebratory trances of *The Bacchae of Euripides,* so *The Road* had already opened up the uncertainties that remain half-submerged in the threnodic essence of *Death and the King's Horseman.* At the center of *Death and the King's Horseman* Elesin's ecstatic dance renders an apparent approach to the abyss: "Elesin Oba, can you hear me at all? Your eyelids are glazed like a courtesan's, is it that you see the dark groom and master of life?" (44–45). Only later do our questions about the approach and the abyss multiply beyond those of the Praise-Singer. At the end of *The Road,* accompanied by a confused fight and the driver's dirge, the ecstatic *egungun* dance renders the problematic nature of both approach and abyss. "Breathe like the road," says the dying Professor, "be even like the road itself" (*Collected Plays, vol. 1* 229). In this pairing, however, the oppositions are less extreme and the affinities more profound. Each play engages, amid cultural conflict and religious uncertainty, the meaning of vocation. And each conjures up a "choric reality" that enables us to share the protagonists' exploration of a most problematic ecstasy. What can it mean, in our ignorance and faithfulness, to insist on death as the price of creative life? What is implied by this ambiguously willed and destined movement toward an "abyss of transition" about which no person or tradition can make final pronouncements? Accepting the pertinence of such questions, but not distancing itself from the mystery of the *egungun* trance, *The Road* allows us variously to celebrate the will of Ogun, whose name is here one of many "accidents" that point to an unnameable "essence," or Word.

Although I have already placed *The Road* in relation to Beckett's work, we must look more broadly at its Euro-African exploration of Soyinka's ritual paradigm. Its landscape of social satire, psychological projection, and metaphysical interrogation identifies it as a Nigerian offshoot of the allegorical-expressionist line that runs from *Everyman, Faust,* and Ibsen's *Peer Gynt* to Strindberg's *The Great Highway,* Kaiser's *From Morn to Midnight,* and Beckett's *Waiting for Godot.* During the episodic day at Professor's "Aksident Store" time races onward. (An hour of stage time actually passes before the first word is spoken.) Within that swift movement Murano inhabits a mute suspension of time between death and dissolution. (He had been run down, as we will discover, by a lorry at the Drivers' Festival while possessed by the *egungun* mask.) And other episodes seem to transcend time and place: Samson and Kotono, for example, rewitness an accident at the bridge and reenact their encounter with the Drivers' Festival, at which Murano had been run down and Kotono had put on the *egungun mask.* In other episodes Samson's hilarious playing of a millionaire, of Professor, and of the dead Sergeant

Burma also takes us toward an eerie loss of identity and location. Through fortuitously synchronized accompaniments the organist in the nearby church and the chorus of layabouts contribute to this recurrent canceling of time and place. And a slithering among several languages—Yoruba, Pidgin, and an English that ranges from drivers' argot to high Victorian—suggests that any identity can be a momentary function of the words we use. Within this protean field the drivers' celebration of death, Professor's search for "the elusive Word" and our own participation in the action of performance begin to converge (*Collected Plays, vol. 1* 184). We share in the hallucinatory movement toward an abyss that can annihilate anyone's most recent identity in giving fresh energy to a new and perhaps supratemporal role. An actor's playing of Samson, Samson's playing of himself or Sergeant Burma, Kotonu's wearing of the *egungun* mask, Murano's miming, and Professor's attempt to discover its hidden meaning—these all become versions of a single action.

These complexities delighted Nigerian audiences (Banham 10–11) as much as they bewildered some Londoners (Billington 31–35). And from them emerges a gamut of attitudes toward the abyss. Say Tokyo Kid hurtles with bravado toward a death that gives him a self-consciously epic identity. Disappearing like Murano in the middle of the road after a murderous accident, he returns to trigger the final mêlée, knife Professor, and be smashed down by the *egungun* mask. Salubi, in contrast, sneaks toward a death that gives him almost no identity. Wearing a dead driver's uniform, begging for a forged license, nearly throttled after spying on Murano, he finally slips his knife to Say Tokyo Kid. The histrionic Samson, vacillating between ebullient improvisation and anxiety about loss of his identity as a driver's mate, dances on the edge of the abyss. He plays roles until they threaten to undo him and urges Kotonu to save them at the Driver's Festival by wearing the mask of the freshly killed Murano. Kotonu himself, who has killed Murano by accident or by Ogun's designing and has been possessed by the death mask, now tries to abandon his driver's identity and withdraw from the abyss. Like some road-shocked and sleepy Mother Courage, this man conceived in a push truck and born in a lorry now settles for a mammy wagon, trading in death.

For Professor these are all ways of groping toward Murano and the Word. Having survived his former Christian calling and identity ("when Professor was Professor" [162]), he is a master-forger and producer of accidents who travels about like some ironic and demented *symboliste,* collecting words that might contain a clue to the Word that is trapped in demonic bondage. The advent of Murano, the dead man and god-apparent who offers evening communion from the palm tree, tempts Professor to make a leap beyond all such mediation—to "anticipate the final confrontation," to "cheat fear, by foreknowledge" (223f., 227). Like a more intellectual Serjeant Musgrave, he tries to provoke direct disclosure of a Word that can be known only in a dance of death. In doing so, he draws together the play's themes, including the flux of identity and the relativity of language, and focuses them on the liminal figure of Murano, with "one leg in each world," the big toe of whose left foot is alleged to rest on "the slumbering chrysalis" within which mutates "the moment of our rehabilitation" (187).

The "plot" of *The Road* is the accident-strewn path toward discovery of who Murano "is"—the ecstatic goal of our playing. His attraction is a music subtler than that of Dionysus in *The Bacchae* and more pervasive than that of the Yoruba abyss in *Death and the King's Horseman*. In his coiling sleep, swift attack, ritual service, or ecstatic dance, he masks what remains in principle beyond us. First seen during that swift hour of stage time before the beginning of the play's verbal, histrionic, and choric participation in death, he returns at the end of part 1, having mistaken a funeral hymn for vespers, and nearly silences the foolish Salubi who would stalk him down. When he returns again at the end of part 2, for a vesper communion that will become a dirge, we have more fully understood the circumstantial identity of the dead palm wine tapper and his symbolic resemblances to willful dogs getting in the way of lorry wheels and a goat that has been stolen by a hit-and-run driver. But we have also more fully sensed the magnetism of absence that has led to Kotonu's entrapment in the bloody death mask and to Samson's discovery that in Sergeant Burma's uniform he has been playing death.

This magnetism now emanates from what *was* Murano as the *egungun* dance begins. A few swift moves—willful? hysterical? accidental?—and Professor learns the meaning of his leap: the attempt to cheat fear by foreknowledge, anticipating the final confrontation, is self-defeating. Professor's lying benediction recapitulates some of the play's most pregnant images: the mirage, the ghost lorries, the reflected identity of living and dead, the serpentine road maker who is also the road and who gives both death and life. But the play's final disclosure is beyond words: the spinning mask collapses into nothingness, Professor's head falls forward, and from the falling darkness wells the dirge. In this music of the god's presence-in-absence we may experience what G. Wilson Knight had called the "positive quality of death."

IV

Reflecting on how the "life impulse" has led Soyinka to shape and reshape theatrical paradigms, we may be led to sobering thoughts about his progression. More powerfully than any of his later plays, *The Road* invites us to share a richly ambiguous descent into the abyss. Within terms provided by an agonized postcolonial culture, this complex masterpiece explores a fundamental romantic and modernist problem: the meanings of an anxiously self-conscious search for creative death. It confronts us with a difficult paradigm, in which ritual drama assumes a spectral intensity. Realism and expressionism combine in a proliferation of analogous actions that variously refract the meaning of our death-haunted action of performance. It seems impertinent to ask more than this of a playwright who said, "To dare transition is the ultimate test of the human spirit" (*Myth, Literature and the African World* 158). But Soyinka's later development may give us pause. Although *Madmen and Specialists,* after the civil war, enacts a further and more sardonic descent into that abyss, *The Bacchae of Euripides* and *Death and the King's Horseman* retreat to politicized versions of a more traditional paradigm—classical tragedy understood as ritual. They restate the spiritual problem with greater craftsmanship, assurance, and cultural scope but with a less probing acknowledgment of its complexities.

Indeed, if we compare the rich obscurity of Soyinka's yet earlier attempt at a major play, *A Dance of the Forests,* which contains in embryo so many of his themes, with the reiterative and mind-numbing polemics of the much later *A Play of Giants,* a satirical attack upon the corruption and cruelty of four African leaders, we may be saddened by the evident price that Soyinka has paid for survival as a playwright. To be sure, the author of *The Man Died* (1972), *Aké: The Years of Childhood* (1981), *Ìsarà: A Voyage around Essay* (1989), and *Ibadan: The Penkelemes Years* (1994) has continued to give us memoirs of extraordinary vividness, balance, and historical resonance. We may hope, however, that some new approach to the abyss of re-creative energies might bring a surprising life to his work for the theater. *The Beatification of Area Boy: A Lagosian Kaleidoscope* (1995), reminiscent of *The Road* but more simply mixing the satirical and the celebratory, may point in this direction. There an insanely prophetic vagrant called Judge, who is somewhat reminiscent of Brecht's Azdak in *The Caucasian Chalk Circle,* journeys toward death but leads "a charmed life" (106). Addressing a Prisoner whom he invites to share his journey, Judge tells him that he is "a mere shell of being, nothing more. A no-man's wilderness inhabited by phantoms.

Your fate is to become a born-again, the genuine thing. A hideous bore. Revelation will come to you on a forlorn road" (74). More than thirty years ago, in *A Dance of the Forests,* the ambivalent Forest Head had understood such a possibility to be his aim as a cosmic playwright. "My secret is my eternal burden," he said, "—to pierce the encrustation of soul-deadening habit, and bare the mirror of original nakedness—knowing full well, it is all futility" and yet "hoping that when I have tortured awareness from their souls, that perhaps, only perhaps, in new beginnings" (*Collected Plays, vol. 1* 71).

Chapter 8

Brook and the Purpose of Playing

I

Wole Soyinka has sought in his major plays to move through several paradigms to an "abyss of transformation" from which playwright, actors, and audience might emerge transformed by the creative energies. For Peter Brook the directorial art itself, to which he has brought a more disciplined eclecticism and internationalism, has offered a field of self-transformation that leads through various paradigms toward the open secret of playing. His assimilation of many genres and styles—drawn most notably from Shakespeare, Beckett, Brecht, and Genet—led to major productions of *King Lear* and *Marat/Sade.* His later work, with scripts and companies both English and international, has seemed perhaps a strange mix of theatricalism, pessimism, mythology, and clinical observation. But he has always understood with Meyerhold and Brecht that the audience is part of the performance, and his often unpredictable course has been an increasingly rigorous means of holding the mirror up to our playing.

What is the purpose of playing? No contemporary director has more fully engaged that question than Brook, and none has more clearly understood that today more than ever before we must respond to a diversity of paradigms and presences. Since 1962 his productions have suggested a repeated abandonment of already mastered styles and forms, a continuing search for the new. He has believed that the director "will find that all the time new means are needed: he will discover that any rehearsal technique has its use, that no technique is all-embracing" (*Empty Space* 124). Since 1970, based in Paris and journeying to Iran, Africa, and around the world with a group of actors diverse in race, national origin, language, and theatrical style, he might seem to have been seeking what he had called "a world style for a world theatre" (135). But he has warned: "We never aimed to discover some synthetic international style, although we worked on all styles. The whole of our work has been to purify, to clarify, to simplify. In fact, what we have striven for is an absence of style" (Carrière and Brook, preface).

For such reasons Brook's theater has often been misunderstood. After seeing *The Ik,* Simon Trussler declared that *A Midsummer Night's Dream* had been "a benign blink, as it were, in the narrowing focus of his misanthropic (and politically myopic) vision" (Selbourne, *The Making of "A Midsummer Night's Dream"* xxix). Brook's next production, *The Mahabharata,* would prove him wrong. But it is not easy to account for a progression that includes *King Lear* (1962), *The Marat/Sade* (1964), *A Midsummer Night's Dream* (1970), *Orghast* (1971), *The Conference of the Birds* (1973–79), *The Ik* (1975), *The Mahabharata* (1985), *The Man Who* (1994), and *Qui est là?* (1996)—with notable productions along the way of *Oedipus, The Tempest, Timon of Athens, Ubu aux Bouffes, Measure for Measure, The Cherry Orchard, The Tragedy of Carmen,* and *Woza Albert!* Who's there, indeed? A formidably eclectic director, a persistent interrogator of playing—but to what end? On that question Brook has often seemed quite vague. "I don't think of myself as a theater artist," he said in 1980. "I'm not particularly interested in theater or art as such. I'm a traveler, an explorer whom life has thrust into this field . . . It's all part of a process I hope is getting richer and richer in human material—and human discovery" (E. T. Jones 12). Two years later he said: "The theater is a search for an expression that is directly concerned with the quality of living and, in that search, one can find great purpose" (Carrière and Brook, preface). What quality? What purpose?

The most detailed account of Brook's career, by Albert Hunt and Geoffrey Reeves, who worked with him in the late 1960s and early 1970s, provides no clear answers to those questions. Indeed, their readings of performances are astonishingly reductive. Brook's process in *King Lear* "goes round and round and ends up—on the empty stage" only to tell us "that our predicament is one of pointless despair" (55). His *Marat/Sade* asks us "to ignore the intelligence, to be swamped by illusion" (94). And in *A Midsummer Night's Dream* he "locked himself, so far as was possible, inside his Chinese box with his actors and asked them to look inside themselves to solve the 'mystery.'" (153) In the early years, they say, Brook seemed to seek "variety of experience," in the 1960s "the nature and purpose of theatre," and in recent decades what he "perceives as 'truth.'" Although Hunt and Reeves aim to "put a magnifying glass on the nature of this 'truth'" (2, 4–5), they have little patience with it. As admirers of the Brook who "belongs to the practical world of showbiz" and "wants his work to be seen on a world stage" (274), they sum him up as "a theatre magician" (95) who can produce "from his voluminous conjuror's sleeves" either "grandiose projects which take us into realms of mysticism into which some of us find it hard to follow him" or a synthesis of theater experience and abstract art that is "at the same time both mysterious and lucid" (278).

Others have offered more penetrating interpretations of part of Brook's work. Shomit Mitter has shown how he assimilated Grotowski's relentless *via negativa,* "a means of emptying the self so that it may be filled by a 'force'" (120), but redirected it through a commitment to a difficult "wholeness" in the theater, the self, and the community (124, 126). Mitter seems to understand that when Brook says, "A play is play," he invokes *Lila,* the cosmic play in which we participate (132; *Empty Space* 141), but his nonchronological analysis repeatedly misses Brook's approach to that process. His account of Brook's dialectical response to Brecht, based on rehearsals for *US* in 1966, ignores the far more complex "play" elicited in 1964 from Peter Weiss's *Marat/Sade.* His examination of rehearsals for *A Midsummer Night's Dream,* focusing on somatic work as an answer to Stanislavsky, scants Brook's interest in the "playing-within-playing" offered by Shakespeare's text. And, finding the climax of Brook's career in *The Mahabharata*'s "unity of indiscriminate amalgamation" that generates "an authentic image of life's plurality," Mitter concludes only that Brook has "an inimitable lack of individuality, a second-hand genius of formidable synoptic power" (5).

On Brook's work since founding the Centre International de Recherche Théâtrale in 1971, we have more useful studies: A. C. H. Smith's account of *Orghast,* John Heilpern's of the African journey, David Williams's essays and edited volumes, and Georges Banu's and Yoshi Oida's personal meditations. Williams shows that *The Mahabharata* gives us a direct taste of the Hindu "*lila:* the world as cosmic illusion and play" (*Peter Brook and "The Mahabharata"* 186). Banu shows how the "cycle" from *Timon d'Athènes* in 1974 to *La Tempête* in 1990 involves a continuing alliance between what Brook has called the "rough" and the "holy" theaters (44). We need, however, to place the later career in a context that can shed further light on Brook's central quest.

We might begin with his admiration for Shakespeare, "a model of a theatre that contains Brecht and Beckett, but goes beyond both" (*Empty Space* 85–86). Although recognizing the "rough" in Shakespeare, Brook sees his fundamental aim as "holy, metaphysical." (62) Like Beckett, he belongs to "The Theatre of the Invisible-Made-Visible" (42). Brook grants that "we shy away from the holy," and that all "the forms of sacred art" have been "destroyed by bourgeois values," but he insists that it is "foolish to allow a revulsion from bourgeois forms to turn into a revulsion from needs that are common to all men." If "the need for a true contact with a sacred invisibility through the theatre still exists, then all possible vehicles must be re-examined" (48).

We must therefore take seriously what can only be called the religious meaning of Brook's quest. We need not dwell on his work in the 1950s, which included some Christian plays that (perhaps congenially) approached the light by way of a labyrinthine darkness: Christopher Fry's *The Dark is Light Enough, The Power and the Glory* adapted from Graham Greene's novel, and T. S. Eliot's *The Family Reunion*. But we should not reduce his "Theatre of Ritual" of the early 1960s merely to an avant-garde reliance "on extreme audience participation in an attempt to tap the subconscious" (Innes 129–44, 5). Brook's perspective has always been broader than that. He once said, "Such is the complete breakdown of the word that I can't make the simple statement that all great theatre is religious with the faintest hope of communicating clearly what I mean" (Hunt and Reeves 71). Irving Wardle found himself uneasy with that notion. Describing Brook as "a man with an urgent message to deliver who finds himself wandering about in a labyrinth," he said:

> I am trying to avoid religious imagery. From one aspect this is the story of a spiritual quest. But as soon as you begin describing it like that, it starts sounding ridiculous. Brook, a pilgrim? What spiritual exercises lead to his productions of *The Little Hut, Irma la Douce,* and *The Perils of Scobie Prilt?* Still more absurd, of course, would be to view him as a commercial entertainer, cunningly applying the techniques of Shaftesbury Avenue to the sacred texts of India and Persia. (Williams, *Casebook* xvi)

Of course, Brook does not believe that theater is a religion, setting itself up in rivalry with Christ, Mohammed, and Buddha or claiming to create a new ritual. He made that clear during a 1966 forum on *Marat/Sade.* Nevertheless, he has remained commited to the "religious" power of great theater—but in what sense?

In his own work Brook has long sought for moments through which the invisible might become manifest. "We know that the world of appearance is a crust—" he could say; when talking of his experimental work in 1963–64; "under the crust is the boiling matter we see if we peer into a volcano. How can we tap this energy?" (*Empty Space* 52). After directing *A*

Midsummer Night's Dream, he said: "It's from the hidden inner life of the performer that the magic, the unfolding possibilities of the play, must emerge" (Ansorge 18). But he also could say, with reference to the "impersonal acting" required by *Oedipus:* "It is not enough for the actor . . . to be open blindly to impulses from sources inside himself that he cannot understand. He needs an understanding that must in turn ally itself to a wider mystery. He can only find this link through a tremendous awe and respect for what we call form" (*Seneca's Oedipus* 7). And yet Brook has always resisted translations of the "invisible" into theological or metaphysical abstractions. Although aware that Attar's *The Conference of the Birds* is a Sufi allegory of the soul's journey to the Divine, he chose to say: "*Conference* speaks in the language of the god, the bird, the serpent. It is the simplest and deepest way of communication, and it cannot be translated. When you say the serpent is a symbol of something, you are not getting more clarity, you are getting less" (Williams, *Casebook* 226). He had made the same point about Beckett's "symbols": "a true symbol is the only form that a certain truth can take" (*Empty Space* 58). For him truth is always concrete, experiential.

In *The Empty Space* Brook offered a concise definition of the "holy" theater. "All religions assert that the invisible is visible all the time," he said. "But here's the crunch. Religious teaching—including Zen—asserts that this visible-invisible cannot be seen automatically—it can only be seen given certain conditions. The conditions can relate to certain states or to a certain understanding." He granted that "to comprehend the visibility of the invisible is a life's work." But holy art, he said, "is an aid to this, and so we arrive at a definition of a holy theatre. A holy theatre not only presents the invisible but also offers conditions that make its perception possible" (56).

An important presence behind these formulations, not named in *The Empty Space,* is G. I. Gurdjieff, whose life and work have guided Brook more than has been generally recognized. A consummate role-player, both shaman and showman, Gurdjieff had devoted himself to the discovery (in Christian Gnosticism, Tibetan Buddhism, the Jewish Kaballah, Hinduism, and Sufi orders) and the teaching (in St. Petersburg, Tbilisi, Constantinople, Paris, and Fontainebleau) of "certain states" or "a certain understanding" through which human beings might awaken from the hypnotic trance of ordinary life. In 1976 Brook rather astonishingly described Gurdjieff as "the most immediate, the most valid and the most totally representative figure of our times" (Moore 1). He had clearly found in Gurdjieff an alliance between the "holy" and the "rough" that could inform his own quest. "Is the saint," he asked,

> the man who withdraws furthest from the squalor and the action of the market place, who artificially lops off the undesirable aspects of human experience to make more room for the holy ones? . . . All of Gurdjieff's life and teaching make an opposite statement . . . In his own spiritual search he was constantly moving, and bringing others with him, through the most rich and intense participation in life. (Moore 57)

We may recall Brook's similar confession: "I'm a traveler, an explorer . . . It's all part of a process I hope is getting richer and richer in human material—and human discovery."

Gurdjieff's "Fourth Way" is a discipline of attention, self-observation, self-remembering, and self-transformation aided by psychological and physical exercises and by music and sacred dances. As in Buddhism and in the teaching of Krishnamurti, the key for Gurdjieff is self-remembering (Ouspensky 117–22; Speeth 76–80), a repeated or persistent awareness that enables detachment from the animal drives, ego, and multiple personas. That discipline can rouse us from our "consensus trance," make us aware of our "identity states" (Tart, *States of Consciousness* 163–70, and *Waking Up* 85–106, 115–25; Speeth, *Gurdjieff Work* 75), enable us to discover the "objective" awareness they mask—and so free us to perceive the world and act in it with fresh intensity. James Moore, placing such practice in a philosophical context, has said that William James had "offered the dictum 'my experience is what I agree to attend to,' but it was Gurdjieff who extrapolated this insight into a *pratique* for the mobilization and direction of attention, within the context of a persuasive phenomenology of consciousness" (342). Gurdjieff sometimes called his teaching "esoteric Christianity" (Ouspensky 102; Webb 519–25). James Webb called it "a particular form of psychodrama" (537). Under whatever name, it has important analogies to Brook's attempt to "make possible" the perception of the invisible. Brook's statement in opposition to Stanislavsky that "preparing a character" is not a "building" but rather a "demolishing" of what stands between the actor and the part is as close to Gurdjieff's understanding of the psyche as it is to Grotowski's *via negativa* (*Shifting Point* 7–8). Brook's rehearsal techniques, too, have been Gurdjieffian: they require an observation of one's habitual movements and responses, a spontaneous opening to "that which comes in the instant when something comes toward you," and, as David Williams has recognized, a retaining of "that essential faculty that Gurdjieff called 'self-remembering,' an objective, critical awareness of self" (*Casebook* 202, 206). The hardest task for the actor, Brook believes, "is to be sincere yet detached" (*Empty Space* 117).

"Everything we do on this journey," he said to John Heilpern as they headed into the Sahara in 1973, "is an exercise. It's an exercise in heightening perception on every conceivable level" (51). After Heilpern took part in some concentration exercises, he said in a Brookian fashion: "I was learning to jolt myself out of my everyday condition. I had to remember myself." He then quoted a passage from a letter by René Daumal (160), author of *Mount Analogue,* the first French testament to Gurdjieff's teaching (Moore 273). Just as Gurdjieff, by remaining aloof, providing glimpses of enigmatic truths, and setting difficult challenges, required his students to discover their personal initiative, so an enigmatic Brook has often given only negative or provocative critiques, requiring the actors to find the appropriate creative moves. "The director is there," he has said, "to attack and yield, provoke and withdraw until the indefinable stuff begins to flow . . . At best a director enables an actor to reveal his own performance, that he might otherwise have clouded for himself" (*Empty Space* 109). Robert Langdon Lloyd, who has worked with Brook over many years, confessed that he used to be terrified when Brook looked at him with "Gurdjieff's eyes" (O'Connor 149). Brook's interest in the nonverbal also accords with Gurdjieff's emphasis on movement, dance, and music as approaches to "mobilized attention equipoised among intellect, feeling, and body" (Moore 352). In *The Empty Space* Brook proposed the orchestra conductor as an analogy for the "mediumistic" process of "total relaxation" and "possession" (109–10): "we are aware that he is not really making the music, it is making him—if he is relaxed, open and attuned, then the invisible will take possession of him; through him it will reach us" (42). Music, said Brook, is "a language related to the invisible by which a nothingness suddenly is there in a form that cannot be seen but can certainly be perceived" (120). Again like Gurdjieff, Brook has fastened on certain works—Shakespeare's plays, Attar's *The Conference of the Birds*–as offering an enigmatic but objective meaning. "Objectivity," David Williams has said, is "Brook-speak for universality" (*Peter Brook and "The Mahabharata"* 16). That is because it is Gurdjieff-speak (Ouspensky 27).

Here, as elsewhere, however, Brook has avoided doctrinal limitations. By 1977 he was in Afghanistan, shooting a long-planned film version of Gurdjieff's semiautobiographical work, *Meetings with Remarkable Men,* with the help of Mme Jeanne de Salzmann, to whom Gurdjieff on his deathbed had given his final instructions (Moore 315). That beautiful film has been criticized by some because its vague and minimal dialogue seems to evade the specific substance of Gurdjieff's search—or leave it to be supplied by viewers who already know. It does contain a glimpse of his famous "Stop!" exercise, a Sufi technique of self-remembering that he thought crucial to the work of changing our thinking and feeling by changing our repertory of postures and movements (Ouspensky 351–56). The principle behind that exercise informs many of Brook's rehearsal techniques. The film also contains the only fragment so far publicly available of the filming of Gurdjieff's Sacred Dances (Moore 353), movements that are variously echoed in Brook's rehearsals. But the absence of explicit doctrine is quite intentional. In recounting its story for *Parabola*—a publication whose founding editor had known Gurdjieff in Paris (Reyner 78)—Brook told a version of his own personal story. The film, he said, is about a "searcher" who "begins to search and as he goes on, his search changes color, changes register, changes tone, but it always goes forward until it reaches a certain intensity." This "is not the tale of a man who searches and finds an answer. The end of the story shows us, quite directly, how a man who searches finds the material that enables him to go still further" (*Shifting Point* 212–13).

By 1991, speaking to a Japanese audience, Brook was willing to outline more clearly what he has meant by the holy theater. "There are," he said, "several layers of invisible." In our century "we know only too well the psychological layer," the "Freudian underworld." This level, however, "has nothing to do" with "Holy Theatre," which "implies that there is something else in existence, below, around and above, another zone even more invisible, even farther from the forms which we are capable of reading or recording, which contain extremely powerful sources of energy" (*Open Door* 70). He related that understanding to the Hindu term *sphota:* "Between the unmanifest and the manifest," he said, "there is a flow of formless energies, and at certain moments there are kinds of explosions which correspond to this term: '*Sphota!*'" (60).

> Although the invisible is not compelled to manifest itself, it may at the same time do so anywhere, and at any moment, through anyone, as long as the conditions are right. I don't think there is any point in reproducing the sacred rituals of the past which are not very likely to bring us towards the invisible. The only thing which may help us is an awareness of the present. (71)

Such "receptivity," he said, can "make sacred the most mundane of objects," for the "sacred is a transformation in terms of quality, of that which is not sacred at the outset." Hence the possibility of a holy theater: "The life of a human being is the visible through which the invisible can appear" (72). For "within us at every moment, like a giant musical instrument ready to be played, are strings whose tones and harmonies are our capacity to respond to vibrations from the invisible spiritual world which we often ignore, yet which we contact with every new breath" (98). A play is "the building of a bridge between ourselves as we usually are, in our normal condition . . . and an invisible world that can reveal itself to us only when the normal inadequacy of perception is replaced by an infinitely more acute quality of awareness" (103).

During a Paris workshop in the same year Brook stressed the actor's need to "open himself to the unlimited possibilities of emptiness." One must conquer the "fear" of "this unfamiliar void," must recognize "that one can be totally 'there'; apparently 'doing' nothing" (*Open Door* 24, 25). It is "hard for the Western mind to accept," he said, "having turned 'ideas' and the mind into supreme deities for so many centuries." But the "only answer is in direct experience, and in the theatre one can taste the absolute reality of the extraordinary presence of emptiness, as compared with the poverty-stricken jumble in a head crammed with thinking" (26). That insight may be found in Buddhism and Vedanta—as well as in Gurdjieff's version of the Sufi tradition: we must quiet the "monkey-mind," confront the void, and let the invisible manifest itself. Brook has often given actors a challenge that, like a Zen koan, forces them beyond the answers provided by the rational mind. Here the "empty space" of theater and the"emptiness" of some of Brook's stage worlds find a fuller meaning.

In what Brook, echoing Jean-Louis Barrault (Innes 111–29), has called a "total theater" manifestations of the invisible should be available to all participants. Here Brook agrees with Meyerhold, who said: "There is a fourth *creator* in addition to the author, the director, and the actor—namely, the spectator . . . from the friction between the actor's creativity and the spectator's imagination, a clear flame is kindled" (qtd. in the Stratford program in *Dream,* Acting ed. 112). Meyerhold claimed that a nonnaturalistic and festive theater could realize a genuine community. "The *truth* of human relationships," he said, "is established by gestures, poses, glances and silences. Words alone cannot say everything. Hence there must be a *pattern of movement* to transform the spectator into a vigilant observer" (Braun 38). And he taught his actors "to imbue every action on stage with joy—the tragic as well as the comic" (128). Meyerhold was deeply impressed by Georg Fuchs's *The Stage of the Future,* which called for the restoration of the theater as festive ritual, with the audience as close as possible to the stage. "By virtue of their origins," said Fuchs, "the player and the spectator, the stage and the auditorium, are not opposed to each other, they are a unity" (Braun 48).

Charles Marowitz has said that, despite Brook's "flirtations with Artaud and Brecht," Meyerhold has "always been the most durable influence" on him (Williams, *Casebook* 160). In "America today," said Brook in *The Empty Space,* "the time is ripe for a Meyerhold to appear, since naturalistic representations of life no longer seem to Americans adequate to express the forces that drive them" (27). He insisted that there is "only a practical difference between actor and audience, not a fundamental one" (134), and he endorsed Brecht's view "that the action of putting together a play is always a form of playing, that watching a play is playing" (77). As he would later say in Paris, the audience "does not need to intervene or manifest itself in order to participate. It is a constant participant through its awakened presence" (*Open Door* 19). Text and stage world are vehicles for a revelatory action that must be found freshly in the present moment. That is why, after a rich elucidation of *King Lear,* Brook could say: "The meaning will be for the moment of performance" (*Empty Space* 94). In order to reach the broadest spectrum of audience interest and response, a Shakespearean "total theater" is drawn toward an amalgamation of themes, forms, and styles. But even the epic synthesis of *The Mahabharata* is primarily what Brook called a "carrier" for moments of awareness of the invisible (*Seneca's Oedipus* 8).

Such moments are beyond description, but we can chart Brook's approach to them: it is a stripping away of the old, an immersion in the new, an integration of body, mind, and spirit, a quest that has indeed been a "shifting point" moving through "empty space" toward an "open door." The end approached is no more evident in the epic synthesis of *The Mahabharata* than in the spareness of the recent chamber piece *The Man Who,* which probes our hidden identity. The quest is open, and the end is always "now" and "here."

II

In 1962 Brook's production of *King Lear* came as a surprise, even though he had been directing Shakespeare since 1945 with increasing emphasis upon death-haunted darkness (*Shifting Point* 11–12; Gilbert 43–55), a bare stage (Trewin, *Peter Brook* 33; *Shakespeare on the English Stage* 205), a correlation of the holy and the rough, and a making visible of the invisible (*Empty Space* 88, 89). For *Titus Andronicus,* in 1955, he had designed a set and written music that assisted in the "expression of a powerful and eventually beautiful barbaric ritual" (95). Lavinia's entrance with scarlet ribbons streaming from her mouth and shoulders, representing her severed tongue and limbs, conveyed a horror that, paradoxically, could strike a spectator as "quite abstract and thus totally real" (Trewin, *Going to Shakespeare* 39). Yet none of this quite prepared for *King Lear,* with its whitish rectangular flats, dangling metal objects, leather costumes, and corroded thunder sheets. Reviewers were reminded of medieval, Brechtian, and Oriental theater. Many were disturbed by the lack of conventional grandeur, moral affirmation, and what Charles Marowitz has called "a reassuring catharsis" (qtd. in Williams, *Casebook* 15). Kenneth Tynan, however, praised what he called "a standpoint of moral neutrality," a readiness to let Scofield's Lear be an irascible, obtuse, and crazy old man and let the usually "unsympathetic" characters "project themselves from their own point of view" (qtd. in Williams, *Casebook* 23). Later remarking upon Brook's use of Jan Kott's "*King Lear* or *Endgame,*" Tynan said that the "production is amoral because it is set in an amoral universe," the play being a "mighty philosophic farce" that presents a "world without gods, with no possibility of hopeful resolution" (25). Accepting that line of interpretation, Hunt and Reeves have complained that "it is difficult to see in what way Brook's *Lear* leads us to a better understanding of our human plight" (55).

Surely, however, a refusal to glorify Lear and a sympathy for Goneril, Regan, and Edward can hardly be called "amoral." Brook also thought the Fool should be an "inspired zany," a "medium through which wit and intuition express themselves" (Williams, *Casebook* 12). How could an amoral universe "inspire" such a character? Although Beckett's *Endgame* as interpreted by Kott was behind the "germinal" scene for the production, in which Edgar leads Gloucester to the cliffs at Dover (Williams, *Casebook* 6), and Brook's strategically cut text did preclude a hopeful resolution, his production was no amoral farce—in itself a contradiction in terms—but, as Marowitz said, a certain kind of tragedy: "not Lear's but ours" (Williams, *Casebook* 19).

Brook began work on the play by recognizing that it is about "blindness" and "insight." In rehearsal he discovered its concern with "sclerosis opposing the flow of existence" and "cataracts that dissolve . . . rigid attitudes that yield, while at the same time obsessions form and positions harden" (*Empty Space* 92). He came to view it as "a vast, complex, coherent poem designed to study the power and the emptiness of nothing" (94). In effect, its characters are what Gurdjieff would call sleepwalkers, determined for the most part by their "blindness." But what enables their "insight"? And our "study"? Brook encountered here the paradox that, as I have shown, inheres in plays by Sartre, Beckett, Genet, and Pinter:

> Beckett's dark plays are plays of light, where the desperate object created is witness of the ferocity of the wish to bear witness to the truth . . . When we attack Beckett for pessimism it is we who are the Beckett characters trapped in a Beckett scene. When we accept Beckett's statement as it is, then suddenly all is transformed . . . Beckett's audience . . . leaves his plays, his black plays, nourished and enriched, with a lighter heart, full of a strange irrational joy. (58, 59)

As Meyerhold said, every action must be imbued with joy—the tragic as well as the comic. Such emptiness, accepted and joyfully performed by the truth-seeking intelligence, is a plenitude, a momentary waking from our consensus trance.

In Lear's world the role-playing runs from deceptive ploys (Edmund), to derangement by obsessive insight (the Fool), to enforced, agonized, therapeutic, and heroic masking (Edgar), to the hysterical release of bleak awareness (Lear on the heath). The Fool, Edgar, and Lear suggest that the rigors of "truth" may come to us, if devastatingly, through the mode of play. The characters provide clues, therefore, to the process in which Brook's actors and audience were participating. (The filming of *King Lear* in 1969 made that point yet more forcefully through some remarkable camera work and editing.) Although Shomit Mitter has claimed that the production was driven by rational analysis (26–28), the company's exploratory playing was crucial. Brook believes that a director's ideas must "evolve continually, thanks to the process he is going through with the actors, so that in the third week he will find he is understanding everything differently" (*Empty Space* 106). He had preliminary thoughts about *King Lear* and made later decisions about its coherence and pace, but he remained astonishingly open, even to the point of almost entirely abandoning his set design in the last week of rehearsals (Williams, *Casebook* 4). Even Marowitz, an American director grounded in Stanislavsky and more experimental than the British actors, was struck by the fact that Brook was "relentlessly (and at times, maddeningly) experimental. He believes that there is no such thing as the 'right way' . . . If what is wrong today is wrong tomorrow, tomorrow will reveal it, and it is through the constant elimination of possibilities that Brook finally arrives at interpretation" (10). Agreeing with Brook that the "work of rehearsals is looking for meaning and then making it meaningful" (8), Marowitz noted Brook's "Oriental Cheshire-cat" openness to the eruption of destructive energies during improvisation (15) and his wish that audiences would listen to plays "with the same intensity as concert audiences listen to Oistrakh," for then "the performance of a play would be so much richer" (18).

Neither "amoral" nor "politically myopic," Brook found the best audience for this austere production in Europe, between Budapest and Moscow, where recent experience

> had enabled them to come directly to the play's painful themes. The quality of the attention that this audience brought expressed itself in silence and concentration, a feeling in the house that affected the actors as though a brilliant light were turned on their work. As a result, the most obscure passages were illuminated; they were played with a complexity of meaning and a fine use of the English language that few of the audience could follow, but which all could sense. (*Empty Space* 22)

In the 1960s he increasingly believed in that Gurdjieffian "quality of the attention," a nonverbal participation in the process of "bearing witness" to a devastating truth. He was under no illusion that this strategically pruned and brilliantly lighted *King Lear* would give in its stage world alone, dominated by rigid and destructive attitudes, the whole truth about the human condition. Its characters were closed in upon themselves, having turned away from the invisible except in moments of psychic distress. That is why the performed action was ruled by "the power and emptiness of nothing." But the shared action of performance, transcending the closed world to which it bore witness, offered an opportunity here and now to discern the invisible. Those who claim that such a production offers no "better understanding of our human plight" simply fail to grasp the difference between rhetoric and art.

III

For Brook the theater had always begun with an image. "If I find the image through the design," he could say, "I know how to continue with the production" (Trewin, *Peter Brook* 32). But his search was now changing color or register: "I think for me everything shifted around the time of *King Lear*

. . . I began to see why theatre was an event. Why it did not depend on an image or a particular context." He became increasingly interested in "whatever is a direct element in performance," and when you set off on that path, "everything else falls away" (*Shifting Point* 12–13).

He increasingly believed, moreover, that traditional "characterization" in the theater solidifies a falsehood:

> What are we—you and I? Things enclosed in solid, stolid frames? Rather, we are at any instant a flow of mental pictures that stream from us and superimpose themselves on the outside world, sometimes coinciding with it, sometimes contradicting it. We are all at once voices, thoughts, words, half-words, echoes, memories, impulses. We change purpose from instant to instant . . . I do not recognize myself or my neighbor in those closed and finite dummies that "characterization" gives us. ("Search for a Hunger" 50, 95)

Again he is in harmony with Gurdjieff, who had said: "One of man's important mistakes . . . is his illusion with regard to his I . . . His I changes as quickly as his thoughts, feelings, and moods, and he makes a profound mistake in considering himself always one and the same person; in reality he is *always a different person,* not the one he was a moment ago" (Ouspensky 59). Because most of us are trapped in the illusion of an unchangeable I, a personal "character," Brook was finding it difficult to work with certain actors:

> Time after time I have worked with actors who after the usual preamble that they "put themselves in my hands" are tragically incapable however hard they try of laying down for one brief instant even in rehearsal the image of themselves that has hardened round an inner emptiness. On the occasions that it is possible to penetrate this shell, it is like smashing the picture on a television set. (*Empty Space* 29)

Such views led to the experimental season at the LAMDA Theatre in 1963–64, which pushed the actors—and indeed Brook himself—beyond learned techniques and protective clichés toward a greater openness to their own untapped resources.

Their improvisations, Marowitz has said, emphasized discontinuities and disruptions that forced the actors "to dip into deep wells of fantasy and absurdity that lay on the threshold of their consciousness" (Williams, *Casebook* 44). Brook's own description points to a process rather like Gurdjieff's training of the attention—an exercise, for example, demanding that the actor express an idea through minimal means of communication. At best, "without any physical change at all," an "invisible idea was rightly shown" (*Empty Space* 51). Such improvisations were followed by a demonstration of work-in-progress, with the Artaudian title "Theatre of Cruelty," and a performance of the first twelve scenes of Genet's *The Screens*. Hunt and Reeves are somewhat ironic about the results (65–83), but we should not forget their serious purpose: "Our aim for each experiment, good or bad, successful or disastrous," said Brook, "was the same: can the invisible be made visible through the performer's presence?" (*Empty Space* 52).

The production of *The Screens,* in fact, was far more than what Hunt and Reeves call a "cartoon history of Algeria" (82). It was, said Tom Milne, a production "to restore one's faith in a theatre which excites, which really matters, and which *is* only in collaboration with its audience." He was aware of "a subtle alchemy between play, actors, theatre and audience" and also of "the extreme complexity of the levels of fantasy (or reality) spread out in the play" (Williams, *Casebook* 57–60). I have laid out in chapter 4 the dialectic of those levels of imagined reality, which moves through a "negative" playing of a negative world toward a theatrical and ritual celebration. Genet understood this to be a way of transforming a world of power and emptiness into a celebration of what can manifest itself in performance. So, too, did Brook. (And so, years later at the Tyrone Guthrie, did Joanne Akalaitis and her company.) The production of *The Screens* was therefore not just part of a "search for a ritual theatre" (Innes 132). It was the next step beyond the closed world of *King Lear* in Brook's search for the purpose of playing.

That production would have been impossible if Brook had not been pushing himself toward a synthesis of performance modes. Already grounded in Meyerhold and Gurdjieff, he could absorb and move beyond Stanislavsky, Brecht, Artaud, and Grotowski. His readiness to do so was partly a pretheoretical openness: "As always," he said of a moment in 1961, "I was so far from any theoretical approach to theatre that I had not the remotest idea who Artaud might be" (*Shifting Point* 41). But he also knew that any theory reduces and distorts the theatrical event. In 1964 he said that there is no "possible theatre today that is *not* a theatre of synthesis." Finding more in Brecht than the Brechtians could admit, he claimed "that the nearest thing to an Artaud theatre we have had was the Brecht theatre . . . What he was actually doing in his best work as a director was creating forms and rituals, and in his most remarkable work you can read off many levels of meaning" (Williams, *Casebook* 31, 33). Brecht's "alienation effect," Brook would later argue, is "above all an appeal to the spectator to work for himself." The "whole range of rhetoric" is open to this "purely theatrical method of dialectical exchange" (*Empty Space* 72, 73). To "discover where, how, and at what level" the "opposition" between Brecht and Artaud "ceases to be real" was therefore something he "found very interesting" during the period in between the "Theatre of Cruelty" and the production of *Marat/Sade*. "For Artaud, theatre is fire; for Brecht, theatre is clear vision; for Stanislavsky, theatre is humanity. Why must we choose among them?" (*Shifting Point* 42, 43).

Brook's understanding of the "group work" of Grotowski, with whom he developed a deep friendship, can put this response into perspective:

> we saw we shared the same aim. But our paths were different. Grotowski's work leads him deeper and deeper into the actor's inner world, to the point where the actor ceases to be actor and becomes essential man . . . For me, the way of the theatre goes the opposite way, leading out of loneliness to a perception that is heightened because it is shared. A strong presence of actors and a strong presence of spectators can produce a circle of unique intensity in which barriers can be broken and the invisible become real. Then public truth and private truth become inseparable parts of the same essential experience. (*Shifting Point* 41)

Following that way, Brook came across *Marat/Sade*—a play that he co-created in his spectacular and controversial production of 1966.

About that production many conflicting statements have been made. Christopher Innes said that it "distorted Weiss' intentions by stressing the Artaudian images of sadism, violence, and insanity" (132). The playwright, however, thought for a time that Brook's production was "definitive," despite the fact that the German production had been closer to the original text. Marowitz suspected that Weiss approved Brook's production for that very reason: "Left to its own devices, the play doesn't stand very tall. But jacked up and made to prance (as it is by Brook), it can pass for an elaborate profundity—which it is not!" (Williams, *Casebook* 71). In fact, Weiss had shown considerable interest in Artaud while working on the play, but in the next two years he abandoned his "third standpoint" of political dubiety, distanced himself from Brook's production, and emphasized a Marxist didactic intention that would favor the idealist Marat rather than the skeptic Sade. And yet he recognized that the form of *Marat/Sade* "contains so many theatrical possibilities" that it could undermine his own later intentions (McKenzie 308). Unlike Marowitz, Richard Gilman saw in Brook's production not even the illusion of profundity: "Flattering our sense of the fashionable, our desire to be at wicked, important happenings, but offering no light and no resurrection, *Marat/Sade* is to be seen but not believed" (169). Walter Kerr said, however, that "we left the theater, feeling that the matter of the play needed scarcely to be investigated" because our focus "at all times was upon the mindless eyes, the spastic mouths, the cracked-egg skulls of the inmates of Charenton asylum . . . We said to ourselves 'How marvelous the actors are!'" The "manner of performing was all we attended to or remembered" (61). And yet Hunt and Reeves have claimed that "the American critics forgot about the actors" because Brook "wanted the illusion of madness to be total" (94).

As a member of that New York audience, I am somewhat bemused by this cacophony of voices. They are partial responses to a dialectical process of playing-with-and-against-the-text, playing-within-playing, and playing-against-playing that was indeed difficult to take in as a whole. I was riveted by three actors-as-characters-as-actors-as-characters, who embodied the complexity of what I came to call "playing the player" (*Fields of Play* 9ff.): Glenda Jackson as the narcolept playing Charlotte Corday, Ian Richardson as the paranoiac playing Marat, and Patrick Magee as the perverse and seductive Sade playing himself and staging the others. They were three powerful versions of our consensus trance. No doubt Brook's production was a partial transformation of Weiss's text. Adrian Mitchell's verse adaptation and Richard Peaslee's music brought a fresh and edgy verve. And, as David Richard Jones has made clear in his thoughtful account of both rehearsal and production (228–33), Brook treated the text not as a blueprint but as provocation or invitation. Having recognized the violence within himself, he began with a workshop on madness, sought in various ways to make the actors face their own violence, and was continually finding new angles of approach. He later insisted that Weiss had opened a head full of contradictions and served up its contents to the audience (243–44). The director's work here, as with Shakespeare's *Titus Andronicus,* "was to take the hints and the hidden strands of the play and wring the most from them, take what was embryonic perhaps, and bring it out" (*Shifting Point* 5).

From Weiss's text Brook elicited our participation in a dialectic of playing that puts in doubt each intellectual position or version of history, because all are consciously or unconsciously histrionic, and all bear the signs of a murderous insanity. Marat's hope for history leads to mass bloodshed; his idealism seems a function of paranoid role-playing; his rhetoric is provided by an opponent who relishes such violence; and his pseudo-engagement with Sade is sponsored by Coulmier for the minor rehabilitation of the inmates and the major delectation of his family. As performed by the inmates, this play-within-the-play is given a Brecht/Artaud stylization, while the "primary" playing of those inmates by Brook's actors has an astonishing Stanislavskian fidelity to the real. In those actors we can sense the violence that they mime in the inmates and that the play-within-the-play discloses as the burden of our history. No doubt Brook thought that by "presenting the violence in themselves to an audience, the performers could make the spectators confront their own violence" (Hunt and Reeves 93). And yet the stylization repeatedly distances us (as Sade has distanced himself) from a violence that has suddenly become an aesthetic object. Sade knows, and this production demonstrates, that we are all participants in a violent and manifold ritual of scapegoating. (Perhaps the most profound comments on such ritual in our culture have been made by René Girard in *Things Hidden since the Foundation of the World.*) As a member of the audience, I could hardly dissent from the sweeping accusation, not to be found in the German text (Weiss, *Die Verfolgung* 47), that erupts from a Patient:

> A mad animal
> Man's a mad animal
> I'm a thousand years old and in my time
> I've helped commit a million murders.
>
> (*Marat/Sade* 32)

Can a production be both symptom and diagnosis? Hysterical insight, mediated or channeled by role-playing, was central to Brook's *King Lear* and *The Screens*. But, what *King Lear* confined to the roles of the Fool, Edgar, and Lear and what *The Screens* shaped according to Genet's negative and visionary dialectic, *Marat/Sade* adopts as the continuing burden of a more-than-Pirandellian dialectic of ambiguity. This Weiss/Brook production was neither a "muddle of sensations" (E. T. Jones 80) nor an illusory "mirror image of our world" (Hunt and Reeves 95) but a self-consciously histrionic structure of "criss-crossing planes" that "thicken the reference at each moment and compel an activity from each member of the public" (*Empty Space* 74). In that Brechtian phrase, of course, Brook pointed to the fact that the mad sanity of the historical play-within-the-play, the riddling texture of the Marat/Sade opposition and collusion, and the evident participation of the actors in the violence they mime do not convey a final pessimism. It is quite wrong to say that in this elaborately choreographed production, this twist on the Brechtian paradigm of actor-audience participation, Brook was "cheating" by hiding the "intelligence" of the actors and the director (Hunt and Reeves 94). That intelligence was evident to any alert observer from beginning to end. But it presented itself as an intelligence that Gurdjieff would call "fallen" or "sleepwalking," an intelligence subject to mass-hypnosis that must speak through the baffles and distortions of its radical illness, its innate predilection for deception, self-deception, and violence. In the Weiss/Brook *Marat/Sade* our obsessive playing turned against itself and revealed its darkest secrets. That for me in 1966 was how the invisible was evident in the massive dialectic of the whole production, but especially in the haunting body languages and cadences of Glenda Jackson, Ian Richardson, and Patrick Magee, who with remarkable control were channeling what seems beyond control.

The recognition of such interior darkness is where any spiritual quest must begin—at least according to Gurdjieff, the Sufi tradition, and Jungian psychology. Irina Tweedie had hoped that her Sufi master would offer instructions in Yoga, "but what the Teacher did was mainly to force me to face the darkness within myself, and it almost killed me" (*Daughter of Fire* x). Jung stressed our need to confront the "shadow," our rejected and unacknowledged impulses and proclivities. "One does not become enlightened by imagining figures of light," he said, "but by making the darkness conscious. The latter procedure, however, is disagreeable and therefore unpopular" (qtd. in Vaughan-Lee 81). To the dismay of some of his critics Brook's own preliminary work upon himself, his actors, and us was of that kind. He was engaging in "shadow work," inviting us to acknowledge all the darkness we repress and project upon others.

IV

The plays that followed *Marat/Sade* continued to make the darkness conscious and to celebrate playing as a way of revealing the invisible. The Vietnam play *US,* with the Royal Shakespeare Company in 1966, which struck many as polemical, is better described as a production of intense concern. Brook explained to journalists "that America is our concern because she is part of us, her atrocities are committed in both our names" (Brook et al. 209). A major aim of the production, through its violence and immediacy, was silence. Brook had said to the actors, "Our job in this performance is to lead our audience—and ourselves" from a "curious, expectant silence" to "the silence of genuine concern, not just attentiveness, indignation, despair, impotence" (141–42). At the end of the play the actors "stopped acting and remained still, switching their attention to a private task in which they evaluated their own personal views in the light of the day's events and the evening's performance." Not aggressive in the manner of the Living Theater, this silence was a sudden and rather unsettling Quaker-like gathering of attention. (The play had already included as one scene a Quaker meeting in memory of Norman Morrison, who had set fire to himself on the steps of the Pentagon.) As Brook expected, the responses were various:

> some audiences saw in their immobility nothing but hostility, self-righteousness, accusation. Some took the silence as an insult, others as an evasion. Some took it as pro-American laisser faire. Some took it as rabid communist propaganda . . . Sometimes, after sitting for 10 or 15 minutes, total strangers began to talk to one another, and would leave the theatre together. Silence becomes a sheet of white paper on which anyone who wishes can watch his prejudice write its name. (211)

In leading the actors toward that silence, Brook had urged the necessity of what he called "burning," their intense engagement with the "brutally splintered actions" and "wildly contradictory characters" in "every part of the show." He told them: "It will be this flame, the intensity of this burning, that will feed whatever solutions each person may wish to put forward to solve the war . . . it will be this burning that will sustain the person who can offer no solutions at all, but does not sink into despair" (142–43). Here was the answer to any feeling that the production lacked a "solution" or was failing to "change the world." "We imagined that we were falling short of something positive," Brook counseled the actors. "But that something was there all the time. It is in the life, the degree of burning you bring to a performance. People leaving at the end weren't crushed" (151). Indeed, the Bishop of Woolwich, deeply moved, suggested that the play was in effect a liturgy, an anamnesis of "the secular crucifixion of our time," from which the Church, if it paid attention, could learn a great deal (Williams, *Casebook* 111–12).

Brook's production of Seneca's *Oedipus,* at the National Theatre in 1968, then tried to transform our murderous hypnotic trance, our denial of responsibility for military violence, and the Lear-like *hysterica passio* of our unconscious guilt, into something like a ritual of recognition and expurgation. Despite the plain stage picture, the immobile actors in dark suits and black roll-neck sweaters, and their impersonal gestures and dispassionate expressions, the ritual elements—including a large golden phallus in the Bacchanalian conclusion—did lead to misunderstandings. Geoffrey Reeves worked with the chorus, some of whom were dispersed among the audience, in using Ted Hughes's powerful text as a libretto for a strange orchestration of sounds, rhythms, and breathing. According to Reeves and Hunt, "Brook wanted the audience to treat *Oedipus* as one possible vehicle to answer the need for a true contact with a sacred invisibility (God?) through the theatre; but the production only seemed to underline the impossibility of making such contact now" (131). Martin Esslin, dubious about "a primitive rite," posed serious questions: "Ritual is only the outward form of the deepest spiritual experience. Can mere theatre evoke such experience? Or should we rather be seeking for the experience itself, i.e. a genuine spiritual awakening before we can validly seek an expression for it in ritual and in theatrical ceremony?" (Williams, *Casebook* 121, 122).

But what awakening, what contact with the invisible, was really in question? Brook had been trying ever since *King Lear* to lead the audience to discover its unadmitted complicity in violence. He now asked that audience to see itself as an archetypal scapegoat who is "consciously innocent while unconsciously judged guilty and throughout unwittingly the cause of his own doom" (Hirschberg 146). The suggestions of the "primitive" may have interfered with that process, but Brook had not gone back on his statement that the theater cannot create a new religious rite. This is, rather, a ritualized recognition of ancient truths. The armies who "marched so bravely away out eastward . . . right away on to the world's rim" but were now "finished rubbished into earth" by the plague that must follow unconscious *hubris* were, in this version, not just Theban but American armies, for which, according to *US,* the British audience bore some responsibility (*Oedipus* 28).

Indeed, Brook's introduction to Hughes's text says nothing about primitive rites but calls the dramatist, poet, and actors "carriers" for a "preexisting pattern." Because Hughes in reworking Seneca had reached the mythical, the text "demands a lost art—the art of impersonal acting." It is not enough for the actor "to cultivate a form of trance to awake his subconscious," and so "think that he is getting close to the level of universal myth." He "needs an understanding that must in turn ally itself to a wider mystery" that he can only find "through a tremendous awe and respect for what we call form." And Brook adds a paradox that became central to his rehearsals of *A Midsummer Night's Dream:* "This form is the movement of the text, this form is his own individual way of capturing that movement" (*Oedipus* 6–7). By eliminating "all unnecessary decoration, all useless expressions of personality," the actor gets to "a form that is both his own and not his own"—and so, like the dramatist, can become a "carrier." That requires him to understand that distance and presence are not mutually exclusive. "Distance is a commitment to total meaning: presence is a total commitment to the living moment: the two go together." Rehearsal exercises can "increase the actor's concern—in body and spirit—for what the play is asking" (*Oedipus* 9). In one exercise designed to make *Oedipus* "a communal experience," everybody was asked to rehearse everybody else's part (Williams, *Casebook* 131). If the actor truly feels the play's question to be his own, said Brook, "he is unavoidably caught in a need to share it, in a need for the audience." From that will come a need for absolute clarity, which "forges the living link with the poet's matrix" (*Oedipus* 9). Here, as elsewhere, the "wider mystery," the invisible, is a disclosure among us of what is beyond us.

In *The Tempest* of 1968, for which Brook first used an international group of actors, he continued to seek a language that might bring the audience into such a shared disclosure. In this "collage," which exhibited greater stylistic freedom than Marowitz's *Hamlet* collage in the "Theatre of Cruelty," there were moments that variously opened on the invisible. Its prelude, for example, was a well-known "mirror" exercise, in which the actors' reciprocal observation and discerning of intent not only brings them into harmony but can also, as Christopher Innes has noted, provide "an image of the ideal feedback between performer and observer" (137). In episodes that dramatized our sexuality and violence Shakespeare's lines were delivered ametrically, in a manner, as Margaret Croyden put it, "to imagize or abstract the driving force *beyond* the symbolic word" (qtd. in Williams, *Casebook* 139). Irving Wardle noted the "potent imagery" of "a blind company reaching out their hands to explore the new world of each other's bodies" and the "unearthly illumination" radiating from "a love quartet of thin spirit voices vibrating in the air" (142, 143). In the epilogue the cast elaborated upon Prospero's phrases—"And my ending is despair" / "Unless it be relieved by prayer"—with a multivoiced echoing that built contrapuntally and then died out in silence.

"After a long series of dark, violent, black plays," said Brook, explaining why he then turned to *A Midsummer Night's Dream,* "I had a very strong wish to go as deeply as possible into a work of pure celebration" (Ansorge, "Director in Interview" 18). Yet he was clearly hoping to lead a wider audience toward the invisible through a celebration that included implications almost as dark as those of *Oedipus* and *The Tempest.* "The first thing the play has running through it is Darkness," he would say. "And from that, everything else stems" (*Dream,* Acting ed. 32). In rehearsal he described the moment of Lysander's bafflement by Puck as "the nightmare coming home to him" (2.2.417–18), as "almost going into tragedy" (Selbourne 73). A torch-lit rehearsal of act 5 brought out for the actors the tragic overtones of Theseus' opening speeches, the play of Pyramus and Thisbe, and Oberon's "Trip away, make no delay" (123–31). In rehearsing act 4, David Waller as Bottom encountered one moment when his own voice, according to Selbourne, "seemed still to speak from deep within the disordered world of terrifying enchantment which, moments before, he had himself created" (147). These would remain as undertones in the final production, but audiences most immediately responded to the impression of circus theater, the "world of marvels and enchantment," the "breathless joy and strange magic" for which Meyerhold had asked (Braun 151). But Brook would say, "I don't think we ever thought of it as a circus." Sally Jacobs's dazzlingly lit white box, the trapeze-borne fairies, the forest of coiling wires, the juggling lovers, a Puck on high French stilts, Richard Peaslee's score of unfamiliar sounds—all this was gradually developed as a vehicle for what Brook called "a celebration of the theme of theatre: the play-within-the-play-within-the-play-within-the-play" (*Dream,* Acting ed. 24). Hence, too, his decision to give a freshly serious treatment to the "mechanicals" and their play of Pyramus and Thisbe and to let otherwise unoccupied actors become (like the dead in *The Screens*) an onstage audience.

For Brook this play brought together many congenial themes: life as playing, as love, as dream, as enchantment, as imagination, as encounter with the invisible, and as an almost unimaginable harmony of discordant feelings. It invites us to explore, in the dark field of opposites, the perplexities of love and awareness—about which Gurdjieff had much to say. Can we understand his maxim, "Outwardly play a role: inwardly never identify" (Moore 38)? Can we awaken from the changeable trance that, for us as for Demetrius and Lysander, dictates our loves and our hates? Can we discover the simultaneity of our apparently sequential feelings, the multiplicity of our actual selves? Can we see, in Theseus/Oberon and Hippolyta/Titania, the complementary nature of our dreaming night life and our dreaming day life? Then we might experience what Gurdjieff called an awakening of "conscience":

> even a momentary awakening of conscience in a man who has thousands of different I's is bound to involve suffering. And if these moments of conscience become longer and if a man does not fear them but on the contrary co-oper-

> ates with them and tries to keep and prolong them, an element of very subtle joy, a foretaste of the future 'clear consciousness' will gradually enter into these moments. (Ouspensky 156)

Those questions and their therapeutic resolution are given a local habitation and a name in this play of enchanted and changeable lovers, newlywed enemies and jealous fairy counterparts (appropriately doubled in Brook's production), an earthy and histrionic man for whom their tale becomes a dream beyond expounding, and our shared realization that these are all figures in our dreaming imagination. Alan Howard, who played Theseus/Oberon, said: "it's a very open-ended question as to *who* is dreaming in this play. And when the dream begins and when it stops . . . It's like one of those dreams where you rise up through various levels of consciousness" (*Dream,* Acting ed. 41, 44). In rehearsal, when the awakened Hermia said, "Methinks I see these things with parted eye, / When everything seems double" (4.1.186–87), Brook said to the cast, much as Gurdjieff might say to his students, "Ask yourselves what is sleeping, and what is waking." Unsatisfied with their answers, he said: "Being awake is more like a dream than sleeping." And when they were puzzled: "Shakespeare is trying to explain something beyond words" (Selbourne 97).

As so often, David Selbourne, in *The Making of "A Midsummer Night's Dream,"* here sides with the most bewildered actors—those who, unlike Howard and John Kane (Puck/Philostrate), did not grasp that Brook's indirections were pointing toward a "secret play" that they must discover (*Dream,* Acting ed. 54). (Kane thought they "brushed momentarily against Peter's 'secret play'" when they were possessed by "some wild anarchic force" [58], but we should not conclude with Christopher Innes that the secret play was simply one of "total 'anarchy' and 'wild joy'" [133].) Reading Selbourne's account, shaped from rehearsal notes made a decade earlier, we must disentangle his genuine insights from all that has led to an almost systematic distortion of Brook's rehearsal process. Selbourne brought with him a "sense of isolation and estrangement" (53), a penchant for self-dramatization as a bewildered and condescending writer, and an acid contempt for both "director's theater" and Peter Brook, whom he describes as defensive and moody, suffering from a "bleak" form of "unexpressiveness" (67), and lacking in "wit" or "humor" (147–49). Brook, in response, has alluded with some acerbity to an unauthorized book "full of inaccurate impressions, and betraying the essential bond of trust which is the basis for the actor and director's capacity to work together" (*Open Door* 120–21). But Selbourne's account is invaluable if one knows how to read *through* his quarrels and misperceptions. In highlighting Brook's obliqueness, contradictoriness, and insistence on freedom from the habitual and in sympathizing with the actors who were nonplussed by this new discipline, Selbourne calls attention to a process that he imperfectly understands—the process of teaching, discovery, and self-discovery that Brook, like Gurdjieff, considered essential.

The actors' difficulties are everywhere apparent as the rehearsals move from attempts to find the meanings of their roles to increasing harmony of the various impulses discovered and finally into the stabilities of blocking, a multileveled set, the discovery of detailed movements, and the refinements of comic business and technique. Brook did have a "view" of the play that "he would like to bring the cast to, though it would have to be done gradually, or they would 'lose their sense of direction'" (Selbourne 43). He told them early on that a "microcosm of the play as a whole is to be found in the mechanicals' play-acting. It raises questions as to the nature of 'reality,' and the nature of acting . . . It asks, 'What is a role? and 'What is the meaning of the actor's transformation?" (3). But he offered little more than questions and oblique references to "something secret and mysterious," "whatever is behind the whole play" (19). "You must be constantly questioning yourselves, others, and me as to what it is about" (95). Gurdjieff too had said to students: "I certainly have an aim of my own, but you must permit me to keep silent about it. At the present moment my aim cannot have any meaning for you, because it is important that you should define your own aim" (Ouspensky 99). John Kane soon understood that "what was novel in working with Peter was that he wanted the play to *do things* with us." The director, in Brook's view, had to be firm in getting rid of what Kane called "*doing something* with a play." Only after eliminating such "useless interventions" could one "reach the level where the actors' truest, most individual creativity really comes into play. When that happens, a group begins thinking and working in one direction" (*Dream,* Acting ed. 26, 27).

With regard to Shakespeare's verse, this involved the paradox, resisted by Selbourne, of "both a rhythm to be found and a particular actor to find it." That is, "what one actor finds will not be what another actor finds" (Selbourne 21). And so, too, with regard to detailed meanings: "I can help you," Brook said, "by eliminating the false experiences you are using. You can only understand, if you use the right experience of your own to draw from. I can know whether it is not right, but I cannot discover the experience for you. This is what Shakespeare is saying too. He is saying, 'my words are only an approximation to my experience, so you must bring your own experience to them.'" The silence, says Selbourne, was "stunning" (101). At the end of two weeks Brook can say the rehearsals have been "interesting." "This is good," he says, because "it is what we are living through." Selbourne adds: "The comment is also too oblique to be immediately understood" (75). At another point—again misunderstood by Selbourne—Brook shouts to the lovers, "The moment you go into pathos, you are playing the wrong line completely. If you cultivate emotional states, you cannot find anything. When your emotions swamp your sense of what is happening second-by-second, you are wrong" (79). About a breakthrough moment at the end of the third week, Brook says: "It cannot however be set, technically, to recur. We will have to find our own way back to it. But the way is now open" (131). Later on, in a moment that invites Selbourne's overwrought prose ("Gimlet-eyed and pushing his pressure upon them"), Brook tells the lovers, "In playing this truly, you should be able to improve the quality of your own, real, relationships with others." "What is the difference," he asks Christopher Gable, "between you and Lysander? . . . Christopher Gable as Lysander must be totally alive and therefore totally free." Selbourne comments, "The *non-sequiturs* are daunting." Gurdjieff would have understood at once. And Brook explains: "Your personal jadedness, cynicism, anger, self-pity take energy out of you as an actor. Liveness and open-ness bring energy in. As long as you are alive in the part, the combination of you and the part can never cease from endless creation" (177). Selbourne notes only the tensions of the personal exchange, but we have here a central Brook credo. Late in the rehearsals, urging the actors to discover Shakespeare's spontaneous joy in creation, Brook says: "I cannot tell you to be joyful, I can only eliminate the useless solutions" (259).

The key, of course, is the reciprocity of play, which discloses a realm in which the hidden life of the actor is intertwined with those of other actors. Consistency is not the cause but the product of life. "There is something consistent," Brook tells the cast, "which happens when the play bursts into life. Watch for this . . . After such a moment has passed, it can't be switched on again, or mechanically pieced together. What has to be recalled are the meanings which come out of a burst of life" (Selbourne 101). He surely had in mind Hippolyta's glosses on the play's meanings, which he would cite when explaining his desire "to capture in our net the richest amount of the contradictory, clashing, opposed discordant elements." Theseus and Hippolyta talk about "how the sound of trumpets and hounds barking can make a conjunction of two images . . . It's a concord-discord. In 'The Dream,' in all Shakespeare, it's there—that co-existence" (*Dream,*

Acting ed. 30). Hippolyta, we recall, speaks of the "mutual cry," the "musical . . . discord," the "sweet thunder" of the baying hounds (4.1.114–15)—and later of how

> all the story of the night told over,
> And all their minds transfigured so together,
> More witnesses than fancy's images,
> And grows to something of great constancy;
> But howsoever, strange and admirable.
>
> (5.1.23–27)

Brook sought a performance true to the opposites of experience, in which their invisible matrix would be felt behind every moment. Selbourne himself gradually came to recognize "the overall consistency of Brook's pronouncements," even of his "contradictions and obscurities" (139). But he did not attempt to expound the meaning of that consistency.

The "core" of the *Dream,* Brook said, is in the Pyramus and Thisby play, "which doesn't come at the end of a highly organized play just for comic relief" (Ansorge, "Director in Interview," 18). Rejecting the traditional comic reading of that subplot, with its "nauseating superiority toward workmen trying to do a play" (*Dream,* Acting ed. 31), he invited his actors to enter into the rough solidity, awkwardness, and innocence, and the apprehensions and astonishing discoveries, of these craftsmen-actors (Selbourne, 57, 59, 67–71). A torch-lit rehearsal of act 5, in which nervous players-playing-craftsmen-playing-players were brought before the partying court, unaware of what Brook had in store for them, opened up many of the issues. The honest attempt at tragic playing, with its dignity, absurdity, and suggestions of horror-filled depths, was interrupted by the court's brittle and frivolous jibing, momentarily reversing the actor-audience roles (123–29). Brook would later say: "They are playing Shakespeare to the mechanicals. They have turned the mechanicals, *in the middle of their own play,* into an audience" (163). It was a foretaste of the larger Chinese-box effect of the entire performance, in which the many reversals of playing and watching would be enclosed by a changing array of actors-as-audience, so that even the entry of Puck at the beginning of act 2 would be overseen by courtiers calmly watching from their heights (247).

The reviewers' comments reflected the sense that all share in the play. Peter Ansorge said of the mechanicals' play that, despite a great deal of "unrehearsed comedy,"

> the final result moves its audience to silence—there is an aura of religious ceremony around a scene which is normally played for a purely knockabout effect. As David Waller's Bottom announces "The wall is down that parted our fathers," it is suggested that the actors' art (as much as the fairies') has brought the feuding fathers and lovers of the earlier scenes together—*their* rough magic has brought unity to the Court. This must account for the moving climax as the Company turn towards the audience—to give some of the magic in their hands to *us*. (Ansorge, review of *Dream* 47)

Ronald Bryden described "a miracle . . . the frontiers of the play vanished and we were all a part of it" (20). Bernard Levin described a feeling of "rebirth into a new, cleansed world of love and joy": "the joy must have been there in the play all the time—Mr. Brook has merely (merely!) released it" (14).

All the dark and joyful ironies of an audience watching actors watching actors watching actors, of humans-as-spirits and spirits-as-humans, of shadow selves doubled and redoubled, of visionary dreams and entranced waking, of what Brook called "the goods and ills of the imagination" that snare us in illusion (Selbourne 229–31)—these all come to a focus in the epilogue.

> If we shadows have offended,
> Think but this and all is mended:
> That you have but slumb'red here,
> While these visions did appear.
>
> (5.1.412–15)

Brook told the cast early on that the epilogue is "the most inner portion of the whole drama," the end being "tantalizingly close to something secret and mysterious. We approach here whatever is behind the whole play." Selbourne added, projecting a playwright's anxieties: "That it is Shakespeare, no one is saying" (19). But for Brook it was not Shakespeare—except in the Brookian sense that to play Shakespeare is to play the "world." It was, quite precisely, the invisible.

V

Bottom's "The wall is down" soon became "the key to Brook's entire approach to theatre" (Heilpern 87). In shared spaces—natural settings, carpets in a marketplace, or their theatrical equivalent at the Bouffes du Nord—he now sought ways in which actors can invite the audience to perceive the invisible. But the performances have been remarkably various. In Iran *Orghast* (1971) reconstituted a mythical action in terms designed to communicate across linguistic and cultural differences. Ted Hughes based his syncretic version of the Prometheus story and its sound-language on the assumption that one could drive below our cultural and linguistic differences to an "inner life" expressive to all people. The actors, he said, were working on an almost impossible task: "to become the vehicle for a spirit, not for a bundle of repressed passions, but for those powers much closer to the source, that speak and move so strangely, but who supply everything finally that we really want and need." But there were moments when "a spirit passed before my face, the hair of my flesh stood up" (Smith 244). The result, both overwhelming and elusive for those who attended, has been called "a vindication of Brook's Theatre of Ritual," though one "unrepeatable in the normal theatre" (Innes 144). The pragmatic Brook took a very different line. "If . . . somebody says, 'Ah, it is ritual theatre,' my heart sinks, because the person is investing the generalization with a superstitious meaning . . . What we must do is find something specific, then it doesn't matter a damn what you call it" (Smith 256).

Without "believing that the theatre can become a substitute for a spiritual way of life," Brook did claim that "an actor who lives a humdrum and confused life like everyone else in his society has a unique possibility . . . of touching at certain short moments a quite genuine but fleeting experience of what could be a higher level of evolution . . . It is the shadow on the wall through which a reality can be perceived" (251). It followed, as he said, that

> we've been acutely conscious all the time that *Orghast,* in fact, is not something we want to develop for work. It's obvious that it's a sketch of Ted's work, and that if Ted were to work on it another year a very remarkable work would appear, Ted's *Ring* would appear. But neither he nor I would be interested in consolidating the *Orghast* position. We want to use it as a stepping-stone to something simpler and freer, which will begin to reconcile in one the experience of the high moments of *Orghast* and tombs at sunset, with the audience falling about with laughter in the village, and the children. (253)

That statement, made just before the Center went to Africa in the autumn of 1972, suggests the combination of holy and rough that would result a decade later in Brook's own yet more un-Wagnerian *Ring* cycle, *The Mahabharata.*

The journey to encounter village audiences in Africa, though romantic in some of its cultural assumptions, shot through with internal tensions, and mixed in its results, was a sustained exercise in perception and transformation. Of the physical exercises Heilpern said, "the real aim isn't physical but spiritual" (181), and his description of the group's larger aim suggests not only Grotowski's relentless *via negativa* but also Gurdjieff's understanding of the "work":

> Truth, a truthful life and vitality, bursts from the centre . . . But to arrive at the centre, the actors must undertake the most intense life of self-exploration. They must strip away their outward personalities, mannerisms, habits, vanity, neuroses, tricks, clichés and stock responses until a higher state of perception is found. To watch a piece of theatre performed truthfully is to see in a different way. Perhaps we awaken. We are shaken out of our everyday condition and we see life differently. Sometimes our lives are changed. But the actor must change first. He must shed useless skins like a snake. He must transform his whole being. (157–58)

Heilpern describes Brook as so deeply affected by this research that "he no longer had a role which could be clearly defined. He had become a participant in his own work, and a victim. In many ways, I saw him as a man who'd lost his identity . . . Struggling to transform theatre, he transforms himself." He was "a man in search of something more essential to him than performing" (26–27), who "would like to wake up on the other side of his identity" (28). "He was trying to enter his own void, like his actors" (266).

The year's major project, *The Conference of the Birds,* was expected to synthesize the popular qualities of the group's improvised carpet shows. But Farid ud-Din Attar's poem about the birds' quest for the Simorgh, who turns out to be not only the Divine but also their essential selves, was also a metaphor for the group's own quest. Almost certainly studied by Gurdjieff (Lefort 57) and translated into English by the Gurdjieffian C. S. Nott, *The Conference of the Birds* clearly embodies Gurdjieffian patterns of aspiration (Moore 366). On the African journey, and in ensuing years, it focused for the group its continuing search for attentiveness, simplicity, and openness and for what is hidden most deeply in oneself. As a dramatic form, it also encouraged an understanding of the actor as narrator-participant with a sympathetic detachment less Brechtian than Muslim, African, or Hindu—a detachment that would later inform the more complex texture of narrative in *The Mahabharata.*

Improvisations in Africa and North America led to the versions of *The*

Conference presented at the Brooklyn Academy of Music in 1973. In demonstration sessions Brook linked the actors' exercises with the imaginative awareness of "birds." The process, "as Brook tactfully makes us aware when he comments on our own efforts, is a spiritual discipline, involving simplification, concentration, purification—a labor that turns out to be very much like that of the birds in his story" (Goldman, *Actor's Freedom* 105). On each of five evenings a pair of actors would take the role of storytellers, and the others would follow their directions (Oida 113). On the final night three versions were presented: one, led by Yoshi Oida and Michele Collison, had the joyful and comic verve of a carpet show; another, led by Bruce Myers and Natasha Parry, returned to the Sufi delicacy of Attar's text; a third, led by Andreas Katsulas and Elizabeth Swados, incorporated the audience in ritualistic choral work and abstract improvisations (Williams, *Casebook* 232). Brook would hope in some way later to combine them.

Although the group then dispersed, seven of the actors soon joined others in a permanent Centre International de Créations Théâtrales at a derelict theater, the Bouffes du Nord, which now became Brook's base. Over the next five years they continued to work on *The Conference of the Birds,* never losing sight of its challenges, even as other productions stressed other modes of playing and other aspects of the human condition. The first, in 1974, was *Timon d'Athènes.* Even without seeing it, Kenneth Tynan called its selection a symptom of the "ritualistic misanthropy" that "has been the driving force behind Brook's work from the early sixties onwards." In Brook's view, said Tynan, "human beings, left to themselves, stripped of social restraints, are animals and are inherently rotten and destructive" (qtd. in Hunt and Reeves 221). Their next production *Les Iks* (1975), with its naturalistic portrayal of a tribe dehumanizing itself in response to dislocation and famine, struck Albert Hunt as a further indication of Brook's "despairing vision of the human condition," his "faith in the futility of human action based on intelligence" (208, 209). The next production, *Ubu aux Bouffes* (1977), a composite text drawn from all four of Jarry's *Ubu* plays, was generally patronized in England and the United States as "lovable and harmless" (214). The austere *Mesure pour Mesure* (1978), which lacked the intensity of Brook's earlier production and the teeming invention of *Ubu,* struck Irving Wardle as a play diminished "by being presented as an ironic fable" (223). What was happening to Brook's quest for the invisible?

Once again, such misunderstandings of Brook's work followed from the assumption that we can infer a play's meaning from its stage world alone. In returning to "negative" visions, Brook kept his faith in "playing" as the optimistic component of performance that complements and counters the bleakness or grotesqueness of the stage world being played. No doubt he viewed the surrounding society as destructive, exploitative, and decaying. *Timon* reflects "the degradation of a humanity fragmented by the cancer of capital" (Williams, "Place Marked by Life" 43). *Les Iks*, in Brook's view, gave "the image of a world that is betraying its possibilities" (54). *Ubu aux Bouffes* was filled with images of peasant misery, economic oppression, and the inhumanity of war. But if Brook's theater mimed the world as a house in ruins like Timon's, it was also, as David Williams has amply shown, "a place marked by life" (40). In *Timon* "the life of the text was released by means of vocal capacities the group had developed on their journeys . . . Words became actions charged with their own energy" (46). In *Les Iks* the disciplined improvisations were based on intense observation of the minutest details of tribal life. Brook later called it "a celebration of detail." In *Ubu* the grotesque comedy was for him "a celebration of energy" (74). In his view these productions set against the dark implications of their stage worlds the sheer fact of performance itself and its human implications.

Brook did not reject "human action based on intelligence" or think human beings unredeemably "rotten and destructive," though indeed he shared Gurdjieff's understanding that a social order shaped by inattentive egos is cruel and self-destructive. His search has long been for a heightened perception, a mutual awareness, indeed a spiritual transformation of individuals and groups—without which the social engineering espoused by Marxists or liberals would merely produce the old problems in new forms. That is why he has seen his work at Bouffes du Nord as an attempt to "reunite the community, in all its diversity, within the same shared experience" (41). For him the theater, even when focusing upon the bleaker aspects of our society, is a scene of artless art in various styles that can introduce its audience to the meaning of a playful community. Far from being despairing or misanthropic, this vision is astonishingly optimistic about what may be produced in the human spirit through the theater. And yet that optimism is understandable in the light of the demands that Brook makes upon playing, as a discipline through which we may glimpse the truly revolutionary import of attention, self-remembering, heightened perception, alertness to the invisible, and celebration of life. Brook stands with those who believe that any transformation of the human condition must begin with the difficult work of the individual in a group and that such transformations will have a contagious power. In that respect he is staunchly at one with the deepest meanings of every religious tradition.

We can therefore see why *The Conference of the Birds* continued to be at the center of the group's activities and why Brook asked Jean-Claude Carrière to prepare a text for the Festival d'Avignon in 1979 in a production that would combine the aspects given separately in the final night at the Brooklyn Academy of Music in 1973. Brook had said then: "We are trying to make a work about theater and about life. It has to be true in a theater form, and yet be something far beyond theater." Only if we "serve something other than our egos," he said, does theater take on "the promise of something more than just a poor thing to get involved in" (Carrière and Brook, preface). *The Conference* was always presented along with *L'Os,* a farce by the African playwright Birago Diop that portrays the materialistic base from which any journey of the ego must start (Banu 186–87). And in 1980 Brook decided to perform *Ubu, Les Iks,* and *The Conference of the Birds* in Adelaide, Australia, as "one three-part play," the third part being a "celebration of the possibility of crossing barriers" (Williams, "Place Marked by Life" 74). David Williams has described in detail the work with storytelling, masks, and puppets required by that final version of *The Conference,* as it mediated between marketplace theater and the supreme mystery (62–72). There were portrayals of earthbound squabbles, mask-induced approaches to the self beneath the outward persona, choreographed disclosures of archetypal realities, enactments of the death of the old self, and a conclusion in which the actors "see" as they advance toward the light. Georges Banu has described with delicacy the effect of that conclusion, with its momentary hint of what we might some day become (200). Brook put it this way: "Perhaps you might say that we are looking for passages—passages that connect the inner and outer worlds" (Carrière and Brook, preface).

The production was no mere allegory: it disclosed the invisible in theatrical terms. In harmony with Sufi thought, the action of performance embodied the meaning to be discovered by the birds at the end of their visionary journey. Carrière's highly condensed text, therefore, does not need to give all of Attar's explication. The Hoopoe says simply that the birds asked the Simorgh "the great secret" (79), whereas Attar had called it explicitly "the secret of the mystery of the unity and plurality of beings" (Attar 132). That secret informed the entire performance. The protean actors, as they presented the birds' story and those told to them in transit by the Hoopoe, assumed a variety of roles and dramatic functions. Each found himself now a character, now a spectator, now quite clearly an actor in the very midst of a radical self-transformation. The reviewers' accolades—"astonishing," "spellbinding," "sublime" (Hunt and Reeves 201)—testified to the skill and authenticity of those transformations. But they also point to the fact that the birds' final discovery that "they were the Simorgh" had already been realized in the choreography of a performance that has shown each to be many and the many to be one. As Attar's Simorgh had put it: "Although you are now completely changed, you see yourselves as you were before" (Attar 132). The action of performance had made visible the mystery evoked by the Sufi master Mahmûd Shabistarî: "Since in the Unity there is no distinction, the Quest and the Way and the Seeker become one" (Vaughan-Lee 78).

This is the context, the realm of the invisible-as-visible, in which we should approach *The Mahabharata,* the stylistic and thematic variety of which has often been called "Shakespearean." When asked how he felt about that description, Brook said:

> Well, some years ago I did a production of *King Lear* and a journalistic cliché spread that this was Shakespeare in the light of Beckett. For me it was the other way round. I found that the very extraordinary quality I greatly admired of Beckett can already be found in Shakespeare. And I say in exactly the same way that the extraordinary quality of Shakespeare can already be found in *The Mahabharata,* so that it really depends in which direction you point your time machine. (Williams, *Peter Brook and "The Mahabharata"* 56–57)

Indeed, we can play various games with the time machine. We could hardly imagine Brook's commitment to the stylistic and narrative variety of *The Mahabharata* without his having explored, at an earlier point in his career, Brecht's epic and dialectical paradigm, which so easily assimilates various narrative forms and shifts of perspective both Western and Eastern. And we might even think of *The Mahabharata* as Brook's semi-Brechtian *Ring of the Nibelungenlied*—a participatory narrative spectacle that embodies a total statement, a mythological synthesis.

The Wagnerian analogy may seem too heavy, at odds with the taste of this former director of productions at Covent Garden, who would later reduce Bizet's *Carmen* to its powerful dramatic spine. But Brook himself had thought of Wagner's *Ring* in connection with Hughes's *Orghast,* and he and Carrière now found in the Hindu text an analogous "world history" unfolding through subordinate narratives. Wagner's four-part dramatization of the life of gods and men from initial fall to ultimate catastrophe uses the orchestra itself as primary "narrator," through a motivic sequence that places and interprets the lyric-dramatic episodes. Brook's and Carrière's three-part dramatization takes us from initial fall to ultimate catastrophe through

Vyasa's story to a young boy, which expands to include a range of homely, complex, and ambiguous narrative-dramatic actions. What this technique loses in grandeur, it regains through our intimate participation in the unfathomable. Instead of "the play-within-the-play-within-the-play-within-the play" of *A Midsummer Night's Dream,* we now follow "the story-within-the-story-within-the story-within-the story"—for Brook's understanding of how the invisible becomes visible has now led to Chinese boxes of narrative. Carrière himself seems to have been influenced less by Wagner's musical vision of northern European mythology than Hugo's poetic treatment of Vedic mythology in *Suprématie,* which encouraged him to provide what Garry O'Connor has called a relativized Western perspective upon *The Mahabharata,* a "sense of unfinished formulation, of tentative seeking, of finding that one element is always contradicting and crossing out another" (51). No doubt such traits must fail to satisfy those who want to see in the complexities of the Hindu text—or in its primary jewel, the *Bhagavad Gita*—a consistent philosophical or religious doctrine.

Once again the Gurdjieff connection is important. In 1975, even as Brook was planning his film on Gurdjieff, he and Carrière were introduced to stories from *The Mahabharata* by the orientalist Philippe Lavastine (Williams, *Peter Brook and "The Mahabharata"* 61), who had been in the 1930s a key figure in the Gurdjieff group that met in Sèvres and Paris (Moore 258, 273). *The Mahabharata* had been an enthusiasm of A. R. Orage, editor of the *New English Weekly* and an important promulgator of Gurdjieff's teaching (Webb 199, 304). A verse from *The Mahabharata* (*Bhagavad Gita* 2:16) was carved by Eric Gill on the headstone for Orage's grave in Hampstead Churchyard (Webb 378):

> The unreal has no being
> The real never ceases to be.

Although not included in Carrière's drastic condensation of Krishna's speech—which Arjuna has later "forgotten" (Carrière 159–61, 231), so losing the supreme confidence of that great poem in the immanence of our being in the one Self—that verse does pose the enigmatic relation between the visible unreal and the invisible real that this production assumes and explores. Permeated with what Brook called "living contradictions" (Williams, *Peter Brook and "The Mahabharata"* 55), it probes through its story of search and through its surprises, stylistic variety, and what Vincent Dehoux has called "musical bricolage" (81) a transient human existence that is everywhere surrounded and permeated by an invisible reality.

Carrière's text, worked out with Brook and the actors in rehearsal, provides many clues to the invisible that we may discern in performance. At the outset of this "poetical history of mankind," Vyasa tells the young boy who is the proof of survival (and in whom we are to find ourselves as innocent auditors and witnesses): "If you listen carefully, at the end you'll be someone else" (Carrière 3, 55). As in *The Conference of the Birds,* though more deviously, we are to enter a narrative process, a field of the invisible, that has transforming power. As Vyasa (or, for the mask is transparent, Robert Langdon Lloyd) tells this story, he increasingly becomes, like the actors in *The Conference,* a narrator-participant, rendering the combination of distance and presence that for Brook has long been the key to both theater and life. He tells of a process in which "each day brings us closer to barrenness, to destruction" and yet "all depends on the hearts of men and there I can't see clearly" (25). He is not even sure that his poem "has an end" (55). Others attribute to him a creative power that he seems not to have: "Vyasa has abandoned us" (179). "Vyasa, you find too much beauty in men's death" (156). But, like his characters, he is hedged round by the invisible. It is uncertain whether he has invented Krishna or Krishna has invented him (107). This invisible field, in which the story seems to write itself through Vyasa, contains both the force of destiny and the unpredictable energies of choice. Both, in fact, are subsumed in the "dharma"—a concept that traditionally means both "the way things are" and "the way things should be"—that Vyasa wants to engrave "in the hearts of men" (107). Here *dharma* may mean "the way of truth, of the order of the world" (60), but it also implies a personal destiny and duty. That slippery notion comes to its sharpest focus in Krishna, whose powers most often seem overshadowed by human ignorance, awareness of moral ambiguity, and laissez-faire. Posing to Bhishma the possibility that his race may have to be destroyed "so as to save dharma," Krishna asks him not to intervene in the game of dice: "Let each one go to his limit" (61). Indeed, Krishna himself, who is "born to destroy the destroyers" (192), is a trickster, a liar, even as he shows Arjuna "the path of freedom, of true, right action" (231). He deceives and kills in order that "a light" may be "saved" (229). As Draupadi says, "sometimes the only way to protect dharma is to forget it" (198).

In order to inhabit this paradoxical and incompletely discernible field with the characters, we must become alert to surprises, frustrations, unpredictable incursions of the invisible. We must adopt toward each moment of uncertainty and bewilderment a stance of passionate commitment and detached acceptance. That is precisely what Peter Brook had been urging upon his players for more than two decades with his teaching of presence and distance. Throughout *The Mahabharata,* as the actors teach us how to play within the invisible, they underline the fact that the norms of this theatrical world are, for Brook, the norms of playing itself. At the Brooklyn Academy of Music in 1987, Ryszard Cieslak seemed to me a pathetic shell of the passionately self-denuded actor whom I had seen in Grotowski's *The Constant Prince* in London in 1969. And yet, as the blind Dhritarashtra, he was a living image of one for whom the enigmatic complexities of the visible world must remain invisible. "I must forget the light," he told Garry O'Connor. To portray the blindness, he looked inside himself, so his playing "became an 'autobiographical' process" (90). Vittorio Mezzogiorno, who learned English in order to continue as Arjuna in this production, brought to his character's Zen-like archery—during which the entire visual field has disappeared except the vulture's head (30)—just such an actor's focus. It clearly derived from the Gurdjieffian discipline that he had learned from Brook: "Performing means being right there with your mind, body and words in the same instant," he had told Maria Shevtsova—adding pertinently: "I'm saying something that seems to be quite natural, but it isn't" (Williams, *Peter Brook and "The Mahabharata"* 96). After an initial bewilderment when confronted by Brook's nondirective direction, he had understood that "the actors were not supposed to execute certain prescribed things so much as to participate with their whole being in the creation of something" (Williams, *Casebook* 376). Bruce Myers, who had shifted from the role of Karna to replace Maurice Bénichou as Krishna, was by contrast almost casual in manner. How to play one who is clearly divine and yet fully human? "The key to being Krishna," Myers told O'Connor, was that, "if you know something is going to happen, you are calm." The more he worked with Brook, said Myers, "the more I see what can be achieved through calmness than through dynamism" (84). Maurice Bénichou had put the same psychological and spiritual point differently: "You must not act Krishna, but be present" (85).

But it was Yoshi Oida playing Drona, instructor in martial arts for the Pandavas, and Kichaka, an ostentatious and farcical general, who seemed to me most fully to render the paradox of presence and distance in his clean stylizations, somewhat reminiscent of Noh or Kabuki, more intense than reality yet intensely real. Oida is the actor who may have learned most from Brook and from such cognate disciplines as Zen Buddhism, one who over the years has destroyed his "actorly" persona to reveal himself ever more clearly. He believes "that we are not merely products of our ordinary daily existence, but that inside us all there is an invisible energy, and that this energy is both a part and a reflection of the vast universal energy" (Oida 142). In what he calls "true theatre":

> the actor's technique consists of the ability to provoke the audience into participating in the creative process . . . Ideal acting is the expression of the metaphysical world through physical acts: ideal theatre is the creation of an invisible world through visual presentation. You don't necessarily realize how the actors have affected you; you only know that you have been changed." (158–59)

He told John Heilpern, with characteristic simplicity: "Acting has become a way to find God. It's normal" (Heilpern 92).

Such different styles of acting could hardly consort with each other except within the bare yet elegant staging—carpets, sand, a river—and the stylistic and international eclecticism of this production, which established a milieu of playing in which almost any event, any style, can appear on the horizon. If we adopt the Western or skeptical point of view that Carrière's script often seems to encourage, we may conclude with Michael Kustow that "the deepest attitude of *The Mahabharata,* and of Brook's idea of theatre," is

> that reality is deliquescent, so that there is no single way, political, psychological or moral, to seize it; that we live in a superimposed plurality of worlds and that the truest wisdom—which live theatre is uniquely placed to explore—is never to lose touch with alternative and contradictory universes, while devoting yourself completely to the demands of the world you inhabit. (Williams, *Peter Brook and "The Mahabharata"* 254)

And Kustow is surely right to say that for Brook "the play's the thing, and playing is the root of all" (261). But if we give full value to a playing hedged round by the invisible, to the hints dropped by a Krishna who "is sometimes guided by a force we can't understand" (Carrière 202), and to a conclusion in which the aged Yudhishthira passes through a paradise where "all hates vanish" (236) and enters the "last dwelling," where "words end, like thought" (238)—then we may see beyond "alternative and contradictory universes." We may learn with Yudhishthira, the emergent quest hero of this epic, that all the playing—including the retributive justice—has been "illusion," a waking dreamwork through which we may intuit the enigmatic reality that is our true home. At that moment our theatrical illusion collapses, the characters become actors who sit down beside the accompanying musicians, and Vyasa's story comes to its end.

VI

In 1986, in the wake of *The Mahabharata,* Brook and his actors held six days of meetings at the Bouffes du Nord for an invited audience. There, through exercises and commentary, they offered some provisional conclusions from their work. They emphasized ways of approaching the invisible—through silence, attention, intuition, and the freeing of the body (Banu, *Peter Brook* 223–37; trans. in Williams, *Peter Brook and "The Mahabharata"* 268–79). After stressing the actor's necessary "fidelity" to one's own concentration, to one's partner, and to the audience, Brook went on to say that "the invisible can only reveal itself through the body. And for that to happen the body must be trained to open itself up to the invisible." This requires the abandonment of "any kind of psychological approach" and the creating of "an empty space" by placing oneself "in a situation of imitation." "The body has caves, hidden passages . . . one must learn to allow energy to flow through it. This would enable an infinite series of possibilities to arise, and one could really start to listen to the invisible" (Williams, *Peter Brook and "The Mahabharata"* 270–71). One is "looking for absolute freedom and at the same time for absolute discipline; for the bridge that links them" (273). In describing that bridge, Brook stressed the primacy of intuition, which grasps the invisible, and the necessary support of intelligence, which can lead to a "disciplined precision once a choice is made" (274). What is most striking in his exercises—especially given the widespread impression of Brook as a director concerned with large-scale spectacle and showmanship—is their emphasis on the smallest units, the most minute details. These are the necessary starting points for freeing the body, emptying oneself, and opening oneself to "heterogeneity" or "impurity." Brook restaged certain moments—a scene from *The Conference of the Birds* when Arabic and French are combined simultaneously, the death of Duryodhana from *The Mahabharata,* when song and words are overlaid. He wanted to show that nothing "need be excluded, as long as one succeeds in preparing the empty space, so as to be able to open oneself up, in a sensitive way, to invisible currents" (271–72). That actor's discipline is the corollary of what he would later describe for a

Japanese audience as the purpose of playing—"the building of a bridge between ourselves as we usually are . . . and an invisible world that can reveal itself to us only when the normal inadequacy of perception is replaced by an infinitely more acute quality of awareness" (*Open Door* 103).

That purpose, bound by no single "theory" or "method" but open to all, has guided Brook's work since 1962. It has most recently led him to a new phase, specifically devoted to the brain, mind, and spirit. "The worst disease today is reductionism," he has said. The question of the spirit "is simply laughed out of court, and I think many people want it back. Certainly, that sort of materialism sets off a deep wish in me to go in the opposite direction" (Nightingale 4). The first of these projects, *The Man Who,* is based on several years of research, improvisation, and dramatic shaping provoked by the clinical tales in Oliver Sacks's *The Man Who Mistook His Wife for a Hat,* a work about the marvels of the mind revealed through its deficits or derangements. *The Man Who* does not dramatize Sacks's narratives but offers a poetic exploration of that subject through a series of doctor-patient encounters. In the New York production four actors—David Bennent, Sotigui Kouyate, Bruce Myers, and Yoshi Oida—switched back and forth between their roles as doctors and patients with each new episode, and Mahmoud Tabrizi-Zadeh provided a continuing musical accompaniment. In this chamber piece the performed action may be puzzling, horrifying, amusing, pathetic, or strangely beautiful. But the action of performance is always exhilarating, as the actors variously lead us to become sensitive to the nuances of behavior through which the invisible is manifest. At the Brooklyn Academy of Music in 1995 I was fascinated by how the actors-as-patients provided us with a series of double images. The patients—not so much characters as people there before us—were blocked from full awareness and expression by neurological deficits; the actors who played them were expanding their normal awareness and expressiveness to lead us into those occulted identities. Sometimes the double image required attention to the subtlest movement of eyes and facial muscles, as when Yoshi Oida inhabited a man who, while shaving, could not perceive one side of his own face in a mirror. Sometimes that doubleness made possible a riff of virtuoso comedy, as when Bruce Myers exploded into a positively Joycean display of glossolalia that the patient himself could not understand when it was played back to him. Always it was clear that the real subject of *The Man Who* is not the pathological but the mysterious reach of the mind that includes our derangements, our almost preternatural abilities, and our ability to share them with one another. Finally, *The Man Who* is about playing itself, as a self-reflexive mirror that may become an open door upon our shared and invisible identity.

It is only a step to the second project in this phase of "theatrical research," *Qui est là?* which was playing at the Bouffes du Nord in January 1996. The title, which like *The Man Who* points to our problematic identity, is drawn from the opening words of *Hamlet:* this implicitly retrospective piece is a theatrical reflection upon the issues central to Brook's career. It dramatizes "the search and struggle within rehearsals" by having seven actors take on a dozen roles from a condensed version of *Hamlet* even as they also play the "anonymous" parts of five theorists—Stanislavsky, Meyerhold, Gordon Craig, Brecht, and Artaud—who make suggestions as to staging and interpretation and discuss their ideas of theater. The result, as Alan Riding has said, is "something of a jigsaw puzzle" because "the theorists are not identified onstage and at times the actors speak their lines while seemingly performing *Hamlet*" (C13). But, for those familiar with Shakespeare's play and with the theorists whom Brook has been assimilating for decades, this is a remarkable commentary on his own position. Although following in the tradition of Charles Marowitz's collage *Hamlet* and Brook's own collage *The Tempest,* it emphasizes no single directorial interpretation but the process of search. Through the contributions of the actors and the directorial voices a production of *Hamlet* is gradually constructed and interpreted before our eyes. "I don't believe a director is there to give his personal interpretation of a work," Brook now says. "We weren't even asking these unknown voices to tell us how to do it, but simply to accompany us" (Riding C14). Who's there, indeed? *Qui est là?* makes clear, as it holds the mirror up to the inner process of playing, that Brook remains open to many paradigms, many presences, in a quest that is genuinely open-ended. As he had said of his film about Gurdjieff, "The end of the story shows us . . . how a man who searches finds the material that enables him to go still further" (*Shifting Point* 213).

It is appropriate, therefore, that Brook has at long last paid explicit tribute to the presence who has for many years informed that search. In "The Secret Dimension"—an essay published in French in 1992 and later translated in Jacob Needleman's and George Baker's *Gurdjieff: Essays and Reflections on the Man and His Teaching*—Brook praises the teaching of Gurdjieff as "firmly rooted in a very ancient, lost tradition" but "bitingly contemporary." It "analyzes the human predicament with devastating precision" (30) and provides a way of self-transformation beyond the ego toward the harmony of "true individuality" (33). It "works simultaneously on all the aspects of the psyche: on the mind, the feelings, and the body," and it "rejects the passivity that can come from a naive dependence on the teacher" (34). Brook here defines "the mystery of quality" in Gurdjieffian terms as a function of our ability to reach a source from which "energies descend to meet and interact with the energies we know" (32). That approach to "quality" also involves the paradoxical simultaneity of what Brook, like Gurdjieff, had called "objectivity" and "presence"—which is why Gurdjieff himself could use the actor as "a metaphor for the fully developed human being." "The better the actor . . . the less he is identified with his role, and . . . the less he is identified, the more deeply he can be involved" (33–34). Brook proceeds to redefine in these terms the holy theater, the revelation of the invisible to the audience. There are moments of "very special silence" that occur when "actors and audience unite, the division between stage and auditorium dissolves and individual egos make no barrier to shared experience." Those moments can lead us "to discover in ourselves new levels of awareness that mount to an ultimate field of consciousness in which all images are no more than vanishing shadows." So understood, art is a mode of "spiritual experience" that reveals a nameless "void": "it is infinite and timeless, and from its absolute vibrancy, step by step, the finest of energies can flow into the world of time" (35).

As Brook now fully acknowledges, Gurdjieff's teaching has been for him a necessary approach to the complementary goals of Stanislavsky, Meyerhold, Craig, Brecht, and Artaud. Other pieces in the same collection—Jean-Claude Carrière's "An Inner Journey: The Actor as Companion" (148–55) and an interview with Jerzy Grotowski, "A Kind of Volcano" (87–106)—testify to the importance of that teaching in Brook's theatrical milieu. As Brook says, it can lead to a "clarity of understanding" that is not theory but vision—and "vision is alive." "It shows us the unending and inevitable movements toward and away from quality. There is a joy in quality found and a suffering in quality betrayed, and these two experiences become the motors that constantly renew our search" (36). Yet more personal statements in Brook's memoirs, *Threads of Time: Recollections,* which appeared after this study was already in press, confirm the importance for him of Gurdjieff's vision, as transmitted through Jane Heap, Mme de Salzmann, and others (59–61, 69–71, 75–76, 108–11, 181). "It seemed to me at the very first meeting," he says, "to contain essential truths, and this seems equally so more than forty years later" (61). Through that vision, which orients us toward a "silent wakefulness, informing and uniting the organism from moment to moment" (110), Peter Brook continues to seek the purpose of playing.

Afterword

Angels in America

I

When I had completed this manuscript, my wife, Joan—with whom I had recently shared the Shaw Festival's production of Granville Barker's *The Secret Life* and James Luse's studio production at Yale of Tony Kushner's *Millennium Approaches*—gave me a copy of Peter J. Gomes's *Sermons: Biblical Wisdom for Daily Living*. In the foreword by Henry Louis Gates Jr.—who some years ago had encouraged me to write about Wole Soyinka—I came across some words that effectively summarize the deepest ethical bearing of the mirrors of our playing:

> The committed life, according to [Gomes], is not about policing the boundaries but about breaking those boundaries down and acknowledging the fluid and interactive nature of all our identities. By word and by example he attests that there is not only one way of being, and that the more strongly one nurtures a sense of the contingent nature of all identities, the less likely it is that one will be harmed by them, or in their name inflict harm upon others. (xi)

With the burden of that text in mind, let me recapitulate and extend my argument.

II

A play is not just an observed stage action in an observed stage world. Its full meaning is constituted by the relations between its "performed action" and its "action of performance," in which both actors and audience participate. In performance, therefore, a play is manifold mirror of the playing that constitutes our lives, shaped by the interaction of playwrights, directors, actors, and audiences with one another, with "presences" from the past, and with one or more theatrical paradigms. Participating in that mirroring performance, we may freshly perceive the contingency of our multiple identities, acknowledge their fluid and interactive nature, and take some small but important steps toward at least a fleeting realization of the one Self that inhabits us all.

Part 1 has set forth several major paradigms in modern drama and many of their variations. Synge's *The Playboy of the Western World,* which blends farce, romance, tragicomedy, satire, and allegory, is a kind of paradigm of paradigms, continually refocusing the relations between the grotesque onstage community and our community of performance. In the mirror of *The Playboy* we come to understand our role-playing not only as a continual temptation but also as a means of ironic self-recognition, personal growth, and the discovery of mutuality. Wilde's *The Importance of Being Earnest,* Shaw's *You Never Can Tell,* Orton's *What the Butler Saw,* and Stoppard's *Travesties* offer variations upon the paradigm of serious farce, which can subsume the satirical, sentimental, savagely grotesque, and didactic and can sweep them beyond apparent chaos into a shared music of performance. In Shaw's *Heartbreak House,* as in Granville Barker's *The Secret Life,* in plays by O'Casey, Odets, Hellman, Storey, Machado, Wilson, and Friel, and in the performance art of Anna Deveare Smith, we find transformations of a Chekhovian paradigm, the community of heartbreak, in which the panorama of isolation, blockage, and waste in the performed action is set against an implicit and necessary faith in the community resources that inform our action of performance. In Sartre's *No Exit,* Beckett's *Play,* Genet's *The Screens,* and Pinter's *No Man's Land* there is a more extreme tension between the explicit negations in the performed action and the implicit affirmations in our action of performance. Such "playing hell" depends upon an action of performance that radically qualifies, and indeed overturns, the bleakness and entrapment of the actions represented onstage.

In showing how those paradigms are transformed by encounters with various styles, genres, and thematic concerns, I made allowance for the mediating participation of personal presences. And I selected, in part 2, certain of those presences for special attention. The spirit of the nineteenth-century poet-playwright Lord Byron, quite evident in much of the work surveyed in part 1, has also entered other plays from Yeats, Eliot, and Auden to O'Neill, Williams, Linney, and Brenton. Reinventing Byron's "mental theater," they have brought his romantic passion, self-conscious damnation, and satirical verve into relation with more beneficent powers of playing. Samuel Beckett, who might seem to have carried the negations of the

Byronic theater to a point of no return, has remained a vital presence in more explicitly affirmative plays by Fugard, Soyinka, Shepard, Mamet, and Friel, which overcome the self-conscious finality of his minimalism, sustain the community life implicit in his actions of performance, and move toward more expansive images of social concern. Wole Soyinka, in aiming toward an ecstasy of transformation, has pursued a difficult course through several ancient and modern paradigms of playing, modifying them as he has related European theater to his Nigerian heritage. And Peter Brook, for whom directing has been a field of self-transformation, has boldly moved through many genres, styles, and paradigms of acting and witnessing in search of the meaning of playing itself. In his international art we can discern the commitment to individual transformation and community realization that informed *The Playboy of the Western World.*

Toward the end of this century the most creative playwrights and directors have become increasingly aware of the diverse paradigms and presences on which they may draw and have also become, at least in the United States, increasingly uncertain about their relation to any specific community aside from that constituted by the performance event itself. Individual theaters, mainstream or avant-garde, have become more eclectic, and there are few current plays of importance that do not combine certain of the paradigms and presences that I have described. Some director-playwrights offer a chameleonlike instance of this process. Peter Brook brings together onstage, or banishes from the stage, a world of paradigms in order to introduce us to the invisible through a performance that holds the mirror up to playing. Richard Foreman constructs, in *Pearls for Pigs,* a visual-auditory symbol of the creative process itself, bringing together Pirandellian transformations, motifs from abstract art, and self-referential allusions to embody among us the lure and the danger of histrionic narcissism. When Foreman directs Suzan-Lori Parks's *African Venus,* her play becomes another Foreman exercise in the self-referential, now by way of the narrated and symbolized historical predicament of an ostensibly antithetical gender. A rather extreme eclecticism is also evident in many other playwrights. Communities of heartbreak indebted to Chekhov, for example, have been variously transformed in Caryl Churchill's *Cloud Nine* and *Mad Forest,* Maria Irene Fornes's *The Danube* and *Fefu and Her Friends,* and George P. Walker's *Escape from Happiness.* Churchill and Fornes have learned from Brecht and from the avant-garde theater of fantasy. Walker has drawn upon kitchen-sink realism, Shaw, Shepard, Orton, and even Kaufman and Hart—for *Escape from Happiness* is sometimes a hilarious conflation of *Heartbreak House,*

Buried Child, What the Butler Saw, and *You Can't Take It with You.* Fornes may have spoken for a fair number of quite experimental contemporary playwrights when she said, while rehearsing *Uncle Vanya* in 1987, "Chekhov is the writer I most admire" (qtd. in Cole 36). And the more-than-Brechtian Tony Kushner has not only listed Chekhov among his "favorite writers in prose" (*Tony Kushner in Conversation* 126) but also adapted and extended Chekhov's panoramic vision of self-closed worlds.

Such combinations and transformations suggest that the most comprehensive theatrical paradigm—as old as Aristophanes but always to be renewed—will lead us into a pattern of dialectical and dialogical interactions. It will combine several perspectives on the action, indeed several recognizable paradigms, as it explores the dialogical relations among the participants. Modern versions of that paradigm have been developed in Hofmannsthal's festival theater, Claudel's total theater, Pirandello's mirrors of the theater, Artaud's theater of cruelty, Brecht's epic or dialectical theater, and Grotowski's poor theater. Of these self-reflexive, shifting, or kaleidoscopic mirrors of our playing, Brecht's is among the most capacious. It is also the most flexibly self-reflexive and the most influential in the United Kingdom and the United States. I introduced this book with one instance of that paradigm of paradigms: the collaborative production of *Children of Paradise: Shooting a Dream* by the Théâtre de la Jeune Lune. In conclusion, I want to point to a more ambitious and more powerful instance, Tony Kushner's *Angels in America.*

III

David Savran has rightly called *Angels in America* "a promiscuously complicated play that it is difficult to categorize generically" (15). The most probing accounts of this play, including Savran's, emphasize its Brechtian orientation. After seeing productions in California and New York, Janelle Reinelt put the matter in a way congenial to my own account of "presences": "Suddenly Brecht seemed like a specter, like Ethel Rosenberg and Roy Cohn in the play: A specific historical presence conjured up, but as a dramatic fiction, to haunt the play through both limitation and aspiration" ("Notes on *Angels in America*" 235). Art Borreca has succinctly summarized the ways in which "a Brechtian spirit resides at the center of the work": it is evident in "such classic Brechtian techniques as episodic structure, emblematic and 'ideological' characters, and theatrical montage, and in the use of these techniques to 'estrange' or 'defamiliarize' sociohistorical conditions in a particular place and time" (245). This sprawling play in two parts, *Millennium Approaches* and *Perestroika,* emerges in part from Kushner's interest in the "multifocal, the multiple perspective" action in *Mother Courage,* which he has called "the greatest play written in the twentieth century" (*Tony Kushner in Conversation* 107, 119). For similar reasons Kushner admires "the interconnectednes and the complexity" of Robert Altman's *Nashville* (50), and he has said that "the labor of synthesizing disparate, seemingly unconnected things" has "become for me the process of writing a play" (*Angels in America* 2:153). This play emerges also from his admiration for Brecht's hardheaded and ironic focus on historical process in *Mother Courage* and *The Good Person of Setzuan* (115), his interest in the problematics of virtue in *The Good Person* (119–20) and elsewhere, and his enthusiasm for the explicitly participatory dimensions of the *Baden Play for Learning: On Consent,* with its urgent question: "How are we to remake ourselves into people who are fit to remake the world?" (118).

But *Angels in America* is also counter-Brechtian and meta-Brechtian. Against the material reality of Brechtian history is set the possibility of interaction with spirits who are understood by Kushner to be "bits of wonderful *theatrical* illusion" (2:7). Such spirits, often not clearly distinguishable from psychic projections (not just the Angel with whom Prior Walter must wrestle but also the Mr. Lies who appears to the disturbed Harper Pitt, the Ethel Rosenberg who so gently haunts Roy Cohn, and the Prior 1 and Prior 2 who visit Prior Walter), as well as the mutual permeability of Prior's dream and Harper's pill-induced hallucination, strongly recall the Expressionistic paradigm in which, as in Strindberg's *The Ghost Sonata* or *To Damascus,* a protagonist's conscious and unconscious awareness is projected into the surrounding stage action. The stage world, which may also be explicitly theatricalized or rendered as "mental theater," as in Strindberg's *A Dream Play,* then becomes for us a mirror of our own potential conscious-and-unconscious awareness. In *Angels in America* it is not just Prior and Harper who mutually recognize "Threshold of revelation" (1:33, 34; 2:67). The entire play puts us all, as actors and witnesses, in that liminal position, without committing itself to any "literal" account of the unconscious or spiritual realm so revealed.

The arrival of Prior's Angel specifically reflects, as David Savran has shown most clearly (15–16), Kushner's fascination with Walter Benjamin's counter-Brechtian interpretation of the millennium, not as a Marxist-Hegelian end point toward which the historical dialectic moves but as a difficult apocalyptic incursion into the historical process. Prior Walter's name derives in fact from Kushner's wordplay in conversation with his friend Kimberly Flynn, who liked to think of herself as "Walter Benjamin reincarnated" (*Essays on Kushner's Angels* 145). The Angels, of course, also have other ancestors in Jewish and Mormon tradition—and poetic ancestors as well, which Kushner is translating into stage terms. He has said that his "great antecedent" in this respect "is James Merrill's *The Changing Light at Sandover,*" which is "a constantly opening series of doors into ever deeper and deeper chambers of the sublime. That's a fun, sort of Blakean thing" (*Tony Kushner in Conversation* 210). Blakean, indeed! As Kushner does not say, Prior's Angel is quite Blakean in ancestry. When she says, "I I I I am Your Released Female Essence Ascendant" (2:41), she is talking like one of Blake's fallen Emanations in *Jerusalem*. But the meaning of the angelic incursion, which remains in doubt throughout *Millennium Approaches,* is disclosed in *Perestroika* to be a call to stasis, to immobility, to the end of creative life—which is very much like the passivity that Blake considers angelic in *The Marriage of Heaven and Hell,* in which the angel's "Reason" or "Good" is at odds with the creative "Energy" called "Evil."

But Kushner can also say that his theater "is completely of" the American narrative tradition that includes Eugene O'Neill and Tennessee Williams (*Essays on Kushner's Angels* 136). That paradigm of poetically heightened narrative, which remains close to "fourth-wall" realism, is most evident when we focus on the story line involving Louis Ironson's betrayal of his AIDS-afflicted lover Prior Walter, Joe Pitt's uneasy relation to Roy Cohn, and Joe's abandonment of his neurotic wife, Harper, as he explores his newly acknowledged gay identity. The main scenes in that story line, in fact, could easily be extracted from *Angels in America* and shaped into a rather Williams-like play.

But there is more. For several reasons the subtitle of *Angels in America,* "A Gay Fantasia on American Themes," echoes that of Shaw's *Heartbreak House,* "A Fantasia in the Russian Manner on English Themes." Kushner has said, "I love Shaw" (*Tony Kushner in Conversation* 40), and we can find in his play, as in Shaw's plays, a remarkable ensemble of characters who are quite stereotypical, histrionically heightened, and ideologically freighted or even overdetermined—in this instance, gay and straight, Mormon and Jewish, Anglo-American and African-American. What Rabbi Chemelwitz says of the deceased Sarah Ironson in the thematically central funeral address at the outset of *Millennium Approaches*—"She was . . . not a person but a whole kind of person" (*Angels in America* 1:10)—is in fact true of every character.

Like Shaw's plays, *Angels in America* gives us an often astonishingly articulate world of socially and psychologically determined masks through which we may explore the most urgent and paradoxical issues of contemporary life. And Kushner's masks, like Shaw's, do often represent paradoxes, dialectical antitheses or mixtures of such antitheses—each with its more or less eloquent self-justification—that the play itself, as David Savran has recognized, does not presume to resolve in a rational manner, even though they may be resolved on another level (14–15, 18). Prior Walter recognizes this for us when he says to Joe Pitt's Mormon mother, Hannah: "I wish you would be more true to your demographic profile. Life is confusing enough" (2:102). The pause that follows this remark, as they look at each other, is a prelude to their intimate—and, for Prior, supportive—talk about AIDS, prophets, and angels. Confusion and difference have been resolved by mutuality—a movement that, as I shall suggest, characterizes the larger trajectory of the play as a whole. Of course, Kushner has also said that he did not realize where the subtitle for his play came from. "I wanted a title that had a musical sound to it. Every playwright probably wants their plays to have a kind of musical structure, its themes and interweaving" (*Tony Kushner in Conversation* 40). No doubt that is true. But much of the music in this play is clearly the Shavian or Chekhovian music of heartbreak. The epigraph for *Millennium Approaches,* drawn from Stanley Kunitz's "The Testing Tree," establishes the centrality of precisely that theme:

> In a murderous time
> the heart breaks and breaks
> and lives by breaking.
>
> (1:7)

Angels in America proceeds very largely by positing such a community of heartbreak and then moving toward its resolution in both the performed action and the action of performance.

These affinities and a good many others are all subsumed within the meta-Brechtian dialectical and dialogical paradigm that Kushner likes to call (shifting gears from Charles Ludlam's Theater of the Ridiculous) the Theater of the Fabulous (*Tony Kushner in Conversation* 75). Far more expansively than *The Playboy of the Western World,* Kushner's paradigm of paradigms invites us into a multidimensional action that we must observe from a variety of perspectives. Roy Cohn is a fascinatingly comic villain, but by act 5, scene 3, of *Perestroika,* when Belize and Ethel Rosenberg both forgive and curse him (2:122–23), we understand that grandiose archetype of self-torturing evil (as we do such Shakespearean villains as Richard III or Macbeth) from a perspective that includes the tragic. Comic tonalities mix with pathos in the portrayal of Prior Walter, his ambivalent lover, Louis Ironson, the frustrated Harper Pitt, and her moralistic and agonized husband, Joe, and they complicate our attitudes toward the African-American ex-ex-drag queen, Belize, who serves as an ethical center for the play, and Hannah Pitt, who comes to seem to Prior (and to us) a maternal mentor—indeed, a *dea ex machina,* the machine here involving a transcontinental flight and a Mormon diorama. Like *The Playboy, Angels in America* commits itself wryly to tragicomedy, lyrical but flawed romance, wide-ranging satire, pervasive allegory, and moments of sheer farce. Both plays, as we find ourselves in their characters, show us that we are constituted by a multiple (even schizoid) role-playing, which establishes our predicament and our path to healing.

In doing so, *Angels in America* can subsume or thematize the major paradigms that I have sketched, partly, as Art Borreca has recognized, because all of the play's styles "are suffused with camp" (251). As in the serious farce of Wilde, Shaw, Orton, or Stoppard, this play offers a stage world of ideologically freighted images of absurdly missed connections, misunderstandings, and doublings, which moves to fortuitous meetings, fresh understandings, and newly discovered identities, allowing us to hear in a painful chaos the music of our fundamental harmony. Within such a world we accept the doubling of Belize with Mr. Lies, so that the same stage presence can assist both Prior and Harper, as we accept the journey eastward of Hanna Pitt, to arrive fortuitously (thanks to the directions given by a psychotic and prophetic woman) at the Mormon Visitor's Center at 65th and Broadway—where Harper, Joe, and Prior all converge.

As in the communities of heartbreak, this play establishes a stage world of isolation, blockage, and frustration in which several characters quite different in social status or background and psychological type, and quite unaware of one another's predicaments, play out analogous actions. Where Chekhov presents this through group scenes on a panoramic stage, Kushner gives us "split scenes" in which analogous events take place. The effect, as in Chekhov, is to establish our perception of the larger pattern of blockage and suffering of which the individual characters are largely ignorant. But Kushner moves beyond this paradigm in two significant ways. On the level of our action of performance he increases our awareness of the larger analogical pattern by calling for the doubling of characters throughout the play.

The specifically cross-gender doubling—Rabbi Chemelwitz, Roy's doctor Henry, and Aleksii Prelapsarianov played by the actor playing Hanna; Martin Heller played by the actor playing Harper; and Sarah Ironson played by the actor playing Louis—is a procedure that partly derives from what David Savran calls the "genderfuck" of Caryl Churchill's *Cloud Nine* (23). Kushner himself has said: "Churchill is like . . . God. The greatest living, English-language playwright and, in my opinion, the most important English-language playwright since Williams" (*Essays on Kushner's Angels* 138).

Savran ignores Louis's doubling as his dead grandma in the optional act 5, scene 6, of *Perestroika* and claims that, because the cross-gender doubling works only one way, it does not "denaturalize gender" (23). The important effect, nonetheless, is that both cross-gender and same-gender doublings keep before us the various world of the performed action as a function of the collaborative will of the performers. Kushner has said: "The play benefits from a pared-down style of presentation, with minimal scenery and scene shifts done rapidly (no blackouts!) employing the cast as well as stagehands—which makes for an actor-driven event, as this must be" (*Angels in America* 2:7). In that event we all participate. The opening funeral sermon "constructs the audience as part of Louis's family" (Solomon 127), as Rabbi Chemelwitz addresses us as part of the melting pot in which nothing melted (1:9–11). Harper addresses to us her first interior complaint (1:16). And Prior, at the end of *Perestroika,* will be—as Arnold Aronson has recognized (218–19)—an *Our Town*-like narrator who addresses us as he closes the story. As *Angels in America* proceeds, it comes to seem our shared "mental theater." The very same actor who played Rabbi Chemelwitz at the beginning of *Millennium Approaches* can chart at the end of *Perestroika* our movement from the melting pot in which nothing melted to this emergent vision. Hannah Pitt completes Louis Ironson's reference to "the sprawl of life, the weird" by adding ". . . interconnectedness" (2:144).

It is therefore appropriate that the performed action, too, after exploring the blockage and isolation in *Millennium Approaches,* should move in *Perestroika* beyond deaths and betrayals to an explicit unblocking and a reaching for community. What is merely implicit in the Chekhovian community of heartbreak becomes the explicit burden of Kushner's play. Some critics have been dissatisfied with this movement, finding Prior's statements at the end of the play disturbingly sentimental or regretting Kushner's apparent relapse from a radical critique (as in Brecht or Benjamin) to an endorsement of "liberal pluralism" (Savran 27) or "bourgeois individualism" (Reinelt, 243). But that, I think, is to miss or underestimate the ways in which the play's dramatic texture supports its conclusion—and to miss or underestimate also the ethical positives that the play keeps increasingly before us. One clue to this dramatic transformation is the gradually developing mutual understanding of Prior and Harper and of Prior and Hannah. Another clue is the combination of love and judgment with which Prior finally dismisses Joe (2:140) and the combination of acceptance and judgment with which Harper dismisses him: "Sometimes, maybe lost is best. Get lost. Joe. Go exploring" (2:139). Most important, as David Román (53) and Framji Minwalla (104–5, 109–10) have recognized, is the role of Belize, who in his early debate with Louis can speak of the "hard law of love" and of a "forgiveness, grace," that he cannot help Louis to learn (1:100) and who after Roy Cohn's death will ask Louis to say the Kaddish for Cohn: "He was a terrible person. He died a hard death. So maybe . . . A queen can forgive her vanquished foe. It isn't easy, it doesn't count if it's easy, it's the hardest thing. Forgiveness. Which is maybe where love and justice finally meet. Peace, at least. Isn't that what the Kaddish asks for?" (2:122). It is through such recognitions of the difficult centrality of love and forgiveness in a world in which there is much to forgive that Prior, Harper, and even to some extent Joe and Louis move through alienation and frustration toward the rudiments of self-knowledge and a recognition of community.

What, then, can Kushner's play do with the paradigm of "playing hell"—our ironic and fictively self-deceptive playing of a meaningless world of stasis, even as we implicitly celebrate the rich human resources that are required for its actualization in the theater? *Angels in America* makes of that paradigm its disturbing counter-theme. "The ultimate expression of this Age of Anomie," Graham Dixon has said, "is Beckett's '*they do not move,*' but the Angel pleads with Prior to persuade Man to do precisely this; to do precisely nothing" (*Essays on Kushner's Angels* 116). Indeed, *Angels in America,* like Blake's *The Marriage of Heaven and Hell,* inverts our perspective and puts that Hell in Heaven. Act 5, scene 5, of *Perestroika* takes us to that hellish Heaven, from which God Himself has defected—a Heaven very different of course from that which Belize envisions: "Race, taste and history finally overcome" (2:78). The angelic voices of this hellish Heaven, though Kushner calls them "very Benjaminian and Rilkean angels" (*Essays on Kushner's Angels* 144), might well inhabit one of Beckett's dramatic worlds or the icy world of Pinter's *No Man's Land.* "This radio is a terrible radio." "The reception is too weak." "A vacuum tube has died." "Can it be fixed?" "It is Beyond Us" (2:128). And the Angel's final speech—an evocation of human and cosmic wasting away and death—is, in effect, Kushner's reworking of the theme of Lucky's speech in *Waiting for Godot.* On that hellish vision in a self-described heaven Prior turns his back: "Bless me, anyway. I want more life." And he adds, with reference to the derelict Deity that Blake had called Nobodaddy or the Prince of this World: "And if He Returns, take Him to Court. He walked out on us. He ought to pay" (2:133).

So Kushner himself would say, at the Cathedral of St. John the Divine on the Episcopalian National Day of Prayer for AIDS in 1994, in his angry prayer to the presumably controlling Power who seems to have absented Himself: "Your silence . . . is outrageous to me, it places you impossibly among the ranks of the monstrously indifferent" (*Thinking about the Long-standing Problems of Virtue and Happiness* 220). Kushner's prayer moved, however, through anger toward a remarkable resolution on the edge of accepting a different kind of Deity: "I almost know you are there. I think you are our home. At present we are homeless, or imagine ourselves to be. Bleeding life in the universe of wounds. Be thou more sheltering, God. Pay attention" (224). *Angels in America* also moves beyond such anger toward a vision of more life and, in so doing, translates the angels of death into the angel of healing who is called Bethesda (2:145). The approach to that telos shapes the "Epilogue: Bethesda," in which the fountain in Central Park that will soon begin to flow is Kushner's more tough-minded, urban, contemporary, and yet both Jewish and Christian version of Don Quixote's dream fountain in Tennessee Williams's *Camino Real.* The Bethesda Fountain points toward the Temple fountain where the descent of Prior's "favorite angel," the angel Bethesda (which means "house of mercy"), made healings possible—and where (though Kushner does not choose to make this explicit) Jesus of Nazareth said to a man, "Rise, take up thy bed, and walk" (John 5:8). The original fountain of Bethesda, which ran dry when the Romans destroyed the Temple, will flow again, according to Hannah Pitt, "when the Millennium comes." Then, she says, "We will all bathe ourselves clean" (2:145). In that final and yet immediately historical context Prior blesses us and calls for "*More Life*" (2:146). Art Borreca has described the import of this moment from a point of view that is somewhat less Brechtian than it may sound:

> In this moment the play refuses Benjamin's visionary leap beyond historical dialectics, choosing, instead, the uncertainty of the historical future that is in the process of being shaped by those dialectics. The moment is the culmination of the play's teleological vision of history and society: it implicitly calls for the spectator to make his or her own choice for more life while remaining aware of the contradictory sociohistorical forces that the play has dramatized.

> The moment affirms this choice as one by which the destructive course of history might be altered, the impasse between ideal and reality transcended, and society redeemed—all *from within.* (259)

But again there is more. I have said that in *Angels in America,* as in Synge's *Playboy,* we may find ourselves in characters that show us how we are constituted by a multiple role-playing that establishes our predicament and our path to healing. Here, as also in *The Playboy,* we who participate in the performance with sympathy and irony may find ourselves led toward a vision more comprehensive than any single character's self-knowledge and recognition of community. For that vision "liberal pluralism" and "bourgeois individualism" and "his or her own choice" are quite inadequate phrases. *Angels in America* offers no specific program of radical political action—any more than Brecht does in *Mother Courage* or *The Caucasian Chalk Circle.* But through its mode of dramatic art it directs itself to what Kushner calls the question Brecht wrestled with: "How are we to remake ourselves into people who are fit to remake the world?" (*Tony Kushner in Conversation* 118). Or, as he once put it more fully: "how do we remake . . . [the individual] ego in a way that isn't itself masochistic? Is there a form of unmaking that isn't destructive?" (*Essays on Kushner's Angels* 149). And for him theater itself is one key to such unmaking of the separate ego: "I believe that everybody in a room together having the same experience creates something. It creates an energy. It creates a community . . . and in almost a mystical way creates good in the world, and it also empowers people and makes it more likely that they will act" (*Tony Kushner in Conversation* 208).

That is why, for Kushner, even a social or historical theater continually verges upon an unnamable religion. In its polyphonic performed action, as in its action of performance, *Angels in America* shows us an interpersonal and intrapersonal reality very different from that ideological mirage of the isolate individual on which so much of our art and our economy is founded. Kushner has said: "I think the play has become—and I didn't intend this when I started writing it—a play about the extent of a community's embrace" (*Tony Kushner in Conversation* 21). *Angels in America* shows us onstage and in ourselves a reality of interpenetrating presences that requires of us now, as Prior tells us, the acceptance of us all as "citizens" and "fabulous creatures" (2:146) and that will ultimately disclose—when the Millennium comes—that we are fundamentally one. Indeed, that is the burden of the dream vision that Harper Pitt has of the tropopause:

> Souls were rising from the earth far below, souls of the dead, of people who had perished, from famine, from war, from the plague, and they floated up, like skydivers in reverse, limbs all akimbo, wheeling and spinning. And the souls of these departed joined hands, clasped ankles and formed a web, a great net of souls, and the souls were three-atom oxygen molecules, of the stuff of ozone, and the outer rim absorbed them, and was repaired. (2:141–42)

As Kushner has said in his own afterword: "From such nets of souls societies, the social world, human life springs. And also plays" (2:155). What he asked of God, he therefore asks of us—as do all the important plays that mirror our playing: "Be more sheltering. Pay attention."

Works Cited

Ansorge, Peter. "Director in Interview: Peter Brook." *Plays and Players* 18 (Oct. 1970): 18–19.

———. Review of *A Midsummer Night's Dream. Plays and Players* 18 (Aug. 1971): 47.

Attar, Farid ud-Din. *The Conference of the Birds.* Trans. C. S. Nott. Boston: Shambhala, 1993.

Auden, W. H. "Byron: The Making of a Comic Poet." *New York Review of Books,* 18 Aug. 1966: 12–13.

———. *Collected Poems.* Ed. Edward Mendelson. New York: Random House, 1976.

———. *Complete Works: Plays.* Ed. Edward Mendelson. Princeton: Princeton University Press, 1988.

———. "Don Juan." *The Dyer's Hand.* New York: Random House, 1968. 386–406.

———. "Foreword: Brand *versus* Peer." *Brand.* By Henrik Ibsen. Trans. Michael Meyer. Garden City, NY: Doubleday, 1960.

Baker, Stuart E. *Georges Feydeau and the Aesthetics of Farce.* Ann Arbor: UMI Research Press, 1981.

Banham, Martin. "Playwright/Producer/Actor/Academic: Wole Soyinka in the Nigerian Theatre." *New Theatre Magazine* (Bristol) 12, no. 2 (1972): 10–11.

Banu, Georges. *Peter Brook: de "Timon d'Athènes" à "La Tempête."* Paris: Flammarion, 1991.

Barnes, Hazel E. *Sartre.* Philadelphia: Lippincott, 1973.

Barnett, Gene A. *Lanford Wilson.* Boston: Twayne, 1987.

Beckett, Samuel. *Collected Shorter Plays.* New York: Grove Press, 1984.

———. *Disjecta.* Ed. Ruby Cohn. London: John Calder, 1983.

———. *Endgame.* New York: Grove Press, 1958.

———. *Happy Days.* New York: Grove Press, 1961.

———. *Waiting for Godot.* New York: Grove Press, 1954.

Bentley, Eric. *The Playwright as Thinker.* New York: Meridian, 1955.

———. *What Is Theatre? Incorporating the Dramatic Event and Other Reviews, 1944–1967.* New York: Atheneum, 1968.

Bermel, Albert. *Farce.* New York: Simon and Schuster, 1982.

Berst, Charles A. *Bernard Shaw and the Art of Drama.* Urbana: University of Illinois Press, 1973.

Bigsby, C. W. E. *Joe Orton.* London: Methuen, 1982.

Billington, Michael. "Commonwealth Arts Festival: Drama Section." *Plays and Players* 13, no. 2 (Nov. 1965): 31–35.

Bogard, Travis. *Contour in Time: The Plays of Eugene O'Neill.* Rev. ed. New York: Oxford University Press, 1988.

Booth, Michael R., ed. *English Plays of the Nineteenth Century.* Vol. 3. London: Oxford University Press, 1973.

Borreca, Art. "'Dramaturging' the Dialectic: Brecht, Benjamin, and Declan Donnellan's Production of *Angels in America.*" *Approaching the Millennium: Essays on* Angels in America. Ed. Deborah R. Geis and Steven E. Kruger. Ann Arbor: University of Michigan Press, 1997. 245–60.

Bottoms, Stephen J. *The Theatre of Sam Shepard: States of Crisis.* Cambridge: Cambridge University Press, 1998.

Bourgeois, Maurice. *John Millington Synge and the Irish Theatre.* London: Constable, 1913.

Brask, Per, ed. *Essays on Kushner's Angels.* Winnipeg: Blizzard Publishing, 1995.

Brater, Enoch. *Beyond Minimalism.* New York: Oxford University Press, 1987.

Braun, Edward. *Meyerhold: A Revolution in Theatre.* 2d ed. London: Methuen, 1995.

Brenman-Gibson, Margaret. *Clifford Odets: American Playwright.* New York: Atheneum, 1981.

———. "The Creation of Plays: With a Specimen Analysis." *Psychoanalysis, Creativity, and Literature.* Ed. Alan Roland. New York: Columbia University Press, 1978. 178–230.

Brenton, Howard. *Bloody Poetry.* London: Methuen, 1985.

Brook, Peter. *The Empty Space.* New York: Atheneum, 1968.

———. *Meetings with Remarkable Men.* Libra Films, New York, 1979. (Available as a Corinth Video Release, 1987.)

———. *The Open Door.* New York: Pantheon Books, 1993.

———. *The Shifting Point.* New York: Theatre Communications Group, 1987.

———. *Threads of Time: Recollections.* Washington, DC: Counterpoint, 1998.

Brook, Peter, et al. *US: The Book of the Royal Shakespeare Theatre Production.* London: Calder and Boyars, 1968.

Browne, E. Martin. *The Making of T. S. Eliot's Plays.* New York: Cambridge University Press, 1969.

Brustein, Robert. *The Theatre of Revolt.* Boston: Little, Brown, 1964.

Bryden, Ronald. "Stripping Down the Dream." *Observer,* 13 Dec. 1970: 20.

Bryer, Jackson, ed. *Lanford Wilson: A Casebook.* New York: Garland, 1994.

Byron, George Gordon, Lord. *Byron.* Ed. Jerome J. McGann. Oxford: Oxford University Press, 1986.

———. *Byron's Letters and Journals.* Ed. Leslie A. Marchand. 10 vols. Cambridge, MA: Harvard University Press, 1973–80.

Calderwood, James L. *Shakespeare and the Idea of a Play.* Minneapolis: University of Minnesota Press, 1971.

Caputi, Anthony. *Buffo: The Genius of Vulgar Comedy.* Detroit: Wayne State University Press, 1978.

Carpenter, Humphrey. *W. H. Auden: A Biography.* Boston: Houghton Mifflin, 1982.

Carrière, Jean-Claude. *The Mahabharata.* Trans. Peter Brook. New York: Harper and Row, 1987.

Carrière, Jean-Claude, and Peter Brook. *The Conference of the Birds,* based on the poem by Farid Uddi Attar. Chicago: Dramatic Publishing Co., 1982.

Chabrowe, Leonard. *Ritual and Pathos: The Theater of O'Neill.* Lewisburg: Bucknell University Press, 1976.

Champigny, Robert. *Stages on Sartre's Way, 1938–1952.* Bloomington: Indiana University Press, 1959.

Charney, Maurice, ed. *Classic Comedies.* New York: New American Library, 1985.

———. *Joe Orton.* London: Macmillan, 1984.

Chekhov, Anton. *Anton Chekhov's Plays.* Ed. and trans. Eugene K. Bristow. Norton Critical Edition. New York: Norton, 1977.

———. *Three Sisters.* Trans. Brian Friel. Dublin: Gallery Press, 1981.

———. *Three Sisters.* Trans. Lanford Wilson. New York: Dramatists Play Service, 1984.

Clark, Barrett. "'The Playboy' in Paris." *Colonnade* 11 (Jan. 1916): 23–26.

Clarke, Eric O. "Shelley's Heart: Sexual Politics and Cultural Value." *Yale Journal of Criticism* 8 (Spring 1995): 187–208.

Claudel, Paul. *Break of Noon.* Trans. Wallace Fowlie. Chicago: Henry Regnery, 1960.

Clurman, Harold. *On Directing.* New York: Macmillan, 1972.

Coe, Richard N. *The Vision of Jean Genet.* London: Owen, 1968.

Cohn, Ruby. *Just Play.* Princeton: Princeton University Press, 1980.

———, ed. *Four Contemporary French Plays.* New York: Random House, 1967.

Cole, Susan Letzler. *Directors in Rehearsal.* New York: Routledge, 1992.

Colum, Padraic. *The Road Round Ireland.* New York: Macmillan, 1926.

Corbett, Martyn. *Byron and Tragedy.* London: Macmillan, 1988.

Corrigan, Robert W., ed. *Comedy: Meaning and Form.* 2d ed. New York: Harper and Row, 1981.

Coughlin, Matthew N. "Farce Transcended: George Fitzmaurice's *The Toothache.*" *Eire-Ireland,* 10, no. 4 (1975): 85–100.

Crompton, Louis. *Shaw the Dramatist.* Lincoln: University of Nebraska Press, 1969.

Crum, Jane Ann. "Stanley Kauffmann on the Unknown Shaw: *You Never Can Tell, Misalliance, Androcles and the Lion, Too True to Be Good.*" *Shaw: The Annual of Bernard Shaw Studies* 7 (1987): 31–44.

Cusack, Cyril. "A Player's Reflections on *Playboy.*" *Modern Drama* 4 (Dec. 1961): 300–305.

Dasenbrock, Reed Way. *Imitating the Italians: Wyatt, Spenser, Synge, Pound, Joyce.* Baltimore: Johns Hopkins University Press, 1991.

daVinci Nichols, Nina. "Pirandello and the Poetics of Desire." *Annals of Scholarship* 9 (1992): 307–25.

Davis, Jessica Milner. *Farce.* London: Methuen, 1978.

Dearlove, J. E. *Accommodating the Chaos: Samuel Beckett's Non-Relational Art.* Durham, NC: Duke University Press, 1982.

Delaney, Paul, ed. *Tom Stoppard in Conversation.* Ann Arbor: University of Michigan Press, 1994.

DeRose, David J. *Sam Shepard.* New York: Twayne Publishers, 1992.
Donoghue, Denis. *The Third Voice: Modern British and American Verse Drama.* Princeton: Princeton University Press, 1959.
Driver, Tom F. *Romantic Quest and Modern Query: A History of the Modern Theater.* New York: Delacorte, 1970.
Dukore, Bernard. *Bernard Shaw, Playwright.* Columbia: University of Missouri Press, 1973.
Dutton, Richard. *Modern Tragicomedy and the British Tradition.* Brighton: Harvester Press, 1986.
Eliot, T. S. *Collected Poems, 1909–1962.* New York: Harcourt Brace, 1963.
———. *Complete Plays.* New York: Harcourt, Brace, 1970.
———. *On Poetry and Poets.* New York: Farrar, Straus, and Giroux, 1957.
Ellis-Fermor, Una. *The Irish Dramatic Movement.* 2d ed. London: Methuen, 1954.
Ellmann, Richard. *Oscar Wilde.* New York: Knopf, 1988.
Erdman, David. "Byron's Stage Fright." *ELH* 6 (1939): 219–43.
Fay, W. G., and Catherine Carswell. *The Fays of the Abbey Theatre.* London: Rich and Cowan, 1935.
Felheim, Marvin. "*The Autumn Garden:* Mechanics and Dialectics." *Modern Drama* 3 (Sept. 1960): 191–95.
Fergusson, Francis. *The Idea of a Theater.* Princeton: Princeton University Press, 1949.
Fisher, James. "Harlequinade: Commedia dell'Arte on the Early Twentieth-Century British Stage." *Theatre Journal* 41 (Mar. 1989): 30–44.
Friel, Brian. *Dancing at Lughnasa.* London: Faber and Faber, 1990.
———. *Faith Healer.* Loughcrew, Ireland: Gallery Books, 1991.
———. *Wonderful Tennessee.* London: Faber and Faber, 1993.
Frye, Northrop. *Anatomy of Criticism.* Princeton: Princeton University Press, 1957.
———. *T. S. Eliot.* Edinburgh and London: Oliver and Boyd, 1963.
Fugard, Athol. *Boesman and Lena and Other Plays.* Oxford: Oxford University Press, 1978.
———. *Notebooks, 1960–1977.* New York: Knopf, 1984.
———. *The Road to Mecca.* London: Faber and Faber, 1986.
Fugard, Athol, and Winston Ntshona. *Statements: Three Plays.* Oxford: Oxford University Press, 1974.
Gale, Stephen. *Butter's Going Up.* Durham: Duke University Press, 1977.
Ganz, Arthur. *George Bernard Shaw.* London: Macmillan, 1983.
Gelb, Arthur, and Barbara Gelb. *O'Neill.* New York: Harper and Row, 1973.
Genet, Jean. *Letters to Roger Blin.* Trans. Richard Seaver. New York: Grove Press, 1969.
———. "A Note on Theatre." *Tulane Drama Review* 7 (Spring 1963): 37–41.
———. *The Screens.* Trans. Bernard Frechtman. New York: Grove Press, 1962.
Gibbs, A. M. *The Art and Mind of Shaw.* London: Macmillan, 1983.
Gibbs, James, ed. *Critical Perspectives on Wole Soyinka.* Washington, DC: Three Continents, 1980.
———. *Wole Soyinka.* London: Macmillan; New York: Grove, 1986.

Gilbert, Miriam. *Shakespeare in Performance: Love's Labour's Lost.* Manchester: Manchester University Press, 1993.

Gilbert, W. S. *The Complete Operas.* Preface by Deems Taylor. New York: Random House, 1932.

Gilbert, W. Stephen. "Directors Bearing Gifts." *Plays and Players* 20, no. 12 (Sept. 1973): 24–25.

Gilman, Richard. *Common and Uncommon Masks: Writings on Theatre—1961–1970.* New York: Random House, 1971.

Girard, René. *Things Hidden since the Foundation of the World.* Trans. Stephen Bann and Michael Metteer. Stanford: Stanford University Press, 1987.

Gleick, James. *Chaos: Making a New Science.* New York: Viking, 1987.

Goldman, Michael. *Acting and Action in Shakespearean Tragedy.* Princeton: Princeton University Press, 1985.

———. *The Actor's Freedom: Toward a Theory of Drama.* New York: Viking, 1975.

Gomes, Peter J. *Sermons: Biblical Wisdom for Daily Living.* Foreword by Henry Louis Gates Jr. New York: William Morrow, 1998.

Granville-Barker, Harley. *The Exemplary Theatre* (1922). Freeport, NY: Books for Libraries Press, 1970.

———. "The Heritage of the Actor." *Quarterly Review* 240 (July 1923): 53–73.

———. *Plays: One.* Intro. Margery Morgan. London: Methuen Drama, 1993.

———. *The Secret Life.* London: Chatto and Windus, 1923.

Granville Barker and His Correspondents. Ed. Eric Salmon. Detroit: Wayne State University Press, 1986.

Greene, David H., and Edward M. Stephens. *J. M. Synge, 1871–1909.* New York: Macmillan, 1959.

Gregory, Isabella Augusta, Lady. *Our Irish Theatre: A Chapter of Autobiography.* New York and London: G. P. Putnam's Sons, 1913.

Grene, David, and Richmond Lattimore, eds. *The Complete Greek Tragedies.* Chicago: University of Chicago Press, 1959.

Grene, Marjorie. *Sartre.* New York: New Viewpoints, 1973.

Grene, Nicholas. *Synge: A Critical Study of the Plays.* London: Macmillan, 1975.

Gruber, William E. *Comic Theaters: Studies in Performance and Audience Response.* Athens: University of Georgia Press, 1986.

Gugelberger, Georg, ed. *Marxism and African Literature.* Trenton, NJ: Africa World Press, 1985.

Guicharnaud, Jacques, and June Guicharnaud. *Modern French Theatre: From Giraudoux to Genet.* New Haven: Yale University Press, 1967.

Gurewitch, Morton. *Comedy: The Irrational Vision.* Ithaca: Cornell University Press, 1975.

Gussow, Mel. "A Conversation (Pause) with Harold Pinter." *New York Times Magazine,* 5 Dec. 1971: 132–33.

Hay, Eloise Knapp. *T. S. Eliot's Negative Way.* Cambridge, MA: Harvard University Press, 1982.

Heilpern, John. *Conference of the Birds: The Story of Peter Brook in Africa.* Rev. ed. London: Methuen, 1989.

Hellman, Lillian. *The Collected Plays.* Boston: Little, Brown, 1972.

Hilgard, Ernest R. *Divided Consciousness: Multiple Controls in Human Thought and Action.* New York: Wiley Interscience, 1977.

Hirsch, Edward. "The Gallous Story and the Dirty Deed: The Two *Playboys.*" *Modern Drama* 26 (Mar. 1983): 85–102.

Hirschberg, Stuart. *Myth in the Poetry of Ted Hughes.* 2d ed. Totowa, NJ: Barnes and Noble, 1981.

Hofmannsthal, Hugo von. "A Prologue to Brecht's *Baal.*" Trans. Alfred Schwarz. *Tulane Drama Review* 6 (Autumn 1961): 111–22.

Hogan, Robert. *The Experiments of Sean O'Casey.* New York: St. Martin's Press, 1960.

Holloway, Joseph. *Joseph Holloway's Abbey Theatre.* Ed. Robert Hogan and Michael J. O'Neill. Carbondale: Southern Illinois University Press, 1967.

Holmes, Richard. *Shelley: The Pursuit.* London: Weidenfeld and Nicolson, 1974.

Honegger, Gitta, Rassami Patipatpaopong, and Joel Schechter. "An Interview with Athol Fugard." *Theater* 16, no. 1 (Fall–Winter 1984): 33–39.

Howe, P. P. "The 'Playboy' in the Theatre." *Oxford and Cambridge Review* 7 (July 1912): 37–51.

Hudson, Lynton. *The English Stage, 1850–1950.* London: Harrap, 1951.

Huneker, James. *Iconoclasts.* New York: Charles Scribner's Sons, 1905.

Hunt, Albert, and Geoffrey Reeves. *Peter Brook.* Cambridge: Cambridge University Press, 1995.

Huston, Hollis. *The Actor's Instrument: Body, Theory, Stage.* Ann Arbor: University of Michigan Press, 1992.

Hutchings, William, ed. *David Storey: A Casebook.* New York: Garland, 1992.

———. *The Plays of David Storey: A Thematic Study.* Carbondale: Southern Illinois University Press, 1988.

Innes, Christopher. *Holy Theatre: Ritual and the Avant Garde.* Cambridge: Cambridge University Press, 1981.

James, William. *Pragmatism* and *The Meaning of Truth.* Intro. A. J. Ayer. Cambridge, MA: Harvard University Press, 1978.

———. *The Principles of Psychology.* 2 vols. Cambridge, MA: Harvard University Press, 1981.

Jenkins, Ron. *Acrobats of the Soul: Comedy and Virtuosity in Contemporary American Theatre.* New York: Theatre Communications Group, 1988.

Johnstone, Keith. *Impro: Improvisation and the Theatre.* New York: Theatre Arts Books, 1979.

Jones, David Richard. *Great Directors at Work: Stanislavsky, Brecht, Kazan, Brook.* Berkeley: University of California Press, 1986.

Jones, Edward Trostle. *Following Directions: A Study of Peter Brook.* New York: Peter Lang, 1985.

Joyce, James. *Finnegans Wake.* New York: Viking, 1939.

Jung, Carl G. *Psychology and the East.* Trans. R. F. C. Hull. Princeton: Princeton University Press, 1978.

Kalb, Jonathan. *Beckett in Performance.* Cambridge: Cambridge University Press, 1989.

Katrak, Ketu. *Wole Soyinka and Modern Tragedy.* Westport, CT: Greenwood, 1986.

Kazin, Alfred. *Starting Out in the Thirties.* New York: Random House, 1980.
Kennedy, Andrew L. *Dramatic Dialogue: The Duologue of Personal Encounter.* Cambridge: Cambridge University Press, 1983.
Kennedy, Dennis. *Granville Barker and the Dream of Theatre.* Cambridge: Cambridge University Press, 1985.
Kenner, Hugh. *Samuel Beckett: A Critical Study.* 2d ed. Berkeley: University of California Press, 1968.
Kern, Edith, ed. *Sartre: A Collection of Critical Essays.* Englewood Cliffs, NJ: Prentice-Hall, 1962.
Kerr, Walter. *Thirty Plays Hath November: Pain and Pleasure in the Contemporary Theater.* New York: Simon and Schuster, 1969.
Kiberd, Declan. "Brian Friel's *Faith Healer.*" *Irish Writers and Society at Large.* Ed. Masaru Sekine. Totowa, NJ: Barnes and Noble, 1987. 106–22.
———. *Synge and the Irish Language.* London: Macmillan, 1979.
King, Bruce. *New English Literatures.* London: Macmillan, 1980.
King, Mary C. *The Drama of J. M. Synge.* London: Fourth Estate, 1985.
Knight, G. Wilson. *Ibsen.* Edinburgh and London: Oliver and Boyd, 1962.
———. *Poets of Action.* London: Methuen, 1967.
———. *Principles of Shakespearean Production.* London: Faber and Faber, 1936.
Knowles, Ronald. "From London: Harold Pinter 1993–1994." *The Pinter Review: Annual Essays, 1994.* Tampa: University of Tampa Press, 1994. 115–29.
Knowlson, James. *Samuel Beckett: An Exhibition.* London: Turret Books, 1971.
———. *Damned to Fame: The Life of Samuel Beckett.* New York: Simon and Schuster, 1996.
Knowlson, James, and John Pilling. *Frescoes of the Skull: The Later Prose and Drama of Samuel Beckett.* London: John Calder, 1979.
Kosok, Heinz. *O'Casey the Dramatist.* Totowa, NJ: Barnes and Noble, 1985.
Kott, Jan. *Shakespeare Our Contemporary.* Trans. Boleslaw Taborski. New York: Norton, 1974.
Kuhn, Thomas S. *The Structure of Scientific Revolutions.* Chicago: University of Chicago Press, 1962.
Kushner, Tony. *Angels in America.* Pt. 1, *Millennium Approaches.* New York: Theatre Communications Group, 1993.
———. *Angels in America.* Pt. 2, *Perestroika.* Rev. version. New York: Theatre Communications Group, 1996.
———. *Thinking about the Longstanding Problems of Virtue and Happiness.* New York: Theatre Communications Group, 1995.
———. *Tony Kushner in Conversation.* Ed. Robert Vorlicky. Ann Arbor: University of Michigan Press, 1998.
Ladipo, Duro. *Three Yoruba Plays.* English adaptations by Ulli Beier. Ibadan: Mbari Publications, 1964.
Lahr, John. "The Bacchae," *Plays and Players* 21, no. 1, (Oct. 1973): 59.
———. "Brian Friel's Blind Faith." *New Yorker* 17 Oct. 1994: 107–10.
———. "Pinter and Chekhov: The Bond of Naturalism." *Pinter: A Collection of Critical Essays.* Ed. Arthur Ganz. Englewood, NJ: Prentice-Hall, 1972. 60–71.
———. *Prick Up Your Ears.* New York: Limelight Editions, 1986.

Langbaum, Robert. *The Mysteries of Identity*. New York: Oxford University Press, 1977.
Lavelle, Louis. *Manuel de Méthodologie Dialectique*. Paris: Presses Universitaires de France, 1962.
Lederer, Katherine. *Lillian Hellman*. Boston: Twayne, 1979.
Lefort, Rafael. *The Teachers of Gurdjieff*. London: Victor Gollancz, 1966.
Levin, Bernard. Review of *A Midsummer Night's Dream*. *Times* (London), 30 Sept. 1971: 14.
Linney, Romulus. *Childe Byron*. New York: Dramatists Play Service, 1981.
Lyons, Charles R. *Samuel Beckett*. New York: Grove Press, 1983.
Machado, Eduardo. *The Floating Island Plays*. New York: Theatre Communications Group, 1991.
MacKenna, Stephen. *Journals and Letters*. London: Constable, 1936.
Magarshack, David. *Stanislavsky: A Life*. New York: Chanticleer, 1951.
Manderino, Ned. *The Transpersonal Actor: Reinterpreting Stanislavski*. Los Angeles: Manderino Books, 1989.
Mamet, David. *Sexual Perversity in Chicago* and *The Duck Variations*. New York: Grove Press, 1978.
Mann, Thomas. *Past Masters*. Trans. H. T. Lowe-Porter. New York: Alfred Knopf, 1933.
Marchand, Leslie A. *Byron: A Biography*. 3 vols. New York: Alfred Knopf, 1957.
Marowitz, Charles. *The Marowitz Shakespeare*. New York: Drama Book Specialists, 1978.
Marranca, Bonnie, ed. *American Dreams: The Imagination of Sam Shepard*. New York: Performing Arts Journal Publications, 1981.
McDonagh, Martin. *The Beauty Queen of Leenane*. Portsmouth, NH: Methuen Drama / Heinemann, 1996.
McDowell, Frederick P. W. "Shaw's 'Higher Comedy' Par Excellence: *You Never Can Tell*." *Shaw: The Annual of Bernard Shaw Studies* 7 (1987): 63–83.
McKenzie, John R. P. "Peter Weiss and the Politics of 'Marat-Sade.'" *New Theatre Quarterly* 1, no. 3 (Aug. 1985): 301–12.
Meisel, Martin. *Shaw and the Nineteenth Century Theatre*. Princeton: Princeton University Press, 1963.
Mendelson, Edward. *Early Auden*. New York: Viking Press, 1981.
Mendelsohn, Michael J. "The Heartbreak Houses of Shaw and Chekhov." *Shaw Review* 6 (Sept. 1963): 89–95.
Mercier, Vivian. *Beckett/Beckett*. New York: Oxford University Press, 1977.
Merleau-Ponty, Maurice. *Signs*. Trans. Richard C. McCleary. Evanston: Northwestern University Press, 1964.
Miles, Patrick, ed. and trans. *Chekhov on the British Stage*. Cambridge: Cambridge University Press, 1993.
Minwalla, Framji. "When Girls Collide: Considering Race in *Angels in America*." *Approaching the Millennium: Essays on* Angels in America. Ed. Deborah R. Geis and Seven E. Kruger. Ann Arbor: University of Michigan Press, 1997. 103–17.
Mitter, Shomit. *Systems of Rehearsal: Stanislavsky, Brecht, Grotowski, and Brook*. London: Routledge, 1992.

Morgan, Margery M. *The Shavian Playground*. London: Methuen, 1972.
Morton, John Maddison. *Box and Cox. English Plays of the Nineteenth Century*. Vol. 4, *Farces*. Ed. Michael R. Booth. London: Oxford University Press, 1973. 205–32.
Moore, George. *Hail and Farewell*. 2 vols. New York: Appleton, 1925.
Moore, James. *Gurdjieff: The Anatomy of a Myth*. Shaftesbury, Dorset: Element Books, 1991.
Müller, Heiner. *Hamletmachine and Other Texts for the Stage*. Ed. and trans. Carl Weber. New York: Performing Arts Journal Publications, 1984.
Needleman, Jacob, and George Baker, eds. *Gurdjieff: Essays and Reflections on the Man and His Teaching*. New York: Continuum, 1996.
Nethercot, Arthur H. *Men and Supermen: The Shavian Portrait Gallery*. 2d ed. New York: Benjamin Blom, 1966.
New Statesman and Nation 17 (Feb. 4, 1939): 169.
Nietzsche, Friedrich. *The Birth of Tragedy and the Case of Wagner*. Trans. Walter Kaufmann. New York: Random House, 1967.
———. *The Portable Nietzsche*. Trans. Walter Kaufmann. New York: Viking, 1951.
Nightingale, Benedict. "Peter Brook Voyages to Inner Space." *New York Times*, 5 Mar. 1995: 2:1, 4.
Norman, Sylvia. *Flight of the Skylark: The Development of Shelley's Reputation*. Norman: University of Oklahoma, 1954.
O'Casey, Sean. *Three Plays*. New York: St. Martin's Press, 1957.
O'Connor, Garry. *The Mahabharata: Brook's Epic in the Making*. San Francisco: Mercury House, 1990.
Odets, Clifford. *Six Plays of Clifford Odets*. New York: Grove Press, 1979.
Oida, Yoshi, with Lorna Marshall. *An Actor Adrift*. London: Methuen, 1992.
O'Neill, Eugene. *Complete Plays*. Ed. Travis Bogard. 3 vols. New York: Library of America, 1988.
Orton, Joe. *The Complete Plays*. New York: Grove Press, 1977.
Ouspensky, P. D. *In Search of the Miraculous: Fragments of an Unknown Teaching*. New York: Harcourt, Brace and World, 1949.
Paikert, Charles. "A Playwright Who Fashions Then into Now." *New York Times*, 3 Dec. 1989: H5, 28.
Parham, Sidney F. "*The Screens*." *Theatre Journal* 42 (May 1990): 249–51.
Peacock, Alan J. ed. *The Achievement of Brian Friel*. Gerrard's Cross: Colin Smythe, 1993.
Peacock, Ronald. *The Poet in the Theatre*. 2d ed. New York: Hill and Wang, 1960.
Pearce, Howard D. "Synge's Playboy as Mock Christ." *Modern Drama* 8 (Dec. 1965): 303–10.
Performance Group. *Dionysus in 69*. Ed. Richard Schechner. New York: Farrar, Straus, and Giroux, 1970.
Perl, Jeffrey M. *Skepticism and Modern Enmity*. Baltimore: Johns Hopkins University Press, 1989.
———. *The Tradition of Return: The Implicit History of Modern Literature*. Princeton: Princeton University Press, 1984.
Pilling, John. *Samuel Beckett*. London: Routledge and Kegan Paul, 1976.

Pine, Richard. *Brian Friel and Ireland's Drama.* London: Routledge, 1990.
Pinter, Harold. *Collected Works: One.* New York: Grove Press, 1977.
———. *Collected Works: Three.* New York: Grove Press, 1978.
———. *Moonlight.* New York: Grove Press, 1993.
———. *No Man's Land.* New York: Grove Press, 1975.
———. *The Proust Screenplay.* New York: Grove Press, 1977.
Pirandello, Luigi. *Naked Masks.* Ed. Eric Bentley. New York: E. P. Dutton, 1952.
Pound, Ezra. *Translations.* New York: New Directions, 1963.
Reinelt, Janelle. *After Brecht: British Epic Theater.* Ann Arbor: University of Michigan Press, 1994.
———. "Notes on *Angels in America* as American Epic Theater." *Approaching the Millennium: Essays on* Angels in America. Ed. Deborah R. Geis and Steven E. Kruger. Ann Arbor: University of Michigan Press, 1997. 234–44.
Reyner, J. H. *The Gurdjieff Inheritance.* Wellingborough, Northamptonshire: Turnstone Press, 1984.
Richards, Kenneth, and Peter Thomson, eds. *Essays on Nineteenth Century British Theatre.* London: Methuen, 1971.
Richardson, Alan. *A Mental Theater: Poetic Drama and Consciousness in the Romantic Age.* University Park: Pennsylvania State University Press, 1987.
Riding, Alan. "For Peter Brook, 'Hamlet' as Starting Point." *New York Times,* 16 Jan. 1996: C13—14.
Righter, Ann. *Shakespeare and the Idea of a Play.* London: Chatto and Windus, 1962.
Robinson, Marc. *The Other American Drama.* New York: Cambridge University Press, 1994.
Rollyson, Carl. *Lillian Hellman: Her Legend and Her Legacy.* New York: St. Martins' Press, 1988.
Román, David. "November 1, 1992: AIDS / *Angels in America.*" *Appproaching the Millennium: Essays on* Angels in America. Ed. Deborah R. Geis and Steven E. Kruger. Ann Arbor: University of Michigan Press, 1997. 40–55.
Rorty, Richard. *Consequences of Pragmatism (Essays: 1972–1980).* Minneapolis: University of Minnesota Press, 1982.
———. *Philosophy and the Mirror of Nature.* Princeton: Princeton University Press, 1979.
Rosen, Carol. *Plays of Impasse: Contemporary Drama Set in Confining Institutions.* Princeton: Princeton University Press, 1983.
Rosen, Steven J. *Samuel Beckett and the Pessimistic Tradition.* New Brunswick, NJ: Rutgers University Press, 1976.
Ross, Colin A. *Multiple Personality Disorder: Diagnosis, Clinical Features, and Treatment.* New York: John Wiley and Sons, 1989.
Rossi, Ernest Lawrence. *The Psychobiology of Mind-Body Healing.* New York: Norton, 1986.
Ruddick, William. "Lord Byron's Historical Tragedies." *Essays on Nineteenth Century British Theatre.* Ed. Kenneth Richards and Peter Thomson. London: Methuen, 1971. 83–94.
Rutherford, Andrew, ed. *Byron: The Critical Heritage.* London: Routledge and Kegan Paul, 1970.

Sacks, Oliver. *The Man Who Mistook His Wife for a Hat.* New York: Summit Books, 1985.

Saddlemyer, Ann. "'A Share in the Dignity of the World': J. M. Synge's Aesthetic Theory." Robin Skelton and Ann Saddlemyer, eds., *The World of W. B.Yeats.* Rev. ed. Seattle: University of Washington Press, 1967. 207–19.

———. "Vision and Design in *The Playboy of the Western World.*" *Craft and Fiction: Essays in Honour of William Blissett.* Ed. H. B. de Groot and A. Leggatt. Calgary: University of Calgary Press, 1990. 203–16.

Salmon, Eric. *Granville Barker: A Secret Life.* London: Heinemann, 1983.

Sartre, Jean-Paul. *Being and Nothingness.* Trans. Hazel E. Barnes. New York: Philosophical Library, 1956.

———. *No Exit and Three Other Plays.* Trans. Stuart Gilbert. New York: Vintage Books, 1955.

———. *Saint Genet, Actor and Martyr.* Trans. Bernard Frechtman. New York: George Braziller, 1963.

———. *Sartre on Theater.* Ed. Michel Contat and Michel Rybalka. London and New York: Pantheon, 1976.

Savran, David. "Ambivalence, Utopia, and a Queer Sort of Materialism: How *Angels in America* Reconstructs the Nation." *Approaching the Millennium: Essays on* Angels in America. Ed. Deborah R. Geis and Steven E. Kruger. Ann Arbor: University of Michigan Press, 1997. 13–39.

Scenarios of the Commedia dell'Arte: Flaminio Scala's "Il Teatro delle favole rappresentative." Trans. Henry F. Salerno. Foreword by Kenneth McKee. New York: New York University Press, 1967.

Schechner, Richard, ed. "Marat/Sade Forum: Peter Brook, Leslie Fiedler, Geraldine Lust, Norman Podhoretz, Ian Richardson, Gordon Rogoff." *TDR* 10 (Summer 1966): 214–37.

Schiller, Friedrich. *On the Aesthetic Education of Man.* Trans. Reginald Snell. New York: Ungar, 1965.

Schnitzler, Arthur. *Anatol, Living Hours, The Green Cockatoo.* Trans. Grace Isabel Colbron. One-Act Plays in Reprint. New York: Core Collection Books, 1977.

Schwarz, Alfred. *From Büchner to Beckett.* Athens: Ohio University Press, 1978.

Selbourne, David. *The Making of "A Midsummer Night's Dream."* London: Methuen, 1982.

Seneca. *Seneca's Oedipus.* Adapted by Ted Hughes. Intro. by Peter Brook. New York: Doubleday, 1972.

Shakespeare, William. *A Midsummer Night's Dream.* Ed. R. A. Foakes. Cambridge: Cambridge University Press, 1984.

———. *Peter Brook's Production for the Royal Shakespeare Company of " A Midsummer Night's Dream": Authorized Acting Edition.* Ed. Glenn Loney. Chicago: Dramatic Publishing Co., 1974.

Shaw, Bernard. *Bernard Shaw's Letters to Granville Barker.* Ed. C. B. Purdom. London: Phoenix House, 1956.

———. *Candida.* Harmondsworth: Penguin Books, 1956.

———. *Complete Plays with Prefaces.* 5 vols. New York: Dodd, Mead, 1963.

———. *Heartbreak House.* Harmondsworth: Penguin Books, 1964.
———. *Plays Pleasant.* Harmondsworth: Penguin Books, 1946.
———. *Shaw on Theatre.* Ed. E. J. West. New York: Hill and Wang, 1958.
———. *The Works of Bernard Shaw.* Vol. 1. London: Constable, 1931.
———. *You Never Can Tell: A Facsimile of the Holograph Manuscript.* Ed. Daniel J. Leary. New York: Garland, 1981.
Shepard, Sam. *Fool for Love and Other Plays.* New York: Bantam Books, 1984.
———. *Seven Plays.* New York: Bantam Books, 1981.
Sidnell, Michael J. *Dances of Death: The Group Theatre of London in the Thirties.* London: Faber and Faber, 1984.
Smith, A. C. H. *Orghast at Persepolis.* London: Eyre Methuen, 1972.
Smith, Anna Deveare. *Twilight: Los Angeles, 1992.* New York: Doubleday Anchor, 1994.
Smith, Grover, Jr. *T. S. Eliot's Poetry and Plays: A Study in Sources and Meaning.* Chicago: University of Chicago Press, 1956.
Solomon, Alisa. "Wrestling with *Angels:* A Jewish Fantasia." *Approaching the Millennium: Essays on* Angels in America. Ed. Deborah R. Geis and Steven E. Kruger. Ann Arbor: University of Michigan Press, 1997. 118–33.
Soyinka, Wole. *Art, Dialogue and Outrage.* Ed. Biodun Jeyifo. Ibadan: New Horn, 1988.
———. *The Beatification of Area Boy: A Lagosian Kaleidoscope.* London: Methuen, 1995.
———. *Collected Plays, Vol. 1.* London: Oxford University Press, 1973.
———. *Collected Plays, Vol. 2.* London: Oxford University Press, 1974.
———. *Death and the King's Horseman.* New York: Norton, 1975.
———. *Ibadan: The Penkelemes Years.* London: Methuen, 1994.
———. *Idanre and Other Poems.* London: Methuen, 1967; New York: Hill and Wang, 1968.
———. *The Man Died: Prison Notes of Wole Soyinka.* New York: Harper, 1972.
———. *Myth, Literature and the African World.* London: Cambridge University Press, 1976.
Spacks, Patricia Meyer. "The Making of the Playboy." *Modern Drama* 4 (Dec. 1961): 314–23.
Speeth, Kathleen Riordan. *The Gurdjieff Work.* New York: Jeremy P. Tarcher / Putnam, 1989.
Spoto, Donald. *The Kindness of Strangers: The Life of Tennessee Williams.* Boston: Little, Brown, 1985.
Steffan, Truman Guy. *Lord Byron's "Cain": Twelve Essays and a Text with Variants and Annotations.* Austin: University of Texas Press, 1968.
Steiner, George. *The Death of Tragedy.* New York: Knopf, 1961.
Stoppard, Tom. *Arcadia.* London: Faber and Faber, 1993.
———. *Jumpers.* New York: Grove Press, 1973.
———. *Rosencrantz and Guildenstern Are Dead.* New York: Grove Press, 1967.
———. *Travesties.* New York: Grove Press, 1975.
Storey, David. *Plays: One.* London: Methuen Drama, 1992.
Strasberg, Lee, ed. *Famous American Plays of the 1950s.* New York: Dell, 1988.

Styan, J. L. *Chekhov in Performance: A Commentary on the Major Plays.* Cambridge: Cambridge University Press, 1971.

———. *Drama, Stage, and Audience.* Cambridge: Cambridge University Press, 1975.

———. *The Elements of Drama.* Cambridge: Cambridge University Press, 1963.

Synge, John Millington. *Collected Works.* Ed. Robin Skelton, Alan Price, and Ann Saddlemyer. 4 vols. London: Oxford University Press, 1962–68.

Szondi, Peter. *Theory of the Modern Drama: A Critical Edition.* Ed. Michael Hays. Minneapolis: University of Minnesota Press, 1986.

Taborski, Boleslav. *Byron and the Theatre.* Salzburg: Universität Salzburg, 1972.

Takahashi, Yasunari. "The Theatre of Mind: Samuel Beckett and the Noh." *Encounter* 58 (Apr. 1982): 66–73.

Tart, Charles T. *States of Consciousness.* New York: E. P. Dutton, 1975.

———. *Waking Up: Overcoming the Obstacles to Human Potential.* Boston: Shambhala, 1986.

Taylor, John Russell. *The Rise and Fall of the Well-Made Play.* New York: Hill and Wang, 1967.

Temkine, Raymonde. *Grotowski.* Trans. Alex Szogiyi. New York: Avon, 1972.

Thody, Philip. *Jean Genet: A Study of His Novels and Plays.* New York: Stephen and Day, 1969.

———. *Jean-Paul Sartre: A Literary and Political Study.* London: Hamish Hamilton, 1960.

Trelawny, Edward John. *Recollections of the Last Days of Shelley and Byron. The Life of Percy Bysshe Shelley.* Ed. Thomas Jefferson Hogg. London: Dent, 1933. 2:151–301.

Trewin, J. C. *Going to Shakespeare.* London: George Allen and Unwin, 1978.

———. *Peter Brook: A Biography.* London: MacDonald, 1971.

———. *Shakespeare on the English Stage: 1900–1964.* London: Barrie and Rockliff, 1964.

Tweedie, Irina. *Daughter of Fire: A Diary of a Spiritual Training with a Sufi Master.* Inverness, CA: Golden Sufi Center, 1986.

Valency, Maurice. *The Cart and the Trumpet: The Plays of George Bernard Shaw.* New York: Oxford University Press, 1973.

Vanden Heuvel, Michael. *Performing Drama / Dramatizing Performance: Alternative Theater and the Dramatic Text.* Ann Arbor: University of Michigan Press, 1991.

Van Laan, Thomas F. *Role-Playing in Shakespeare.* Toronto: University of Toronto Press, 1978.

Vaughan-Lee, Llewellyn. *Sufism: The Transformation of the Heart.* Inverness, CA: Golden Sufi Center, 1995.

Weales, Gerald. *Clifford Odets, Playwright.* New York: Pegasus, 1971.

Webb, James. *The Harmonious Circle: The Lives and Work of G. I. Gurdjieff, P. D. Ouspensky, and Their Followers.* Boston: Shambhala, 1987.

Weintraub, Stanley. "Genesis of a Play: Two Early Approaches to *Man and Superman.*" *Shaw: Seven Critical Essays.* Ed. Norman Rosenblood. Toronto: University of Toronto Press, 1971. 25–35.

———. *The Unexpected Shaw.* New York: Ungar, 1982.

Weiss, Peter. *Die Verfolgung und Ermordung Jean Paul Marats dargestellt durch die*

Schauspielgruppe des Hospizes zu Charenton unter Anleitung des Herrn de Sade. Frankfurt am Main: Suhrkamp Verlag, 1964.
———. *The Persecution and Assassination of Jean-Paul Marat as Performed by the Inmates of the Asylum of Charenton under the Direction of The Marquis de Sade.* English version by Geoffrey Skelton. Verse adaptation by Adrian Mitchell. Intro. by Peter Brook. New York: Atheneum, 1965.
Whitaker, Thomas R. *Fields of Play in Modern Drama.* Princeton: Princeton University Press, 1977.
———. *Tom Stoppard.* London: Macmillan, 1983.
Wilde, Oscar. *The Artist as Critic: Critical Writings of Oscar Wilde.* Ed. Richard Ellmann. New York: Random House, 1969.
———. *The Importance of Being Earnest.* Commentary by Patricia Hern. London: Methuen, 1981.
———. *Plays.* Harmondsworth: Penguin Books, 1954.
Wiles, Timothy J. *The Theater Event: Modern Theories of Performance.* Chicago: University of Chicago Press, 1980.
Williams, David. "'A Place Marked by Life': Brook at the Bouffes du Nord." *New Theatre Quarterly* 1, no. 1 (Feb. 1985): 39–74.
———, ed. *Peter Brook: A Theatrical Casebook.* London: Methuen, 1988.
———, ed. *Peter Brook and "The Mahabharata": Critical Perspectives.* London: Routledge, 1991.
Williams, Philip Middleton. *A Comfortable House: Lanford Wilson, Marshall W. Mason, and the Circle Repertory Theatre.* Jefferson, NC: McFarland, 1993.
Williams, Tennessee. *Camino Real.* New York: Grove, 1953.
———. *The Notebook of Trigorin.* New York: New Directions, 1997.
Wilshire, Bruce. *Role Playing and Identity: The Limits of Theatre as Metaphor.* Bloomington: Indiana University Press, 1982.
Wilson, Lanford. *Fifth of July.* New York: Dramatists Play Service, 1982.
———. *5th of July.* New York: Hill and Wang, 1979.
Worth, Katherine. *Oscar Wilde.* London: Macmillan, 1983.
———. *Revolutions in Modern English Drama.* London: G. Bell, 1972.
Worthen, William B. *The Idea of the Actor.* Princeton: Princeton University Press, 1984.
Wright, William. *Lillian Hellman: The Image, the Woman.* New York: Simon and Schuster, 1986.
Yeats, John Butler. *Essays: Irish and American.* New York: Macmillan, 1918.
Yeats, William Butler. *The Autobiography of William Butler Yeats.* New York: Macmillan, 1953.
———. *Collected Plays.* New York: Macmillan, 1953.
———. *Essays and Introductions.* New York: Macmillan, 1961.
———. *Explorations.* New York: Macmillan, 1962.
———. *The Letters of W. B. Yeats.* Ed. Alan Wade. New York: Macmillan, 1955.
———. *The Poems.* Vol. 1 of *The Collected Works of W. B. Yeats.* Ed. Richard J. Finneran. New York: Macmillan, 1989.
———. *The Variorum Edition of the Plays of W. B. Yeats.* Ed. Russell K. Alspach. New York: Macmillan, 1966.

———. *A Vision*. London: Macmillan, 1937.

York, Richard. "Friel's Russia." *The Achievement of Brian Friel*. Ed. Alan J. Peacock. Gerrard's Cross: Colin Smythe, 1993. 164–77.

Young, Stark. *Immortal Shadows*. New York: Hill and Wang, 1958.

Zinman, Toby Silverman. "Inside Lanford Wilson." *American Theatre* 9 (May 1992): 12–18, 63.

Index